SILENCES AND SECRETS

ABOUT THE AUTHOR

Kay Dreyfus is an Adjunct Research Fellow in the School of History (SOPHIS), Monash University. Her background is in musicology and history and she holds doctorates in both areas. As curator of the Grainger Museum (Melbourne), she edited *The Farthest North of Humanness, Letters of Percy Grainger 1901–1914* (1985). She is particularly interested in everyday musical experience in Australia, and her publications include *Sweethearts of Rhythm: The Story of Australia's All-Girl Bands and Orchestras to the End of the Second World War* (1999) and a biography of the Australian violinist Alma Moodie (*Die Geige War ihr Leben: Drei Frauen im Portrait*, 2000).

SILENCES AND SECRETS

The Australian Experience of the Weintraubs Syncopators

KAY DREYFUS

© Copyright 2013 Kay Dreyfus

All rights reserved. Apart from any uses permitted by Australia's Copyright Act 1968, no part of this book may be reproduced by any process without prior written permission from the copyright owners. Inquiries should be directed to the publisher.

Monash University Publishing
Building 4, Monash University
Clayton, Victoria 3800, Australia
www.publishing.monash.edu

Monash University Publishing brings to the world publications which advance the best traditions of humane and enlightened thought.

Monash University Publishing titles pass through a rigorous process of independent peer review.

National Library of Australia Cataloguing-in-Publication entry:

> Author: Dreyfus, Kay, 1942- author.
>
> Title: Silences and secrets : the Australian experience of the Weintraubs Syncopator / Kay Dreyfus.
>
> ISBN: 9781921867804 (paperback)
>
> Notes: Includes bibliographical references.
>
> Subjects: Weintraubs Syncopators (Musical group)--History; Jazz--Germany--History; Jazz--Australia--History; Big bands--Germany--History; Big bands--Australia--History; Jazz musicians--Germany; Jazz musicians--Australia; Germans--Australia--Evacuation and relocation, 1940-1946.
>
> Dewey Number: 781.65092

www.publishing.monash.edu/books/sands-9781921867804.html

Design: Les Thomas

Front cover image: The Weintraubs Syncopators joining local musicians on tour. The presence of Freddy Wise and Fritz Goldner places this photograph before the band's arrival in Australia. Private collection, with permission.

Back cover image: The Weintraubs Syncopators, Berlin c. 1930. State Library of New South Wales MLMSS 7164X. Scrapbooks concerning the Mercury Theatre, 1940s–1950s [Sydney John Kay], with permission.

Printed in Australia by Griffin Press an Accredited ISO AS/NZS 14001:2004 Environmental Management System printer.

The paper this book is printed on is certified by the Programme for the Endorsement of Forest Certification scheme. Griffin Press holds PEFC chain of custody SGS - PEFC/COC-0594. PEFC promotes environmentally responsible, socially beneficial and economically viable management of the world's forests.

CONTENTS

List of illustrations vi
Abbreviations viii
Acknowledgements ix

PART ONE: SILENCES AND SECRETS

Introduction 3

1 'Truth' and the telling of the past in the bio-documentary film *Weintraubs Syncopators: Bis ans andere Ende der Welt* 25

PART TWO: THE ENCOUNTER WITH THE MUSICIANS' UNION

Introduction 47

2 'Quite candidly, we don't want them' 63
3 'One of the finest small bands in Australia' 89
4 The Weintraubs Syncopators, the Jewish question and the Musicians' Union of Australia 1937–1953 115
5 Breaching the profession 147

PART THREE: THE ENCOUNTER WITH THE STATE

Introduction 177

6 'No shadow of doubt' 195
7 'I cannot find a corner in the world where I am welcome' 229

PART FOUR: CONCLUSION

8 Claims to be Jewish 259

Bibliography 269
Index 297

LIST OF ILLUSTRATIONS

Figure 1. The Weintraubs Syncopators, Berlin, 1929–31

Figure 2. The Weintraubs Syncopators on stage, Berlin, c. 1928

Figure 3. The Weintraubs on tour in Czechoslovakia

Figure 4. The Weintraubs on tour in Holland

Figure 5. The Weintraubs on stage with a kickline, Berlin, n.d.

Figure 6. A selection of what the band could offer

Figure 7. Clowning in the studio

Figure 8. Constant movement was part of the Weintraubs' mystique

Figure 9. Clowning on stage

Figure 10. Clowning around at Prince's Restaurant, Sydney, n.d. [late 1930s]

Figure 11. Playing for dancing at Prince's, late 1930s or early 1940

Figure 12. A musician's dream of Australia invaded by foreign musicians, 1935

Figure 13. Comfortable with celebrity

Figure 14. Promotional sheet music of a popular song

Figure 15. Diagrammatic representation of MUA-related discourse: fields of action, genres and topics

Figure 16. George Molnar's cartoon 'State of the Nation', 1949

Figure 17. Entertaining at Prince's, late 1930s to early 1940

Figure 18. The musical boxing match

Figure 19. A themed presentation at Prince's

Figure 20. The 'Midnight Sextette' at Prince's, 1941

Figure 21. The Fisher brothers rehearse a Venetian interlude

Figure 22. Mannie Fisher's party trick, playing two trumpets at once

Figure 23. 'Looking for spies?'

Figure 24. The band had its own bus on tour in New Zealand, early 1938

LIST OF ILLUSTRATIONS

Figure 25. 'I'm no Kreisler but I'm an Aussie …' John Frith's cartoon captures the dispute between the Union and Eugene Goossens, 1949

Figure 26. 'Is he an Aussie?' A. Stuart Peterson caricatures Union insistence on a preference for Australian musicians, 1949

Figure 27. William Muir Augustus Erskine Buchan, Shanghai, 1929

Figure 28. The internees

Figure 29. Bad timing? The Weintraubs' seasonal greetings advertisement, January 1940

Figure 30. Tony Hudson's cartoon drawing of the Weintraubs Syncopators [1937?]

ABBREVIATIONS

AAJUS	Australian Archive of Judaica, University of Sydney
ABC	Australian Broadcasting Commission (later Australian Broadcasting Corporation)
AdKB	Akademie der Künste, Berlin
ASIO	Australian Security and Intelligence Organisation
CIB	Commonwealth Investigation Branch
MPI	Military Police Intelligence
MSO	Melbourne Symphony Orchestra
MU	British Musicians' Union
MUA	Musicians' Union of Australia
NAA	National Archives of Australia
NBAC	Noel Butlin Archives Centre, Australian National University
NFSA	National Film and Sound Archive
NLA	National Library of Australia
NSW	New South Wales (Australian state)
RMK	*Reichsmusikkammer* [Reich Music Chamber]
RSSILA	Returned Soldiers' and Sailors' Imperial League of Australia [June 1916 – November 1940) then RSSAILA [+ 'and Airmen's'] (to October 1965)
SLNSW	State Library of New South Wales
SSO	Sydney Symphony Orchestra

ACKNOWLEDGEMENTS

This book started life as a doctoral thesis in the School of Philosophical, Historical and International Studies (SOPHIS) at Monash University. My first and best thanks go to my supervisors, Professors Andrew Markus and Alistair Thomson, for their wise teaching, thoughtful feedback and steady encouragement. I count myself privileged to have been able to learn from them. Thanks to the Monash Research Graduate School and SOPHIS for giving me the opportunity to do so.

I am grateful in particular to the librarians and staff of the Noel Butlin Archive Centre, Australian National University, Canberra, for their courtesy and helpfulness over my many visits. I have also benefited from assistance given by reference librarians in several state offices of the National Archives of Australia, in State Records NSW, the State Library of NSW, the Archive of Australian Judaica (Sydney University) and the National Library of Australia. Years ago, Matthew Stuckings (NLA) helped me 'crack the ice' in Butlin and the NAA. Dr John Whiteoak shared some insights and information early on; Edzia Fisher was generous with photographs and memories. Adrienne Simpson checked the New Zealand newspapers for me and Judith Hampel translated Russian- and German-language material in the Akademie der Künste, Berlin (October–November 2009). I am indebted to Douglas Hermann, who located William Buchan's son David, and to David himself who, without prejudice, shared information and documents about his family's business and other activities in Shanghai. Charles Phippen found the sheet music. Dorothy Graff, Horst Graff's second cousin and only living blood relative, has been most supportive. Professor Sheila Fitzpatrick supported a real but unsuccessful attempt to locate information in Russia.

Earlier versions of some sections of the book have appeared as journal articles elsewhere. Full details of these publications are included in the bibliography.

I have made all reasonable efforts to secure copyright permissions for third-party content included in this book and have not knowingly added copyright content to my work without the owner's permission. Photographs are reproduced with permission of the holding institutions or individuals and copyright owners.

My colleague and friend Dr Suzanne Robinson (University of Melbourne) was always willing to read and critique different chapters. At home, my son Jonathan listened, read, discussed and reassured. And then there was George who, over several decades, made me aware of what it meant to be a Jew in Hitler's Germany, a refugee, and a musician of European sensibilities in postwar Australia.

Finally, my best thanks to Nathan Hollier and his staff at Monash University Publishing for making this book.

PART ONE

SILENCES AND SECRETS

Figure 1. The Weintraubs Syncopators, Berlin, [1929–31]

Left to right: Stefan Weintraub (drum kit), Freddy Wise (Eb contrabass saxophone), Cyril Schulvater (banjo), Franz Wachsmann (piano), unidentified trumpet player [Arno Olewski?], Horst Graff (saxophone) and John Kurt Kaiser (trombone). Schulvater joined in 1929; Leo Weiss became the piano player in 1931. Notice the lineup of instruments beside each player.

State Library of New South Wales. MLMSS 7164X. Scrapbooks concerning the Mercury Theatre, 1940s–1950s [Sydney John Kay], with permission.

INTRODUCTION

Idealised Australian migration stories tend to emphasise positive outcomes: successful integration and productive contributions to the new society. The experience of the Weintraubs Syncopators, as recounted in this book, is more complex. Exiled from Germany by the antisemitic ideologies of the Third Reich, this band of (then mainly) Jewish musicians embarked on a four-year journey that took them around Europe, across Russia from Moscow to Vladivostok, from Korea to Japan and finally, through the Far East (Shanghai, Manila and Singapore) to Sydney. They entered Australia as contracted musicians, not refugees, and the decision of the Jewish members of the band to try and stay in this country brought them into immediate conflict with the aggressively protectionist Musicians' Union of Australia. In spite of Union opposition, the band obtained employment at a high-class Sydney nightclub, but when war came the musicians struggled to understand their change of status from celebrities to aliens and enemy aliens. Denounced for alleged espionage activities in Russia, three were interned and the band broke up. Some of the musicians survived into postwar careers in music; others left the profession, discredited.

Even in outline, the story of the Weintraubs Syncopators is an extraordinary one. The band started life in Berlin as the Tanzkapelle Stefan Weintraub in 1924. The brainchild of Stefan Weintraub and Horst Graff, it was initially a 'student' outfit, made up of young men trying to make some money on the side while otherwise engaged in various occupations. According to Horst Graff, it began as an amateur jazz orchestra playing for dancing, but in time developed an act that blended vaudeville and music.[1] From the beginning, the musicians determined that 'music was to be used as the vehicle for expressing humour'. Stefan Weintraub, interviewed in 1981, described the band's approach: 'We didn't just sit on stage and play our music. We performed the music as a pantomime or a comedy show. We became a so-called number, a variety number'.[2]

---

[1] Transcript of Hearing at the Aliens Tribunal No 1, Melbourne, 21 March 1941, p. 3, NAA C329, 402.
[2] *Australian Music Maker and Dance Band News*, November 1937, p. 19; the Weintraub interview is excerpted in the documentary film Klaus Sander and Jörg Süssenbach,

SILENCES AND SECRETS

Figure 2. The Weintraubs Syncopators on stage, Berlin [c. 1928?]
Left to right: Friedrich Hollaender (piano), Paul Aronovici (banjo), John Kay [Kurt Kaiser], Horst Graff, Ansco Bruinier (trumpet) and Stefan Weintraub. There were several changes of personnel in the early days. According to Bergmeier, Aronovici played with the Weintraubs from the autumn of 1926 until Cyril Schulvater took his place sometime early in 1929. Bruinier joined in August 1926 and retired from musical life in October 1930. Franz Wachsmann replaced Hollaender in the band on tour from Spring 1928; he left for the US in 1934.

Akademie der Künste, Berlin, Bestand Weintraubs Syncopators, Item 32, with permission.

Acclaimed as the best jazz band in Berlin by 1927, the Weintraubs' reputation was given a boost by its association, from early 1927, with Friedrich Hollaender, a leading composer and performer in the Berlin cabaret scene.[3] In following years, the band appeared with Hollaender in his 'cabaret-revues' and, through him, found an entrée into sound film, the new medium that was to present a significant challenge to live theatre from the late

---

Weintraubs Syncopators: Bis ans anderes Ende der Welt ([Berlin]: Cine Impuls KG for WDR TV in collaboration with Arte Media, 2000).

[3] *Berliner Börsencourier*, 12 September 1927, cited in Horst J. P. Bergmeier, *The Weintraub Story. Incorporated The Ady Rosner Story*. JAZZFREUND No. 16 (Menden: der JAZZFREUND, 1982), p. 11. Michael Kater says the Weintraubs had become a legend by the late 1920s. Michael H. Kater, *Different Drummers: Jazz in the Culture of Nazi Germany* (New York: Oxford University Press, 1992) p. 6.

PART ONE: INTRODUCTION

1920s, both as entertainment and as a source of employment for musicians.[4] Not only did the collaboration with Hollaender give the Weintraubs an international presence, but it seems that this partnership allowed the band to consolidate its distinctive ensemble style, since many of the elements attributed to the Weintraubs were also features of Hollaender's creative personality. Hollaender was a master of pastiche who excelled at spoofing other people's styles.[5] His songs, many of which the Weintraubs recorded, display his talent for parody and express what Alan Lareau calls an impudent stoicism, sometimes laughing in the face of death, sometimes laughing and crying simultaneously.

The Weintraubs are immortalised as the on-stage band in *The Blue Angel* (1930), the classic Josef von Sternberg movie that elevated Marlene Dietrich to stardom. But if the film eventually brought international fame to both Friedrich Hollaender (the pianist and composer) and the Syncopators, it also attracted Joseph Goebbels' opprobrium. Goebbels, who was instrumental in shaping the Third Reich's new cultural policies, described the film as "'offal", spewed out by the fetid city [Berlin]'.[6] The Weintraubs left Berlin for a tour of Czechoslovakia and Switzerland in March 1933, as the Nazi regime began systematically to exclude non-Aryans from Germany's professional and cultural life. At the completion of a series of engagements in Holland in January 1934, they elected to continue touring and not to return to Germany.

At the time of the band's second tour of Russia, the troupe was made up of nine men (seven musicians, a manager and a stage assistant) and four accompanying women; this was the group that arrived in Sydney in 1937. The touring group comprised Stefan Weintraub, Horst Graff, John Kurt Kaiser (known as John Kay), Cyril Schulvater, Leo Weiss, Emanuel Frischer (known as Mannie Fisher), Freddie Gordon Wise, Fritz Goldner

---

[4] Alexander L. Ringer, 'Dance on a Volcano: Notes on Musical Satire and Parody in Weimar Germany', *Comparative Literature Studies* 12/3 (1975), p. 253. According to Erik Levi, (*Music in the Third Reich* [New York: St Martin's Press, 1994], p. 120), 12,000 musicians were made redundant by the introduction of the sound cinema in Germany and the consequent disintegration of cinema orchestras. Levi reads the Nazi interdiction of jazz from April 1933 as thus not merely ideological (because of the inferred connection between jazz and negro or Jewish musicians and the view of jazz as an alien culture undermining German national values) but also as an effort to protect the domestic light music industry (pp. 120–121).

[5] Alan Lareau, interviewed in '"From Where? And Where To?" Episodes in the Life of the Musical Clown Friedrich Hollaender', two-part radio documentary produced by Andrew McLennan for ABC Radio National's *The Listening Room* (February 2007).

[6] The comment, from Goebbels' diaries, is cited by Kater, *Different Drummers*, p. 23 and note 141.

Figure 3. On tour in Czechoslovakia

Max Brod was a German-speaking Czech Jewish writer and journalist.

Akademie der Künste, Berlin, Bestand Weintraubs Syncopators, Item 184, with permission.

Figure 4. On tour in Holland

German comedic actor Hans Albers played alongside Marlene Dietrich in *The Blue Angel*.

Akademie der Künste, Berlin, Bestand Weintraubs Syncopators, Item 78, with permission.

PART ONE: INTRODUCTION

(stage manager) and Henry Barger (formerly Heinz Baruch, tour manager). The women were Gerty Pfund (later Gerty Kaiser), Gertrud Bergmann (later Gertrud Weintraub), Margot Graeme (actually Margot Graff) and Antoinette Paris (later Antoinette Wise).[7] Three of the women were common law wives at the time of their arrival in Australia, though the Weintraubs and the Kaisers were to marry in Sydney shortly after war was declared. The Graffs concealed the fact that they were married from Australian officials so that Graff's wife would not lose the advantages that came with her British nationality (wives took their husband's nationality on marriage). The women's stories have their own interest, largely centring on issues of nationality and how this is defined, and the wives were on occasion the subjects of hostile scrutiny. All the musicians in the group that eventually came to Australia, except Freddy Wise, were Jewish; they were not, however, all German, though all except Wise had spent their youthful years in Germany.

The Weintraubs arrived in Australia in July 1937 as entertainers contracted to the cinema firm of Snider and Dean and, in the face of strenuous resistance from the Musicians' Union of Australia (hereafter MUA or 'the Union'), were subsequently engaged at Prince's, a stylish 'Continental' cabaret in Sydney. By the time the band settled in at Prince's in December 1938, it comprised the six musicians who were to be of interest to the Australian security services: Mannie Fisher (trumpet, violin, mellophone, trombone, vocals), Horst Graff (alto, soprano and tenor saxophones, clarinet, flutes, oboe, trumpet, vocals), John Kay (trombone, saxes, clarinet, bass clarinet, vocalist, arranger), Adolphe (Ady or Eddie) Normand ([Adolf Frischer], string bass, tenor saxophone, clarinet, trombone, vocals), Leo Weiss (pianist, arranger) and Stefan Weintraub (drums and percussion).[8] Cyril Schulvater, although no longer in the band (he had played banjo, guitar, cello, trombone and accordion), was still linked to it in the eyes of military intelligence since both he and his brother Ernest had been in Russia. The Weintraubs' appointment at Prince's consolidated their local reputation as sophisticated

---

[7] NAA A6126, 1236, doc. 60. See also NAA K269/4, 'Incoming passenger list "Gorgon" arrived Fremantle', 14.7.1937. Freddie Wise, an American, joined the band around 1930 (Bergmeier, *The Weintraub Story*, p. 23–24). Kater (*Different Drummers*, p. 27) writes that 'a German band's overall attraction and financial success would be enhanced by the presence of just a few American colleagues' and that after 1923 many band-leaders tried to include American musicians in their lineups (p. 6). Bergmeier states that before joining the Weintraubs, Wise was freelancing in Berlin without a firm contract.

[8] Weintraub excelled on piano, drums, guitar, xylophone, vibraphone, celeste and ukulele. Initially he played piano with the band, but after Hollaender joined the group, he switched to drums (Bergmeier, *The Weintraub Story*, p. 9).

European musicians, but the conspicuous foreignness that was so much part of their appeal was to make them vulnerable once war was declared.

In September 1939, a British businessman called William Muir Augustus Erskine Buchan, a resident of 9 McDonald Street, Potts Point (a suburb of Sydney), and neighbour of two of the musicians, made the first of two statements to officers of the No.10 Police Station in Paddington. Buchan claimed that he had been in Russia at the same time as the Weintraubs and that the musicians had been charged with espionage when a complete set of the plans of the naval fort at Kronstadt—the seat of the Russian admiralty and the base of the Russian Baltic Fleet—had supposedly been found in their possession.[9] One of the women travelling with the group had accepted responsibility, Buchan said, whereupon she had been imprisoned and the band expelled from the country. The police officers reported the matter at once to the Military Police Intelligence Section of the New South Wales (NSW) Police. Security files were immediately established on each individual musician, and although errors in Buchan's statements quickly became apparent and the allegations were never substantiated, the effects of the denunciation were profound, long-lasting and ultimately destructive of the group, impacting on their wives, and on family members who had not even been in Russia and were implicated only by association. Most immediately, Buchan's statements were used to justify the internment of three of the four German nationals in the band. Denunciation was to have a continuing role in the progressive disintegration of relationships within the group and one may observe how, in struggling to establish and maintain their bona fides against consequent threat and duress, the individuals involved also at times turned against each other as their fear and distress grew.

The Weintraubs belonged to the tradition of Berlin cabaret known as *Kleinkunstbühne*, a movement that was 'born out of a youthful spirit of rebellion against the established arts'.[10] In Berlin the band had moved comfortably between the intimate settings of the revue-cabaret and the more lavishly staged spectacles of the larger variety theatres: they performed on and off stage with Rudolf Nelson, at Max Reinhart's second Schall und Rauch Kabarett, established in the basement of his grand German Theatre (where Hollaender was employed as musical director), on stage in

---

[9] See, for example, the summary of Buchan's charges included in Leo Weiss's application for naturalisation. Letter, Deputy Director of Security for New South Wales to Acting Inspector, Commonwealth Investigation Branch, 13 July 1945. NAA A435, 1947/4/2710.

[10] Alan Lareau, *The Wild Stage: Literary Cabarets of the Weimar Republic* (Columbia, SC: Camden House, Inc, 1995), p. 180.

PART ONE: INTRODUCTION

Figure 5. On stage with a kickline, Berlin, n.d.
Peter Jelavich (*Berlin Cabaret*, pp. 180-181, 251), spends some time discussing the appeal of the kicklines: the attenuated femininity of the girls, their cheerfulness and dynamism. The kickline represented the flip side of the (black) American entertainment coin, embodying both military precision and economic rationalisation. For the National Socialists, the Girl shows were 'the epitome of Jewish decadence and perversion'.
Akademie der Künste, Berlin, Bestand Weintraubs Syncopators, Item 31, with permission.

Hollaender's revues at the Komödie and Theater am Kurfürstendamm or with Trude Hesterberg at the Deutsches KünstlerTheater. They accompanied Josephine Baker in her revues[11] and appeared in the more lavish production numbers of Eric Charell's variety shows at the Wintergarten (alongside the American-style kickline, the Tiller Girls). On tour the band played in theatres, hotels, cafés, even the restaurants of department stores.

Contrary to the popular image of Weimar cabaret (largely shaped by *The Blue Angel*, or by Joel Grey and Liza Minelli in *Cabaret*), cabaret entertainment of this period (the late 1920s to early 1930s) was neither radically political nor artistically revolutionary. Alan Lareau has described it as two-edged: wanting at once to be avant-garde, edgy and shocking, and on the other hand to cater to audience taste for a certain kind of entertainment, and to

---

[11] Stefan Weintraub, 'Answers to an Interview', n.d. [1981]. Bestand Weintraubs Syncopators AdKB Item 102.

pay the bills.[12] It was frequently satirical, occasionally topical, but essentially aimed at amusing a middle-class audience in search of distraction. Lareau asserts that it was strongly influenced by American entertainment, though the extent to which this might be actually true and in what way is contested by other scholars. Peter Jelavich offers an explanation: 'The music of the prewar [First World War] revues had derived from waltzes, polkas, mazurkas, folk songs and marches … After the war, however, American music flooded the stages. The specifically Central-European musical elements receded, and the melodies of revues came to be dominated increasingly by fox trots and jazz rhythms'.[13] '[J]azz to Weimar Germany was an all-embracing cultural label attached to any music from the American side of the Atlantic, or indeed to anything new and exciting', writes J. Bradford Robinson, even if all that was known were 'diluted commercial imitations'.[14] The sounds of jazz in themselves were satirical or parodic: 'The shrill sound of the clarinet and the trumpet, the wailing of the saxophone and the syncopated rhythms of the drums, banjo, and piano all seemed to portend a breakdown of cultural order'.[15] Jazz was the link to modernity and a sign of the break with the musical past; whereas the triple metre of the waltz had defined operetta, the duple metre of the foxtrot defined the revue.[16] At the same time, however, the continuing presence of stringed instruments (Mannie Fisher's violin and Cyril Schulvater's cello in the case of the Weintraubs) preserved a link with older styles of coffee-house and salon dance music.

Michael Kater argues that the persistence of these and other 'residues of the continental salon dance style' prevented German jazz musicians from ever acquiring quite the right American touch, but that is another story.[17] Debate over whether what the Weintraubs played was authentically jazz or not is less important than the perception of jazz as modern, parodic and potentially anarchic. The Weintraubs did not entirely cast off the musical legacy of the prewar years. Their stage repertoire ranged over a variety of genres from American 'swing' and gipsy melodies to Viennese waltzes and Cossack songs, all of which could be made either the subject or carrier of

---

[12] Lareau, "From Where? And Where To?".
[13] Peter Jelavich, *Berlin Cabaret* (Cambridge, Mass. & London: Harvard University Press, 1993), p. 169.
[14] J. Bradford Robinson, 'Jazz Reception in Weimar Germany: In Search of a Shimmy Figure', in Bryan Gilliam (ed.), *Music and Performance During the Weimar Republic* (Cambridge: Cambridge University Press, 1994), pp. 113–114.
[15] Jelavich, *Berlin Cabaret*, pp. 169–170.
[16] Triple metre means three beats (strong-weak-weak) in each measure; duple meter means two (strong-weak).
[17] Kater, *Different Drummers*, pp. 15–16.

PART ONE: INTRODUCTION

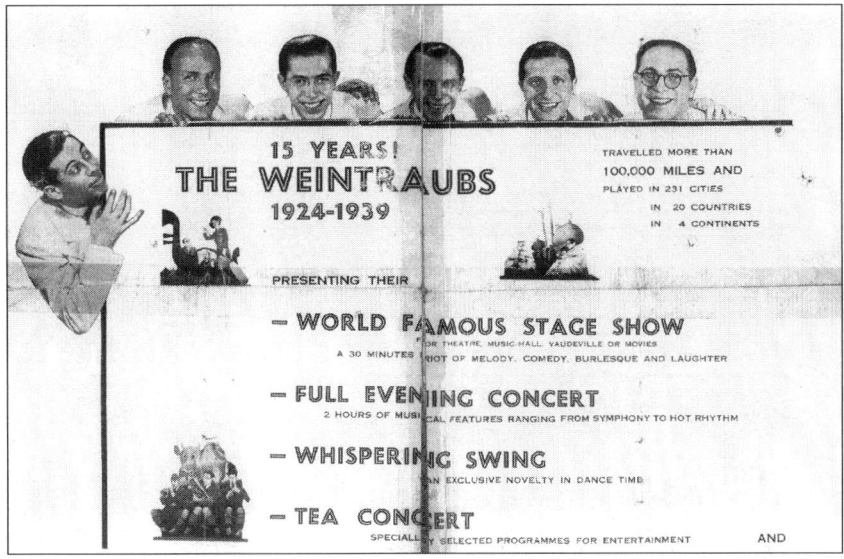

Figure 6. A selection of what the band could offer
Promotional pamphlet, Australia, 1939.
National Archives of Australia A434, 1944/3/690, with permission.

parody. More than that, however, applying the styles of former times to the popular music of the day became itself a form of parody. As will be shown, the musicians' ability to play all types of music and their multi-instrumental prowess later made the band remarkable in the Australian context.

The core element of the Weintraubs' performance was the three- to five-minute song or instrumental number and since this format was equally suited to the variety theatre, the cabaret revue, film (on and off camera), the recording industry (fitting the length of a 78 rpm disc) and to dancing, the Weintraubs were able to move with ease between these venues and genres. A promotional pamphlet from 1939 gives an idea of what they could offer: a 30-minute stage show (comedy, burlesque, melody), a two-hour full evening concert (symphony to hot rhythm), whispering swing (for dancing), a tea concert (entertainment programs) and radio broadcasts.[18] Their act drew on the traditions of music hall and vaudeville, favouring short novelty numbers with a strong element of visual comedy, underpinned by an absolute musical precision and a high level of versatility (of instruments and musical genres).

---

[18] NAA A434, 1944/3/690.

Figure 7. Clowning in the studio
The Weintraubs were comedy miming artists and gagsters and the visual element displayed in this promotional photograph was an important part of the Weintraubs' appeal.

Private collection, with permission.

This combination of musical and comedic elements was not, perhaps, as unusual as it might sound. Kater writes that jazz-band musicians were, by definition, expected to provide a good time, tell jokes and engage in the 'distorting humour' that characterised so-called 'nut jazz'.[19] There is some suggestion that the Weintraubs took this feature to an extreme; Kater cites one German musician as being so disillusioned by the Weintraubs' 'constant gimmickry' that he left the group after a few months.

We may glimpse something of the style the band brought to Australia through contemporaneous descriptions of its 'unusual entertainment'. One critique, of a performance at the Theatre Royal (of an unidentified city) in New Zealand in early 1938, is particularly illuminating: the act struck a balance between buffoonery ('as of masters who take the liberty of laughing at their art') and a 'mercilessly efficient' playing of jazz tunes and harmonies—the one aimed at entertaining those who might have

---

[19] Kater, *Different Drummers*, p. 15.

PART ONE: INTRODUCTION

found a whole program of jazz tedious, the other at satisfying those who had actually come to listen to the jazz. The performers were found to be at once 'comedians of an original type' and musicians capable of undertaking a performance of a 'serious' piece like George Gershwin's *Rhapsody in Blue*. Just what their buffoonery consisted of is harder to ascertain. They 'leapt from instrument to instrument with the most amazing dexterity' and they could all sing. Comic relief came from instruments imitating each others' sounds and from the speed of the act, the virtuosity and versatility of the musicians and their 'infectious good humour'. 'Their fun is so exuberant that the cleverness of their playing is almost overlooked', commented another reporter.[20] Much of the humour of the act derived from lighting effects (designed by Ray Goldner, a trained electrician), allied to the instrumental changeovers and novel musical variations. There was some patter and jokes, but most of the comedy was in 'dumb show' so as not to interfere with the music. Adaptability was a critical feature of the show: 'It is mainly comic and can be presented over periods of varying lengths from 25–30 minutes to over two hours with the inclusion of chamber music. Mr Dean [of Snider and Dean] finds it difficult to express to what extent the artists are possessed of special qualifications but he knows of no other "act" which can be compared with theirs'.[21] Nonetheless, the combination of comedy routines and high-level musical virtuosity made the band distinctive and versatile: it could be a dance band as well as a show band or stage orchestra that specialised in novelty pieces.

Certain questions occur at this point: to what extent did the kind of musicians the Weintraubs were influence what subsequently occurred in Australia, particularly how they were viewed by the officials with whom they had contact after the war began? To what extent did their iconoclastic onstage personae influence or was perceived to influence, or reflect, their offstage behaviour? Their character as artists is fundamentally important to their Australian reception. They were brought to Australia as an 'act' by the theatrical entrepreneurs Snider and Dean; their subsequent employment at Prince's was specifically linked to the kind of entertainers that they were and their professional success was the basis of their decision to remain. But Australia's geographical isolation from Europe, which made it so attractive

---

[20] From 'Says the Press', a compilation pamphlet of undated clippings from the New Zealand tour, collection Mannie Fisher. A folder of reviews and advertisements from the same tour may be found at AdKB Item 60.
[21] Letter, C.J. Brossois, Investigating Officer to the Boarding Inspector, 2 June 1937. NAA A434, 1944/3/690.

to many (especially postwar) refugees, also produced a parochialism born of cultural and political insularity, ignorance and a fortress mentality that many historians see as essential to contextualising the country's anti-refugee feeling in the 1930s.

Alexander Ringer identifies 'interchangeability'—with the thorough knowledge of musical literature that implied—as one of the most characteristic traits of artistic life in Weimar Berlin. Cabaret-based performers moved with ease from one type of entertainment to another.[22] But what was habitual for the Weintraubs was fundamentally antithetical to the Musicians' Union of Australia's attempts to reorganise the Australian music industry in the 1930s. Not only was the band formidable competition for local musicians, but the act routinely violated Union efforts to prevent musicians from crossing boundaries between discrete performance spaces: from pit to stage, from stage to dance hall rostrum. The ability of each individual to play a number of instruments and to change from one to the other smoothly and quickly was essential to the Weintraubs' sound, since they were thus able to reproduce the timbres of a much larger ensemble. The same skill underpinned their comedy stage routine. Such versatility was, however, also a direct affront to the rules of the MUA which, reflecting the Union's wish to spread available work among a maximum number of musicians, particularly in the difficult Depression-shadowed years of the 1930s, prohibited a musician from 'doubling' (that is, playing on more than one instrument during a single engagement). Unionists were also forbidden from combining instrumental performance with whistling or singing; all the Weintraubs could and did sing. Freddy Wise was also a good dancer.[23]

In a similar way, the counterpoint of nationalities within the group was a source of concern to the Australian authorities and grief to the musicians once war began. Only Weintraub and Graff were unambiguously German nationals. Leo Weiss, though born in Berlin and travelling on a German passport, claimed Polish parentage; his mother was born at Milloslow, Poland, his father in Jarotschin in the district of Posen (a city that moved in and out of German ownership), and both sets of grandparents were Polish.[24] The Schulvater brothers, born in Johannesburg, South Africa, of a German father and an English mother, had returned to Berlin as boys but travelled on British passports; while the Frischers were both born in Berlin

---

[22] Ringer, 'Dance on a Volcano', pp. 253, 256–257.
[23] Bergmeier, *The Weintraub Story*, p. 25.
[24] Letter, C.R. James J.P. to Secretary, Department of Interior, 28 October 1942. NAA A435, 1947/4/2710.

PART ONE: INTRODUCTION

to Polish parents and possessed Polish passports. John Kurt Kaiser's claim to Peruvian nationality was most problematic of all: his father was born in Peru to a German immigrant father; his mother was German and he himself was born in Leipzig. Issues of credibility increasingly permeate official wartime assessments of the musicians. Individual protestations of pro-British patriotic sentiments did not persuade sceptical Australian officers like the one who assessed Graff's evidence at his tribunal hearing for release from internment. The officer wrote, 'Objector's statements as to his pro-British and anti-Nazi sympathies ... cannot be questioned, because these can be known only to himself, but, as his [other] evidence ... show[s] such a propensity for lying, it is conceivable that he would express these sentiments when it was so obviously to his advantage to do so'.[25] Andrew Moore comments that Australian intelligence officers were hardly equipped, either by temperament or education, to understand 'the seams and folds of the exotic political lives that crossed their paths and whose paper work accumulated on their desks'.[26]

According to the German-produced documentary film *Weintraubs Syncopators: Bis ans andere Ende der Welt*, it was the Australian experience of internment, not the band's expulsion from the Third Reich, that destroyed the Weintraubs.[27] Even supposing one can separate the two, this is a discomforting proposition given the received image of Australia as a safe haven, however reluctant, and of Australians as essentially a fair-minded people. The purpose of this book, then, is to examine the reception of the musicians as world-class entertainers, and the effects of their wartime treatment as Jewish refugees by circumstance, using the Weintraubs' story as a lens through which to study aspects of a wider social and cultural landscape. The

---

[25] Document dated 25 August 1941, p. 4, NAA C123, 1213.
[26] Andrew Moore, " ... When the Caretaker's Busy Taking Care"? Cross-Currents in Australian Political Surveillance and Internment, 1935–1941', in Kay Saunders and Roger Daniels (eds), *Alien Justice: Wartime Internment in Australia and North America* (St Lucia, University of Queensland Press, 2000), pp. 60–61.
[27] Production details are as follows: Idee und Buch: Jörg Süssenbach; Regie/Realisation: Klaus Sander, Jörg Süssenbach; Mitarbeit: Axel Fischer; Kamera: Axel Fischer (BVK); Ton: Jan Bendel, Steve Foy; Schnitt: Uli Peschke; Tonmischung: Clemens Grulich; Sprecher: Leon Boden, Jenny Gröllmann, Uwe Müller; Projektentwicklung: Walter Brun, Henrike Maass, Corinna Volkmann; Produktion Australien: Anette Heidenreich, Wendy Oaks, Nimrod Sztern-Adidle; Produktionsleitung: Karl-Bernhard Koepsell, Karl Laabs; Redaktion: Heike Wilke (WDR), Olaf Rosenberg (Arte); Eine Produktion der Cine Impuls KG für den WDR [Westdeutscher Rundfunk (West German Broadcasting)] in Zusammenarbeit mit Arte; Media (Der Vertrieb wird gefördert mit Mitteln der EU [European Union]), 2000; duration 65 minutes. Credits and acknowledgements (including Australian crew and sources) may be found in the Newsletter No 8 of the Film Museum Berlin, May 2000, at http://www.marlenedietrich.org/pdf/News08.pdf, accessed June 2009.

chronological frame of my study is the 18-year period from the time of the band's arrival in July 1937 to the mid-1950s, when John Kay left Australia for the UK and his surveillance, the longest running of those of all the members of the band, came to an end. This timeframe allows some consideration of individuals' postwar efforts at 'normalisation', including naturalisation and professional reinstatement, and enables some assessment of the medium-term consequences of their wartime treatment. The discussion is mainly telescoped at a point of contact between the musicians and the state, as represented by its various bureaucratic agencies, including the Musicians' Union as a registered entity within the country's state and federal arbitration systems.

Although it could be argued that the Weintraubs' experience was in certain respects a fractal of the wider refugee situation, my present purpose is to maintain focus on processes—how events and decisions impacted on the individuals concerned—while examining what was typical and what unique. In pursuit of this objective, the book will examine two elements of the Weintraubs' Australian story: their encounter as foreign professionals with the MUA (in Part Two), and their encounter, as alleged spies and (in some cases) blacklisted security risks, as aliens and enemy aliens, internees and refugees by circumstance, with the state (in Part Three). The first allows a wider exploration of the extent to which economic conditions influenced the Australian response towards refugee immigration throughout the 1930s and a case study of the impact of a group of established musicians on the profession at large and of the profession's response, official and informal. The second personalises the effects of public letter-writing and security information gathering, exploring the motivations of those initiating and investigating allegations and complaints and seeking to differentiate between those driven by essentially personal concerns and those ostensibly motivated by feelings of patriotic loyalty.[28]

Understanding the two parts of the story has required two different approaches. Perhaps because it is numerically small, the MUA has attracted little attention in the secondary literature on trade unions, nor has it been much noticed in writings about Australian music history. Consequently, the approach taken in Part Two has a threefold purpose: to document the formation of Union policy on foreign musicians as it affected the reception of the Weintraubs Syncopators, as contracted imports, from 1937; to understand

---

[28] Robert Gellately characterises these two types of motivations as 'affective' (essentially personal) and 'instrumental' (system-loyal). See his 'Denunciation as a Subject of Historical Research', *Historical Social Research* 26/2–3 (2001), p. 23.

PART ONE: INTRODUCTION

the Musicians' Union's place within the Australia arbitration system and to acknowledge commonalities of strategy and response between the MUA and other unions; and to present a narrative account of the Weintraubs' interaction with the Union. Although the Weintraubs did not arrive in Australia as refugees, in the eyes of the MUA they became emblematic of the entire refugee problem as it presented in the late 1930s, largely because of their high public profile. In this section of the book the Weintraubs are viewed through the prism of that larger story.

In order properly to understand the MUA's response to the arrival of Jewish refugee musicians in the 1930s, including the Weintraubs, it has been necessary to expand the chronological frame of the narrative to include the origins and development of a policy on foreign musicians through the 1920s, to explore briefly the application of essentially the same ideas in the very different context of government-sponsored postwar migration in the late 1940s and early 1950s, and to note the eventual decline of this particular aspect of Union policy by 1960. According to Paul Bartrop, the 'impact of the Depression ... overshadowed Australia in the 1930s more completely than [did] anything else'.[29] The Depression impacted profoundly on the music profession, coinciding as it did with the advent of sound film. Bronwen Arthur writes that of the MUA's 5,000 members in 1927, an estimated 95 percent of whom were employed in picture theatres, four-fifths had lost their jobs by late 1930. The Union estimated that 4,000 members, or 80 percent of professional musicians in Australia, were unemployed, most of whom never found re-employment in cinema or theatre pits.[30] In consequence, from the late 1920s, the MUA became highly protectionist, institutionalising its adherence to the principles of the White Australia policy and pursuing a policy of total exclusion of foreign musicians that persisted until the late 1950s. Nonetheless, Union policy took shape within a strictly regulated framework, supervised by legally constituted industrial commissions in both Commonwealth and State jurisdictions.

My book traces the process by which a relatively benign and rational posture towards foreign musicians took on a highly prejudicial and discriminatory aspect. Fortuitously, the judgment that resulted when John Kay summonsed the MUA before the Industrial Commission of New South

---

[29] Paul Bartrop, *Australia and the Holocaust 1933–1945* (Melbourne: Australian Scholarly Publishing, 1994), p. 26.
[30] Bronwen Arthur, '"Ban the Talkies!" Sound Film and the Musicians Union of Australia 1927–1932', *Context* 13 (Winter 1997), pp. 47–48; 'Industrial Relations', in John Whiteoak and Aline Scott-Maxwell (eds), *Currency Companion to Music and Dance in Australia* (Strawberry Hills, NSW: Currency Press, 2003), p. 348.

Wales (discussed in Part Two) was profoundly influential through the 1950s. Analysis draws primarily on the archives of the MUA, preserved in the Noel Butlin Archives Centre at the Australian National University, supplemented by records of correspondence between the Union, various government departments and the Australian Broadcasting Commission (ABC) held in the National Archives of Australia (NAA) and elsewhere.

In Part Three, I view the larger story through the prism of the Weintraubs' wartime experience; chapters in this section examine the impact of the Buchan denunciation, the effects of internment, and the process of collective and individual self-redefinition that followed. Although the role of denunciation in a liberal democracy has not received much attention, the Australian experience of internment and political surveillance has been well studied, as has the government's wartime treatment of Jewish refugees. My discussion in this section is primarily based on the individually named files that have so far been identified in the NAA, and my focus is on the impact of policy rather than its formation, as the latter is thoroughly documented. Particular attention is given to the effects of the Buchan denunciation, which shaped these musicians' collective and individual evaluation by the security services for the duration of the war, provided the rationale for internment and the frame for interrogation before the Appeals Tribunal that heard applications for release, and affected applications for naturalisation, alien reclassification and military service. My study demonstrates how wartime anxieties allowed for the development of a potent culture of denunciation, arising out of a conflation of allegiance and nationality and targeting foreign nationals, which was countenanced and implemented as a mechanism for the defence of the nation. The wartime setting is critical to the unfolding of some parts of this narrative, since, even in this country 'at the other end of the world',[31] the war produced a set of changed and changing circumstances, as a consequence of which the whole society's sense of what was normal was destabilised[32] and the Weintraubs' collective self-representation was fundamentally challenged. Allowing for the fact that war, or a perceived

---

[31] The phrase is from an interview with Fritz Goldner that provided the title of the documentary film *Weintraubs Syncopators: Bis ans anderes Ende der Welt* [Weintraubs Syncopators: Right to the Other End of the World] and probably reflects the musicians' sense of their destination at the time.

[32] Although I am prefiguring here the provisions of alien registration and control, Guyatt points out that, after 1942, Australians accepted an unprecedented amount of Governmental interference in their private lives, including conscription for overseas service and for industrial and construction purposes. Joy Guyatt, 'A Study of the Attitudes to Jews and of the Jewish Stereotype in Eastern Australia, 1938 to 1948, as reflected by Government policies, parliamentary debates and public opinion as

PART ONE: INTRODUCTION

threat to national security, clearly offered a fertile environment in which denunciation could flourish, my research nonetheless asks why a single, unsubstantiated accusation was so wide-ranging and so potently destructive in its consequences, though not equally (or even reasonably) so for all the individuals implicated. I examine the factors that shaped official assessments of the relative credibility of denouncer and denounced.

The outbreak of war created a rupture in the Weintraubs' narrative, though its consequences were not evident at once. Some effects were immediate: along with all other resident foreign nationals, the musicians were at once required to register as aliens or, in the case of the German nationals, as enemy aliens, but their employment was not affected despite protestations from the Musicians' Union. And though the first of Buchan's influential statements alleging that the band had been engaged in espionage while touring in Russia was made as early as 11 September 1939, the security services did not proceed beyond a routine follow-up investigation until June 1940, when Graff, Kay and Weintraub were interned. Before the war, and indeed until that critical moment in the middle of 1940, the musicians were primarily concerned with consolidating and extending their careers within Australia. After September 1939, however, they were confronted with a much more complicated series of accommodations. The National Security Regulations governing the behaviour of alien residents were very different from the rules and regulations of the Musicians' Union; whereas the latter could be and largely were ignored with impunity by the Weintraubs, the former were enforceable at law and punishable in the breach. It is clear from the files that the musicians did not at first understand that, in the altered situation of war, their celebrity status and the attitudes that apparently came with it were not helpful.[33] Not surprisingly, the fate of individuals was tied to the fortunes of the war, but this realisation came slowly to the musicians.

One of the objectives of this study is to trace the impact of the discrepancies that arose between the group's public self-representation, collectively and individually, and the official view of their status and reliability, individually and generically (as refugee aliens, foreign nationals and Jews), as the war progressed. These were initially very confident people who, over the previous several years and more, had become accustomed to viewing the world from

---

expressed by newspapers, journals and sundry publications'. MA qualifying thesis, University of Queensland, 1967, p. 87, n. 179.
[33] See, for example, police reporting of Horst Graff's behaviour and attitude in connection with the band's application for travel permits for a function at Government House in Canberra, April 1940. NAA C123, 1213. The incident is discussed in detail in Part Three, Chapter Seven.

Figure 8. Constant movement was part of the Weintraubs' mystique
This illustration accompanied James Lucas's interview, 'Played Around the World: Story of the Weintraubs' (*Australian Music Maker and Dance Band News*, 1 November 1937), which emphasised the band's peripatetic lifestyle.

Magazine held in the Mitchell Library, State Library of New South Wales, reproduced with permission.

a position of privilege, not used, as visitors and foreign celebrities, to being subject to the same rules as ordinary citizens in the countries through which they travelled. This study documents their efforts to come to terms with the social, political and economic realities of late 1930s and wartime

PART ONE: INTRODUCTION

Australia—its cultural conservatism and isolation, its pro-British national thinking—and with varying Australian responses. How the members of the Weintraubs Syncopators collectively and individually reconfigured their social and personal identities,[34] and how they seem to have understood and responded to the process, as evidenced through an examination of pivotal events in the biographical narrative, is a central concern. For example, in an interview with *Tempo*, the monthly music trade magazine, in December 1938–January 1939, the band claimed to have 'played in 459 places, in 230 cities, in 21 countries' and to have 'travelled 105,000 miles'.[35] Constant motion was part of their celebrity mystique. Later, this peripatetic lifestyle would be viewed with some suspicion by Australian military intelligence.[36] Asked, during the same *Tempo* interview, whether the political situation in Germany had had anything to do with the band's touring, the musicians dismissed the idea as 'quite ridiculous, as long before any change of regime was contemplated in Germany, this band was touring Europe'—a statement which is technically true, but camouflages and trivialises the connection between Nazi antisemitism and the band's decision not to return to Germany from its Dutch tour in 1934, a connection Weintraub and Graff subsequently struggled to prove during hostile interrogation before the Aliens Tribunal hearing their appeals for release from internment.

Linked to the above enquiry is the question of how important it was in Australia, to the musicians and to others, that they were Jewish, given the denial implied in the *Tempo* interview just quoted. In postulating an answer to this and other questions, my study offers a perspective on some wider issues of Australian historiography. First, it problematises the extent

---

[34] For a discussion and definition of these two different kinds of 'identity projects', see Sheila Fitzpatrick, 'Becoming Soviet', in *Tear Off the Masks! Identity and Imposture in Twentieth-Century Russia* (Princeton: Princeton University Press, 2005), pp. 11–12, and n. 19.

[35] *Tempo*, p. 8. Details of their journeys are scattered across individual NAA files, often accompanying applications for naturalisation, which required applicants to identify countries lived in or visited before Australia. The Weintraubs Collection (Bestand Weintraubs Syncopators) in the Musikarchiv of the Akademie der Künste Berlin (AdKB) contains a number of the band's European contracts and lists of engagements completed, which taken together map its European tours. One such list (Item 75), printed in 1935 and including the first Russian engagements but not the return tour, identifies 141 cities in 13 countries. It is likely that the figures cited in *Tempo* are not exaggerated.

[36] Letter, Director-General of Security, Canberra to Deputy Director of Security, Sydney, 22 December 1942, on the subject of E. Frischer's application for naturalisation: 'the itinerant nature of his profession as disclosed in the Statutory Declaration signed by him does not suggest that his motives are inspired by a strong sense of nationalism'. NAA C123, 1211.

to which prewar professional attitudes towards Jewish refugee musicians were shaped or driven by antisemitism. The often prejudicial discussions of the Jewish refugee issue in the late 1930s involve an interaction of ideas of race and nation that are time- and place-specific (White Australia in the 1930s), but the rhetoric displays features that universally characterise what Ruth Wodak and her colleagues call a 'discourse of prejudice', incorporating but distinguishing elements of racism, xenophobia, antisemitism and ethnicism.[37] My analysis questions assumptions about Australian working-class antisemitism by proposing that Union rhetoric was essentially opportunistic in its choice of a foreign 'Other'. I postulate a link between pre- and postwar practices of professional exclusion and the growth of an initially unregulated, ethnically-based sector within the music industry from which, within two or three decades, public musical multiculturalism emerged.

Up until June 1940, it is possible to tell the story of the Weintraubs as a collectivity. After June 1940, when three of the musicians were interned and the band broke up, it is not. Paradoxically, however, the dissolution of the band and the very different responses of its members to their subsequent experiences make it impossible to represent the Weintraubs' story as a victim narrative, though it is certainly true that some of the musicians were 'victimised', or felt themselves to be. It was unquestionably difficult for Weintraub and Graff to avoid that perception when they found themselves interned, together with a small group of German and Austrian Jewish men, in Tatura 1, at that time under the internal governance of German nationals who were either Nazi sympathisers or members of the NSDAP in Australia. Victim narratives are as pervasive in one kind of migration discourse as enrichment narratives are in another, growing out of efforts to analyse historically the politics and institutions of contemporary multiculturalism and to critique ideas of nation that grew up around Australia's long-standing, racially-based, exclusionary immigration policy. Along with other common migration metaphors, victim paradigms can minimise the importance of personal agency, of an individual's capacity to influence events and outcomes or assert their own sense of self or identity. The challenge is to create a narrative that recognises both 'the existence of individual agency and [the] forces with potential to curtail it'.[38]

---

[37] For example, Richard Mitten and Ruth Wodak, 'On the Discourse of Racism and Prejudice', *Folia Linguistica* 27/2–4 (1993), pp. 191–215; Martin Reisigl and Ruth Wodak, *Discourse and Discrimination: Rhetorics of Racism and Antisemitism* (London: Routledge, 2001).

[38] Andrew Markus, *Australian Race Relations 1788–1993* (St Leonards: Allen & Unwin, 1994), p. xv.

PART ONE: INTRODUCTION

The broad spectrum of reactions within the group to essentially similar circumstances, and the apparent anomalies that emerge, make the Weintraubs a fertile migration case study, rich in irony and ambiguity. Why was it, for example, that Stefan Weintraub was made the scapegoat of the group, became the primary target of the Musicians' Union and the object of the security services' darkest suspicions, while Leo Weiss, named in the Buchan denunciation and also a German national, apparently avoided all difficulties with the authorities and remained undisturbed in his job at Prince's for the duration of the war and beyond? How was it that John Kay was able to rejoin the profession following his release from internment while Graff and Weintraub essentially could not? Kay (formerly Kurt Kaiser, who had had his own band in Berlin but joined the Weintraubs in 1926) went on to create a significant place for himself in Australian cultural life, as a composer of high repute for the Commonwealth Film Unit and as the prime mover in Sydney's Mercury Theatre—in which latter role he continued to be of interest to ASIO as a suspected communist sympathiser—though Australia could not keep him. He left for London in 1955. This book will explore these and other paradoxes in the Weintraubs' story.

Chapter One

'TRUTH' AND THE TELLING OF THE PAST IN THE BIO-DOCUMENTARY FILM
WEINTRAUBS SYNCOPATORS: BIS ANS ANDERE ENDE DER WELT

My interest in the Australian experience of the Weintraubs Syncopators originated towards the end of 2000 when the documentary film *Weintraubs Syncopators: Bis ans andere Ende der Welt* was screened for the first time at the Melbourne Jewish Film Festival. I was aware of the band from my readings about Weimar cabaret and from the film *The Blue Angel*, but it was in my peripheral vision; I did not know much about the musicians nor what might have happened to them. A few seconds into the opening frames of the film, shots of Bondi Beach, the Sydney Harbour Bridge and the Sydney Opera House appeared on the screen. I was absolutely startled: I had no idea that these musicians had anything to do with Australia, let alone that they might have ended up in Sydney. My attention was captured. The rest of the film unfolded and I was charmed and disarmed by the appeal of the story and the music. But I came away with the disheartening idea that Australia, supposed to be a safe haven, had 'destroyed' the band. I wanted to find out more, since the film was not strong, to an Australian viewer at least, on explanations as to how and why this might have been so. Now that I am more aware of what it includes and leaves out I view the film more critically, but its charm remains undiminished, even though it is highly conventional in its narrative structure and approach. To some extent, then, the following discussion has taken on a life of its own, as an examination of the nature and obligations of film documentary as a form of historical discourse.

Perhaps because they were interpreters rather than creators, the Weintraubs appear in most accounts of Berlin cabaret as adjuncts to the major creative personalities of the day with whom they were associated—figures such as Rudolf Nelson, Friedrich Hollaender, Otto Strasser, Franz Wachsmann, Mischa Spoliansky and Trude Hesterberg—rather than as central characters, despite their celebrity.[1] Thus the film warrants critical attention as the only publicly available extensive account of the story of the band, from its beginning in 1920s Berlin to its point of dissolution in Sydney, Australia, in mid-1940. As a documentary, not a dramatic reconstruction, the film implicitly has a specific obligation towards the telling of the past. More than that, in both chronology and the way it is put together, the film's narrative reproduces, almost exactly, that of the only other published account of the band's history, namely, a 41-page booklet by discographer H.J.P. Bergmeier, who is named in the credits of the film.[2] Bergmeier's chronicle, published in typescript in 1982 by the author and *der JazzFreund*, Menden (Germany), starts from discography and known performance venues, and reconstructs chronology and changes in the band's personnel from evidence provided by recordings, programs and tour lists, supplemented by information assembled over the course of an extensive correspondence (in German and English) between the author and Stefan Weintraub.[3] Though particular musicians are highlighted in brief vignettes, the biographical subject of the film, as of Bergmeier's account, is the band as a group, not its constituent members. Snippets of biography are interpolated, but the main purpose is to document and celebrate the recorded heritage. In the case of the film, this emphasis produces one consistently authentic historical element, the musical soundtrack, which is assembled from the band's recordings (including some made in Russia and Japan) and includes extracts from sound and promotional films in which it featured.

Bergmeier's version of the band's history is given authority and a wide public dissemination by its absorption into the film, whether the viewer is aware of the connection or not. To my knowledge the film has screened in venues as disparate as the Jewish film festivals in Berlin, Sydney and Melbourne and at a jazz festival in the USA.[4] The film not only incorporates

---

[1] For example, there are three references to the Weintraubs in the 300+ pages of Peter Jelavich's definitive English-language study of Berlin cabaret.
[2] H.J.P. Bergmeier, *The Weintraub Story. Incorporated The Ady Rosner Story* (1982).
[3] Correspondence between Bergmeier and Weintraub, 1978–1980, is preserved in the AdKB Item 88.
[4] The film is listed at http://www.jewishfilm.com, accessed August 2012, a site whose purpose is to highlight notable films and videos of Jewish interest to aid in Jewish

the shape and focus of Bergmeier's account but reproduces and implicitly endorses his version of the cause of the dissolution of the band, a problematic feature which will be discussed in detail below. The film thus begins that process of consolidation by means of which, in the absence of evidence to the contrary, assertions become 'true' through mere repetition. In December 2007, the Neuköllner Oper Berlin produced Hans-Peter Kirchberg and Ulrike Gärtner's nostalgic (and necessarily ephemeral) music-theatre piece *Jazz Odyssee—Die Legende einer Showband*, stimulating a degree of interest in the German media. Although this theatre piece had neither the reach nor the potential influence of the film, it nonetheless perpetuated another of Bergmeier's errors, namely, that Leo Weiss was one of the three musicians who were interned.[5]

If, as Dan Sipe asserts, the medium of the documentary film is arguably a 'major influence on the public's historical consciousness',[6] then what are this film's obligations in its retelling of the past? My analysis starts from, but also interrogates, the assumption that a documentary film shares with other forms of historical discourse a commitment to truth-telling. The discussion acknowledges the accepted notion that there is a fictive element involved in any structured retelling of the past,[7] and recognises the complex layers of signification and interaction that can exist, in a film, between spoken text, images and music, the purposive ordering of which constitutes the film's 'rhetorical project'.[8]

The film positions itself in relation to two generic paradigms, in accordance with its targeted constituencies: primarily audiences at Jewish or music/jazz film festivals.[9] On the one hand, the film is a musical 'tribute',

---

      film festival programming. In 2008, it was also screened at the Lionel Hampton International Jazz Festival, University of Idaho.

5   Compare Bergmeier, *The Weintraub Story*, p. 41 and Gerhard Müller, 'Weintraubs Jazz Odyssee'. Programmheft Nr. 33, 11 December 2007. http://www.berlinerphilharmoniker.de/konzerte/kalender/programmdetails/konzert/2994/termin/2007-12-11-20-00/, accessed February 2010.

6   Dan Sipe, 'The Future of Oral History and Moving Images', in Robert Perks and Alistair Thomson (eds), *The Oral History Reader* (London and New York: Routledge, 1998), p. 379.

7   Robert A. Rosenstone, *History on Film/Film on History* (Harlow, UK: Pearson Education Limited, 2006) p. 91; Bill Nichols, *Representing Reality: Issues and Concepts in Documentary* (Bloomington: Indiana University Press, 1991), p. 107; Carolyn G. Heilbrun, 'Is Biography Fiction?', *Soundings* 76/2–3 (Summer/Fall 1993), pp. 295–304.

8   The term is from Carl R. Plantinga, *Rhetoric and Representation in Nonfiction Film* (Cambridge: Cambridge University Press, 1997), p. 169.

9   For a discussion of the impact of sponsoring and distribution agencies on the conventions and ideologies of documentary film production, see Bill Nichols, *Introduction to Documentary* (Bloomington: Indiana University Press, 2001), pp. 22–25.

the function of which is to celebrate, record, recover and restore, and the dominant mode of which is nostalgia—understood in this case simplistically but seductively as a dream of a past that is better than the present reality but is irretrievable. On the other hand, it seeks to recount the historical story of the Weintraubs, a story which also evokes a paradigm instantly recognisable to a Jewish audience: the axis of exile, the journey towards survival, loss and dislocation. The film succeeds as a tribute film because the musicians it celebrates were first-class entertainers and because the European context in which the band flourished is lovingly recreated through period footage, original recordings and evocative contemporaneous images. The account of the band's story, however, and in particular its Australian wartime experience, is less convincingly handled. There is no contemporaneous Australian footage, no attempt to explain Australia's internment policy. Instead, the filmmakers rely on second-hand testimony for explanation, and do not redress any of the misconceptions or reductions which arise from serious (though almost certainly unwitting) flaws in these accounts.

The structure of the film is conventional: two decades in the life of the band are organised into a unitary, chronological story line, in which larger historical events are represented through their impact on this small group of individuals. The journey metaphor is powerfully encoded into the Weintraubs' story between 1933 and 1937, and is represented in the film by images of maps and rolling trainstock: Czechoslovakia (March–November 1933), Austria, Switzerland, Holland (November 1933–January 1934), Belgium, Switzerland (February–June 1934), Sweden, Denmark, Switzerland, Italy (July 1934 – July 1935), Austria and back to Czechoslovakia (February–March 1935). The band arrived in Moscow from Prague on 22 May 1935 for a 50-day series of engagements in Moscow and Leningrad, returning with an extended contract in September (after a sojourn in Sweden, August–September 1935). In the Australian file sources, the most comprehensive and perhaps the most reliable reconstruction of the band's travels between May 1935 and November 1936 comes from a statement made by John Kay, 'compiled of [*sic*] old diaries and notes'.[10] From another statement in Kay's file, we learn that, because its 'enormous salary became uneconomical for the [sponsoring] Moscow organisation' ('GOMEZ' [GOMETs], the State Organisation for Music, Variety Theatre and Circus), the band was

---

10 NAA A6126, 1236, doc. 65 dated 21 June 1945. Russian contracts are preserved in the Bestand Weintraubs Syncopators AdKB (see in particular Items 269 and 272).

re-contracted for twelve months, from December 1935, to the Gofilegt State Philharmony and Vaudeville Trust in Tiflis [Tblisi], Georgia, which sent it on 'a concert tour through approximately 30 different Russian cities'.[11] The musicians left Russia temporarily for Bucharest, Romania in May 1936, and permanently on 1 November 1936, for engagements in Japan (November 1936 – March 1937) and China (May 1937 – June 1937), finally arriving in Australia in July 1937.

The allocations of time in this film are worth noting. The film covers two decades in 65 minutes: the account of the first decade of the band's life takes up thirty minutes, the four-year journey from Berlin to Sydney is covered in seventeen minutes, and the Australian chapter of their story occupies eleven minutes, of which three are taken up with a nostalgic recollection of the film *The Blue Angel*. Insofar as the film indexes itself as a music tribute film, this is reasonable enough; Berlin in the 1920s and early 1930s was a fascinating city, culturally and musically, and the band's early film clips and recordings produce absorbing visuals and an attractive soundtrack. The journey through Russia and Japan is enlivened by humorous anecdotes of the musicians' on- and off-stage shenanigans from Ray [Fritz] Goldner, the surviving musician who was there, while recordings made with Russian and Japanese singers add an exotic touch of local musical colour. This was no harassed flight of traumatised refugees, as is evidenced by this Russian cameo from a 1962 interview with Henry Barger:

> We were really spoiled. We were chauffeured around the city in flashy Cadillacs. There were hardly any cars on the streets in Moscow or Leningrad back then and the taxis were ancient open-topped Fords. The life of average Russians looked completely different and decidedly less attractive than all those receptions and banquets they organised to impress us foreigners…

These boys were stars; earning fabulous money, attracting glamorous women, they clowned and partied their way across the world. Australia is probably the least interesting part of the story musically since there are no Australian recordings, though the film incorporates some live performance footage from a three-minute promotional newsreel 'Weintraubs Bring Novel Musical Act to Australia: Sydney', released in August 1937 to be shown in

---

[11] NAA A6126, 1236, doc. 62. This undated document appears to be a transcript of Kay's answers to a series of questions about the band's Russian tour. The Gofilegt contract (AdKB Item 272) confirms that the contract with GOMETs was cancelled in June 1935.

Snider and Dean's cinemas ahead of the Weintraubs' appearances.[12] And yet the filmmakers attribute enormous significance to events that occurred in Australia.

Exile (1933) and internment (1940) frame the narrative—the band's early career is recounted through an extended flashback—and substantial rhetorical and dramatic weight attaches to the underdeveloped account of internment as the cause of the group's dissolution. Additionally, by virtue of the fact that the story begins with exile and ends with internment, a structural link is established between these two injustices, indirectly but noticeably establishing a comparison between two regimes seen as hostile to an element within their populations ('Jews' in Germany, 'enemy aliens' in Australia). When I first saw this documentary, I was captivated by the music and intrigued by the story, but under-informed. When I watch the film now, having spent some years on a close analysis of Australian material relating to the Weintraubs' wartime experience (and particularly of files preserved in the National Archives of Australia), I observe the ways in which film artifice blurs the distinction between what is historically authentic and what is reductive, the ways in which it 'create[s] a fiction in the name of truth'.[13] I notice in particular how the filmmakers' handling of two elements—music and witness testimony—that may be seen to enhance the film's claim to represent actuality, ultimately serve to disarm critical response through their appeal to subjectivity. I ask what the film's purpose is and how important absolute historical accuracy is to that purpose, as well as what kind of 'truth' the viewer is invited to take away.

The layered narrative: chronicle, story and the film's 'rhetorical project'

The introductory opening sequence of the film quickly and clearly establishes its parameters and its mode. To an accompaniment of one of the band's many recordings and a succession of still photographs of the musicians and iconic images of cities (some including the musicians, others not), the film's thematic content is set in place by five brief scene-setting statements, edited out of what were clearly longer interviews with protagonists in and witnesses to the story.[14] Two concern the journey from Berlin

---

[12] Cinesound Productions, 1937. National Film and Sound Archive (NFSA), Canberra, Title No: 70618.
[13] Rosenstone, *History on Film*, p. 71.
[14] I did contact Dr Jörg Süssenbach, one of the film's writers, and Herr Karl Laabs, from the production company Cine Impuls Berlin, and asked if I could view the unedited

to Australia and three relate to the music, establishing the musicians' versatility, uniqueness and celebrity. The sequence also introduces the two survivor protagonists (Ray Goldner and Ady Fisher [Adolf Frischer]) and two 'experts' (a German jazz historian and a Japanese record collector). Goldner, the youngest of the troupe (he was born in 1915), joined the band as a stage assistant in Vienna in February 1935;[15] Fisher came to Australia from Beirut in May 1938.

In imposing a narrative structure on the bare bones of Bergmeier's chronology, the film gives purposive shape to its arrangement of sounds and images, the means by which it projects its interpretation of the story. Particularly formulaic are the strategies used to establish and conclude the narrative. The 'motif of inauguration',[16] introduced by the unseen 'voice-over' as he begins his narration, posits 'an initial "steady" state that is violated and must be set right', or explained[17]: 'Berlin 1933 ... the Weintraubs Syncopators are one of the city's most popular jazz and show bands. But the young musicians cannot suspect that their lives are about to change dramatically'. The film ends with what Plantinga identifies as a common 'terminating motif', a (ritual) celebration[18]—in this case, a reunion, organised by Mannie Fisher's then wife in 1975. A group photograph of the now elderly musicians appears briefly on the screen.

An element of ambiguity attaches to the account of this latter event and the preceding narrative, but it is an ambiguity that results from what is left out, not from what is said. No hint is given that not all the members of the band were present at the reunion and no reference is made to the two musicians who did not attend: Leo Weiss and John Kay. Perhaps coincidentally, these are two who were able to continue successfully in musical careers—a fact that is also missing from the film's end narration, which describes how, after the war, 'most of the musicians' went on to do other things. In fact, Weiss continued, without interruption until 1952, to direct an orchestra at Prince's, the Sydney cabaret at which all the Weintraubs

---

interviews. Eventually Herr Laabs informed me that most of the documentary material was lost due to a flood in the company's storage cellar in 2002. Email, Karl Laabs to Kay Dreyfus, 9 September 2009.

15 Application for naturalisation, 21 July 1947; Letter to Inspector, Commonwealth Investigation Branch, 24 March [1943]. NAA BP242/1, Q15366.
16 The term is adapted from Hayden White, *Metahistory: The Historical Imagination in Nineteenth-century Europe* (Baltimore & London: The Johns Hopkins University Press, 1973), p. 5; such inaugurating motifs effect the transformation of chronicle into story.
17 Plantinga, *Rhetoric and Representation*, p. 126.
18 Plantinga, *Rhetoric and Representation*, p. 93. 'Terminating motif' is also taken from White.

were performing between December 1938 and June 1940, when three of the musicians were interned. On his release from internment, John Kay took up a lucrative position as musical director for the Colgate-Palmolive Radio Unit; he later established and managed the Mercury Theatre (with Peter Finch in the early 1950s) and wrote a number of scores for Australian feature and documentary films before relocating to London in 1955.[19] The effect of this omission is two-fold. First, it allows nostalgia (represented as a sentimentalised longing for a lost past, see below) to be the dominant affect at the end of the film, in lieu of the complexities that might arise from the inclusion of contradictory elements. Secondly, it preserves the hegemonic integrity of the text as a victim paradigm, reinforcing a thematic motif introduced at the start of the film.

I can only speculate on the possible reason why all mention of these two individuals is avoided and whether or not this was intentional. The omission could be read as reflecting one of the ideological conventions embedded in what film theorists call the 'classic text', namely, to present a 'well-defined chain of cause-and-effect which ends in satisfying closure'.[20] According to such a view, 'closure usually signals the ultimate containment of matters brought out in the narrative—the network of cause-and-effect is resolved, and the narrative returned to a final state of equilibrium'.[21] To admit exceptions to this formula is to disrupt closure and cloud the transparency of the explanation of the band's break up that constitutes the film's epistemological ending. Klinger notes 'the expulsion of any feature which would distract from the hegemony of the narrative line'.[22] Perhaps also for this reason Goldner's departure for Brisbane is situated chronologically in the postwar commentary, implying that his departure was somehow a consequence of the war, though in fact he went to Brisbane before the band's New Zealand tour early in 1938.

Music and the bath of affect

Film historian Robert Rosenstone insists that some information about the past—for example, landscape, sounds and strong emotions—can be better represented on film than in any merely verbal account.[23] Where musical

---

[19] For John Kay, see http://www.imdb.com/name/nm0443190/bio, accessed February 2008. He died in 1970.
[20] Barbara Klinger, '"Cinema/Ideology/Criticism" Revisited—The Progressive Text', *Screen* 25/1 (January–February 1984), p. 37.
[21] Ibid., p. 38.
[22] Ibid., p. 37.
[23] Cited in Hayden White, 'Historiography and Historiophoty', *The American Historical Review* 93/5 (December 1988), p. 1194.

Figure 9. Clowning on stage
A Bavarian or Austrian theme is suggested by the mock *Lederhosen*, no place, no date.
State Library of New South Wales MLMSS 7164X. Scrapbooks concerning the Mercury Theatre, 1940s–1950s [Sydney John Kay], with permission.

performance is the subject of the discourse, film has a particular value; in the case of a band like the Weintraubs Syncopators, who incorporated an essentially visual style of comedic behaviour into their musical act, the vintage live performance footage is a historically valuable element in the film. It tells the viewer what the musicians were like, where their comedy was, and how their clowning was linked to the music they played. Moreover, many of the visual elements of their performance, apparent only in the surviving footage, clearly show how their musical act could be transplanted between cultures that did not share language, a feature which distinguishes them from many other ensembles and individuals whose flight from Nazi Germany also signalled the end of their careers.

How, then, is the music imagined in this film, and what is its interpretive function? Despite the fact that the film is, purposively at least, supposed to be *about* music, its soundtrack is not for the most part intrinsic to the events of the narrative; neither is the music consistently the 'subject' of

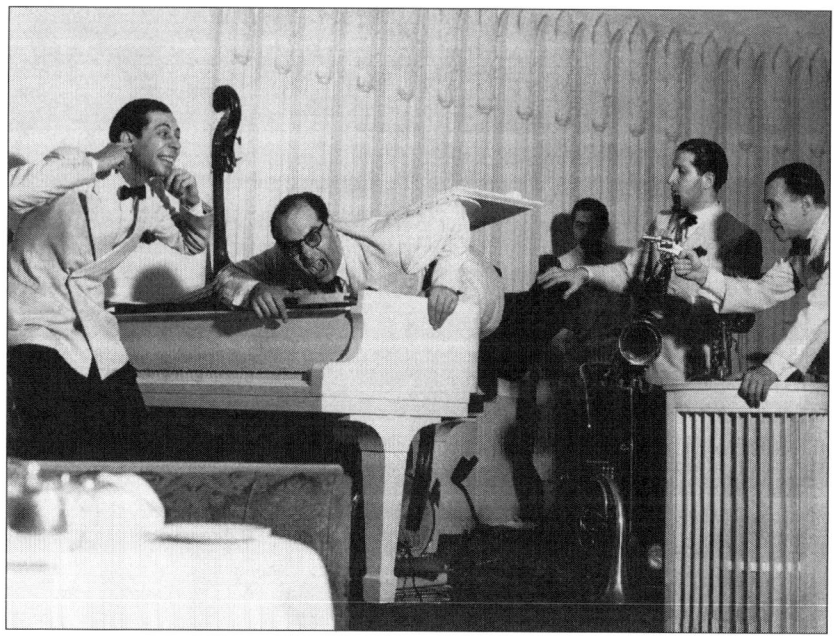

Figure 10. The Weintraubs Sycnopators clowning around at Prince's Restaurant, Sydney, n.d. [late 1930s]
Left to right: Leo Weiss, John Kay, Mannie Fisher, Ady Fisher, Stefan Weintraub.
State Library of New South Wales MLMSS 7164X. Scrapbooks concerning the Mercury Theatre, 1940s–1950s [Sydney John Kay], with permission.

the commentary.[24] The only occasions on which music and image are synchronised in real time are when archival filmed performance excerpts are included. For the rest, music serves as 'background' to the narration and the images, acting as all background music does to intensify affect (whether comic, melancholic or nostalgic) and 'draw the viewer further into the diegetic illusion'.[25] It could be argued that the film is not really about the music; no effort is made to explain, for example, why the band was so popular outside Germany or how it fitted—or failed to fit—into the music and entertainment industry of late 1930s Australia, a very different cultural

---

[24] One must distinguish here between 'expert' discussion of the Weintraubs as musicians, their performance skills and style, and the music itself.
[25] Claudia Gorbman, *Unheard Melodies: Narrative Film Music* (Bloomington: Indiana University Press, 1987), pp. 30, 59. The film's diegesis is the total world of the story action; music that arises from a source within the film's world, as in this case, enhances and reinforces the evocation of the sounds and ambience of the period.

milieu from that of 1920s Berlin. Within the film, music facilitates smooth transition between different layers of narrative, voices and expressions of time. Covertly, by reinforcing nostalgia as the 'experiential envelope' within which the spectator views the film,[26] the music helps to elicit empathy and disarm the viewers' critical faculty, and contributes towards the affective appeal of its ending. Gorbman writes that by acting to 'bathe the listener in affect', music 'lessens defenses against the fantasy structures to which narrative provides access' and 'increases the spectator's susceptibility to suggestion'.[27] While Gorbman is primarily speaking of the dramatic fiction film, Plantinga's observation of the documentary's indebtedness to the conventions of classic fiction cinema must surely also apply to its use of music.

Gorbman emphasises music's role in reinforcing the narrative at the key points of its beginning and ending.[28] Two musical features of the closing sequences of this film are worth comment. One concerns the placement of a short segment devoted to the band's participation in the classic 1930 film *The Blue Angel*, in which it accompanied, on stage, the singing of the film's star, Marlene Dietrich. The other concerns the choice of the song that accompanies the final passages of commentary that describe the breakup of the band. Situated chronologically, *The Blue Angel* segment would have occurred earlier in the film, during the flashback to the band's career in Berlin cabaret before the advent of the Nazi regime, and particularly in the extended discussion of its defining relationship with the composer and pianist Friedrich Hollaender. Instead, it is the only element that appears out of chronological sequence, shown some five minutes before the film ends and after the narrator has described how 'most of the Weintraubs take up new professions'. The frame is unapologetically nostalgic: a Sydney record collector describes how, as an older man, Stefan Weintraub would come to the collector's house to listen to the old tunes and reminisce.[29] 'The exciting times have all become memories now', we have just been told. The past has become an old man's dream.[30] A link with 1930s Berlin is re-established in a context of rupture and loss.

---

[26] Plantinga, *Rhetoric and Representation*, p. 166.
[27] Gorbman, *Unheard Melodies*, p. 5.
[28] Ibid., p. 82.
[29] A narrative connection is established by the fact that the collector, Ian Manfred, met Stefan Weintraub at a screening of *The Blue Angel* in Sydney.
[30] A similar idea is developed in an untitled, undated Australian article (in German) about Weintraub, probably from the 1970s: *'Lächeln kann er eigentlich nur noch, wenn er die alten Schallplatten auflegt, und ihn seine 50 Jahre alte Musik zum Träumen bringt.*

The personal nostalgia associated with Stefan Weintraub's memories becomes generalised through the use of the refrain of the popular song *My Melancholy Baby* as the underpinning of the final ten minutes of the film, preceding and following *The Blue Angel* segment and continuing under the closing credits. Sung in English, the refrain is the final textual element of the film:

> Come to me my melancholy baby,
> Cuddle up and don't be blue
> All your fears are foolish fancies, maybe
> You know dear, that I'm in love with you.
>
> Ev'ry cloud must have a silver lining;
> Wait until the sun shines through.
> Smile my honey, dear, while I kiss away each tear,
> Or else I shall be melancholy too.[31]

Gorbman coins the term 'metadiegetic' to describe this foregrounded use of music as a secondary narrator that represents (as did the primary voice-over narrator) a particular point of view and to some extent controls the audience's response.[32] Here the music expresses feelings that the audience is invited to identify as Weintraub's and, by implication, the group's as a whole.

In his article 'Rock'n'roll Sound tracks and the Production of Nostalgia', David Shumway argues that 'music is the most important ingredient in the production of the affect of nostalgia or the recollection of such affective experience in the viewer'.[33] Rosenstone notes that documentaries speak quite

---

Denn Träume kosten nichts'. [He can only smile when he puts on the old gramophone records and his fifty-year-old music brings him to dreams. Dreams cost nothing.] AdKB Item 67.

[31] Words and Music by George A. Norton and Ernie Burnett, 1912. The song was recorded by the Weintraubs in Tokyo in 1936, featuring a trumpet solo by Mannie Fisher and vocals by Freddy Wise, both of which are heard on the film soundtrack. Paradoxically, the arrangement heard is an upbeat and cheerful one, though this only mildly undercuts the intended tone established by the lyrical content.

[32] Gorbman, *Unheard Melodies*, p. 22. For a further discussion of this idea, see Robynn J. Stilwell, 'The Fantastical Gap between Diegetic and Nondiegetic', in Daniel Goldmark, Lawrence Kramer and Richard Leppert (eds), *Beyond the Soundtrack: Representing Music in Cinema* (Berkeley. Los Angeles and London: University of California Press, 2007), 194–196.

[33] David R. Shumway, 'Rock 'n' Roll Sound Tracks and the Production of Nostalgia', *Cinema Journal* 38/2 (Winter 1999), p. 40.

regularly in 'a specifically visual tense we might dub "nostalgia", a tense whose emotional appeal can pull in a huge audience … '[34] However, Shumway argues that 'nostalgia is a particular attitude toward or construction of the past, and not all representation of the past or its artifacts is nostalgic'.[35] What comment does this choice of song make on the narrative at this point? In context it would seem that the formulaic clichés of the song's lyrics overlay grief with romantic melancholy, neutralising the impact of the darker realities of 1930s Germany, the heart-breaking revelations of the postwar era for many German-Jewish refugees, or even the more profound layers of loss that are intimated within the film.[36]

Witness testimony and the thinning of evidence

In a compilation documentary such as this, spoken word combines with images and music not just to evoke the past (though the film does this quite powerfully), but to make us feel something about the story being told: '[Film] does not simply provide an image of the past, it wants you to feel strongly about that image … Film does more than want to teach the lesson that history hurts; it wants you, the viewer, to experience the hurt (and pleasures) of the past'.[37] The witness-centred 'voice of testimony' is used to substantiate or provide evidence for the filmmakers' or text's argument and to elicit feelings from the viewer. Onscreen witnesses testify to or describe the events depicted, enriching the expressive texture of the narration with their empathetic appeal while the onscreen close-up of the expressive human face allows us to register the power of past events by observing their impact in the present.[38] The use of real people, so-called 'social actors' (as distinct from theatrical performers), reinforces the film's 'claim to be an authentic recreation of the world as it was for these people', even though we no longer witness them 'engaged in historical situations and events but in reflection and recall of such events'.[39] The visual element is critical: 'We not only benefit from *what* is said, but from the visual and aural information available in *how* it is said—from facial expression to gestures to inflections

---

[34] Rosenstone, *History on Film*, p. 17.
[35] Shumway, 'Rock 'n' Roll Sound Tracks', p. 50 n. 10.
[36] As may be inferred, for example, from Bonnie Weintraub's statement that Stefan did not see much of the others after the war.
[37] Rosenstone, *History on Film*, p. 16.
[38] Nichols, *Introduction to Documentary*, p. 42.
[39] Nichols, *Representing Reality*, p. 252. 'Social actors' is from Nichols, *Introduction to Documentary*, p. 5.

of the voice'.[40] So, for example, at the start of the film's main narrative, Ady Fisher, one of the two surviving musicians interviewed live, describes how, shortly after the Nazis took control of government, a young girl spat at him in a tram and called him '*Jude*' ['Jew']. 'We loved what we did,' he says, 'but they just didn't want us any more'. This simple sentence, spoken by an old man with tears in his eyes, resonates with everything we know about the subsequent fate of Germany's Jews during the 1930s and 1940s.[41] Given the power of the affect, it may seem that the person on screen speaks directly to the viewer but in fact his contribution is significantly mediated by what Plantinga calls 'propositional editing'.[42] Only extracts from interviews are included (sometimes no more than single sentences), the questions are not heard and the questioner is not present, so the viewer has no knowledge of the larger content of the interview, either in terms of the give and take of dialogue or of the structuring role of the interviewer.

Though editing operates to 'maintain logical continuity between individual viewpoints'[43] and create a uniform perspective, there is, in fact, a complex hierarchy of subjectivities among the witnesses in this film. Only two 'subject-protagonists' appear in the film: Ray [Fritz] Goldner (the only witness to have been with the band in Russia) and Ady Fisher (who did not join the band until May 1938, in Sydney). Other witnesses include bystanders (people who knew the musicians personally or heard them play) and experts (principally jazz historians who can 'place' the music and musicians in a wider musical and cultural context or substantiate claims about the quality of the musicianship). Archival interviews recorded in the past with now deceased protagonists are absorbed into the voice-over narration.

Not all individuals speak of events of which they have direct knowledge, so that at times hearsay replaces testimony at key points of the narrative. The explanation of why the Weintraubs broke up, for example, is divided between Stefan Weintraub's widow Bonnie, and Mannie Fisher's wife Edzia, neither of whom was together with her musician husband at the time of the events of which she speaks:

> (hesitantly) The Weintraubs broke up on account of the War … and … um … they were called in Australia displaced persons of course

---

[40] Plantinga, *Rhetoric and Representation*, p. 162.
[41] Fisher tells the same story, clearly a defining experience of rupture, in his interview for the Shoah Foundation (interview 17168, 4 August 1996).
[42] Plantinga, *Rhetoric and Representation*, p. 151, citing Paul Messaris.
[43] Nichols, *Representing Reality*, p. 45.

and ... ah ... life began to be a little more difficult for them here. (Bonnie Weintraub)

Around the middle of 1940 ... Stefan Weintraub, Horst Graff and John Kaiser get turned in as Germans into the internment camp in Victoria. It's based on the belief that they are transmitting on Thursday nights through the radio some secret codes as spies to the Japanese. As hard as it is to believe, that's what the Australians are claiming and sending them off to an internment camp. (Edzia Fisher)

Bonnie's hesitations are intriguing, as is her evident discomfort in talking to the camera (a discomfort not evident in her earlier appearances). Her description of the musicians as 'displaced persons' is inaccurate (though probably not deliberately intended to mislead), since 'displaced persons' is the term used for postwar refugees. Its effect, though, is curious: 'displaced persons' are clearly victims, of circumstance and the events of war; 'enemy aliens', which is how Stefan Weintraub was classified, justly or unjustly, at the time of his internment, designates a group to which suspicion could hypothetically attach itself (and did). Her statement that the Weintraubs broke up on account of the war, while ultimately true, is so broad as to be largely uninformative, and also seems to contradict her earlier remark that Australia was a 'safe country to be in ... far removed from Europe where trouble was and that's why they stayed'. No further explanations are offered of what changed or what difficulties the musicians encountered.

The choice of Edzia Fisher to explain the circumstances surrounding the internment of three of the musicians in June 1940 is even more intriguing since not only was she not married to Mannie Fisher at the time, but he was not one of the three interned.[44] Moreover, Stefan Weintraub is the implicit subject of the end of the film: his memories frame *The Blue Angel* flashback and his estrangement introduces the postwar reunion. Why did Bonnie Weintraub not speak about her husband's internment?

There is indeed a link between an (unproven) allegation of espionage and the internment of the three musicians named by Mrs Fisher, but the charge involved the band's activities in Russia and is not mentioned in the film. Mrs Fisher's recollection is, I believe, based on another, later, incident that is recorded in the Fisher brothers' wartime security file in the National Archives of Australia. As is mentioned in the film, Ady and

---

[44] As Edia Sztern, Mrs Fisher interviewed both Mannie and Ady Fisher for the Shoah Foundation in July and August 1996.

Mannie Fisher, together with Leo Weiss (a German national who was not interned), continued in their employment as musicians for some time *after* the other members of the band had been interned. In March 1942, after Pearl Harbour, an internal military security memo, reporting a phone call from a local Passport Guard, noted that a group under the name of 'Manny Fisher's Sextet' was broadcasting from radio 2UW on Thursdays. The memo concludes, 'as the majority of the band must be subject to suspicion, perhaps an inquiry might be made as to the facts and the material broadcast ascertained'.[45] Inquiries into the content of the broadcast were duly made and Mannie was interviewed by military intelligence,[46] but there is no record of any further action on this matter.

With its historical inaccuracies left unscrutinised, Mrs Fisher's anecdote serves only to trivialise the legitimate military and national security concerns that shaped Australia's internment policy in 1940, however prejudicially applied. The most cursory examination of a Sydney newspaper would have alerted the filmmakers to the reality of domestic concerns about the war in the middle of 1940, and of the internment operation that took place on 6 June 1940, the day on which the three musicians were arrested. Page 1 of the *Sydney Morning Herald* on that day carried a report of heavy German bombing in central France. High levels of anxiety attached to the apparent ease of the German conquest of Europe and the pressure on British and Dominion forces (witness the evacuation from Dunkirk). The film's writers would have noted how, after the fall of the Low Countries in May 1940, fears of fifth column activities among 'phony' refugees, particularly those of German and Austrian nationality (so-called 'enemy aliens'), had triggered vigorous local debate over whether or not *all* refugees should be interned for the public good.[47] Historian Paul Bartrop cites a secret government memorandum from 20 June which, in addressing the possibility of enemy agents 'travelling as refugees on neutral ships', concludes, 'Where there seems any ground for doubt, authority can take no risks, and we must ask those who are placed under restrictions, which in their case appear to them quite unnecessary and undeserved, to bear with the inconvenience for the common good'.[48] The problem is that internment was not universal, and the

---

[45] Initialled memo, 9? March 1942. NAA C123/1, 1211.
[46] Handwritten note, dated 20 March 1942. NAA C123/1, 1211. A transcript of the broadcast, reports of the interview and detailed notes on the individual musicians are included in the file.
[47] *Sydney Morning Herald*, 6 June 1940, p. 9.
[48] Bartrop, Paul R. 'Enemy Aliens or Stateless Persons? The Legal Status of Refugees from Germany in Wartime Australia', *Journal of the Australian Jewish Historical*

policy was selectively applied. Inconsistencies and injustices often arose from this selectivity, particularly in the treatment of Jewish refugees, who were targeted and often interned, as indeed were Graff and Weintraub, along with Germans associated with the Nazi Party. In the eyes of the Australian authorities, significant doubt attached to the reliability of the musicians collectively in consequence of the allegation that the band had been expelled from Russia for engaging in espionage on behalf of the German Government, and individually because refugees with family remaining in Germany were considered to be susceptible to pressure from the Nazi regime. However unlikely the espionage charge may seem to us to be in hindsight, prevailing ideologies that influenced official assessments of the reliability of the denouncer (a British national and First World War veteran) and the denounced must be acknowledged.

Various issues cluster around the relationship of filmmaker and witness in a documentary film. First there is the historical status of the evidence itself. As in oral history, witnesses claim the authority (or surrogate authority, as in the case of the wives and widows) of a first-hand knowledge of events that results from 'having been there'. In film, however, because of the way they are subsumed into the narration, 'oral histories tend to function ... as pieces of argumentation rather than as primary source material still in need of conceptual organization'.[49] Ethical considerations attend the filmmaker's relationship to witnesses as real people: how is the testimony of witnesses to be contested or qualified within a film 'without running the risk of appearing to disbelieve, discredit or mock them'?[50] On the other hand, the absence of oppositional testimony or contesting voices, as here, raises the question of whether the filmmaker has chosen to extrapolate only those opinions that reinforce the dominant point of view, 'casting suspicion on the veracity of the film'.[51]

The brief, out-of-context witness statements included in this film are too mediated to support a discussion of the vexed relationship between memory, witness and testimony. At issue here is not the reliability of the witnesses, but the effect of the statements as they are included and the filmmakers'

Society X, Part 4 (November 1988), p. 274. Figures reproduced in Neumann show that the numbers of internees increased from 253 to 2095 between March and June 1940. *In the Interest of National Security: Civilian Internment in Australia during World War II* (Canberra: NAA 2006), p. 7.

[49] Nichols, *Representing Reality*, p. 252.
[50] Nichols, *Introduction to Documentary*, pp. 5–13; Nichols, *Representing Reality*, p. 252.
[51] Plantinga, *Rhetoric and Representation*, p. 162.

failure to navigate between memory as it survives within families and the detailed historical record as it survives in public archives.

What does this documentary document?

The documentary film, by taking what Plantinga calls an 'assertive stance' in relation to actuality, makes a claim to represent *the* world (not 'a' world) as it was,[52] and our complicit belief in or acceptance of this claim is essential to the communication of the filmmaker's view or argument.[53] If this film is to be taken seriously as a contribution to the history of its topic, then truth has to matter. But while such an affirmation is easy to make, it is less easy to apply in all the situations generated within the complex medium of film.

Rosenstone, for example, problematises the proposition by asking what kind of truth it is that we should look for: factual, narrative, emotional, psychological or symbolic.[54] In his many essays on the relationship between memory and actuality, Alessandro Portelli argues for the value of 'wrong' versions of historical events, asserting that it is the very discrepancies between fact and memory that gives oral testimonies their worth, since such discrepancies arise out of the witnesses' efforts to discover meaning in the events described.[55] It is not difficult to read the subjective 'truth' underpinning Ady Fisher's and Bonnie Weintraub's statements. Ady Fisher's statement 'they just didn't want us any more', enhanced as it is by temporal placement at the start of the film, undoubtedly carries emotional 'truth'. Is it consequential, then, that the 'we' of whom he speaks cannot be the Weintraubs, despite the contextual implication that it is, since Ady Fisher did not join the band until May 1938 in Sydney? Does it matter that he did not leave Berlin in 1933, as the commentary implies, but in 1935? We respond because, irrespective of such details, his comment encapsulates all the gratuitous and arbitrary lawlessness and localised brutalities of the early months of the Third Reich. Similarly, the manifest discomfort and hesitancy of Bonnie Weintraub's attempt to explain why the Weintraubs broke up has an implicit psychological truth, aimed at protecting the memory of her husband.

---

52 Ibid., p. 19; Nichols, *Representing Reality*, p. 109.
53 Plantinga, *Rhetoric and Representation*, pp. 18, 220.
54 Rosenstone, *History on Film*, p. 28.
55 Alessandro Portelli, 'What Makes Oral History Different', in Perks and Thomson (eds), *The Oral History Reader* pp. 63–74 and esp. p. 67.

Based on her language and demeanour, one might speculate that, in the case of her anecdote about internment, historical correctness was perhaps less important for Edzia Fisher than the wish to characterise the actions of the Australian authorities as absurd. It could indeed be argued that the detention of the Weintraubs, as Jews, was 'absurd', but that absurdity was not so apparent at the time, and an official case was assembled against each individual.[56] No distinction was made in the official classification of Jews and non-Jews of German and Austrian nationality as 'enemy aliens' until 1942, when a class of 'refugee aliens' was created, or more comprehensively in 1944, when the definitions in the National Security (Aliens Service) Regulations were amended.[57] That the filmmakers were not motivated to question Edzia Fisher's testimony is perhaps explained by the fact that Bergmeier also attributes the internment of three of the musicians to concerns about the Japanese following Japan's entry into the war.[58] However, in its reliance on recollection (witness and testimony) *to provide explanations*, the film appears to offer a somewhat naïve form of endorsement to opinions that remain at times self-protective, partial, or incomplete.[59]

There is one aspect of the Weintraubs' story that makes it rather different from many other exile stories, inasmuch as their career did not end when they left Berlin. Already established as a successful touring ensemble when the musicians took their decision not to return to Germany, they simply continued doing what they had always done, albeit with local variations that may be appreciated from recordings used in the film.[60] In terms of the film's erotetic narrative—that is, the questions it poses and then answers[61]—it is internment, not exile, which marks the end of the group as an entity. It is Australia's treatment of the musicians, not Germany's that emerges as responsible for the group's artistic destruction.[62] It matters, therefore, whether Edzia Fisher's three sentences are enough to do justice to the complexities of Australia's wartime internment policy.

---

56 Documents outlining the individual cases for internment may be found in NAA C123/1213 [Horst Graff]; NAA MP529/2, WEINTRAUB/S; NAA SP1048/7, S56/1/1041 [John Kurt Kaiser].
57 Bartrop, 'Enemy Aliens or Stateless Persons?', pp. 275, 278.
58 Bergmeier, *The Weintraub Story*, p. 41.
59 Nichols, *Representing Reality*, 252.
60 The Weintraubs added a Russian flavour to their music in Russia and recorded with Japanese popular vocalists in Japan.
61 Plantinga, *Rhetoric and Representation*, p. 107, citing Noël Carroll.
62 Plantinga, ibid., p. 131 writes that 'Formal endings guide the backward-directed activity of the spectator in comprehending the film'.

For most theorists of film as history, the reductive pressures within the textual narrative, its 'thinning of data',[63] are the single most problematic feature, especially when allied to a strong drive towards presenting 'a unified representation of a subject marked by a clear contextualization of knowledge within a relatively conventional structure'.[64] For me, this film's usefulness as a historical document is undermined by its (probably unwitting) pro-German cultural bias as reflected in its allocations of time and in its attributions of causality, and by a simplistic appeal to the uncritical subjectivities of its target (Jewish or musical) audience. Most difficult, even if largely unnoticed, is the implied synchronicity between the film's opening—Nazi treatment of the Jews (expulsion, exile)—and its ending—Australian treatment of the same group of Jews (arbitrary internment, loss of profession). Though Australia's Second World War refugee policy has deplorable aspects (which are well documented in the scholarly literature), there are no parallels to be made between a totalitarian regime with murderous racial policies and even a temporarily de-liberalised wartime democracy.

---

[63] The phrase is from White, 'Historiography and Historiophoty', p. 1197, citing Rosenstone.
[64] Plantinga, *Rhetoric and Representation*, p. 115.

PART TWO

THE ENCOUNTER WITH THE MUSICIANS' UNION

INTRODUCTION

On 1 December 1938, Frank Kitson, secretary of the NSW District of the Musicians' Union of Australia, wrote to all district secretaries on the subject of the Weintraubs who, being 'all foreigners and, I understand, mainly Jews … are of course not eligible as members of this organisation', but who, despite these obstacles, had secured a highly sought-after job at Prince's, a lavish, new, Continental-style dance restaurant and cabaret venue for the 'ultra-discriminating' in Martin Place, Sydney.[1] Kitson detailed his interaction with J.C. Bendrodt, the manager of Prince's, over the prospective employment of the Weintraubs, which Kitson had vigorously attempted to prevent. After several lengthy interviews, Bendrodt agreed to employ, in addition, a local, fully unionised band led by New Zealand-born Craig Crawford. Kitson endeavoured to persuade Bendrodt to use the Weintraubs as a stage attraction only and not as a band for dancing but the matter ended in a stalemate: 'I have not agreed to them being used even to an infinitesimal degree for dancing and Mr Bendrodt has not agreed that he will employ them entirely as an attraction'.[2] However, the appointment of an Australian band to Prince's curtailed Kitson's ability to pursue his campaign against the Weintraubs publicly, and affected the response of the various government officials with whom he continued to correspond on the matter.

It is the purpose of Part Two of this book to contextualise the Union's treatment of the Weintraubs Syncopators as part of an ongoing tension between a union dedicated to protecting its membership by restricting the 'importation of competitive wage-earners', and the commercial interests of entrepreneurs who argued that Australian musicians could not, of themselves, satisfy either public demand or the needs of the industry. For four decades of the twentieth century, from about 1918 to the end of the

---

[1] The phrase is from the advertisement for the opening, *Sydney Morning Herald*, 8 December 1938, p. 35.
[2] Noel Butlin Archive Centre, Australian National University, Canberra: Archive of the Professional Musicians' Union of Australia (NBAC MUA) E156/2/2/(ic) (Kitson letter). The union could reasonably hope that the Weintraubs would have a limited tenure as a specialty stage act, whereas popular dance bands were known to remain in venues for years.

Figure 11. Playing for dancing at Prince's, late 1930s or early 1940
The Union lost its battle to make management engage the Weintraubs as a fixed contract 'speciality' act only.

Akademie der Künste, Berlin, Bestand Weintraubs Syncopators, Item 205, with permission.

1950s, the MUA attempted, as one of its key policy objectives, to prevent any foreign musicians from working in Australia. For most of the twentieth century, membership of the professional musicians' union was mandatory for any musician hoping to work in the mainstream music industry. Australia's arbitration system legislated preferential employment for union members, and many if not most employers were bound by the determinations of either the Federal Conciliation and Arbitration Court or the states' industrial tribunals and commissions. Musician unionists were prevented by the Union's rules from playing with non-members.

The engagement of the Weintraubs at a prestigious venue like Prince's thus exposed a number of fault lines in the Australian music profession. The problem was to some extent an historical one. Foreign musicians have been part of Australia's musical landscape since the European colonies were founded. Although British traditions shaped the country's manners

PART TWO: INTRODUCTION

and its social, administrative and legislative structures, the musical culture was European and international. As Katharine Brisbane has written, 'A few years after European settlement, Australia and New Zealand became staging posts in a world circuit of performers who kept their audiences in close touch with events and progress abroad'.[3] Opera singers (sometimes whole companies), concert virtuosi, popular entertainers of various kinds, conductors, band leaders and their bands supplemented the small reserve of resident performers. Some of these visitors came and went, some returned many times; others came and stayed. The taste for the foreign took on different aspects at different times. A public enthusiasm for American dance bands and Italian opera companies characterised the 1920s; in the 1930s, the sophisticated appeal of the Continental—in venues, décor and music—advantaged European entertainers like the Weintraubs over local musicians.

Once the Australian Broadcasting Commission emerged as the single largest employer of musicians across a range of styles from the mid-1940s, the argument in favour of the employment of foreign musicians shifted from commercial advantage to cultural advancement, but the Union remained adamant that Australian musicians could supply all that was needed just as potential employers insisted that they could not. Battles were fought on a case by case basis, with the Union maintaining that only a blanket embargo could prevent the country from being flooded with foreign musicians. Bendrodt, as an influential entrepreneur and employer on the Sydney scene, was an example of the perils of precedent, as Kitson advised in a circular letter to government ministers and parliamentarians in 1935:

> On 23rd ult. I received a letter from Mr J.C. Bendrodt who has been an employer of dance musicians in this City for a number of years, to the effect that … if such importations were permitted, he would be enforced by competition, though appreciating the quality of Australian bands, to capitalise the publicity values involved by importing musicians. You will see therefore that one successful application to the Government for permission to import, will be merely the forerunner of many similar applications and that not only would an avenue of employment be closed to Australian musicians, but the position of musicians in employment would be jeopardised.[4]

---

3   Katharine Brisbane, 'The Hidden Australia: An International Culture', in *Entertaining Australia*, ed. Katharine Brisbane (Paddington, NSW: Currency Press, 1991), p. 10.
4   Frank Kitson (as Secretary of the MUA NSW District), to various parliamentarians, 5 February 1935. NAA A444, 1952/2762. For Bendrodt, see Iain McCalman, 'Bendrodt, James Charles (1891–1973)', *Australian Dictionary of Biography* 13 (Melbourne:

SILENCES AND SECRETS

Figure 12. A musician's dream of Australia invaded by foreign musicians, 1935

In this cartoon by Jim Russell, published in the *Australian Music Maker and Dance Band News* of January 1935, a despondent musician imagines Australia in the shape of a tiny island invaded by foreign musicians.

Magazine held in the Mitchell Library, State Library of New South Wales, reproduced with permission State Library of New South Wales and Ingrid Mackenzie.

The Weintraubs' success in securing the job at Prince's immediately elevated their profile in the music profession. It led to a twelve-month contract to broadcast with the Lever Brothers' sponsored show 'Rinso [a laundry

---

Melbourne University Press, 1993), pp. 161–162.

PART TWO: INTRODUCTION

Figure 13. Comfortable with celebrity
The Weintraubs endorse Conn saxophones. *Australian Music Maker and Dance Band News*, May 1939.

Magazine held in the Mitchell Library, State Library of New South Wales, reproduced with permission.

powder] Melody Riddles' every Thursday evening on radio 2FC and to broadcasting spots on radio stations 2CH and 2GB. Photographs of the group appeared in the pages of the music magazines promoting products such as the Conn saxophones or the Ajax 'New Century' Dual Snare model side drum, while the musicians' confident self-representation of their own

Figure 14. Promotional sheet music of a popular song
The small inset publicity photograph shows the six members of the Prince's band being silly around the microphone of radio 2CH (Sydney) in the late 1930s. Only the top bands would be pictured on sheet music in this way.
Author's collection.

celebrity was projected through their annual 'season's greetings' promotional advertisements. By entering into competition with Australian musicians in other areas of work, the Weintraubs became, for the MUA, a prototype for the refugee musician 'menace' that increasingly gave shape to Union policy through the 1930s.

On 29 July 1938, in a context of increased public debate on the Jewish refugee question that followed Australia's participation in the Evian

PART TWO: INTRODUCTION

Conference in June–July, the *Sydney Morning Herald* canvassed a range of professions on the possibility of finding employment for European refugees. The survey revealed conflicting opinions. While architects, engineers and accountants were sympathetic, the Musicians' Union joined with doctors and dentists in definite opposition to an influx of refugee professionals. Frank Kitson, speaking as NSW District secretary of the MUA, stated that his union was strongly opposed to the importation of foreign musicians 'exiled from Germany as a result of the Hitler regime'. The following day Kitson gave an interview to the *Telegraph* in which he expressed himself unambiguously on the question of refugee musicians: 'We are clearly specifying Jews', he said, just to make his position perfectly plain.[5] Kitson was responding to a speech made by visiting English conductor Malcolm Sargent, who declared that 'the development of orchestral talent in Australia was being retarded by union regulations, which prevented the employment in orchestras of skilled performers from overseas'. 'Only imported players who are British will be acceptable to local musicians', Kitson retorted, echoing the Australian Medical Association's declared preference for British doctors. In the following month, at its meeting in August 1938, the NSW District 'closed its ranks to foreigners', both local and overseas.[6]

It would be easy to read this and Kitson's earlier remark about the Weintraubs being 'mainly Jews' as evincing the antisemitism that historian Michael Blakeney and others have claimed was so influential in shaping Australia's response to the Jewish refugee crisis of the late 1930s; they certainly suggest that the MUA was singling out 'Jews' as an ethnicity within its exclusionary policy in the 1930s.[7] The Union itself steadily maintained, throughout the 1930s, that its policy was in no way more pronounced in the case of expatriated European Jews than in the case of other foreigners:

> On the contrary this organisation sympathises very strongly with these unfortunate exiles who are the victims of Hitlerism. Applications from

---

[5] 'Refugees. Professions' Attitude', *Sydney Morning Herald* 29 July 1938, p. 13 (survey); 'Will Welcome only British Players', *Telegraph*, 29 July 1938 (Kitson's rejoinder); 'Unions and Music. Progress Retarded', *Sydney Morning Herald*, 28 July 1938, p. 13 (Sargent's speech reported). All in the scrapbook 'Press cuttings 1938–52', NBAC MUA Z401 Box 13.

[6] Minutes of the NSW committee, 5 August 1938. NBAC MUA T7/1/10.

[7] Michael Blakeney, *Australia and the Jewish Refugees 1933–1948* (Sydney: Croom Helm Australia, 1985). The idea that pre- and postwar Jewish refugee policy was shaped by a prevailing antisemitism has been critiqued, for example, by Bartrop (*Australia and the Holocaust* p. xi) and W.D. Rubinstein, ('Australia and the Refugee Jews of Europe, 1933–1954', *Journal of the Australian Jewish Historical Society* X, Part 6 (May 1989): pp. 500–523).

some of these gentlemen have been rejected, not because they are Jews but because the policy of the organisation is opposed to the admission of foreigners each one of whom would undoubtedly secure work which could be taken by our own people, many of whom are in dire need of work.[8]

Jewishness was neither the ground for particular discrimination nor for special treatment despite, in some cases, the applicants' heart-rending personal stories. Paul Bartrop agrees that prejudicial Australian thinking extended more widely than simple Jew-hatred. But the matter was more complex; as he writes: 'Decidedly anti-alien, Australians could not always steer a course between hatred of foreigners and hatred of Jews, particularly when the aliens in question happened also to be Jewish'.[9]

To the extent that the policy on foreign musicians articulated by Kitson in 1938 had been formed over the two preceding decades in different circumstances, and prevailed until the early 1960s, my study would endorse Bartrop's assertion. A number of different ethnicities were identified as the foreign 'other' between 1918 and 1960—Italians and Americans in the 1920s, German and Austrian Jewish refugees in the 1930s, Jewish survivors and non-Jewish displaced persons of various nationalities in the postwar period. Facile conclusions are complicated by the fact that, although one of its fighting slogans was to 'keep orchestras British', and although it expressed a nominal preference for imported British musicians over non-British (as in Kitson's 1938 interview cited above), in reality the Union also opposed the importation of musicians from Britain and other Commonwealth countries for most of this period, and imposed restrictions on their admission to membership. (While it is true that Australians at this period were legally British subjects, as no separate category of Australian citizenship existed until 1948, the term 'British' is used somewhat variously in Union rhetoric. The MUA distinguished 'British' from 'non-British' in the discussion of the category of foreign musicians; but in relation to Australian-born musicians as, for example, in the Union's rules, 'British' meant born in Britain or another Commonwealth country.) To characterise the policy as antisemitic, however, is to limit its wider application, to Jew and non-Jew alike, whatever the personal views of individual Union officials might have been.

---

[8] Secretary MUA to K Cargill Renkin Esq, 5 March 1935. NBAC MUA E156/2/2(xx) (1938–48).
[9] *Australia and the Holocaust*, p. 17.

PART TWO: INTRODUCTION

Union policy on foreign musicians took shape over a decade between 1918 and 1929. In September 1929, the General Secretary of the MUA announced in *The Professional Musician*, the Union's official journal, 'there are no orchestras of any foreign nationality here now … the fight is over', an extraordinary statement given that the non-indigenous musical traditions of this former British colony are entirely transplanted. The proximity of the date to the advent of sound films suggests a causal relationship, but here, too, the facts are more complex. The issue of foreign musicians became the site of a struggle for control of the labour market, a struggle rooted in the institutionalised racism of the *Immigration Restriction Act* of 1901 (the so-called White Australia policy), legitimised by the distinctive structures of the arbitration system and sanctioned by legal recognition of trade union autonomy with regard to membership regulation. Chapter Two examines the evolution and consequences of the MUA's policy on foreign labour through the 1920s and its efforts to mobilise legislative support by appeals to popular concerns—in this decade, about Italian migration. The focus in the chapter is on the institutional framework provided by the state-supported arbitration and conciliation system, and on the development of an organisational culture of rule-making within the Union, as part of a transformational process of consolidation.

A parallel process of myth-making accompanied the process of rule-making that the MUA undertook in the decade of the 1920s: 'myths' in this case being understood to include those stories an organisation tells itself and its members about its history, in which its explicit assumptions and tacit values are embedded, as well as the stories that the organisation tells to the various interest groups whose support it seeks to enlist. But whereas rule-making produced a mindset of 'literal legalism', much concerned with minutiae, myth-making, paradoxically, called for an entirely different set of skills: rhetorical opportunism, an ability to argue several positions simultaneously and a flexible approach to the truth. Union officials routinely appropriated the language of the current popular immigration debate to legitimise the Union's case against foreign musicians across various fields of action (social and political), in a range of settings (from private to public) and modes (written or oral), and using a variety of genres. The scope of Union discourse and the contexts in which it occurred may be represented diagrammatically (Figure 15).[10] Arguments and vocabulary remained

---

[10] Diagrammatic representation and terminology in the preceding sentence are derived from Reisigl and Wodak, *Discourse and Discrimination*, see in particular Chapter 2.

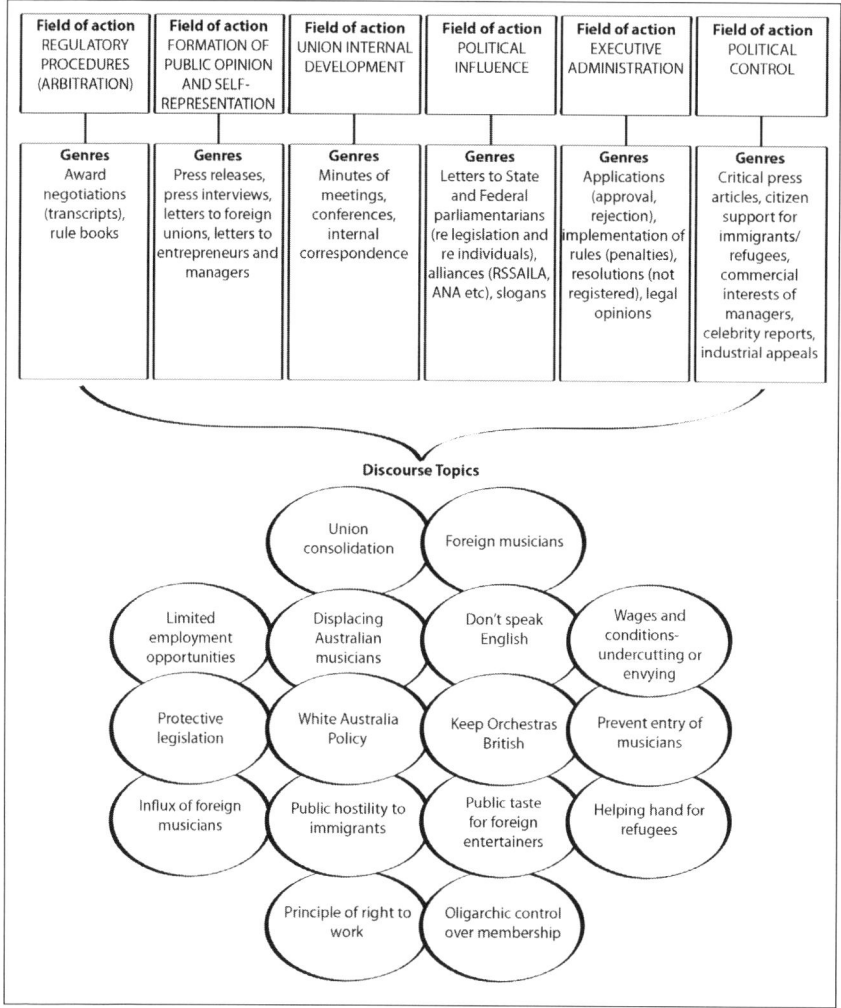

Figure 15. Diagrammatic representation of MUA-related discourse: fields of action, genres and topics

Drawn by Kara Rasmanis, Arts Imaging, Monash University.

remarkably constant across all fields, though with varying degrees of circumspection and formality.

Essentially the Union promulgated a nativist jobs discourse in which a very small number of topics clustered around formulaic slogans such as 'Australian jobs for Australian workers'. The Union expressed its opposition to foreign musicians generically in the press, but opposed the employment of foreign

PART TWO: INTRODUCTION

musicians on a case by case basis through direct approaches to management and government. The Union's engagement with refugee musicians in the 1930s and 1940s was thus at the same time a highly personalised one, aimed at specific individuals and groups, as may be seen in the discussion of two incidents involving the Weintraubs in Chapter Three. Since the objective was so clearly dismissal, prohibition, deportation or repatriation, the campaigns against individuals can appear startlingly deliberate, amounting at the time to a professional persecution not dissimilar to the one they were escaping in Europe. Public rhetoric reflected prevailing attitudes towards and constructions of specific European groups, relying heavily on the emotional value of stereotypical metaphors of 'flooding' and 'swamping' and persistent applications of that universal cliché of anti-migration rhetoric, the 'influx'.[11] Although these strategies worked well in the decades before the Second World War, the Union found itself increasingly out of step with changes in public opinion towards so-called 'New Australians' in the 1950s, and its ideological positions came under challenge from within and without. Chapter Five, a postwar postscript, looks briefly at the changing situation of the 1950s.

Federal Council of the Union comprised perhaps eight individuals for most of the period covered by my study. However, one cannot fail to note the extent to which the development and implementation of policy on foreign musicians is linked to Frank Kitson personally. His name first appears as a member of the NSW committee in the minutes of the meeting of 26 April 1915. He was elected to the committee, though not every year between 1916 and 1923, and fulfilled various other roles such as Trades Hall representative in 1918, delegate to the Labour Council in 1920 and to Federal Council in 1923, Returning Officer in 1925. From 1924 until his death in 1951 he acted as secretary for the NSW District and Federal President; he died in office in November 1951. He was the Union's delegated representative at arbitration so fulfilled a key role in arguing the Union's cases to government and the courts. As President and official spokesperson, he presented the Union's position to the public through the press. He was a diligent, vigilant and hard-working career official; his quarterly printed secretary's reports to members of the NSW District from 1934 to the end of the 1930s summarise ongoing Union concerns. Most of the correspondence for the period of my study thus involves him in one role or other. His turn of mind was literal and inflexible, an approach of technical legalism that placed first priority on the

---

[11]   For discussion of negative stereotypical metaphors, see ibid., p. 59.

'enforcement of the rules as set out in the constitution'[12] and precluded any possibility of making exceptions. Admired by his Union colleagues for his steely resolve, he declined to make any personal information available to the public, beyond admitting, when interviewed by the *Sunday Sun* late in 1949, that he was 'a professional musician once, but I am not going to say what I played'.[13]

Union officials like Kitson occupy a particular place in my analysis: they are not part of the machinery of government and yet they operate in a semi-official capacity as elected office-bearers motivated by concern for and solidarity with the community of people they represent (the Union membership). By examining Union interaction with government, either about specific individuals or more general issues, my study documents the efforts of the MUA to influence government policy on the admission of immigrant musicians and the extent to which these efforts were successful, either in the design or the implementation. Embedded in the exchanges between Union and government is the larger issue of the immigrant musician's right to work once admitted to the country and a question concerning the point at which exclusion should occur. Kim Rubenstein argues that the latter question impacts on the very concept of citizenship, citing Henry Parkes, who observed that it was better 'to prevent the arrival of immigrants than to discourage or harass them after they arrived'. Unless immigrants are permitted 'to have the same rights and privileges as you possess to the full measure of citizenship, then you are simply supporting them in coming here in order to establish a degraded class ... '[14] This is a debate over ethics and responsibilities that underpins the whole history of the Union's engagement with foreign musicians and with government through at least four decades of the twentieth century.

I am aware that the Union officials whose voices dominate my narrative— Frank Kitson, Cecil Trevelyan and, at a lower volume, William Lamble and Victor Massey—are not fleshed out to the same degree or in the same ways as are my subject musicians. There is certainly scope for this to happen, since the influence of these individuals on the culture and development of the Union through the period of my study was profound. But this is not my

---

[12] Minute book April 1918. NBAC MUA T7/1/5.
[13] *Sunday Sun*, 23 [4?] 1949. NBAC MUA Z401 Box 13, Press cuttings 1938-52.
[14] Kim Rubenstein, 'An Unequal Membership: The Constitution's Score on Citizenship', in Laksiri Jayasuriya, David Walker and Jan Gothard (eds), *Legacies of White Australia: Race, Culture and Nation* (Crawley, WA: University of Western Australia Press, 2003), p. 150.

PART TWO: INTRODUCTION

purpose, though it is worth noting the dedication and determination of these individuals at the same time as one observes how, over time and with regard to the matter of foreign musicians at least, high ideals settled into obsession and intransigence progressively distorted the leadership's view. I am also aware that, in concentrating on the single issue of the development and decline of the Union's policy on foreign musicians in the first half of the twentieth century, I have not attempted a comprehensive account of the Union's concurrent efforts to secure and maintain good standards of wages and working conditions for rank and file Australian musicians. I have not detailed the Union's struggle to survive as an effective organisation through a period of technological change that threatened large-scale unemployment in the music industry. Elements of these stories make their way into my account, but they are viewed through a single prism.

It is sometimes hard to avoid thinking that the Weintraubs and other refugee or immigrant musicians were treated with unwarranted harshness. But it is not my intent to engender outrage. MUA officials were not monsters; they were products of their environment, their culture and their time, and I have endeavoured to represent them as such. The MUA, for example, was not the only union to adopt a highly protectionist position towards immigrant workers. Throughout the 1930s and beyond, politicians and union officials reiterated fears that a 'flood of immigration' would undermine working conditions and living standards since refugee workers would not adhere to Australian industrial awards. Protectionist attitudes within the union movement were reinforced in society at large by a fortress mentality in which the isolationism that developed after the First World War, allied to imperialist pro-British sentiments, combined to produce a deep suspicion of all things foreign. In 1948, Arthur Calwell (Minister for Immigration and architect of the postwar mass immigration scheme), described his compatriots as 'notoriously insular and inclined to view the stranger with a great deal of suspicion'.[15]

Some scholars of Jewish migration to Australia before and after the Second World War have noted that, among the professions, music and medicine were the least welcoming. Michael Blakeney, for example, includes the Musicians' Union among the professional groups that emulated the exclusionary objectives and tactics of the doctors, but notes only the requirement that foreign musicians should be naturalised before becoming

---

[15] House of Representatives' Debates, 6 October 1948, p. 1280. Cited in Egon Kunz, *Displaced Persons: Calwell's New Australians* (Sydney: Australian National University Press, 1988), p. 143 and n. 7.

members and that unnaturalised applicants should not work in the music profession while fulfilling the mandatory five-year qualifying residency requirement.[16] But whereas the medical profession has been studied in some detail (for example, by Suzanne Rutland and Egon Kunz), the musicians have not attracted attention to date.

There are similarities of rhetoric and strategy between the MUA and the Australian Medical Association (AMA); most strikingly, arguments about supply and skill were fundamental to the efforts of both organisations to argue their case to the public, to politicians and to related professional bodies. Anti-refugee rhetoric was highly prejudiced, though the musicians' public campaign perhaps failed to achieve what Egon Kunz calls 'the malevolence of the propaganda sustained against foreign doctors'.[17] The AMA, acting as the doctors' union,[18] took the offensive, attacking the ethical standards and credentials of refugee doctors in a manner calculated not only to exclude, but to discredit them, 'to instil a fear and mistrust of the foreigner so that public support might be marshalled against those state governments tempted to liberalise the laws or practices governing the registration of foreign graduates'.[19] In general, the musicians adopted a defensive strategy. 'I think you will agree', wrote the Union's General Secretary to his colleagues on Federal Council on the subject of European Jewish musicians in August 1938, 'that we are all very sorry for these victims of political and racial strife and view their lot with something akin to horror. At the same time we would be failing in our duty as Australians in general and unionists in particular if we failed to resist to our fullest extent any encroachment on our employment by any of these unfortunate foreigners either singly or in numbers'.[20] The secretary's sentiments are reminiscent of the formulaic mixture of ersatz compassion and frontier protectionism reflected in a speech by Senator J. S. Collings (one of Kitson's regular correspondents as Labor Minister for the Interior) on 16 May 1939. He remarked, 'I hope that I shall not be accused of cruelty, but, if I had my way, not one foreign refugee, man or woman, would be admitted until every

---

[16] *Australia and the Jewish Refugees* (Sydney: Croom Helm Australia, 2001), p. 193. Hooper, 'Australian Reactions to German Persecution of the Jews and Refugee Immigration, 1933–1947, MA thesis, Australian National University, 1972, p. 110, also notes the naturalisation requirement.
[17] *The Intruders: Refugee Doctors in Australia* (Canberra: Australian National University Press, 1975), p. 28.
[18] Ibid., p. 46.
[19] Ibid., p. 67.
[20] General Secretary, Musicians' Union of Australia, Circular letter to Federal Council, 2 August 1938. NBAC MUA E156/2/2(xx) (1938–48).

PART TWO: INTRODUCTION

good Australian had been taken off the dole or relief work and given a job under award conditions'.[21]

It is difficult to ascertain with any certainty the numbers of professional musician refugees who entered Australia in the 1930s, since systematic records of applications from foreigners only begin in the postwar period. Most information about prewar musician immigrants is to be gleaned from newspaper reports and personal histories. Kunz identifies 'over fifty' prewar refugee doctors; it is likely that there were no more musicians than that and probably fewer.[22] What is certain is that none of the prewar applicants for membership was successful, since the Union argued that every single foreign musician employed displaced one of its own.[23] There are many ironies involved in Australia's treatment of those German-speaking Jewish refugees who found refuge in this country in the 1930s: that German-Jewish refugees were interned as 'enemy aliens', that they were initially interned with other classes of German nationals including Nazi sympathisers, that their very status as refugees made them suspect. For German and Austrian refugee musicians there was an additional irony in the fact that, while they were excluded from their professions in their home country by the proscriptive regulations of the Nazi regime, they were also excluded from their professions in Australia—nominally, until they had achieved naturalisation. Again, the Musicians' Union was not the only Australian union to make naturalisation into what Egon Kunz calls an 'artificial barrier' to re-establishment for immigrant professionals. Andrew Markus cites the example of BHP, which would not recruit displaced persons for its operating staff, once they had discharged their contractual obligations to the government, until such time as they became naturalised citizens.[24] The naturalisation requirement is a

---

[21] Cited in Bartrop, *Australia and the Holocaust*, pp. 187–188.
[22] *The Intruders*, p. 40. I am speaking here specifically of musicians who attempted to enter the profession by acquiring Union membership. Albrecht Dümling's estimate of 97 prewar German-speaking Jewish refugee musicians needs to be viewed with caution, as it includes amateur or 'hobby' musicians, those who worked in other areas of the industry (for example, as critics, teachers or publishers), involuntary immigrants transported in the *Dunera* who subsequently repatriated and people who arrived as children and later became musicians. A number of around fifty intending to be permanently resident adult professionals emerges within this large group. *Die verschwundenen Musiker: Jüdische Flüchtlinge in Australien* (Köln, Weimar, Wien: Böhlau Verlag, 2011).
[23] W.H.S. Lamble, MUA General Secretary and Secretary of the Victorian District to F. Dambman, General Secretary, Musicians' Union of Great Britain (MU), 13 July 1939. NBAC MUA E156/2/2(xi). The number of Italian musicians who entered the country in the 1920s—probably less than ten—is discussed in Chapter Two.
[24] Egon Kunz, 'Australian Professional Attitudes and the Immigrant Professional', *ANZAAS Congress*, Perth, 1973, p. 7; Andrew Markus, 'Labour and Immigration

barrier of a particular kind, one that projects the implication that rejection is grounded in legal regulations. The assumption was, however, that once full citizenship was achieved, the foreign-born worker proceeded on a basis of equality with his fellow-Australians. In the discussions that follow, both these assumptions are scrutinised in relation to the MUA.

The Weintraubs were fortunate to the extent that, after some periods of unemployment that followed the cancellation of their contract with Snider and Dean (early October 1937) and their return from their tour of New Zealand (May 1938), they were eventually able to secure high-profile and well-paid engagements, despite the fact that the MUA refused to admit them to membership. Other refugee musicians were not so fortunate: some were forced out of the profession altogether; others were obliged to wait out the war and achieve naturalisation before they could work again as musicians. Chapter Four examines the Australian situation in the context of a suggested comparison of the exclusionary tactics of the MUA and those of the Reich Music Chamber (*Reichsmusikkammer*) in relation to foreign musicians. In particular, the chapter discusses John Kay's successful legal challenge against the NSW District of the MUA in August 1944, since the judgment handed down by the state Industrial Commission at this hearing governed the Union's handling of applications from foreign musicians into the 1950s.

1946–9: The Displaced Persons Programme', *Labour History* 47 (November 1984), p. 90. Compare Reisigl and Wodak, *Discourse and Discrimination*, p. 216, on the discursive structure of negative notifications.

Chapter Two

'QUITE CANDIDLY, WE DON'T WANT THEM'[1]

The Foreigner, the Musicians' Union, and the State in 1920s Australia

In February 1929 the Musicians' Union of Australia endorsed an amendment to rule 7d of its conditions of admission to membership which articulated a complete embargo on foreign musicians for a twelve-month period.[2] Ostensibly linked to the unemployment resulting from the introduction of sound films, it was also coincident with two specific events: an application for membership from four musicians in an orchestra of Italians that had been offered a year's employment under contract by the Hoyts theatre chain from March 1928, and a challenge to the registration of new rules affecting Australian musicians working with foreigners, heard in the Federal Court of Conciliation and Arbitration on 22 February 1929. Far from lasting for a single twelve-month period, however, the embargo was renewed annually until, in 1935, a formally registered voting mechanism was introduced for the admission of non-naturalised, non-British applicants. This latter procedure effectively allowed the MUA to exclude all pre- and postwar refugee musicians, displaced persons, and other immigrants from membership until they had achieved naturalisation

---

[1] General Secretary MUA (Cecil Trevelyan) to General Secretary MU, 18 August 1927. NBAC MUA E156/2/4(i).
[2] Put forward by the NSW District, the supporting resolution read, 'That no foreign musician be admitted to this Union for at least twelve months when the position may again be reviewed'. NSW District Minute Book 1926–1930, p. 287. NBAC MUA T7/1/8.

after the regulatory five-year residence period, a mechanism that lasted until 1958 when the rule was rescinded.[3]

Rhetorically and at points of public interface with external organisations—government departments, officials of the arbitration court, overseas unions and the press—the MUA maintained a distinction between musicians who came to the country 'under contract' and so-called 'freelance' musicians, who entered as individuals in free and equal competition with resident musicians. Although frequently blurred in practice—the ultimate objective of a total ban was the same in both cases—the distinction is an important one as it determined the arena of action and delimited the extent and character of the Union's control over the entry of foreign musicians and their reception. The entrepreneurial practice of importing musicians under contract was primarily disputed and negotiated publicly with erstwhile employers; applications from individual musicians, however, were dealt with internally by Union officials. Accountability varied in each situation.

The issue of the importation of foreign bands or contracted foreign musicians was thus situated at the nexus of a conflict of interest between the Musicians' Union on the one hand and various cultural entrepreneurs on the other, with entrepreneurs intent on importing talent from overseas to satisfy what they claimed was a public demand for quality or novelty, and the Union determined to fill all positions with Australian musicians, even though case after case suggests that the supply of local talent was neither sufficient nor as sufficiently capable. Policy took shape in a series of dialectic encounters between the MUA and entrepreneurs within the institutional framework of the State-sponsored conciliation and arbitration system. The system was highly bureaucratic, with a process of regulatory rule-making that extended downwards from government through state and federal tribunals to the registered organisations (employer associations and unions), then upwards again through an arduous process of negotiated settlement and award making. A discussion of the evolution of the MUA's policy on foreign musicians must, therefore, take cognisance of the ways in which the union itself was shaped by its participation in the arbitration process. It must also consider how a small cohort of union officials was enabled to usurp the authority of the system in order to counter the real or imagined threat

---

[3] Michelle Langfield, *More People Imperative: Immigration to Australia, 1901–39*, Guides to the Collection No. 7 (Canberra: NAA, 1999), p. 211 (Commonwealth Naturalisation Act).

'QUITE CANDIDLY, WE DON'T WANT THEM'

Figure 16. George Molnar's cartoon 'State of the Nation' [1949]
Molnar's cartoon ([*Daily Telegraph?*], 15 July 1949) captures the absurdity of the Union's requirement that musicians should work at other professions while waiting five years to become eligible for naturalisation.

Press cuttings 1938–52, NBAC MUA Z401 Box 13. Reproduced with permission, Katie Molnar and NBAC.

of competitive foreign labour through its application or misapplication of discretionary admission clauses in the legislation.

It is in the treatment of individuals that arguments about equity, fairness, and the protection of Australian jobs become tinged with darker elements of bigotry and narrow-mindedness. The Union's attitude towards foreign musicians was driven, and certainly sanctioned, by the racist sentiments of an all-White, all-British Australia as expressed in the *Immigration Restriction Act* of 1901, the so-called 'White Australia policy', which the Union formally endorsed in its revised rule book of 1925.[4] Characteristically, MUA rhetoric attached itself to popular causes as a means of strengthening its appeal. Hence, in the mid- to late-1920s prejudicial aspects of popular concern over Italian migration fortuitously provided a context for political action.

Decisions made in the 1920s may be seen as exerting a profound (and arguably detrimental) influence on the development of musical culture in Australia for several decades, not to mention their impact on the lives of individuals already traumatised by events in Europe in the key decades of refugee migration that preceded and followed the Second World War.

Three pieces of legislation form the backdrop to this discussion. The *Commonwealth Conciliation and Arbitration Act* of 1904 established the institutional framework within which the issues of imported bands and foreign musicians were disputed, debated, and resolved. The *Immigration Restriction Act* of 1901 provided an ideological underpinning for the Union's attitudes towards non-British musicians. The amendments to the latter Act contained in the *Contract Immigrants Act* (1905) served as the basis of the Union's appeal for protective legislation and also for the government's introduction, in July 1928, of a form of application to control the entry of foreign musicians under contract.

Within the tiny literature on industrial relations in the Australian music industry, the MUA's validation of its embargo on foreign musicians from the end of the 1920s by reference to job losses resulting from the introduction of sound film technology is accepted.[5] The advent of mechanical music was certainly catastrophic, and a catalyst for and rationalisation of the final

---

[4] A resolution advocating the formal endorsement of the policy was introduced at Federal Conference in 1923, apparently in response to an application from a coloured musician. Minutes, NBAC MUA E156/6/2, p. 7.

[5] See Bronwen Arthur, '"Ban the Talkies!"', and her entry on 'Industrial Relations' in Whiteoak and Scott-Maxwell (eds), *Currency Companion to Music and Dance in Australia*, p. 348.

stage of the hardening of policy, but it was not the basis for the development of that policy, which, I argue, had begun in the previous decade.

Australia turned inwards in the decades following the First World War, which triggered a resurgence of pro-British nationalistic sentiment allied to strong anti-German feelings that became a widespread xenophobia and opposition to 'foreigners'. In April 1918, acting on an initiative from its New South Wales District, the MUA undertook a purge of its membership. District Secretaries were instructed to suspend 'members who are or who have been at any time subjects of a nation at war with the King', moving at once against all known members and enquiring into doubtful names.[6] In November of the same year, at the Union's federal conference, the meeting was informed that approaches had been made to 'certain members of the Federal Parliament', asking them to influence the ministers concerned to repatriate all alien internee musicians at the end of the war: 'In the concentration camps in N.S.W.', reported the secretary (Alfred O'Brien), 'there are hundreds of musicians, who having little else to do, have kept in good practice and if they are allowed to remain in Australia, will be a very serious menace to our community'.[7]

Though the records do not show the impact of these early actions, several trends can be extrapolated which were prevalent throughout these formative years of MUA policy regarding foreigners: a desire to secure state endorsement of Union resolutions, an exaggerated and probably unrealistic representation of competition and, concealed in this case behind a façade of patriotic nationalism, an ideologically driven agenda aimed at creating a normative membership that was white, British (meaning British Australian), and male.

As His Honour Chief Judge Dethridge of the Commonwealth Court of Conciliation and Arbitration observed in February 1929, the labour market in music in Australia is, more than most others, 'subject to excessive importation of competitive wage-earners'.[8] Within the music industry, the issue of the importation of foreign bands or contracted foreign musicians became a 'frontier of control', as entrepreneurs resisted pressures from the Musicians' Union (representing the profession) to employ only Australian

---

[6] NSW District Minute Book 1911–1918, p. 358 and inserted Notice of the Annual Meeting of the MUA NSW District, 15 April 1918. NBAC MUA T7/1/5.
[7] Secretary's Report to the 1918 Federal Conference of the MUA. Minutes. NBAC MUA E156/6/1.
[8] Murray M. Stewart (ed.), *Commonwealth Arbitration Reports* Vol. 27 (1928–29) (Melbourne: The Law Book Company of Australasia Ltd.), p. 1142.

musicians and Union members.⁹ The employers asserted commercial competitiveness, popular taste, and an inadequate local supply. The Union countered with various arguments, but the basic issue was the difference between a *'pre-entry'* closed shop', in which initial employment must be preceded by membership of the requisite union and the union thus has almost complete control of the labour supply, and the *'post-entry'* closed shop', which allows the employment of individuals—as in the case of foreign musicians—subject to them joining the union after their engagement, a situation which removes the control of the supply of labour from the union.¹⁰ The importation and employment of foreign musicians thus emerged as a site of 'opposition of interest between those who manage and those who are managed'.¹¹ The issue was not one of numbers but of principle, since 'the right to freely contract is … a direct threat to the interests of organised labour'.¹²

Arbitration and rule-making: a state-sponsored institutional framework

Industrial relations in twentieth-century Australia were governed by the Commonwealth Court of Conciliation and Arbitration, a state-regulated system established under legislation passed by the Federal Parliament in 1904 that provided for the compulsory conciliation and arbitration of industrial disputes.¹³ Within a two-tiered institutional framework, one Commonwealth and six state tribunals were invested with powers to obtain control of disputes and enforce decisions ('Awards') on the disputants. The process involved a three-way dialogue between employer, union (representing the employees), and the officials of the court. It was possible for unions

---

[9] The phrase is cited in Stephen J. Deery and David H. Plowman, *Australian Industrial Relations*, (3rd edition, Sydney: McGraw-Hill Book Company Australia, 1991), p. 44 and n. 32.

[10] Richard Mitchell and Stuart Rosewarne, 'Individual Rights and the Law in Australian Industrial Relations' in Kathryn Cole (ed.), *Power, Conflict and Control in Australian Trade Unions*, (Ringwood: Penguin Books, 1982), p. 194.

[11] Deery and Plowman, *Australian Industrial Relations*, p. 43.

[12] Mitchell and Rosewarne, 'Individual Rights and the Law', p. 208.

[13] A copy of the Act may be found at http://www.aph.gov.au/library/INTGUIDE/LAW/docs/CommonwealthConciliationandArbitration Act 1904.pdf, accessed August 2008. For a discussion of the distinctive features of the Australian system and a comparison with those of the USA and Britain, see Richard Mitchell, 'State Systems of Conciliation and Arbitration: The Legal Origins of the Australasian Model', in Stuart Macintyre and Richard Mitchell (eds), *Foundations of Arbitration: The Origins and Effects of State Compulsory Arbitration 1890–1914*, (Melbourne: Oxford University Press, 1989), pp. 74–82, 89–93.

to negotiate agreements with employers outside arbitration but, as Stuart Macintyre and Richard Mitchell affirm, such external negotiations were coloured by the knowledge that the system was available in the event of an agreement not being reached.[14]

Although 'industrial arbitration' meant 'the formal systems of state regulation of industrial disputes in Australia', the process was informed by high-minded liberal notions in which partnership replaced confrontation and disputes were settled 'through legal agency, according not to legal right but according to equity and fairness'.[15] In particular, the system was seen as offering protection to the working man through registered unions, challenging the employers' view that they were 'able to do as they pleased with men simply because they paid them wages'.[16]

The arbitration system 'encouraged changes in the structure and nature of unionism itself'; given that 'the creation of arbitration coincided with the mobilization of workers and employers, [it] *helped to shape their organizational forms* [my emphasis]'.[17] The top officials of a Union acquired the authority of 'lay advocates', since the *Commonwealth Conciliation and Arbitration Act* provided for and the court generally favoured representation by an officer of an organisation in proceedings requiring knowledge of the facts of the industry in dispute.[18] For example, the General Secretary of the MUA, assisted by the Federal President or another nominated delegate, would routinely act as union representative in federal arbitration cases and interstate negotiations and disputes. State secretaries had parallel responsibilities under state arbitration legislation.

Historians have argued, however, that the establishment of tribunals is only one of two key elements of the Australian model, the other being the provision for the registration and regulation of trade unions. As MUA General Secretary Cecil Trevelyan explained to his English counterpart, under the Arbitration Act, 'Unions ... have to register before the Court

---

14 Stuart Macintyre and Richard Mitchell, 'Introduction', in Macintyre and Mitchell (eds), ibid., pp. 1-2.
15 Macintyre and Mitchell, 'Introduction', p. 6 ('formal systems'); Mitchell, 'State Systems', p. 96 ('equity and fairness').
16 Bede Healey, *Federal Arbitration in Australia: An Historical Outline* (Melbourne: Georgian House, 1972), p. 11.
17 Ray Markey, 'Trade Unions, the Labor Party and the Introduction of Arbitration in New South Wales and the Commonwealth', in Macintyre and Mitchell (eds), *Foundations of Arbitration*, p. 170 ('changes in the structure'); Macintyre and Mitchell, 'Introduction', p. 13 ('creation of arbitration').
18 The term 'lay advocates' is from Orwell De R. Foenander, *Trade Unionism in Australia: Some Aspects* (Australia: The Law Book Co of Australasia, 1962), p. 20 and n. 6.

recognises them ... the Court can only bind the Union and Respondents, [namely] employers who have been cited by having the log of claims served on them and [who have been summoned to] the hearing ... The [Act] throws its cloak over both sides protecting their individual interests and compelling observance of the Award ... Both sides have obligations which can be pressed'.[19] Since the system was based on collective bargaining, 'Such regulation was perceived from the beginning to be integral to the purposes of the compulsory arbitration systems, which required the incorporation of unions to act as representative bodies for large groups of employees (or employers) and to supervise and enforce the award-making process'.[20]

Registration of unions compelled employer recognition of union interests and bargaining status and incorporated them into a legislative framework of entitlement that included preferred employment for union members, protection from discrimination, and monopoly of organisation.[21] It provided legal support for a union's internal system of regulation, both its structures and its objectives, since in order to be able to function efficiently within the system, unions needed to be able to discipline and control their membership.[22] Because registration ensured the survival of a union irrespective of its numerical size and industrial power, the MUA was able to hold its own against the major entrepreneurs, who gained commercial muscle in the 1920s through takeovers and merging of interests, and to survive the vicissitudes of the Depression years.[23]

Registration also obliged the Union to develop a set of internal rules to specify, amongst other things, its objectives and the conditions and eligibility for membership.[24] Under the MUA's new rule 93a (added to the rule book of

---

[19] Trevelyan to F. Dambman, General Secretary, (British) Musicians' Union, 25 January 1935. NBAC MUA E156/2/4(i).
[20] Mitchell, 'State Systems', p. 91.
[21] Macintyre and Mitchell, 'Introduction', p. 16.
[22] Mitchell, 'State Systems', p. 91; Richard Mitchell and Esther Stern, 'The Compulsory Arbitration Model of Industrial Dispute Settlement: An Outline of Legal Developments', in Macintyre and Mitchell (eds), *Foundations of Arbitration*, p. 108.
[23] Deery and Plowman, *Australian Industrial Relations*, 251 (numerical size). 'It was in the 1920s that the independent (usually suburban) cinema owner was deliberately squeezed out of business by the two large exhibition chains [Hoyts and Union Theatres]...' Diane Collins, *Hollywood Down Under: Australians at the Movies 1896 to the Present Day* (North Ryde, NSW: Angus & Robertson, 1987), p. 116.
[24] Raj Jadeja, *Parties to the Award* (Canberra: Noel Butlin Archives Centre, Research School of Social Sciences, The Australian National University, 1994), p. 4 and n 23. Schedule B of the *Commonwealth Conciliation and Arbitration Act* required the keeping of a register of members and the provision of rules governing 'the times when, terms on which, persons may become, or cease to be members of the association ...'.

1927), any state district could petition the Federal Council to make or frame any new rule or rescind, vary, or alter any existing rule. Nonetheless, a rule was not binding until registered by the Industrial Registrar, an officer of the Court of Conciliation and Arbitration, who determined its compliance with the requirements of the Act and the law. The progress of a new rule from resolution to registration and formal incorporation was a lengthy and complex one, involving as it did a process of internal consultation, of analysis and review by the Union's solicitors and review and approval by the Registrar, with the possibility of amendment at each stage.[25] For this reason one needs to consider when a rule was proposed rather than when it was registered, when mapping causality, since the procedure of formulation, consultation, legal review, amendment and registration could take several years. Margin dates in the rule books give the dates of registration.

Alteration of the rules to make them non-compliant, failure to *bona fide* observe them or judgment that 'the rules ... or their administration do not provide reasonable facilities for the admission of new members or impose unreasonable conditions upon the continuance of their membership or are in any way tyrannical or oppressive' were all grounds for non-registration or cancellation of registration under Schedule 60c of the Act.

This federal requirement was replicated within the individual states of the Commonwealth since, in order to be able to function within the respective state system (for intra-state disputes), districts of the MUA registered independently of the federal body. State registration created a separate and distinct legal entity which could and did formulate and register its own rules. Cockburn and Yerbury note, in their discussion of the problems of multiple registration, that 'there are often differences in rules, particularly the rules governing who is eligible for membership, and invalidities arise as, for example, when someone who can be a member of the State union cannot be a member of the State branch of the federal organisation, yet votes in State-branch matters, or participates in the election of State-branch officers who then make decisions within the federal union'.[26]

The MUA registered federally as a 'party to the award' in 1911. In a series of letters written to colleagues in various overseas unions, Cecil Trevelyan, the long-serving General Secretary of the MUA, summarised the features

---

[25] Legal opinions on the rule revisions that took place in the 1920s may be found at NBAC MUA E156/8/7.
[26] M.R. Cockburn and D. Yerbury, 'The Federal/State Framework of Australian Industrial Relations', in Cole (ed.), *Power, Conflict and Control*, p. 62.

of the Australian system and reflected on the Union's experience of its merits and demerits:

> The Federal Arbitration Court can not deal with any dispute that is not interstate, i.e. it must cover at least two States. In our industry Messrs J.C. Williamson [the largest theatrical entrepreneur] show in every State, as do Union Theatres and Hoyts (both pictures), B.J. Fuller (Theatrical) etc. and as our Union is in every state the Federal Award is most useful to us ... Each state has some form of Arbitration *within* the State and can give a *common rule* which will cover *everyone not covered* by a *Federal Arbitration Award* ... Our districts also use the state which is beneficial in dealing with casual work ... Whatever this sounds like it is not involved and quite simple in the effect when one is used to the procedure ...[27]

Of the judges and the quality of judicial intervention, Trevelyan wrote,

> Speaking generally I am inclined to the opinion that all judges when first appointed to Arbitration duty have an accepted and well defined *class* consciousness which carries a subconscious class bias. Early environment and education deeproot these tendencies. It is generally accepted that the *master class* is top dog, and has *the right* to do—well almost anything he likes as long as it is legal ... I find that usually after the first year or so their experience develops within them an admission that employers are frequently hardhearted and unfair and mostly determined to maintain the ascendency [sic] they have hitherto held unchallenged, and gradually these judges develop a sense of sympathy and almost as an outgrowth of nausea and determination to give the workers interest *greater practical* consideration.[28]

From the time of his appointment to the reconstituted Commonwealth Arbitration Court in 1926, Judge George James Dethridge heard most disputes involving the entertainment industry (including the Musicians' Union), thus acquiring, over the period of his tenure, a comprehensive knowledge of the industry's special features and requirements. Described by Trevelyan as 'essentially a *fairminded* and reasonable man', Dethridge

---

[27] Trevelyan to Dambman, 25 January 1935. NBAC MUA E156/2/4(i). Trevelyan was General Secretary from 1924 until his death in September 1935, with prior experience as Secretary of the South Australian District.
[28] Trevelyan to Dambman, 25 January 1935. NBAC MUA E156/2/4(i). Grammar and spelling are quoted verbatim.

is assessed as a judge as being 'a cautious but flexible conservative', and is said to have had some sympathy for the position of the working man, offsetting the bias of class and education noted by Trevelyan.[29] At another time Trevelyan commented of the judge, 'I know his Honor is sympathetic towards the musicians but he must take a common sense view point and deal with facts as he finds them'.[30]

Growing hostility in evolving policy on foreign musicians

At the annual conference of the federal body of the MUA held in Melbourne in November 1923, a resolution was passed to redraft the federal rule book (last published in 1914) in order to consolidate rules added in the intervening years.[31] At the Conference in November 1925, with the revised rule book already registered, the meeting determined to work towards new rules.[32] This decision set in motion a process of rule formulation and amendment that occupied the rest of the decade. It was not a trivial decision since, whereas the 1925 rule book reflected the organisation's benign origins as a benevolent society and employment agency, the rule book that took shape from 1925 to the end of the 1920s effected a transformation of its culture into an oligarchic bureaucracy, with all that implies in terms of centralised power and devaluation of individual freedoms.[33]

Up to the 1920s, the membership rules of the federal body were more concerned with outlining general terms of compliance with the requirements

---

[29] Trevelyan wrote, 'Chief Judge Dethridge takes *all* the cases in the Entertainment Industry'. Trevelyan to Dambman, 25 January 1935. NBAC MUA E156/2/4(i); Ian G. Sharp, 'George James Dethridge', in *Australian Dictionary of Biography* Vol. 8, eds Bede Nairn and Geoffrey Serle (Carlton: Melbourne University Press, 1981), p. 293 (assessment as conservative).

[30] Trevelyan to A.A. Greenbaum, Secretary MU San Francisco, 6 December 1932. NBAC MUA E156/2/4(i). It was Dethridge who presided over and ruled on the challenge to the MUA federal rules in 1929 to be discussed below.

[31] The General Secretary Cecil Trevelyan is credited with the achievement of a 'uniform set of rules and one Federal award'. (*Smith's Weekly* n.d. [1931?], Press cuttings 1927–29, NBAC MUA Z401 Box 12); a statement to that effect appears in *Rules of the Musicians' Union of Australia*, 1925, NBAC MUA N93/476.

[32] *Rules of the Musicians' Union of Australia*, 1925, NBAC MUA N93/476; Minutes of the Annual Federal Conference, November 1925, NBAC MUA E156/6/3.

[33] For a summary of the Union's early history, see Arthur, 'Industrial Relations', p. 348. This is not to say that bitter disputes did not take place before the 1920s. See for example the account of the Union's campaign against non-union musicians (mainly women) in the Marshall-Hall Orchestra in Melbourne in 1911. Kenneth Morgan, 'Sir James Barrett, Musical Patron in Melbourne', in Thérèse Radic and Suzanne Robinson (eds), *Marshall-Hall's Melbourne: Music, Art and Controversy 1891-1915* (Melbourne: Australian Scholarly Publishing, 2012), pp. 97–99, 101–102.

of the arbitration legislation than with formulating specific terms of eligibility, since applications for membership were dealt with by the individual districts, which set their own terms and conditions under state registration. The 1921 Rules of the NSW District of the Union, for example, while treating 'visiting professionals' not unreasonably as a separate category, nonetheless allowed for fixed-term membership of six months' duration, and for the possibility of such musicians becoming 'ordinary members' upon payment of an additional fee. This provision at least acknowledged the reality that some visitors, given favourable professional opportunities, might choose to remain in the country. In the revision to the federal rules of 1927, section 4 ('Objects') reiterates the federal body's intention 'to oppose, by all constitutional methods, the admission into Australia from overseas of professional musicians under contract or agreement to contract after arrival in Australia', although the exclusionary thrust of the revisions as they take shape is clearly aimed at *all* foreign musicians, contracted or not. 'We feel that any employment offering should be the prerogative of the native born', stated Federal President and NSW District Secretary Frank Kitson, promoting the Union's latest embargo against foreign-born musicians in 1949.[34]

How is such an attitude to be characterised given that the country was legislatively committed to a racist immigration policy and that discrimination on the basis of country of origin would have a broad base of social support? Is it ultra-nationalism? Or can it be viewed more opportunistically as an attempt to consolidate political power by mobilising 'different coalitions around different issues'?[35]

Insofar as the Union's attitude towards foreign musicians was underpinned by the racial principles embedded in the *Immigration Restriction Act* of 1901, it was no different from that of any other Australian union of the time. Indeed, Julia Martinez has written that '"White Australia" continued as the dominant ideology of Labor unionists'.[36] But there is also a paradox here, for although the MUA organised its discriminatory

---

[34] In November 1949 the Union resolved to restrict membership of orchestras to 90 percent Australians and 10 percent British people who had lived in Australia for ten years. Minutes of the 1948 Annual Federal Conference, p. 8. NBAC MUA E156/6/7. Kitson quote is *Sunday Sun*, 23 April? 1949. Press cuttings 1938–52, NBAC MUA Z401 Box 13.

[35] Macintyre and Mitchell, 'Introduction', in Macintyre and Mitchell (eds), *Foundations of Arbitration*, p. 12.

[36] Julia Martinez, 'Questioning "White Australia": Unionism and 'Coloured' Labour, 1911–37', *Labour History* 76 (May 1999), p. 1.

anti-foreign resolutions around the slogan 'keep orchestras British', British-born or English-speaking musicians from Commonwealth countries were equally unwelcome.

From the mid- to late-1920s, the MUA found itself engaged in particularly hostile exchanges with the British Musicians' Union (MU) over its attitude towards British musicians. It was not so much its campaign of opposing imported bands or excluding foreigners, since the MU pursued similar goals, as the inclusion of British musicians in the category of 'foreigners'.[37] 'Treat the American, the Italian and the German as you will', wrote the editor of *Melody Maker*, a British trade journal, to Trevelyan, ' ... but we Britishers look upon the Commonwealth, by birthright, as being another home, should we have to go there, and you yourselves always literally talk of a journey to England as "going home," knowing full well that all civic privileges are yours because you are in every way members of the same kinship'.[38]

Trevelyan was at pains to point out to his MU colleagues that MUA rules privileged British musicians within the foreigner class, but the British unionists objected to the requirement that British musicians should reside in Australia for six months without working in the profession before becoming eligible for membership or pay the higher overseas musicians' fee of £21, observing that, 'there are many Australian musicians in London and no bar is put up against them so long as they don't undercut our terms. Our people are of [the] opinion that no bar should be put up against our members going out from the Motherland to distant parts of the Empire and vice-versa, always subject to local terms and conditions being observed'.[39] The argument raged on through the 1930s in letters and in the press, with the MUA adamant and the MU asserting that the policy was 'anti-British' and likely to precipitate a change of policy in Britain towards Australians seeking work there (which it eventually did).[40]

---

[37] Cyril Ehrlich, *The Music Profession in Britain since the Eighteenth Century, A Social History* (Oxford: Clarendon Press 1985), pp. 216–7 (similar goals). For a focused study of the British MU, see Beatrix R Hoffman, 'Workers and Players. The Musicians' Union, 1928–1940' (MA thesis, University of Warwick, 1989).

[38] Letter from the Joint Editor of *Melody Maker* to Trevelyan, 12 June 1929. NBAC MUA E156/2/4(i).

[39] General Secretary, (British) MU, to Trevelyan, 21 September 1925. NBAC MUA E156/2/4(i).

[40] Hostile articles appeared in *Era* (January 1928) and *Melody Maker* (November 1929), to which Trevelyan responded in an article in the MUA's journal, *The Professional Musician*, September 1929, 10 and 12. NBAC MUA E156/11/1.

SILENCES AND SECRETS

Various sections of the *Commonwealth Conciliation and Arbitration Act* allowed for the rules of a registered organisation to be challenged if oppressively administered, but to do so presumed a knowledge on the part of the claimant not only of the Constitution and the Act, but, in the case of the MUA, of a federal rule book—which by 1929 comprised some ninety-six pages, 92 sections and their subsections—and of the rules of the district in which a claimant was a member—89 sections with their subsections in the case of the NSW District. Challenges involving rules and appeals to the law were necessarily argued by counsel, a significant expense, and it is not surprising that few were lodged by individual members. However, in February 1929, a summons was issued by the Theatrical Proprietors and Managers Association of Australasia for the suspension or cancellation of awards on various grounds, one being that the Union had adopted improper rules.

Six rules relating to the employment of foreigners in orchestras as developed in the second stage of rule revision (between December 1926 and November 1929) were challenged, among others.[41] Ultimately, the judge's objection to these rules was neither ethical nor ideological but only concerned the wording, which potentially involved complying musicians in a breach of their contracts. The judge concluded that 'there is an industrial struggle for life between similar classes of employees in different countries, and defensive devices are inevitable', finding the rules to be clear in intent 'although not very precisely expressed'. Summing up, he remarked: 'Several of the foregoing rules have been objected to on the ground that they confer discretionary powers on the union, or its various executive organs, which may be improperly used … But some such powers must be allowed, and rules embodying these powers are not bad merely because they are capable of being directed to bad ends'.[42]

Challenges by individuals could only be argued in the state tribunals as individual workers had no status before the Federal Court.[43] One such

---

[41] Only those sections of the judgment dealing with restrictions on foreigners in orchestras were reported in the press (*Evening News* 27 May 1929; *Sydney Morning Herald* and *Daily Guardian*, 28 May 1929). Press cuttings 1927–29, NBAC MUA Z401 Box 12.

[42] The judgment may be found at *Commonwealth Arbitration Reports* 27 (1928–29), pp. 1141–1145.

[43] This situation has been read in two ways: legislatively ('The act favours collective bargaining. Workers individually have no status before the Court … '. [Trevelyan to Dambman, 25 January 1935. NBAC MUA E156/2/4(i)]) and politically ('The feminist

challenge was issued in 1928, when two Italian musicians who had come to Australia under contract to the Gonsalez Opera Company applied to the court for a declaration of their entitlement to membership. The matter was heard in the NSW Industrial Commission, with plaintiffs and Union represented by counsel. At issue were not only the complications arising from the extent of the tribunal's jurisdiction over a federal union with a state branch registered under the laws of the state, but the relationship of various contracts binding the musicians (that between themselves and their employer, and that between the employer and the union).[44]

Frank Kitson, in opposing the application in his role as secretary of the NSW District, informed the Commission that, as they could not speak English, the musicians could not obey an orchestral conductor. 'A conductor couldn't start them', Kitson is reported to have said (*Daily Guardian*, 12 June 1928), 'and if he could he wouldn't be able to stop them',—lively copy, perhaps, and a fair representation of the Union's position, but a distortion of what was, in fact, an extended discussion of the extent to which the musicians' inability to speak English would impact on rehearsals and performances. In the end, however, the court was unable to uphold the appeal because of limitations in its powers. Mitchell and Rosewarne also admit, 'in these cases [of complaints about inability to secure admission to a union], the law has not adopted a strongly interventionist role ... the courts generally will not interfere with the prescribed criteria of membership, no matter how unfair or arbitrary'.[45]

When one of the plaintiffs, who had not worked professionally as a musician in the meantime, reapplied for membership in November 1932, Kitson wrote to Trevelyan with a revealing opportunism,

---

analysis of bureaucracy sees it as purporting to be a politically neutral discourse— of efficiency, rules, roles and procedures—which has the effect of depowering individuals... ' Diane Kirkby, 'Arbitration and the Fight for Economic Justice', in Macintyre and Mitchell (eds), *Foundations of Arbitration*, p. 347). For a discussion of the complications around the legislative protection of individuals under arbitration, see Mitchell and Rosewarne, 'Individual Rights and the Law', pp. 197– 202 and Alan Boulton, 'Government Regulation of the Internal Affairs of Unions', in Cole (ed.), *Power, Conflict and Control*, pp. 231–232.

[44] The first stage of the appeal was reported in *Daily Guardian*, 12 June 1928 and *Sydney Morning Herald*, 13 June 1928 (Press cuttings 1927–29, NBAC MUA Z401 Box 12) and by Kitson in *The Professional Musician*, September 1928, pp. 18–19 (NBAC MUA E156/11/1). The transcript of the hearings may be found at 'Oyoyly vs Musicians' Union', State Records NSW, 6/1433, '1928 Industrial M-R'. For an account of the Fuller-Gonsalez tour, see Alison Gyger, *Opera for the Antipodes* (Paddington, NSW: Currency Press and Pellinor, 1990), Ch. 20.

[45] Mitchell and Rosewarne, 'Individual Rights and the Law', p. 196.

Doubtless, my District would have continued to debar him from the Union, but he has made application to become a naturalised citizen. On producing proof of this application and with the knowledge that such application was about to be granted in a few weeks, my Committee thought it better to admit him at £21 than to charge a naturalised subject £21 or admit him at £5/5/-. It was obvious that the grounds for his non-admittance, viz. 'foreigner' were about to be removed.[46]

One of the touted attributes of the arbitration system was that it elevated industrial disputation to a plane of rational discourse, but currents of prejudice and mean-spiritedness swirl beneath the surface. Not speaking English was an immediate basis for discrimination. As Cecil Trevelyan wrote in 1927 in the letter from which this chapter's heading comes, 'Many foreigners are arriving who cannot speak one word of English. Quite candidly, we don't want them'.

The vexed question of skill

It is difficult to adjudicate issues of skill or to articulate those elements of music performance practice that are passed on by example and consolidated over generations. As Judge Dethridge remarked, 'If this court attempted to determine the rate of pay for artistry it would find itself in a hopeless mess'.[47] According to Kitson, Italian musicians who visited Australia with touring opera seasons of the twentieth century brought nothing that could not be supplied or surpassed by local players: 'That we have the players here is instanced by the last J.C. Williamson grand opera season [of 1924], when imported Italian musicians were relegated by an Italian conductor to a lower position, and Australians placed in advance of them'.[48] There is no way of testing the truth of Kitson's assertion as the listing of musicians in the 1924 season souvenir program is alphabetical by name and not by orchestral desk, but of the four imported Italians (in an orchestra of fifty), one, a double bass player called Luigi Ricci Bitti, could claim that he had worked professionally and consistently in itinerant opera companies throughout Europe and southeast Asia, an experience unlikely to be matched by even

---

[46] Kitson to Trevelyan, 11 November 1932. NBAC MUA Z401 Box 5.
[47] 'High Rates for Radio Musicians', undated, unattributed clipping. Press cuttings 1927–29, NBAC MUA Z401 Box 12.
[48] *Daily Telegraph*, 2 March 1928. Press cuttings 1927–29, NBAC MUA Z401 Box 12.

the best of Australia's players.⁴⁹ A shortage of good players in particular instrumental categories—woodwinds and double basses, for example—was frequently mentioned in the press in the late nineteenth and early twentieth centuries.⁵⁰

Until the establishment of the Elizabethan Theatre Trust in the 1960s, there was no permanent orchestra available to play for opera or ballet in Australia. Instead, 'scratch' ensembles were 'somewhat hastily organised' from the best local talent available, and whether or not the best musicians available were always the best is an open question.⁵¹ Trevelyan once admitted, 'We have the five instruments of the class and quality desired, but our men are earning more in permanent billets and will not play for the money offered'.⁵² The 1924 Melba-Williamson Grand Opera Season is recorded as having included 211 performances of seventeen operas in 28 weeks, with a different opera on each night of the week and minimal rehearsal time, and although orchestras rarely attracted comment in newspaper reports of operatic performances, there is enough to give a sense of the pressures of inadequate rehearsals and unfamiliarity with a constantly changing repertoire.⁵³

In the same year, the Union asked the Industrial Registrar to adjudicate on the question of whether the importation of Harry Yerkes' (white) American band to play at the Wattle Path dance palace in Melbourne constituted discrimination under the Award by threatening the jobs of local musicians ('Discrimination means preferring non-members to members *all other things being equal*' [my emphasis]). The Registrar declined to endorse the Union's argument that it did, accepting instead the entrepreneur's argument that Australian musicians were unable to 'get that rhythm that is essential in the dancing halls nowadays'. The employer argued that public taste was driving his commercial interests: 'We boosted an Australian Band when the Americans were here but the public wanted an American band. We tried very hard to keep the Australian orchestra but public opinion was against it. As a matter of fact our own men were unable to get the same rhythm as the Americans'.

---

49   *Tempo*, May 1949, p. 6 (profile of Ricci Bitti).
50   See, for example, Suzanne Cole and Kerry Murphy, 'Wagner in the Antipodes', *Wagnerspectrum* 02/08 (Bayreuth: Richard-Wagner Museum, 2008), p. 257 (re the importation of oboe, bassoon and double bass players).
51   Gyger, *Opera for the Antipodes*, p. 207 ('hastily organised').
52   Trevelyan to General Secretary, (British) MU, 7 March 1928. NBAC MUA E156/2/4(i).
53   Gyger, *Opera for the Antipodes*, p. 250 (performance statistics).

The Registrar concluded, 'My view is that it is not discrimination as far as the award is concerned, at the same time it is going to be a very disastrous state of affairs for our own citizens if this kind of thing is going to spread throughout the country'.[54] The Union argued that the problem was indeed spreading throughout the country: 'American musicians arrived here in large numbers and supplied dance bands. In almost every case Australians were displaced and … the novelty caught on and became a serious problem … The Americans who came here were paid over the Award rate and displaced Australians …'[55] The President of the American Federation of Musicians, being appealed to, did not share the Australian's view that the situation was critical: 'As I take it that organizations composed of members of the Federation who visit Australia only do so for a limited time and are employed for the reason that they are considered an attraction, the matter will adjust itself when their attractiveness has passed …'[56]

The matter at issue was, as the Secretary to the Prime Minister's Department wrote to Trevelyan in May 1928, 'largely one of fact, i.e. whether it is possible to obtain in Australia musicians whose training and experience render them suitable for employment in orchestras' or whether, as was unsympathetically inferred in a contemporaneous article by a British music magazine, 'Australian musicians needed protection because of their lack of ability'.[57] The recurring argument was not about numbers but about perception: 'the effect [of the importation of six "key instrumentalists"] would be … to foster a belief in the scarcity of talent here and migration would be intensified'.[58] The Union consistently maintained its position that Australian musicians could supply what was needed and refused to differentiate skill within its general protectionist argument against foreign musicians. As the *Sydney Morning Herald* reported on 17 March 1928, 'No objection was made to the employment of specially skilled foreigners, but Australians should come first'. Pursuing the same argument twenty-one years later, in 1949, Frank Kitson defended the Union position: 'Our action [in implementing yet another embargo against foreigners in the Australian Broadcasting

---

[54] This quotation and those in the previous paragraph are from the transcript of the hearing, 21 August 1924. NBAC MUA E156/8/7.
[55] *The Professional Musician*, September 1929, 10. NBAC MUA E156/11/1.
[56] President of the American Federation of Musicians to Trevelyan, 4 June 1924. NBAC MUA E156/2/4(i).
[57] NBAC MUA E156/2/6(ii) (Secretary's letter). *The Melody Maker*, November 1928, reported in *The Professional Musician*, September 1929, p. 12. NBAC MUA E156/11/1.
[58] Frank Kitson to Charles Moses, Chairman of the Australian Broadcasting Commission, 4 August 1939. NBAC MUA E156/2/2(ib).

'QUITE CANDIDLY, WE DON'T WANT THEM'

Commission's (ABC) orchestras] is no different from that of an industry seeking a tariff to keep out goods from overseas'.[59]

The ongoing debate intensified as Australia's orchestral culture began to achieve permanence in the orchestras associated with the ABC. Repeated complaints by visiting artists—some extremely colourful—over the standard of orchestral music-making in the decades of the 1930s and 1940s were simply dismissed by the Union as anti-Australian.[60] But the Union's uncompromising line on the issue was steadily seen as an impediment to progress, even by unpartisan observers: 'It seems that the union, while engaged in the praiseworthy task of safeguarding the industrial interests of its members, has also become a protector of mediocrities and a drag on musical progress', wrote a staff correspondent of a major Sydney newspaper in 1944.[61] Other voices were more forceful. Competition is healthy and admission to the Union should be based on a minimum standard, not national origin, opined Richard Goldner, a viola player who was refused Union membership when he arrived in Australia as a refugee in 1939 and was thus unable to take up an offer of a 'leading position' in an ABC orchestra.[62] Captain H.E. Adkins, director of Britain's prestigious Royal Military School of Music and engaged on a short-term contract in 1933 as the first conductor of the ABC's military band, stated his opinion that the MUA would 'unless curbed in some way, kill musical art in this country'.[63]

Unfortunately, or so Martin Buzacott argues, the legislators and politicians involved in resolving these issues into policy were not always well placed to make judgments: 'for politicians ... the emotional power of the "Australians first" and "secure employment" arguments were compelling in a community in which everybody wanted cultural excellence but very few could notice the difference between, say, the artistic standards of one professional cellist compared with another'.[64]

---

[59] 'How Ban on Oversea Players Will Affect Music Here', undated, unattributed clipping [1949?]. Press cuttings 1938–52, NBAC MUA Z401 Box 13.
[60] For example, visiting pianist Ignaz Friedman brewed up a storm when he commented publicly, 'Some of your brass players ought to be sent to the Far East to break down the walls of Jericho'. 'Pianist Slates A.B.C. Standard of Music', undated, unattributed clipping [1943?]. Press cuttings 1938–52, NBAC MUA Z401 Box 13.
[61] 'Permanent Orchestras. Task for Australians', *Sydney Morning Herald*, 24 March 1944, p. 4. Press cuttings 1938–52, NBAC MUA Z401, Box 13.
[62] *Sydney Morning Herald*, 3 April 1944 and *Daily Mirror*, 10 April 1946. Press cuttings 1938–52, NBAC MUA Z401 Box 13.
[63] 'A Report to the Australian Broadcasting Commission [1934]', NAA SP 1538/2 [Box 46] cited in Martin Buzacott, *The Rite of Spring: 75 Years of ABC Music-Making* (Sydney: ABC Books, 2007), pp. 27 and 410, n. 15.
[64] Ibid., p. 227.

The quest for legislative protection

In the early 1920s, anxieties about foreign musicians attached themselves to the importation of American bands for dancing, as is reflected in Trevelyan's letters to the secretaries of English-speaking foreign unions from early 1925. Beginning at that time, the MUA undertook 'to secure legislation that will prevent the influx of any persons whose admission to Australia may be detrimental to Australians'.[65] It was not the only Australian union to attempt to control or prevent, through legislation, foreign participation in the labour force; Andrew Markus identifies more than thirty separate Acts in Queensland alone between 1901 and 1920 designed to restrict the occupational freedom of foreign workers.[66]

Circular letters were sent to Members of the Commonwealth Parliament and the Union had a Bill drafted for an Act restricting the importation of immigrant musicians under contract, which it attempted to have brought before the House, but the issue lacked political purchase and the legislation failed to pass.[67] The Union tried to argue that imported musicians fell under the tighter provisions of the *Contract Immigrants Act* (the *Amending Immigration Act*) of 1905, whereby employers wishing to bring in labourers under contract had to obtain approval from the Minister of External Affairs, and pressed for similar controls to be introduced for foreign musicians. But Stanley Bruce's National and Country parties' coalition government maintained that the restrictions of the Act applied only to manual labour and thus did not apply to music.[68] The Union tried again in May 1928, but again the government declined to take 'so drastic a step as the prevention of the entry into Australia of bands of foreign musicians .... The international aspect of the matter must be considered and it is almost certain that action such as you suggest would indubitably result in repercussions in other countries, particularly America'.[69] It was, as the Minister for Trade and

---

[65] Clause (t) of the Objects of the MUA, was added to the 1927 Rule Book, p. 13. NBAC MUA N93/477A.

[66] Markus, *Australian Race Relations*, p. 120.

[67] Senator Burford Sampson to Trevelyan, 10 May 1926, NBAC MUA E156/2/6(ii) (re legislation); *The Professional Musician*, September 1929, p. 10, NBAC MUA E156/11/1 (attempt failed).

[68] The argument over the applicability of the *Contract Immigrants Act* was on-going. See, for example, Minutes of the Federal Conference, 1923, NBAC MUA E156/6/2; 'Musicians Union– Importation of Bands–Contract Immigrants Act', Minute Paper, Attorney-General's Department, Commonwealth of Australia, 18 May 1937, NAA A432, 1937/383.

[69] Secretary to the Prime Minister's Department to Trevelyan, 23 May 1928. NBAC MUA E156/2/6(ii).

Customs acknowledged, a situation 'bristling with difficulties'.[70] The Union could do little but rail against the public taste for American bands and insistently refute the notion that only American musicians could play jazz.

However, when, in 1928, Hoyts employed an imported orchestra of thirty Italians for the opening of the luxurious new Regent Theatre in Sydney, and J.C. Williamson concurrently imported twelve Italians for the Williamson-Melba Grand Opera Season (breaking its negotiated agreement with the Union for five), the Union was able to link its feelings of resentment to general public concerns about Italian migration. For although southern Europeans were not specifically excluded under the terms of the *Immigration Restriction Act* of 1901 and thus were entitled to citizenship and union membership, they were regarded as racially inferior and subjected to prejudicial treatment.[71] Trevelyan painted migration as a threat to the union movement as a whole: 'Thousands of foreigners—in all callings—are being brought to this country and Australian workers generally consider there is an organised attempt to swamp the market, break Unionism and install cheap labour'.[72]

Italians made up the largest numbers of non-British or 'alien' immigrants to Australia in the 1920s with some 23,233 arriving in Australia between 1922 and 1930.[73] As the decade progressed and unemployment grew, this 'influx' became a focus of public discussion and resentment. Accordingly, the government introduced various restrictions and controls on Italian migration: quotas, visas, landing fees or guarantor requirements, or nominations by close relatives already resident in Australia. In fact, assisted British migration far exceeded Italian, but this did not alter public perception. Arnaldo Cipolla, an Italian writer who visited Australia during the 1920s, declared that although the total number of Italians arriving in Australia in 1924 was 4,000, as against about 88,000 British, 'to read the newspapers and the parliamentary reports of the day, you would have thought that Italy was about to invade the Commonwealth'.[74] Endorsing

---

[70] Minister for Trade and Customs to Trevelyan, 14 March 1930. NBAC MUA E156/2/6(ii).
[71] For a discussion of discriminatory attitudes towards southern Europeans (including Italians) in the 1920s and 1930s, see Markus, *Australian Race Relations*, pp. 144–151.
[72] Circular letter, Trevelyan to Foreign Musicians Unions, 9 January 1928. NBAC MUA E156/2/4(i).
[73] Gianfranco Cresciani, 'Italian Immigrants 1920–1945', in James Jupp (ed.), *The Australian People: An Encyclopedia of the Nation, Its People and Their Origins* (2nd edition, New York and Oakleigh, Vic.: Cambridge University Press, 2001), p. 500.
[74] Stephanie Lindsay Thompson, 'Italian Migrant Experiences of Australian Culture (1945–1970): Historical Background', in *Australia, The Australians and the*

this view, a clipping from the *Sydney Morning Herald*, preserved in one of the Union scrapbooks, announced that 'It was easy to imagine that after some years of this kind of penetration, Australia and Canada would not retain their traditional aspect as British dominions'.[75]

Though one could argue that the Union's assessment of the Italian musical 'influx' was similarly overstated, it was an issue with significant rhetorical and political potential.[76] The Union could, for example, join other voices in asserting that the Italians were undermining wages and working conditions (untruthfully in the case of contracted musicians, since compliance with Australian Awards was written into negotiated contracts and sometimes the Italian musicians were actually paid more than their Australian counterparts).[77] Or it could support the Theatrical Employees' Union in its threat of industrial action when it was found that the Italian chorus girls in the 1928 Williamson-Melba Grand Opera Season were also being paid more than the Australian girls (an irony apparently lost on Union officials).[78]

On 28 March 1928, W.M. Hughes, maverick politician, former Prime Minister, and avid proponent of a British White Australia, made a speech at the National Party conference in which he attacked the government's policy on Italian migration: 'We believe in a White Australia', he intoned, 'and a British White Australia at that'.[79] Hughes referred to the fact that he had recently introduced a deputation of Australian musicians to the Prime Minister, Stanley Melbourne Bruce, to protest against the importation of foreign musicians.[80] The deputation was undoubtedly prompted by the Union's lack of success in preventing the importation of the Hoyts Italian orchestra.

Italian Migration, ed. Gianfranco Cresciani (Milan: Quaderno di Affari Sociali Internazionale, 1983), p. 30 and n. 11.

[75] 'Italian Migration to Australia', *Sydney Morning Herald*, 23 [month illegible] 1928: Press cuttings 1927–29, NBAC MUA Z401 Box 12. The article cites the opinion of a French publicist, M. Henri Dekorab, that Italy 'had begun a systematic scheme of colonisation'.

[76] Of the c.54 Italian musicians who were brought to Australia in connection with the four major events under discussion in this article, not more than 6-8 seem to have succeeded in remaining in the country and joining the Union.

[77] See, for example, transcript of the hearing in the Principal Registry of the Commonwealth Court of Conciliation and Arbitration, 21 August 1924. NBAC MUA E156/8/7.

[78] *Daily Guardian*, 16 June 1928. Press cuttings 1927–29, NBAC MUA Z401 Box 12. The Australians received redress.

[79] 'Warm Address ... ' *Sydney Morning Herald*, 29 March 1928. Press cuttings 1927–29, NBAC MUA Z401, Box 12.

[80] The deputation was reported in *Sydney Morning Herald*, 17 March 1928. Press cuttings 1927–29, NBAC MUA Z401 Box 12. It was supported by the leader of the opposition Labor party, Matthew Charlton and included James Scullin, who succeeded Stanley Bruce as (Labor) Prime Minister in 1929.

'QUITE CANDIDLY, WE DON'T WANT THEM'

The MUA's efforts were rewarded with limited success in July 1928 when the Homes and Territories Department in Bruce's government finally announced that it was introducing a form of licensing for entrepreneurs wishing to import musicians for pit bands and orchestras, though it was likely less the result of the Union's petitions than of a sexual scandal involving a 'negro' stage band that had occurred in Melbourne in March 1928, since the licences were primarily intended to exclude coloured musicians.[81] Amongst various requirements, the prospective employer was to be asked to disclose whether application had been made to the Union for the class of performer required and whether there was any special reason for employing a foreigner instead of a local musician.[82] Though the Union was able to announce to its members, in September 1929, that 'there are no American or Italian orchestras, nor orchestras of any foreign nationality, here now'—a fact that possibly had more to do with the worldwide economic Depression—it was to some extent a Pyrrhic victory, as the minister had declined to make the Union a party to the decision-making process, retaining his discretionary power to 'consider each case on its merits'.[83]

The above discussion has identified the issue of the importation of foreign musicians as situated at the nexus of a conflict between the Musicians' Union and various theatrical entrepreneurs. Given that 'conflict is essential to the survival of both parties' in the dialectic of work-place relations, conflict over the issue of foreign musicians can be viewed as an inevitable outcome of a set of conditions that prevailed in the industrial relations system in the 1920s, exacerbated by pressures created by technological

---

[81] *Sydney Morning Herald*, 21 July 1928. Press cuttings 1927–29, NBAC MUA Z401 Box 12 (announcement of licence). *Sydney Morning Herald*, 29 March 1928. Press cuttings 1927–29, NBAC MUA Z401 Box 12 ('negro' musicians); Letter, Secretary to the Prime Minister's Department to M. Charlton, MP [Member of Parliament], 11 July 1928. NBAC MUA E156/2/6 (ii): 'The firms … are accordingly being advised that in connection with the administration of the Immigration Act, under which power could be exercised if necessary to prohibit the landing of any person whose admission had not been authorised by the Minister for Home and Territories, application should to be made to that Department and the Minister's approval obtained before arrangements are made in future to introduce into Australia foreign musicians under engagement to perform in orchestras or bands'.

[82] *Sydney Morning Herald*, 21 July 1928. Press cuttings 1927–29, NBAC MUA Z401 Box 12.

[83] *The Professional Musician*, September 1929, 12, NBAC MUA E156/11/1 (no foreigners); Assistant Secretary, Home and Territories Department to Trevelyan, 3 September 1928. NBAC MUA E156/2/6(ii) (each case).

developments within the music industry itself.[84] But to say that would be to ignore the role of systemic racism and generalised xenophobia in validating the Union's policy of discrimination against individual foreign musicians, a policy that prevailed for several decades with degrees of institutional and political support.

In her article on 'Union Strategy: A Gap in Union Theory', Margaret Gardner contends that 'Unions behave in characteristic ways, but not all act alike'.[85] However, at least with regard to its efforts to financially penalise, delay, limit, disenfranchise, and ultimately exclude 'overseas musicians', whether resident or visiting, from membership, the Union's strategies show features in common with those of other unions engaged with foreign labour. The determination that only financial British and naturalised British subjects were entitled to vote in Union elections is reminiscent of the withholding of votes from supporters of Chinese immigration within the furniture trade union in 1880, and British preference quotas recall similar quotas introduced against the Italians in the Queensland sugar-cutting industry in the 1920s.[86] Deputations to the Prime Minister, mass mailings to Members of Parliament, appeals to sympathetic parliamentarians, and approaches to ministers with appropriate responsibilities were all strategies that have parallels in other industries.[87]

Notwithstanding this larger truth, I propose that, because of the distinctive features of the music industry in Australia, the issue of foreign musicians became a 'frontier of control' between the Union and entrepreneurs that was disputed and mediated by the regulatory conventions of Australia's distinctive, State-sponsored conciliation and arbitration system. Not only was that system highly bureaucratic, but the culture it generated had a deeply embedded emphasis on the making of rules and the containing of conflict within a regulatory framework.[88] Within the resultant

---

[84] Deery and Plowman, *Australian Industrial Relations*, p. 45 ('conflict essential').

[85] Margaret Gardner, 'Union Strategy: A Gap in Union Theory', in Bill Ford and David Plowman (eds), *Australian Unions: An Industrial Relations Perspective* (2nd edition, South Melbourne: The Macmillan Company, 1989), p. 49.

[86] On the withholding of votes, see Andrew Markus, 'Divided We Fall: The Chinese and the Melbourne Furniture Trade Union 1870–1900', *Labour History* 26, (May 1974), p. 1; *Rules* 1929, section 41c (amended Dec. 1928), p. 41, NBAC MUA N93/478. On the situation in Queensland, see Markus, *Australian Race Relations*, p. 149 and Cresciani, 'Italian Immigrants 1920–1945', p. 502. On the Union's quotas, see, *Rules* 1927 section 4 (v) (a) and (b), registered Dec. 1927, p. 14, NBAC MUA N93/477A.

[87] See Markus, 'Divided We Fall', p. 5.

[88] Deery and Plowman (*Australian Industrial Relations*, pp. 12, 19) cite different theoretical approaches that view these as defining features of the Australian system.

organisational culture of the MUA, the exercise of power and control through the legalism of the minutiae of the rules was clearly more important than the fate of the individuals who found themselves caught up in it. As Kathy Ferguson has written, 'Bureaucracies proliferate rules as means to their ends, and emphasize adherence to established procedures in order to obtain standardized, reliable progress toward these ends. But the situation is such that the bureaucrats come to see adherence to the rules as itself the goal. Thus the function of the bureaucracy comes to be equated with its purpose'.[89] Though gender issues do not come into this present discussion, it is worth noting that feminist scholars, in critiquing masculinist features of the arbitration culture, have linked competitive ('foreign') labour with women in observing how 'male workers have used the authority of the system to enhance their own position *vis-à-vis* that of competitive labour, women and juniors'.[90]

It is a truism that unions operate for the benefit of their membership, but policy formulation and rule-making is imagined and articulated by very few voices. To some extent this is also an outcome of the system, for while registration gave legal status and recognition to unions, the system devalued participatory styles of union organisation, 'because courtroom methods of operation encouraged specialized skills which did not necessarily depend on interaction with rank-and-file members'.[91] Despite elaborately democratic governance formulae, though presumably with the implicit consent of the membership, the formation of Union policy over foreign musicians was nominally driven by the small cohort of district (state) and general office-bearers that constituted its Federal Council. Policy was, however, articulated, implemented and argued by an even smaller oligarchy of two or three long-serving, full-time, salaried officials within the Federal Executive.

In terms of its culture of rule-making, the arbitration system may be seen as a shaping influence on the organisation and a mechanism for legalisation of its values and policies. Most damagingly, the system's endorsement of discretionary powers for the Union in the implementation of its rules allowed the system's espoused values of equity and fairness to be subverted so that a potentially legitimate industrial concern over the large-scale importation of bands or orchestras of foreign musicians could become a site for the

---

[89] Kathy E. Ferguson, *The Feminist Case Against Bureaucracy* (Philadelphia: Temple University Press, 1984), p. 9 and n. 15.
[90] Kirkby, 'Arbitration and the Fight for Economic Justice', p. 347.
[91] Markey, 'Trade Unions', p. 170.

prejudicial treatment of individuals. The case study of the Weintraubs is offered in the next chapter as an example of the MUA's dealing with a group of Jewish immigrant musicians in the 1930s. The system did, however, allow for remedy, an option that was successfully and influentially exercised by John Kay in 1944, as is discussed in Chapter Four.

Chapter Three

'ONE OF THE FINEST SMALL BANDS IN AUSTRALIA'[1]

The Weintraubs from Arrival to Re-establishment

In a sense, the Weintraubs were accidental immigrants. An interview in *Australian Music Maker and Dance Band News* in November 1937 clearly announced their intention, at the conclusion of their initial Australian contract with Snider and Dean, of 'going to India and South Africa, and so on and on and on in their never-ending quest to play new theatres in new places'. Documents preserved in the Bestand Weintraubs Syncopators of the Akademie der Künste, Berlin, record Horst Graff's efforts (as manager), from late 1937 to May 1940, to secure residencies in the grand hotels of the region—Raffles in Singapore, the Taj Mahal in Bombay, the Eastern and Oriental Hotel, Penang—or tours in South Africa, Java or the USA. But his efforts were unsuccessful and, in the absence of a contract to move on to, the musicians were simply forced to stay. And so began their encounter with the defensive strategies of the MUA, particularly as articulated by its combative NSW District secretary Frank Kitson. Kitson used the example of the Weintraubs to pursue the Union's general arguments against refugee musicians, and these were scrutinised and responded to in various ways by the government departments and ministers with whom he corresponded. The alliances that formed around both the union and the musicians (viewed as refugees) provide instances of Kitson's use of a range of stereotypes in prosecuting the Union's case.

Two specific incidents provide the basis for my analysis. The first is the Weintraubs' participation, on 20 April 1940, in the Government House

---

[1] *Australian Music Maker and Dance Band News* 1 March 1940, p. 4.

Garden Fair and Hotel Canberra Ball in aid of Lady Gowrie's War Fund Appeal. This event provides an opportunity to explore the clashes of values that occurred once war was declared: for example, between the Weintraubs and the Union over participation in patriotic fundraising activities, and between the Union and those advocates in the wider society who believed that the musicians' status as refugees entitled them to special consideration. The second incident concerns Kitson's efforts to prevent Stefan Weintraub and Horst Graff from resuming employment as musicians after their release from internment. It should be noted that Kitson campaigned equally vigorously against a handful of other refugee musicians, concentrating his efforts on 'the names that occur to me as being prominent at the moment', while admitting that 'there are others seeking casual employment with more or less success'.[2]

Frank Kitson's first letter to a government minister on the subject of the Weintraubs dates from 24 February 1939, one week after Horst Graff lodged the band's first application for membership of the MUA, presumably to regularise its position at Prince's.[3] (Though he was, at this time, also Federal President of the MUA, Kitson routinely wrote and spoke as Secretary of the New South Wales District.) Read in the context of the secretary's file of correspondence with state and federal parliamentarians at the time, it was a routine 'protest' in the form of an enquiry to the Hon. J. McEwen, Minister for the Interior in Joseph Lyons' United Australia Party government, as to the form of license under which the Weintraubs (and other named refugee musicians) were accepting employment as musicians in Australia. After several months' delay, several follow-up letters from Kitson, two changes of prime minister and a Cabinet reshuffle, the secretary to the new minister, Senator H.S. Foll, replied with an explanation of the musicians' residence statuses.[4] On 1 June the minister offered the further explanation that 'An Alien musician, if permitted to land in Australia, is either admitted for permanent residence or temporarily for touring purposes'.[5] Kitson, noting that Kay and Graff were still under temporary permits (they applied for

---

[2] F. Kitson to The Hon H.S. Foll, Minister for the Interior, 18 [May] 1939. NAA A444, 1952/16/2762.
[3] NBAC MUA E156/2/2(ic).
[4] J. A. Carrodus to Kitson, 22 May 1939. NAA A444, 1952/16/2762.
[5] H.S. Foll to Kitson, 1 June 1939. NAA A444, 1952/16/2762. J. McEwen was Minister for the Interior from 1937–April 1939, when the death of the Prime Minister occasioned a reshuffle in the governing coalition, and Senator Hatil Foll was appointed to the Department (from 26 April 1939). Paul Bartrop devotes a whole chapter of his book *Australia and the Holocaust* (Ch. 8, pp. 144–168) to an examination of the development of an anti-Jewish bias in the Department under Foll, in particular the imposition of

permanent residency in January and February 1939),[6] responded by quoting back to the minister his departmental secretary's assurance that '"where there is reason to believe that applicants would seek to become members of dance bands or orchestras in Australia to the detriment of Australian musicians," the general policy of the Dept. is not to grant permits', pointing out that this is exactly what the two musicians were doing.[7] The band had taken up its engagement at Prince's in December 1938.

Robert Menzies' UAP government was not immediately or necessarily responsive to this or any other of Kitson's regular arguments, though the latter's complaints were routinely investigated. A Commonwealth Investigation Branch internal report pointed out, for example, that as the Weintraubs started at Prince's at the time the restaurant was opened, they therefore could not be said to have displaced any Australian musicians.[8] Moreover the fact that an Australian band of six—later ten—musicians was engaged to play alongside them, suggested that 'on the whole the presence of the men mentioned has not been to the detriment of Australian musicians in general'.[9] When Kitson shifted ground to protest the importation of British or alien dance band conductors, including of course Stefan Weintraub, the government again disagreed: 'It would appear from the reports received … that the engagement of popular and efficient conductors from overseas is not altogether a disadvantage to members of your Union inasmuch that the increased public support has resulted in most of the cases in the employment of additional Australian musicians'.[10]

Kitson continued to press his point that the Weintraubs were admitted as a stage band and were now operating as a dance combination, prompting the Union to revise the distinction previously maintained between stage acts (as acceptable imports) and dance and pit instrumentalists (unacceptable). Kitson wrote:

> I am aware that combinations of musicians seek to enter Australia as stage or specialty turns and it may be that the Department's

---

migration quotas and the introduction of the notorious 'Jewish race' clause on the Form 47 Application for Permit to Enter Australia.

[6] NAA A434, 1944/3/690.
[7] Kitson is quoting the letter from J.A. Carrodus, 22 May 1939; Kitson's letter is dated 24 May 1939. NAA A444, 1952/16/2762.
[8] Memorandum from J.R. Magnusson, Inquiry Officer, to Inspector, Commonwealth Investigation Branch Sydney, 20 September 1939. NAA A444, 1952/16/2762.
[9] Internal memorandum, (doc 38/2819), 23 November 1939. NAA A444, 1952/16/2762.
[10] J.A. Carrodus, Secretary, Department of the Interior to Kitson, 28 December 1939. NAA A444, 1952/16/2762.

investigators are disposed to consider such applications favourably. (I understand that the Weintraubs were represented as a stage turn.) I wish to point out that the life of such acts, however good, is short in this country, mainly due to the fact that our vaudeville circuit comprises theatres in the Capital Cities only. A repeat visit to each capital is about the life of a good musical act and if the components of such acts are armed with permanent permits they must eventually be thrown into competition with unemployed Australian musicians. I think the Dept. of the Interior should be seized with this aspect of our position.[11]

In his reply, the minister observed, 'It is a matter for your union to decide whether such persons who have been admitted to Australia and who seek to obtain employment in bands or orchestras shall be admitted to membership of the Union'.[12]

Files record two occasions on which the Weintraubs as a group attempted to regularise its situation within the profession by applying for membership of the MUA through the NSW District.[13] In the first letter of application, 17 February 1939, Horst Graff, as business manager of the band, attempted to argue that 'owing to our special turn of work, the question of competition does not arise';[14] Kitson's opinion of this line of argument is outlined in his letter to the Minister of the Interior quoted above. In Graff's second letter, 23 November 1939, he wrote pleadingly to Kitson, 'You will find that since our stay here, we have never broken any of the Union's rules'.[15] Apart from the basic outrage that the Weintraubs, as foreigners and non-unionists, had captured an engagement that Kitson described as possibly the most lucrative of its character in Australia,[16] everything about the musicians and their act was an affront to Union sensibilities and rules.

As has been shown, increasingly proscriptive rules governing the obligations of members had been added to the MUA federal rule book in the

---

[11] Kitson to Foll, 24 May 1939 after receiving advice on the residence status of the Weintraubs NAA A444, 1952/16/2762. One might compare this statement with that in *The Professional Musician*, September 1928, p. 28: 'This embargo is not aimed at orchestra conductors, concert virtuosi, or vaudevillians on tour, but merely at theatre pit musicians etc., whose importation might deprive Australians of employment'.

[12] H.S. Foll to Kitson, 1 June 1939. NAA A444, 1952/16/2762. However, their temporary residence status clearly left Kay and Graff particularly vulnerable.

[13] NBAC MUA T7/1/10: MUA (NSW District) Minute Book No 12, 23/11/34–14/5/41, minutes of meetings 24 February and 10 March (application held over), 13 April (refused); 5 December (refused), all 1939.

[14] Horst Graff to Kitson, 17 February 1939. AdKB Item 103.

[15] NAA ST1233/1, N19220.

[16] F. Kitson to Lady Gowrie, 29 May 1940. NBAC MUA E156/2/2/(ib).

'ONE OF THE FINEST SMALL BANDS IN AUSTRALIA'

Figure 17. Entertaining at Prince's, late 1930s to early 1940
According to the rules of the Musicians' Union, instrumentalists were not supposed to sing.
Private collection, with permission.

late 1920s, no doubt in an effort to ensure that available work was shared equitably among members as employment opportunities declined. Members were not, for example, allowed to play two or more dissimilar instruments in the same orchestra without Union permission. Nor were unionists permitted to move, without permission, between different performance situations. Virtuosity on dissimilar instruments and interchangeability were fundamental to the Weintraubs' act and to their claim to distinctiveness in the Australian context. Some of the musicians developed specialties: Leo Weiss was the band's pianist, Stefan Weintraub its drummer. On the other hand, John Kay played piano, trombone, saxophone, clarinet and bass clarinet in addition to composing and arranging,[17] while Ady Fisher moved between his double bass and microphone, as the band's 'crooner'. Union rules forbade instrumental musicians taking part in any form of acting. The Weintraubs habitually enacted 'little cameos of comedy', many of

---

[17] 'Kay v. Musicians' Union of Australia,' *Industrial Commission of New South Wales* vol. 198, *Transcripts of Proceedings August 1944*, p. 655. SRO NSW NRS 5343, 11/1573.

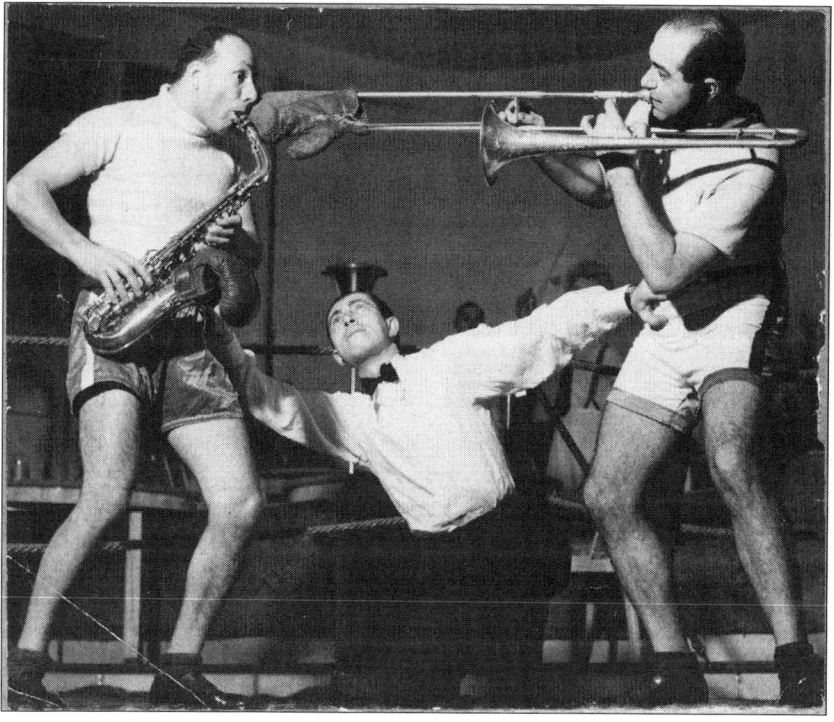

Figure 18. The musical boxing match
Cyril Schulvater (saxophone) faces off with John Kay [Kaiser] (trombone) while Mannie Fisher referees. Place unknown, n.d.
State Library of New South Wales MLMSS 7164X. Scrapbooks concerning the Mercury Theatre, 1940s–1950s [Sydney John Kay], with permission.

which are documented in extant photographs. On stage and for 'themed' entertainments at Prince's, the band appeared in various costumes and matched their musical routines to the theme. In one such stage act, exploiting their differences in size for comic purposes, John Kay (who was tall) and Cyril Schulvater (who was small) mimed a musical boxing match. One boxing glove was attached to the end of Kay's trombone slide and the two musicians wore satin shorts; Mannie Fisher 'refereed'. For a 'Mexicano' floor show at Prince's, the musicians dressed up as Mexican revolutionaries ('Panchos and Villas' [Pancho Villa]);[18] on another occasion the musicians walked the whole distance of the restaurant in convict attire with clanking

---

[18] Jack Meander, 'Two Eyes and a City', *Sydney Morning Herald*, 10 June 1939, p. 11.

Figure 19. A themed presentation at Prince's
Was this the remembered source for Victor Massey's Mexican reference in his letter to Harold Holt, 12 December 1951? Union officials had long memories.

State Library of New South Wales MLMSS 7164X. Scrapbooks concerning the Mercury Theatre, 1940s–1950s [Sydney John Kay], with permission.

chains.[19] For a Polo Ball at Prince's in July 1939, the musicians dressed up in 'incredibly ill-fitting' polo jumpers and riding breeches and performed a 'delightful burlesque on polo', the 'Polo Solo', which seemed to involve the impersonation of half a horse.[20] Kitson was unmoved. 'In passing,' he replied to Graff, 'I cannot agree with your statement that your combination has not broken any of the Union rules; you have certainly done things that would not have been permitted had you been members'.[21]

The MUA, the Weintraubs and the war effort

Nowhere is the clash of values between the Weintraubs and the MUA more apparent than in their respective attitudes towards participation in patriotic fundraising. The moment war was declared, the Weintraubs volunteered to

---

19　Jack Meander, 'The Weekend in Town', *Sydney Morning Herald*, 29 May 1939, p. 4.
20　Untitled clipping, 21 July 1939, SLNSW MLMSS 7164X. Scrapbooks concerning the Mercury Theatre, 1940s–1950s [Sydney John Kay].
21　Kitson to Graff, 29 November 1939. AdKB Item 103.

assist the Australian war effort; Weintraub, Kay and Graff at least entered their names on a list organised by the Jewish Welfare Society through the Maccabean Hall in Sydney, where refugees were able to offer their services (though not to enlist).[22] As aliens and non-nationals, the musicians were ineligible for military service, but the band undertook to perform without payment at a variety of patriotic functions including fundraising events for the Red Cross (in the Sydney Town Hall and Martin Place) and at entertainments for soldiers in the camps (at Warwick Farm and Rosebery).[23] Kay also asserted that, at the time of his internment, he was preparing to donate half his salary from a pending contract for a weekly show on radio station 2GB to the government as an interest free loan. As early as 11 September 1939, Horst Graff approached the Lord Mayor of Sydney when a patriotic fund was initiated, offering to raise one thousand pounds by playing Sunday evening concerts at the different town halls around Sydney, an offer which, once accepted, was duly publicised.[24]

The MUA, on the other hand, had, from the beginning of the war, opposed 'the huge demand on the gratuitous services of musicians for war and patriotic appeals',[25] seeking to exercise some control over the situation by a strict implementation of rule 88(o) of the federal organisation, which prohibited members donating their services gratis without prior permission of their district committee. Permission was withheld, almost without exception, and musicians in breach of the rule were disciplined. At the same time the Union tried to persuade the government to establish properly funded, union-sponsored concert parties to provide entertainment for soldiers. The government declined to take up this suggestion, 'as there are so many patriotic organisations and public societies throughout the Commonwealth

---

[22] This information was tendered by Graff during the tribunal hearing of his appeal for release from internment. The entire transcript is to be found in NAA C329, 402 (see especially p. 6); for Weintraub, see NAA ST1233/1, N19220, second letter from internment, 22 July 1940. According to John Kay, he offered his services to the Commonwealth in any capacity required as early as September 1938, by signing a list for aliens of the Jewish faith in the Maccabean Hall, Sydney. NAA A6126, 197, doc. 64.

[23] John Kay, Statutory Declaration made at Orange, NSW, [?] September 1940. NAA A6126, 197, doc 65. The last patriotic function at which the Weintraubs played was a luncheon for the Returned Soldiers' and Sailors' Imperial League on Empire Day, 31 May 1940. NAA C329, 402, p. 6.

[24] NAA C329, 402, p. 6. For correspondence, see AdKB Item 108; for publicity, see *Tempo*, December 1939–January 1940, p. 2.

[25] Secretary's report to the NSW District, August 1940. NBAC MUA T7/1/10, Minute Book No. 12. Other references to the Union's opposition to members' gratuitous participation in fund-raising or soldier entertainments may be found in the Secretary's reports for November 1939, August and November 1940.

providing free entertainment to the troops any restriction of their efforts could not at present be contemplated'.[26] As the Union remained adamant, the issue routinely erupted into the press.[27]

Internment prevented the realisation of the Weintraubs' more ambitious fundraising plans.[28] However, shortly before three of the musicians were interned, the Weintraubs donated their services to a garden party at Government House in Canberra and a ball at the Hotel Canberra on 20 April 1940, in aid of Her Excellency The Lady Gowrie's War Funds (she was the wife of the Governor-General).[29] The Musicians' Union was doubly aggrieved: on the one hand seeing the presence of aliens ('some ... of which are enemy aliens')[30] as a mockery of the patriotic cause, on the other seeing the gesture of performing without payment as undercutting the legitimate means of livelihood of Union members. For some more enlightened people—and Lady Gowrie was one who enjoyed a reputation as a refugee advocate—the musicians' status as refugees engendered sympathy. Kitson's protest was retrospective, perhaps because, as he wrote to Lady Gowrie on 3 May 1940, 'Society obviously takes the lead from you in such matters and as a result of this engagement it is probably that "The Weintraubs" combination will be offered many social engagements to the exclusion of our own race and the damage done, at the moment, is difficult to assess'.

The Governor-General's personal private secretary replied on 11 May, identifying the three German-Jewish members of the band as 'refugees

---

[26] The Secretary's report to the NSW District, August 1940 contains the text of the Secretary's letter to the Prime Minister, 17 July 1940, and of the reply from the Secretary, Department of the Army, 1 August 1940. NBAC MUA T7/1/10, Minute Book No. 12.

[27] For example, in February 1943, when two enlisted musicians were formally charged (Newcastle District) with breaking rule 88 (o). 'Union and Army Musicians. Non-Payment Dispute', *Sydney Morning Herald*, 4 February 1943, p. 4; follow-up articles titled 'Musicians Union Criticised' appeared in *Sun* and *Herald* of around the same date. See Press cuttings 1938–52, MUA NBAC Z401 Box 13.

[28] NAA C329, 402, p. 6.

[29] Horst Graff to Department of Military Intelligence, Sydney, 17 April 1940. NAA C123, 1213.

[30] This and the following quote are from Frank Kitson's letter to Lady Gowrie, 3 May 1940, protesting the Weintraubs' participation in the Canberra functions. Even though, as mentioned above, the Weintraubs did not arrive in Australia as refugees they could and later did argue that they were made refugees by circumstance. For the whole correspondence see NBAC MUA E156/2/2 (ib). For Lady Gowrie as refugee advocate see Klaus Neumann, 'Fifth Columnists? German and Austrian Refugees in Australian Internment Camps,' Public lecture for the NAA, the Goethe Institute (Sydney) and the Centre for European Studies at the University of New South Wales, Sydney, 17 April 2002, p. 7, at http://www.naa.gov.au/about_us/frederickwatson/Neumann.pdf, accessed 18 May 2006.

from German tyranny, who have been completely ruined by Nazi persecution' and therefore deserving of a 'helping hand'. Kitson responded on 29 May, that in the light of the musicians' long list of successes in Australia and the status of the engagement at Prince's, a helping hand was unnecessary. In general the Union was completely unmoved by arguments that European musicians who found refuge in Australia were entitled to special consideration by virtue of their status as refugees. 'It is a curious anomaly', wrote the General Secretary to his counterpart in the British Musicians' Union in July 1939,

> ... that British people think more of the foreign article than they do of their own production. They are also apt to consider this from a sentimental point of view rather than face the facts as they really are, because they are sorry for the victims of Hitler and Mussolini—and who of us are not sorry for them? They thoughtlessly are liable to clamour for their employment, in their adopted country, quite regardless of the fact that every one so employed dis-places one of their own.[31]

Many refugee advocates were people of high public profile and some social status and position, and the class base of their tolerance bred its own resentments. Interviewed on 16 November 1941 in *Truth*, a favoured mouthpiece for MUA propaganda, Kitson castigated 'Sydney café society, titled and wealthy playabouts [who] have developed a distinct fondness for foreign musicians and entertainers'. In the same interview, Kitson returned to the Lady Gowrie incident, and to the Weintraubs, protesting their continued employment:

> last year my executive instructed me to write to Her Excellency Lady Gowrie, to protest against the appearance of a combination of foreigners calling themselves The Weintraubs, at a garden fete at Government House, Canberra … [The Weintraubs] have been getting most lucrative work despite our protests. They are particularly welcome in the swirl of rich night clubs and at other places where rich and idle people disport themselves, as do many high officials of the Navy, Army, and Air Force… We find them playing at Romano's Café, conducted by Orlando Azalin Romano, and three of them play

---

[31] W.H.S. Lamble, General Secretary of the MUA and Secretary of the Victoria District to F. Dambman, General Secretary, MU, 13 July 1939. NBAC MUA E156/2/2(xi).

'ONE OF THE FINEST SMALL BANDS IN AUSTRALIA'

Figure 20. The 'Midnight Sextette' at Prince's, 1941
Leo Weiss and Ady Fisher are standing at the left, Mannie Fisher is centre front. The other three musicians were Canadian Samuel Lee (drums), and Australians Johnny Weine (guitars) and Mark Ollingham (piano and piano accordion).

Private collection, with permission.

lunch and dinner music at Prince's. Another plays at the Café La Palette at Double Bay.[32]

Class is not an overt feature of Union discussions of this period. More important here is Kitson's use of class-based stereotypes (what Reisigl and Wodak call 'classonyms') to portray a group of social actors ('rich and idle people') as homogeneous and ascribe to them a specific, allegedly shared 'fondness for foreign musicians and entertainers'. Reisigl and Wodak identify the use of such 'particularizing synedoches' as characteristic of stereotypical and prejudicial discourse 'a few decades ago', and acknowledge their political underpinnings. The same pattern of rhetorical stereotyping also produced, at this period, what Reisigl and Wodak call 'one of the historically most discriminating and incriminating collective singulars ... "the Jew"'.[33]

---

[32] '"Society People Prefer Alien Musicians", Union Secretary in Spirited Protest,' *Truth*, 16 November 1941 p. 21. The Newcastle District of the MUA made a similar statement, using similar rhetoric, at the same time. Untitled clipping, Press cuttings 1938–52, MUA NBAC Z401 Box 13. Leo Weiss played at La Palette for a brief period late in 1941. *Music Maker*, 20 December 1941.

[33] Reisigl and Wodak, *Discourse and Discrimination*, p. 63.

Figure 21. The Fisher brothers rehearse a Venetian interlude
No details given.

State Library of New South Wales MLMSS 7164X. Scrapbooks concerning the Mercury Theatre, 1940s–1950s [Sydney John Kay], with permission.

A 'kick in the pants' for the Union

The internment of Graff, Weintraub and Kay in June 1940 signalled the end of the Weintraubs as a combination under this name. It did not, however, mark the end of Kitson's campaign to drive the musicians, collectively or individually, from the profession, since not only did the three who were interned take up musical employment again on their release, but the three musicians who were not interned continued to play at Prince's. In its December 1941 – January 1942 issue, the trade journal *Tempo* announced that Prince's was introducing a special midnight entertainment unit known as the Prince's Midnight Sextette. Though the Union did not approve the combination, Bendrodt (Manager of Prince's) installed it anyway. The line-up of musicians comprised the two Frischer (now known as 'Fisher') brothers and Leo Weiss, 'late of the Weintraubs' (the so-called 'Polish trio'), a Canadian and two Australians. 'The formation of this outfit was a big "kick in the pants" to the Union,' the author of the article reported, 'as a couple of the boys resigned from the Union in order to join the outfit, but you can depend on J.C. Bendrodt to pay his hands better than Union

Figure 22. Mannie Fisher's party trick, playing two trumpets at once
Private collection, with permission.

money, so where's the kick coming from and why?'[34] As such movements of personnel from one group to another were a common feature of the dance band scene, the writer, without mentioning internment, simply moves on to describe the music, noting that 'the band's pleasing style and individualistic arrangements bring much appreciation from the patrons of this lovely restaurant where "Whispering Swing" is having its debut'. The phrase 'Whispering Swing' establishes a direct connection to the Weintraubs' 1939 promotional pamphlet.

The group survived as Mannie Fisher's Sextet, with some further change of the Australian personnel, until the Frischer brothers were drafted into the army in August 1943, despite evidence of further Union efforts to 'get rid' of the musicians. For example, an internal memo to the Deputy Director of Security for New South Wales, reads, 'Information has been received from a completely reliable source that much public criticism is arising from the continued employment of the undermentioned Aliens as musicians at Prince's Restaurant, 42 Martin Place, Sydney [A. and E. Frischer and Leo Weiss are named]. Each of the above is earning from 15 to 25 [pounds] per week. *It*

---

[34] *Tempo*, December 1941 – January 1942, p. 14. The resignation of the three unionists, all members of the NSW District, was reported to Federal Conference on 17 November 1941. Minutes of Annual Conference, p. 8, NBAC MUA E156/6/5.

is rightly considered that women could be more suitably employed in this capacity and without upsetting public morale' (my emphasis).³⁵ Though the Union is not identified as the 'completely reliable source', the reference to the band's earnings and the declared preference for 'women' over 'aliens' (anyone else would be better, even women) all point to Kitson. This is paradigmatic union rhetoric. As discussed earlier in relation to the film *Weintraubs Syncopators: Bis ans andere Ende der Welt*, the Sextet had also attracted the attention of the security services in March 1942, shortly after Pearl Harbour, when a local Passport Guard reported that a group under the name of 'Manny Fisher's Sextet' was broadcasting regularly from radio 2UW. Neither report resulted in any action being taken against the band, though detailed investigations into the status of each of the six musicians were once again carried out.³⁶

Graff and Weintraub were not so lucky. It was arguably Kitson's attempted exploitation of the public perception of internment as a stigma, namely, an attribute that is deeply discrediting to the individual interned, that effectively drove them from the profession within a few months of their release from Tatura. This was particularly the case during the Second World War because individuals were selected for internment and, due to the circumstances and administration of the detention and appeals process, in which no formal charges were laid, it was almost impossible for detainees to prove their innocence (that is, 'loyalty').³⁷

The Romano's incident, November 1941

Graff and Weintraub were released from internment on 4 September 1941 after taking advantage of an appeal mechanism set in place by the government in November 1940. Although the tribunal had recommended

---

35 Memo is signed C.W. Firth, 29 April 1943, and initialled by at least nine other persons, including Army personnel. NAA C123, 16027. Early in 1943, the Sextet was broadcasting nationally on the Horlick's variety show. See, for example, the advertisement in *The Mercury* (Hobart), 11 February 1943, p. 15. 'Boy, can they swing it!', carolled the promotion in the *Australian Women's Weekly*, 13 February 1943, p. 19.

36 See documents dated 9 March 1942 (Passport Guard's report) and 14 April 1942 (report on musicians). A complete script of the pre-recorded broadcast for Thursday 5 March 1942 was placed on file. NAA C123, 1211. Michael Fisher told me that his father used the spelling 'Mannie' for the diminutive of his first name, but official documents and press cuttings often use 'Manny'.

37 For a fuller discussion of these points, see Margaret Bevege, *Behind Barbed Wire: Internment in Australia during World War II* (St Lucia, Qld.: University of Queensland Press, 1993), pp. 26-7; 38f. and Saunders, 'A Difficult Reconciliation: Civil Liberties and Internment Policy in Australia during World War Two,' in Saunders and Daniels (eds), *Alien Justice*, pp. 114–137.

release, army intelligence officers who (secretly) analysed and (negatively) compared the transcripts of their hearings opposed the recommendation. Both men continued to be regarded with deep suspicion, partly arising from their apparently contradictory responses to questioning, and official surveillance continued.[38] All internees were freed on parole, which could be revoked; public perception of internment as a stigma was thus not discharged. Within days of their release, files record the response of former colleagues at Prince's: 'Members of Craig Crawford's band (Australians) have expressed amazement at the release of GRAFF and WEINTRAUB since, they say, both are "Nazis of the Nazi-ist", particularly GRAFF'.[39] Investigating officers considered but dismissed the idea that these comments might have had anything to do with professional jealousy.

Also within days, Graff was again under the notice of the security services; discretion, it would seem, was not part of his nature. On 19 September the intelligence section of Eastern Command received a report, forwarded from the censor's office, in the form of an extract of a letter written to a Hungarian alien named Adulbert Gomprez De Denta by an unidentified writer ('L') on 8 September and describing a recent dinner party, 'On Friday morning Horst Graff returned from internment. He looks extremely well—sunburnt, fat and like after a long vacation in the mountains. He tells the most amazing stories, how well they were treated, fed, etc. About the excellent organization, hygienic—sports—library colleges etc. ... I gave them a splendid dinner party last night, with candles, 6 courses and extra special wine—everything complete, yet it appears hard to beat the camp'.[40] It is generally held in the literature that the Australian Army's humane treatment of internees was one of the redeeming features of the internment story, but this was perhaps not quite the right tone for either describing internment at a time when Australian enlisted men were serving and dying overseas, nor of entertaining at a time of national rationing. The report was investigated thoroughly, though without further consequence to Graff. Graff's picture of camp life certainly sits oddly with the one that emerges later in this book

---

[38] NAA ST1233/1, N19220, contains page 1 only of the army's assessment of the transcript of Weintraub's evidence before the tribunal (internal memo dated 23 August 1941 [the remainder presumably sealed]). The whole assessment of Graff's transcript may be found in NAA C123, 1213 (5 page internal memo, from Captain G.H.V. Newman, Intelligence Section (I.b), Eastern Command, 25 August 1941). The Tribunal's report to GOC Eastern Command, containing its recommendation that Graff should be released and dated 11 August 1941, is also preserved in NAA C123, 1213.

[39] Anonymous report dated 12 September 1941. NAA C123, 1213 and NAA ST1233/1, N19220.

[40] NAA C123, 1213.

(Chapter Seven), but Graff does not present in the documentary record as a person of outstanding sensitivity to his immediate social environment. Charitably, one might view Graff as undertaking a process of normification, and his bravado as an attempt to convert a stigma symbol (internment) into something else, or at least defuse it ('like a long vacation').[41]

Stefan Weintraub's re-entry into civilian life was a more complex process that appears to have involved what Erving Goffman calls 'socialization into the stigma'[42]—an idea premised on the notion that internment was a form of incarceration and that, like other forms of incarceration, it was potentially a stigma, defined as 'an attribute that is deeply discrediting', which individuals might be expected to cope with in different ways according to their particular circumstances and personalities.[43] Files provide an example of a critical phase of transition for Weintraub personally, in terms of remaking his social identity, a 'phase through which he learns he possesses a particular stigma and ... the consequence of possessing it'.[44] It was a lesson for which both Weintraub's former employer and Frank Kitson, speaking for the MUA, were catalysts.

On 12 November 1941, Weintraub himself initiated a police report that was then forwarded to the Commissioner of Police and the Military Police Intelligence section. It contained allegations made by Weintraub against J.C. Bendrodt, manager of Prince's. On his release from internment, Weintraub had approached Bendrodt seeking re-employment at Prince's. Bendrodt offered him one hour's employment a day. This offer being unsatisfactory, Weintraub then approached the proprietor of Romano's Restaurant, Sydney's only other fashionable nightclub and, as such, a rival establishment to Prince's (in the same general location). Together with Horst Graff (also just recently released from internment) and two other 'enemy alien' musicians, he secured a position at Romano's in a Continental Quartet for a remuneration of forty pounds per week.[45] The other two musicians were Hungarian violinist Karoly Szenassy and German pianist Henry Adler, both Jewish refugees.

---

[41] For ideas about individuals coping with stigma, or the possibility of being stigmatised, and the impact of stigma on social identity, see Erving Goffman, *Stigma: Notes on the Management of Spoiled Identity* (London: Penguin Books, 1990 [1963]). For the idea of 'normification,' see ibid., p. 44.

[42] For the idea that an individual's stigmatisation is often associated with admission to a custodial institution, see ibid., p. 50.

[43] For the definition of stigma, see ibid., p. 13.

[44] Ibid., p. 45.

[45] *Music Maker* 20 November 1941, p. 2; document dated 12 November 1941, NAA ST1233/1, N19220.

Weintraub then reported a further conversation with Bendrodt that included the following:

> Well Mr Weintraub I have heard you are going to play at Romano's. Do you know that the Musicians Union will make some trouble? How would you like that the papers write about you—"Former German soldier plays in leading Restaurant"? Of course I cannot blame you for being a German soldier, [but] you know how people are when they read something in the papers. Then they will make trouble ... You were a soldier and people will be against you.

Bendrodt advised Weintraub to look for employment elsewhere, anywhere but with the opposition. He offered Weintraub one hundred pounds to set up in a 'commercial enterprise'. Weintraub inferred that Bendrodt's statements 'were tantamount to preventing him from obtaining employment'.

The police followed up Weintraub's complaint by interviewing all the parties involved in the affair:

> It was learned that the Management of Romano's Restaurant had received communications from Mr Kitson, Secretary of the Musicians Union, and Mr Black, Secretary of the Returned Sailors and Soldiers Imperial League, requesting information as to whether it was a fact that Aliens were to be employed in a Band at that establishment. ... It was gleaned from Mr Kitson that he was adverse to Aliens obtaining employment as musicians when members of his organisation were available ... [Kitson showed the officers his correspondence with Lady Gowrie in support of his opinion "that the services of enemy Aliens should not be utilised in this direction."] ... He contends that Romano might be well advised not to employ Aliens in the Band at his Restaurant seeing that he was dependant [sic] upon the Australian public for his livelihood.

Mr Black, being interviewed, admitted that he did not know Weintraub or any of the other members of his band: 'He indicated that Mr Kitson had communicated with him suggesting that he should write to the management of Romano's thereby giving him support to his objections of Aliens being employed as musicians'. None of the persons interviewed had knowledge of 'anything detrimental' (specifically, subversive activities) on the part of Weintraub or his associates. Graff, then working as a labourer for a firm in Annandale,[46] told the investigating police officers that he 'was desirous

---

[46] See Graff's Refugee Alien form, 27 September 1941. NAA C123/1, 1213.

of joining Weintraub at Romano's but he was apprehensive of taking this course as by so doing it might bring about his re-internment'.

Bendrodt, for his part, gave the appearance of being generous:

> He was satisfied that these people were law-abiding and would become good citizens of this country. ... He pointed out that he could not again employ Weintraub or Graff seeing that they were of German nationality and had been interned, as he had a duty to perform to his patrons, although he would like to do so as he had no personal grievance against them and that they were first class artists. ... [He] pointed out that it was no concern of his should Romano employ Weintraub and Graff but by doing so he may receive publicity through the press, seeing that it was common knowledge that Weintraub had served in the German Army during the 1914–18 war and had been awarded the Iron Cross. He stressed that should this publicity occur it would not be at his instigation.[47]

With or without Bendrodt's complicity but in seemingly magical fulfilment of his threat, these matters were made public by Frank Kitson in the November 1941 interview in *Truth* mentioned above,[48] as part of 'a vigorous campaign' against those foreign musicians and entertainers who, while Australian musicians had either gone to the war or were undergoing compulsory military training, were getting 'plum musical and stage employment' and had suddenly become the darlings of Sydney's rich and influential classes. The debate is not developed in general terms; Kitson names Romano's and the Weintraubs specifically, mounting a direct and personal attack against Stefan Weintraub himself, the only member of the group that he identifies:

> [s]ome of the Weintraubs have been interned. Some of them are out again now ... Stefan Weintraub is said to be the proud possessor of a high military decoration from the last war, given to him by Kaiser Wilhelm. That doesn't enhance the opinion of my executive concerning the Weintraubs and the other foreigners, or those rich and influential people who employ or sponsor them.

---

[47] NAA ST1233/1, N19220. The report, prepared by Sergeant F.P. Fyfe and Det. Serg. John W. Swasbuck for Inspector 2nd Class Wilson, 12 November 1941, is stamped as read by a number of officials including J.H. Wilson for the Commissioner of Police, the Commissioner of Police and Military Police Intelligence.

[48] 'Society Folk Prefer Alien Musicians', *Truth*, 16 November 1941, p. 21.

'ONE OF THE FINEST SMALL BANDS IN AUSTRALIA'

How may this incident be understood, in terms of Frank Kitson's behaviour as Union representative and spokesperson, of Bendrodt's apparent perfidy, and of the consequences for Graff and Weintraub, both of whom left the music profession at the conclusion of their Romano's engagement? In their study of press reporting of the immigrant presence between 1935 and 1977, Naomi Rosh White and Peter B. White found that more references were made to the impact of immigrant *groups* on the *status quo* than to immigrant *individuals*. When individuals were mentioned, a negative evaluation was the least common descriptor.[49] Kitson's public assault on Weintraub may therefore be seen as highly unusual, but not without parallels in other areas of Union campaigning. As has been argued elsewhere in this book, the MUA deployed various strategies in its fight against foreign musicians. While largely carried out in generic terms in the press, the crusade was also, at another level, highly personal; specific groups and individuals were named and targeted (though not always successfully) for dismissal, prohibition or repatriation in the Union's approaches to management and government departments.

The Union's efforts were subject to occasional scrutiny in the music trade press. In an article published on 29 June 1940, for example, the assistant editor of *Music Maker*, Jim Bradley, had complained that union efforts to curb the infiltration of refugees by direct representation to prospective employers had been ineffective. Bradley advocated 'a determined and well-directed system of propaganda' as the means to defeat the refugee menace to Australian-born musicians on the home front and to ensure a 'weeding-out process among certain bands, both large and small, whose aggregations contain a disproportionately large percentage of aliens'.[50] Perhaps in response to such critiques, Union propaganda escalated, in this case, to what amounts to a public denunciation. It is worth noticing, in this connection, the close proximity of the public 'kick in the pants' to the Union delivered by those Australian musicians who resigned their memberships to join Mannie Fisher's Sextet at Prince's, resignations reported to the Union's federal conference on 17 November 1941, one day after the interview in *Truth*. Was Kitson saving face? Whatever his reasons, Kitson's purpose is clear: Weintraub is presented as not only discredited (through internment) but discreditable (a soldier in the German army). Kitson's enlistment of support

---

[49] Naomi Rosh White and Peter B. White, 'Evaluating the Immigrant Presence: Press Reporting of Immigrants to Australia, 1935–77', *Ethnic and Racial Studies* 6/3 (July 1983), p. 299.
[50] Jim Bradley, 'And What of our Home Front?', *Music Maker*, 29 June 1940, p. 3.

from an ultra-nationalistic, pro-British and anti-alien (and anti-Jewish) public pressure group like the RSSAILA may likewise be understood as an attempt to reinforce the effectiveness of his direct approach to management.[51] Significantly, although he is identified as a 'German Jew', it is Weintraub's German nationality, not his Jewishness, that is at issue here. It is a painful irony that a fact intended to destroy Weintraub's credibility in Australia would not, being a Jew, have saved him in Germany.

One crucial detail does not appear in the police report of Weintraub's complaint. A pamphlet in the Weintraubs Collection of the AdKB suggests that Weintraub intended to revive the name of the band he and Graff had founded and call his new combination 'The Weintraubs'.[52] Given his reputation as a hard employer and negotiator, Bendrodt clearly could not tolerate Prince's highly successful speciality act appearing to relocate at a rival establishment.[53] Bendrodt's motivation is transparent: allegedly fearing a volatile public response, Bendrodt would not re-employ Weintraub, but neither was this first-class musician free to keep his good name if he worked for 'the competition'. The betrayal would have been obvious to Weintraub. Only two years earlier, at the musicians' request and presumably with their knowledge, Bendrodt had written to the Secretary of the Minister for the Interior endorsing the Weintraubs as 'desirable citizens in the true sense of the word'.[54] At that time, Bendrodt described the three German nationals as 'German Non-Aryans, who have not been domiciled in Germany … for period of nine years' and who had 'expressed to me on many occasions, strong anti-Nazi political beliefs'.

As the owner of a number of Sydney venues featuring live music, Bendrodt was a major employer who had ongoing dealings with Kitson over a long period of time. Despite their frequent clashes—for example, over the Midnight Sextette discussed above—Kitson kept his good opinion of Bendrodt, writing to MUA Secretary Trevelyan in 1933, 'Bendrodt is

---

[51] Suzanne Rutland writes that the President of the NSW branch of the RSL (known as the RSSAILA in November 1941) became a leading advocate for the cessation of alien and Jewish migration postwar. 'Postwar Anti-Jewish Refugee Hysteria: A Case of Racial or Religious Bigotry?' *Journal of Australian Studies* 77 (2003), p. 75. This alliance was not without precedent. In 1928, the MUA solicited support from the editor of the ANA Journal in its campaign against Hoyts proposed Italian orchestra. Letter, Editor to T.J. Ley, M.P., 9 March 1928. NBAC MUA E156/2/6(ii). At that time the ANA sought a policy of total exclusion of alien immigrants. Bartrop, *Australia and the Holocaust*, p. 8.

[52] AdKB Item 43.

[53] McCalman, 'Bendrodt, James Charles (1891–1973)', p. 161; John Ritchie, 'Romano, Azzalin Orlando (1894–1972)', *Australian Dictionary of Biography* 11 (1988), p. 447.

[54] Letter, 4 September 1939. NAA A434, 1944/3/690.

a particularly good employer and I would not like any unfair treatment of him'.[55] In the case of Weintraub at Romano's, Bendrodt's commercial interests coincided with the Union's political objectives; collusion is implicit between these adversaries in agreement. Complicity extended to Ezra Norton, proprietor of *Truth*. Norton's publicly expressed prewar antipathy towards Jewish refugees is well documented. In October 1938, he had editorialised:

> We do not want Jewish refugees! Not because we do not sympathise with their plight; but because we cannot possibly allow them to undermine our life and economic fabric. As a racial unit they are a menace to our nationhood and standards. As an inflow of migrants, they are a menace to employment ... It is a problem of self-preservation.[56]

Truth's demand that all Jewish refugees be refused admission into Australia was consonant with the Union's desire for a complete embargo on immigrant musicians; the paper's 'social racism' articulated what was concealed in the Union's more extreme applications of employment-based arguments.[57] Less obvious was the link between Bendrodt and Norton. They were, in fact, business partners since Norton was a financial contributor to the Trocadero dance palais and restaurant which Bendrodt had opened in Sydney in 1936.[58]

Weintraub was ambushed. The difficulty was, however, that the allegation was true. The police, in following through on Weintraub's report of his encounter with Bendrodt, ascertained that Weintraub had indeed served in the German Army during the First World War and that he had received the Iron Cross. A translator's report dated 3 December 1941 suggests that the police may have confiscated certain documents from Weintraub (Exhibit 24653/36) at the time of the Romano's incident. These documents yielded the information that ex-prisoner Stefan Weintraub, late of Field Artillery, was given the Iron Cross on 8 November 1918. The file also records—rather

---

[55] Kitson to Trevelyan, 20 October 1933. NBAC MUA Z401, Box 5, Correspondence General Secretary 1932–34.
[56] *Truth*, 16 October 1938. Cited in Rutland, *Edge of the Diaspora* (2nd revised edition) (Sydney: Brandl & Schlesinger, 1997 [1988]), p. 189.
[57] In the context of economic arguments around racial prejudice, Richardson and Wodak define a 'social racist' as one who wants 'neither labour nor the presence of the alien'. John E. Richardson and Ruth Wodak, 'Reconstructing Fascist Ideologies of the Past: Right-Wing Discourses on Employment and Nativism in Austria and the United Kingdom', *Critical Discourse Studies* 6/4 (November 2009), p. 255 (citing Cohen).
[58] Valerie Lawson, 'Norton, Ezra (1897–1967)', *Australian Dictionary of Biography* 15 (2000), p. 295.

extraordinarily given the date—that 'on 13 July 1934 Weintraub was given the Cross of Honour for active service 1914-18'.[59] In Chapter Seven I will argue that the participation of German (and Austrian) Jewish refugees as soldiers in the First World War was a major factor in shaping hostile public and official assessments of their wartime status; once again, Kitson has allied the Union with an issue of public concern. Nonetheless, there is malice in Kitson's attack, and the commercial and political alliances that formed around it, that goes beyond the duty of care of a union official protecting the interests of his membership and speaks of an antipathy that is personal and vengeful, though masked by the semantic move to the anonymous cover of 'my executive'.[60]

Despite Weintraub's exposure and Graff's uncertainty, the musicians hung on at Romano's, though the name 'The Weintraubs' was never used in any publicity. The quality of the music had not changed; *Music Maker* was once again enthusiastic. Noting the installation of a 'very smooth quartette' at Romano's in November 1941, the magazine observed that the group had 'settled down to an assured success amongst luncheon and dinner patrons of this popular rendezvous' supplying 'practically every type of music, including Tzigani, classics and the more dulcet pops'.[61] But there was further unpleasantness. 'Looking for spies?', asks the author of an anonymous note in Weintraub's file, received 10 February 1942. 'Try the Weintraubs, a dance band of Germans. Three are playing at Romano's and three at Prince's Restaurant. Have a look at Mr Graf [sic] (the name speaks for itself) and see if you can see a German officer in mufti looking at you. If there is any "benefit of the doubt," it should be on our side'.[62]

The mention of Tzigani in the *Music Maker* report draws attention to another member of the Romano's quartet, violinist Karoly Szenassy. Szenassy, a Hungarian Jewish refugee who arrived in Australia on 26 July 1938,[63] has his own history with the Union, the ABC and the security services. Twenty-six year old Szenassy presented in Australia as a prize-winning virtuoso concert soloist. As such, in the months before the war,

---

[59] NAA ST 1233, N19220.
[60] On the use of such masking 'semantic moves', see Mitten and Wodak, 'On the Discourse of Racism and Prejudice', pp. 198, 204–205, who argue (after van Dijk) that such moves are employed 'to dissociate oneself from the content of one's statement, should it be in danger of transgressing the boundaries of allowable political discourse [about refugees]'. Of course this particular shift also adds weight and authority to Kitson's statements.
[61] *Music Maker*, 20 November 1941, p. 2.
[62] NAA ST1233/1, N19220.
[63] NAA SP11/2, YUGOSLAVIAN/SZENASSY K (Box 210).

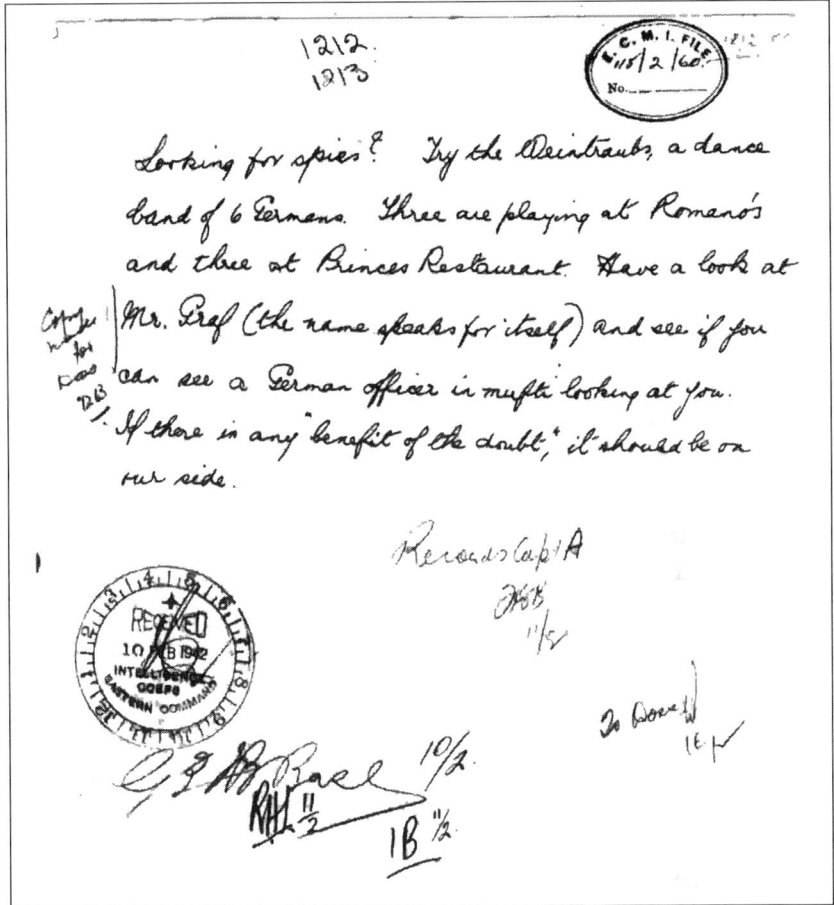

Figure 23. 'Looking for spies?'
A sample of an anonymous denunciation, focusing on the re-employment of the interned musicians after their release, received 10 February 1942.

National Archives of Australia ST1233/1, N19220, with permission.

he made an eleven-week concert tour for the ABC (with Richard Crooks, mid-1939) and broadcast on ABC radio. When he complained about the infrequency of these engagements, the ABC responded that he would simply have to 'take his turn'.[64] To earn his living as a non-member of the Union, he was obliged to take work playing popular music in a Melbourne

---

64   ABC Inter-office memo, T.W. Bearup, 8 October 1940. NAA SP173/1, SZENASSY, KAROLY.

tea-room and in restaurants like Romano's. He complained again when the ABC rejected his gypsy band. More rejections followed advice from the intelligence section that he was 'not a suitable person to appear before a microphone'.[65] After the war, he found himself caught up in the struggle between Eugene Goossens and the Union. Goossens wanted Szenassy for the reformed Sydney Symphony Orchestra, but the Union rejected Szenassy's application for membership, commenting that though he had had ample time to become naturalised, he had not done so.[66] Szenassy announced his intention to leave the country in February 1948 whereupon ABC Chairman W.J. Cleary commented, 'I cannot believe Mr Szenassy would have been overlooked if he is all he says he is. It is possible that he is not as good a player as he was when he won the Vienna Prize'.[67]

Weintraub's band was replaced at Romano's by May 1942—in itself nothing unusual, as bands rotated in high-profile venues—though Weintraub and Graff seem to have left not only the job but the profession. Without naturalisation, neither had any hope of joining the Union. By November 1942, Weintraub was working as a mechanic for Camtran Windings, Sydney; Graff returned to his job with the firm in Annandale.[68] Both Weintraub and Graff found a haven and outlet for their musical skills with the German-language Little Viennese Theatre.[69] Weintraub's name appears regularly in the group's musical presentations up to and including the *Jubilaeums Konzert* of 1971. As an amateur company, run by refugee migrants for the benefit of other refugees and thus out of the entertainment mainstream, its activities were of no interest to the Union. Indeed, only one of the four musicians at Romano's, Henry Adler, seems to have survived in the Australian profession postwar. In an ironic twist, Adler turned up at Prince's in 1949.[70] Asked to explain, in an interview in 1979, why

---

[65] Inter-office memo, J.J. Donnelly, 1 July 1941. NAA SP173/1, SZENASSY, KAROLY.
[66] Kitson to Lamble, 28 July 1948. NBAC MUA E156/2/3(v) (1945–50).
[67] 'No "Welcome" Sign for Gifted Musician', *Sunday Telegraph*, 13(?) February 1949. NAA SP767/1, KAROLY SZENASSY (Box 4).
[68] *Music Maker*, May 1942, p. 12, announced that Harry Whyte was providing the music at Romano's. For Weintraub's employment, see his Application for written permission to possess or use Wireless Receiving Apparatus, 19 November 1942. NAA ST1233/1, N19220. For Graff's employment, see his Application for Naturalisation, 25 February 1944. NAA C123/1, 1213.
[69] The Little Viennese Theatre ('Kleinen Wiener Theater') has been written about in detail by Birgit Lang. See, for example, her *Eine Fahrt ins Blau. Deutschsprachiges Theater und Kabarett im australischen Exil und Nach-Exil, 1933–1988*. Amsterdamer Publikationen zur Sprache und Literatur, Band 163 (Berlin: Weidler, 2006).
[70] NAA SP1011/1, 818, has an ABC publicity photograph of Adler from c.1955; for Prince's, see *Australian Music Maker and Dance Band News*, October 1949, p. 35.

'ONE OF THE FINEST SMALL BANDS IN AUSTRALIA'

the Weintraubs no longer existed as a combination after the war, Stefan Weintraub commented, 'We all took other jobs; we wanted security', a statement that is remarkable for what it does not say about who survived in the industry and who did not, and the reasons.[71]

---

[71] Interview with Stefan Weintraub (1979), NAA C100, 80/7/353 M. Australian Broadcasting Commission Radio Archives Library recording.

Chapter Four

THE WEINTRAUBS SYNCOPATORS, THE JEWISH QUESTION AND THE MUSICIANS' UNION OF AUSTRALIA 1937–1953

Any discussion of the rapidity of the Weintraubs' decision to leave Germany needs to take two things into account: that they were able, with apparent ease, to find employment outside the country, and that Berlin cabaret and revues became one of the prime markers of 'Jewish perversion' in Nazi propaganda. As early as April 1933, the German Government introduced legislation to exclude non-Aryans—both foreigners and Jews—from Germany's professional, intellectual and cultural life.[1] Rudolf Asmis, German Consul-General in Sydney, reassured Australians that these measures had been taken not on religious grounds, but in order to limit 'revolutionary, communistic, destructive, and anti-patriotic Jewish influences in the political, cultural, and economic life of the nation', citing 'the demoralisation of the theatrical life in the capital of Berlin'.[2]

The arts were of fundamental importance to the Third Reich, both to its ideology and its propaganda. Flagship cultural institutions like the Berlin Philharmonic Orchestra were used to promote an international image of the regime as benign and cultivated. Within Germany, efforts to coordinate and reorganise the country's professional associations and unions resulted in the

---

[1] Alan E. Steinweis, *Art, Ideology and Economics in Nazi Germany: The Reich Chambers of Music, Theater, and the Visual Arts* (Chapel Hill and London: University of North Carolina Press, 1993) p. 106 identifies the Civil Service Law of April 1933 as marking the beginning of a systematic and orderly purge of Jews from the art professions.
[2] 'Germany's Defence. Stated by Consul-General', *Sydney Morning Herald*, 21 July 1933, p. 8, cited in Hooper, 'Australian Reactions to German Persecution of the Jews', p. 14.

formation, in September 1933, of the Reich Chamber of Culture, a centralised governing body under the control of Joseph Goebbels' Propaganda Ministry. Efforts at reorganisation proceeded in tandem with the Nazification of the country's cultural life, a process which involved the removal of foreign and Jewish elements. John Kay, in one of his many statements to Australian security forces, described the situation as it affected the Weintraubs:

> After the Reichstag fire (27th January [sic]) and the elections at the beginning of March which brought the Nazis into power, it was impossible, for racial reasons, to obtain further employment; furthermore, contracts with film companies (U.F.A.) were cancelled. An enquiry was made from our manager by the management of this film company as to whether there were any foreigners or Jews in the orchestra and subsequently the film company paid us 800 marks to release them from a contract which should have started about this time. All members of the orchestra left Germany before the Jewish boycott day (1.4.33) and assembled in Prague, Czechoslovakia, from where we continued on our tour of engagements outside Germany.[3]

It is certainly one of the ironies of the Weintraubs' story that, having been excluded from employment by the racial ideologies of the Third Reich, they should encounter such opposition from the Musicians' Union in Australia, an organisation equally determined to exclude them, as foreigners, from employment or even permanent residence. Is there a parallel to be made between the two organisations and how far can it be taken? Writing about Australia's treatment of German-speaking refugee musicians in the November 2008 issue of the *Australian Jewish Historical Society Journal*, German musicologist Albrecht Dümling compared the Musicians' Union of Australia and the Reich Music Chamber (*Reichsmusikkammer*, RMK) in Germany with regard to their exclusion of foreign musicians in the declared interests of 'protecting' native-born musicians.[4]

Dümling is not the only scholar to have drawn parallels between elements of Australia's restrictive immigration policy and its treatment of immigrant refugees, past and present, and aspects of Nazism or apartheid. The introduction to Keith Windschuttle's confrontational critique of scholarly

---

[3] NAA A6126, 1236, doc. 64. No date or identifying details. The Reichstag fire was 27 February 1933.

[4] Albrecht Dümling, 'Uncovering Traces: German-speaking Refugee Musicians in Australia', *Australian Jewish Historical Society Journal* XIX, Part 2 (November 2008), pp. 219–236 and esp. pp. 227–228. The reference to John Kay is on page 228.

readings of the White Australia policy from the 1960s onwards considers several such examples.⁵ Nor is Dümling the only scholar to suggest that at least some of the RMK's regulatory interdictions were as much to do with protectionism as ideology.⁶ Dümling's comparison is challenging, but also deeply thought-provoking, since it invites consideration of unlovely aspects of Australia's treatment of Jewish refugees in the 1930s and 1940s, and of refugee music professionals in particular. The test of the legitimacy of even such a limited link requires the examination of three aspects of the Australian situation: the Union's relationship to government, the extent to which Union policy was underpinned by the racist ideologies of the White Australia policy and the availability of legal remedy to musicians who were excluded from membership. In this context, the notion of 'protection' needs to be problematised around the crucial issue of how much it mattered to the formation and implementation of MUA policy in the 1930s that foreign refugee musicians were Jewish. Whether the MUA can be taken as representative of the profession at large is a question this discussion seeks to address.

Australia was a safe haven in which extermination was never a possibility. Nonetheless, it was, at the same time, a 'reluctant refuge';⁷ some individuals were treated unfairly, others unjustly. The experience of the Weintraubs Syncopators—cited by Dümling as exemplifying one class of refugee musicians—was ultimately destructive of the group, though neither the process nor the outcome was the same for each musician. The case of John Kurt Kaiser (aka Sydney John Kay), the only individual member of the Weintraubs Syncopators mentioned by Dümling, is certainly of importance, by virtue of the legal challenge Kaiser/Kay successfully mounted against the NSW District of the MUA in 1944. It is also fortuitous that comprehensive documentation exists of Kaiser's interaction with various government agencies and the Musicians' Union.⁸

---

5   Keith Windschuttle, *The White Australia Policy* (Sydney: Macleay Press, 2004), pp. 1–3, 12.
6   See, for example, Erik Levi, *Music in the Third Reich*, pp. 120–121 (for the link between the ban on jazz and unemployment) and Michael H. Kater, *Different Drummers*, pp. 27, 36–38 (for a nuanced treatment of the situation of foreign musicians, before and under the RMK).
7   The phrase is from Glen Palmer, *Reluctant Refuge: Unaccompanied Refugee and Evacuee Children in Australia, 1933–1945* (East Roseville NSW: Kangaroo Press, 1997).
8   Sydney John Kay, as he became known professionally in Australia, arrived in the country with a Peruvian passport in which his birth name appears as John Kurt Kaiser, by which name he is generally identified in government files. He was interned under the name Ned John Kurt Kaiser, a name which also appears on other official documents,

By withholding membership from foreign musicians, the MUA, like the RMK, sought to isolate them within the profession and, ideally, to exclude them from employment. Beyond that exclusionary objective, however, there are significant differences in the Australian situation. The first concerns the Union's relationship to government. As will be shown, the MUA was regulated by the state; it was not an instrument of the state, and legal remedy was available to individuals against an 'oppressive or tyrannical' application of a union's rules. The legal setting for Kay's challenge is provided by the general context of the Australian arbitration system, and by formal and informal government policy on the admission of foreign and refugee musicians. The hearing allowed a public airing of the matters at issue between John Kay and the Union, and produced a judgment that was to have ongoing consequences.

The Union's formal endorsement of the so-called 'White Australia policy' would appear to validate Dümling's comparison since, as Andrew Markus points out, the White Australia policy was more than a means of excluding non-European immigrants embodied in the *Immigration Restriction Act* of 1901;[9] the ramifications of the policy's racist ideologies also affected some non-British European immigrant groups including, as Dümling notes, Jewish refugees in the 1930s. Following the First World War, 'White alien' (non-British European) immigration was tightly controlled legislatively and through the implementation of quotas, landing money requirements and discretionary criteria governing the issue of landing permits that preferenced certain groups over others.[10] The *Immigration Act* 1925, for example, gave the Governor-General wide powers to prohibit outright or limit the immigration of 'any specified nationality, race, class or occupation'.[11] Philosophically, the emphasis in the pre-Second World War period was on restriction rather than encouragement of immigration. While

---

such as his application for naturalisation. He seems to have enjoyed playing with his name. His band in 1920s Berlin was known as 'Sid Kay's Fellows' and he also admitted to using the pen-name Raymond Maurice. I will refer to him by his chosen business name, John Kay; footnotes will, however, show his name as it appears in the cited document. Much of the detail in this chapter comes from the named Kay/Kaiser files in the NAA and the NBAC.

[9] Markus, *Australian Race Relations*, pp. 110–111.
[10] See Bartrop, *Australia and the Holocaust*, pp. 27–32; Langfield, *More People Imperative*, Chapter 4, especially pp. 85–86.
[11] Geoffrey Sawer, *Australian Federal Politics and Law 1901–1929* (Carlton: Melbourne University Press, 1972), p. 231. Sawer writes that the 1925 Act 'for the first time broke in on the principle of the dictation test as the sole formal ground for excluding migrants when the real ground was race or colour'. See also Langfield, *More People Imperative*, p. 85.

the MUA excluded 'coloured' musicians without exception, and rhetorically asserted a preference for 'British' immigrant applicants over Europeans, the Union's practical realisation of the ideals of White Australia as 'Australia for Australians' also excluded musicians from other Commonwealth countries.[12] I would argue that, like its opposition to Italian musicians in the 1920s, the Union's resistance to Jewish refugee musicians in the 1930s, though validated by prevailing social concerns and racial attitudes, was driven more by circumstance and a generalised objection to competitive labour.

The MUA and the 'White Australia Policy'

It is a truism of Australian labour history that there was a link between trade union ideology in the first decades of the twentieth century and the discriminatory racial policies of 'White Australia', as expressed initially in the *Immigration Restriction Act* of 1901.[13] The MUA proposed formal allegiance to the principles of the policy at its annual conference in 1923, requiring districts to prevent the admission of coloured races. Once duly registered as one of the Union's 'Objects', this declaration of allegiance remained a pillar of MUA policy until the paragraph was removed from the federal rule book in 1961.[14]

Although the Union had secured the deportation of four 'Phillipino' musicians from the 1916 Gonsalez Opera Company's orchestra,[15] the Australian music industry of the 1920s was not one that was particularly susceptible to infiltration by coloured musicians; minutes suggest that the Union's 'White Australia policy' resolution was a response to a specific application from a musician who was 'said to be a coloured person'.[16] A number of questions occur: What practical and ideological uses was the policy put to by the Musicians' Union? What did the Union take from the idea of a White Australia and how did officials translate its principles into strategy and policy? Julia Martinez identifies Labor PM Andrew Fisher's 'preference to

---

[12] For the idea of 'Australia for Australians' as the popular and practical evolution of 'White Australia', see Jim Bradley, 'And What of Our Home Front?', *Music Maker*, 29 June 1940, p. 3.

[13] Andrew Markus, *Fear and Hatred: Purifying Australia and California 1850–1901* (Sydney: Hale & Iremonger, 1979), p. 228. Peter Love suggests a further link between working class antisemitism and the radical nationalism of labour politics. '"The Kingdom of Shylock": A Case-Study of Australian Labor Anti-Semitism', *Journal of the Australian Jewish Historical Society* XII, Part 1 (November 1993): 54–62.

[14] NBAC MUA Z391/73, File 'Rules 1958–61'.

[15] Secretary's Report to Federal Conference, August 1916, pp. 2–3. NBAC MUA E156/6/6.

[16] Minutes of the NSW District, 1923–1926, p. 58. NBAC MUA T7/1/7.

unionists' amendment of the arbitration legislation as representing a second phase of implementation of the White Australia policy.[17] She is discussing the replacement of coloured workers with Europeans, but can one reasonably deduce that the Musicians' Union equated 'foreign labour' generically with coloured labour for its own purposes?

Of more long-term consequence than the admission of coloured members was that portion of the *Immigration Restriction Act* which prevented the entry of any person under contract to perform manual labour within the Commonwealth, a clause that was amended and superseded in the *Contract Immigrants Act* of 1905.[18] Arguments around the applicability of the *Contract Immigrants Act* to the music profession were renewed, unsuccessfully, by the Union with each change of government from 1923 to at least 1937. In April 1937, just three months before the arrival of the Weintraubs, a deputation was introduced by Melbourne Ports Labor representative E.J. Holloway MP, to argue the musicians' case for protection against competition by imported bands, under the terms of the *Contract Immigrants Act*, 'even though the personnel of these was British'.[19] However, successive Attorneys-General maintained the view that the Act applied only to manual workers, refusing to extend the Act's provisions to include musicians.[20]

The appellant: Sydney John Kay

John Kay arrived in Australia with the Weintraubs from Shanghai in July 1937. The band then comprised a group of seven musicians and was under contract to Snider and Dean, a firm of theatrical entrepreneurs owning or controlling thirty-five cinemas nationwide.[21] In accordance with government regulations introduced in July 1928 as a result of intensive lobbying by the MUA, Snider and Dean were obliged to apply to the Department of the Interior for a licence to import this 'stage and vaudeville act ... all of whom

---

[17] Martinez, 'Questioning "White Australia"', p. 2. Fisher was a 'firm advocate' of 'White Australia'.

[18] Langfield, *More People Imperative*, p. 211.

[19] Memorandum, T. Paterson, Minister for the Interior, to Attorney-General R.G. Menzies, 6 April 1937. NAA A432, 1937/383.

[20] In 1937, the Attorney-General advised the Minister that 'It [the Act] applies to manual labourers only and the introduction of professional musicians into the Commonwealth falls completely outside the intention of the Legislature when passing the Act'. Memo from the Attorney-General (Robert G. Menzies) to the Minister for the Interior, 1 June 1937. NAA A432, 1937/383.

[21] Internal report forwarded to the Secretary, Department of the Interior, 2 June 1937. NAA A434, 1944/3/690. A list of the firm's theatrical interests nationwide is included in the file.

Figure 24. The band had its own bus on tour in New Zealand, early 1938
Akademie der Künste, Berlin, Bestand Weintraubs Syncopators, Item 185, with permission.

are Europeans'.²² The firm gave the requisite undertakings: that the importation of the troupe would not be the cause of displacing any Australians at present employed, that the musicians would not become a charge upon the public purse, and that the firm would be responsible for their maintenance and for their departure from Australia at the conclusion of the contract.

When an outbreak of polio in Melbourne forced a curtailment of the original contract (from the promised sixteen–twenty weeks to eight), Kay remained with the band, accompanying it on its substitute tour of the firm's cinemas in regional Australia and subsequent independent tour of New Zealand. The trip to New Zealand was a turning point for the band. It discharged Snider and Dean from their undertaking to ensure the band's departure at the conclusion of the contract and occasioned some significant changes of personnel after a number of the original group broke away. Of the original seven, (South African) Cyril Schulvater left before the New Zealand tour, having arranged to remain in Australia; (American) Freddy Wise travelled on to Europe from New Zealand. Six musicians left for New

---

22   Snider and Dean to Secretary, Department of the Interior, 29 May 1937. NAA A434, 1944/3/690.

Zealand on 28 January; five returned on 21 May: Stefan Weintraub, Leo Weiss, Horst Graff, Emanuel Frischer and John Kay. All five returning members of the group were granted permission to re-enter the country for a further twelve-month period to fulfil broadcasting engagements.[23] At the same time, Adolph Frischer joined the band as a replacement for Freddy Wise.[24] The band had also severed its connection with its former manager, Heinz Barger, who had returned to Japan.[25]

By January 1938, five of the original group had applied to remain permanently in the country and three of the five who returned from New Zealand had been successful.[26] It is notable that each of the musicians who was granted permission to remain permanently had stated his intention of working in a profession other than music: Weintraub proposed to resume his earlier career as a chemist; Emanuel Frischer thought he might open a café, while Leo Weiss planned to set up as a theatrical entrepreneur.[27] The musicians' declarations of intent with regard to their future careers might seem, at first glance, to provide evidence in support of Dümling's idea that foreign musicians were only welcome in Australia if they gave up their musical professions.[28] It is true that the MUA sought to prevent musicians from entering the country and, when here, from entering the profession; it is also true that the Union prosecuted individual cases with noteworthy determination. But while successive ministers gave assurances to the Union that they would discourage, or even deny, applications for the importation or admission of musicians,[29] the government's consideration

---

[23] Internal memorandum, Department of the Interior, 4 April 1938. They had initially been admitted for a twelve-month period. Secretary, Department of the Interior to Snider & Dean, 8 June 1937. For the curtailment of the contract, see J.A. Tonkin, Acting Australian Government Commissioner in Japan, to Secretary, Department of Commerce, 9 December 1937. All NAA A434, 1944/3/690.

[24] Secretary, Department of the Interior to Horst Graff, 7 April 1938. NAA A434, 1944/3/690.

[25] Copious documentation of their extended New Zealand tour survives in the AdKB. In addition to mapping the complexities of managing the band, coordinating its finances and arranging a touring schedule, these documents confirm that Horst Graff had assumed the role of manager. Many difficulties notwithstanding, Graff managed to prolong the tour from the four weeks originally announced (*New Zealand Radio Record*, 28 January 1938, p. 8) to c. four months, but this involved a constant search for new sponsorship.

[26] Stefan Weintraub, Emanuel Frischer and Leo Weiss. Secretary, Department of the Interior to F. Kitson, 22 May 1939. NBAC MUA E156/2/2 (ic).

[27] Internal memorandum, Department of the Interior, 20 March 1939. NAA A444, 1952/16/2762.

[28] Dümling, 'Uncovering Traces', p. 222.

[29] For example, an internal memorandum to the Collector of Customs, Sydney, dated 28 February 1935 (from the Secretary of an unidentified department) stated that 'it is not the practice to grant authority for the introduction of alien dance band musicians,

of the Weintraubs' situation was relatively benign. The assessing officer observed of Emanuel Frischer that it was unlikely that he would make a success of a café as he appeared to have no experience, and the bohemian class to which he belonged and for which he proposed to cater had no money; it was assumed that he would continue in his career as a musician.[30] Each application was made during a period of uncertain employment for the individual musicians, and their 'false' declarations are perhaps more to do with the need to satisfy the authorities that they would not be a drain on the public purse, in the event of not securing appropriate musical employment.

The importance of the Prince's engagement in securing the short-term future of the band should not be underestimated. In a 'Curriculum Vitae' statement dated 22 July 1940, prepared when he was interned at Orange, John Kay reported that the musicians had been without continuous or permanent work for three months after the Snider and Dean contract was terminated on 4 October 1937, though they had occasional broadcasting work with the ABC. Kay testified to the Industrial Commission of NSW in August 1944 that this radio employment was very difficult to obtain and amounted to about a dozen engagements over half a year. The musicians were then again unemployed for four months following their return from New Zealand in May 1938; a contract with radio 2GM from July 1938 was 'suddenly terminated' in September.[31]

Graff and Kay did not apply for permanent residence in Australia until the early months of 1939 (January and February respectively), by which time, in the face of a heightened demand for admission in the aftermath of the *Anschluss* and the *Kristallnacht* pogrom, government policy and public attitudes towards Jewish refugee migration had changed significantly. In addition to the landing money requirements, '[m]igrants had to pass medical examination, be of suitable character, able to find employment without detriment to Australian workers and undertake not to work below award rates'.[32] Neither Graff nor Kay made pretence in their applications of

---

although due consideration would be given to the question of authorising the temporary admission of a foreign conductor of special standing'. NAA A444, 1952/16/2762.

[30] Inspector D.R.B. Mitchell, to Director, Commonwealth Investigation Branch, 11 January 1938: 'I am of the opinion that he is a musician, and as such would continue to earn his living by joining an orchestra, radio work, etc'.. NAA A434, 1944/3/690.

[31] NAA A1626, 197, docs 45–47 (John Kay statutory declaration). See also letter, Horst Graff to Department of the Interior 5 January 1938 and Statutory Declaration, 17 January 1938, NAA A434, 1944/3/690; 'Kay v. Musicians' Union of Australia' (transcript), pp. 646–647. SRO NSW NRS 5343, 11/1573.

[32] Markus, 'Jewish Migration to Australia 1938–49', *Journal of Australian Studies* 13 (November 1983) p. 18. Numerical quotas on the number of Jewish immigrants were

any intention to sever their connection with the band though each provided an overall summary of their skills, including non-musical ones. Indeed, the band's very public success counted in their favour. By this time, the band was featured at Prince's and appeared regularly on radio. Accordingly, the Weintraubs' direct engagement with the Musicians' Union had begun.

The respondent: the Musicians' Union of Australia

As was shown in Chapter Two, MUA policy on foreign musicians working in Australia took shape through the decade of the 1920s in a series of encounters with entrepreneurs desirous of importing bands and orchestras or groups of musicians under contract, either as attractions in dance palaces or stage acts in theatres and cinemas, or to supplement the orchestras of touring opera companies. Although the Union gave nominal preference to 'British subjects' generally, in fact it opposed all importations with equal resolve, even those from other Commonwealth countries—Canada and New Zealand—and even Britain itself. Because of Australia's constitutional links to the Commonwealth, no government action was possible against British subjects; efforts to obtain protection from government against musicians from America proved equally complex because of the fear of international repercussions. Approaches to government on the question of foreign musicians were potentially more successful when attached to prevailing public concerns about perceived high levels of migration of specific groups. Hence, as noted, the Union linked its campaign against Italian musicians to the public agitation about Italian migration in the mid- to late-1920s. Similarly, in the 1930s, the Union was able to associate its ongoing general opposition to imported or 'foreign' musicians with public concerns about (Jewish) refugee migration and, in the postwar period, about displaced persons and other assisted immigrants. The introduction of mechanical music into cinemas in the late 1920s and consequent large-scale unemployment within the music industry gave weight to the Union's arguments.

The impact of the Depression

Australian musicians were casualties of the global trauma resulting from the coincidence of the introduction of mechanical sound technologies (talking pictures arrived in Australia in December 1928) with the Wall Street

---

set on 9 June 1938; they were reviewed but not changed after the *Kristallnacht* pogrom. Ibid., pp. 19, 21-23.

financial crash (October 1929) that precipitated the Great Depression. As in other countries with comparable music industries, the silent picture theatres in Australia had provided employment for thousands of pit musicians. The rapid and widespread installation of sound equipment in theatres saw these musicians thrown onto the street. Union membership was drastically affected. In Britain in 1928, for example, some 4,000 picture theatres were providing employment to about 75 percent of the 28,000 musicians in the country; by the summer of 1932, there were 4,096 'talkie houses' in the country and only 952 silent cinemas remained. Union membership had fallen from 20,000 (in 1929) to 6,700.[33] US figures were analogous: 26,000 American musicians were employed in picture theatres in 1926; their numbers fell to 5,000 in 1930.[34] In Germany, 30,000 musicians out of a total of around 80,000 were believed to be out of work by July 1932.[35] Though numbers were smaller in Australia, a country of some 5.5 million people (excluding full-blooded Aboriginals) in 1929, the effects were equivalent. MUA General Secretary Cecil Trevelyan wrote to William Hughes in April 1930 that 'out of a membership of 5,000 we now have 4,000 odd unemployed, and of our present membership I doubt if 50% are financial in their organisation, and the finances of our Union are suffering severely'.[36] By mid-1930, the MUA estimated that 80 percent of professional musicians in Australia were unemployed, a number far higher than the national average, which peaked at 30 percent in the second quarter of 1932.[37] Lists of employers cited as respondents to Commonwealth Arbitration Awards vividly chart the contraction in the industry that occurred across the late 1920s and early 1930s.[38]

---

[33] These statistics are from Hoffman, 'Workers and Players', p. 2, p. 15 and p. 25, and Ehrlich, *The Music Profession in Britain since the Eighteenth Century*, p. 199 (75 percent) and p. 210. Ehrlich (p. 210) estimates musicians' unemployment as 'more than double the average and from nine to twenty times worse than that in the professions'.

[34] Hoffman, 'Workers and Players', p. 31 and n. 66.

[35] Michael H. Kater, 'The Revenge of the Fathers: The Demise of Modern Music at the End of the Weimar Republic', *German Studies Review* 15/2 (May 1992), p. 303 and n. 16. Changes from semi-private to civic funding, and general fiscal pressures in the late 1920s also contributed to the German situation (p. 302).

[36] Cecil Trevelyan to Rt. Hon. W.M. Hughes MP, 1 April 1930. NBAC MUA E156/2/6(ii).

[37] Bronwen Arthur, '"Ban the Talkies!"', p. 47. Arthur, p. 50, gives details of musician dismissals town by town.

[38] At the end of the 1920s, as many as 1800 employers could be nominated as respondents to a federal award (for example, *Commonwealth Arbitration Reports* Vol. 28 (1 July 1929–31 March 1930), pp. 141–169.

In most countries, xenophobic attitudes towards foreign musicians and de-liberalising forms of protection against competition were rationalised as a response to high rates of unemployment consequent on the advent of new technologies at the end of the 1920s.[39] However, in Chapter Two I have argued against the idea of a causal relationship, at least in the Australian context, given that the Union's policy on foreign musicians began to evolve from as early as 1918, and persisted with remarkably little modification until the late 1950s, by which time the industry was reformed and full employment had long been restored nationally. Well before sound film technology was introduced, the Union was clamouring against migration, and letters were sent to the secretaries of European unions in an effort to discourage musicians from emigrating. Though actual numbers hardly seemed to validate Union concerns, it maintained its view that 'an overflooded market in any industry always tends to break down Unionism'.[40]

In arguing the Union's protectionist case, officials drew attention to Australia's unique demographic features: the small population, vast distances and widely separated population centres. In most of the smaller towns and cities, music was not a livelihood; professional musicians congregated in the larger cities of the coastal fringe. As Cecil Trevelyan wrote to the General Secretary of the British Musicians' Union, a union to which the MUA shows most similarities of history and development, 'Compared with your Union our members are very few and cover an immense country, whereas you have an immense number covering a very small area'.[41] In consequence of the relatively limited number of employment opportunities available, even in good times, 'we always have more highly skilled musicians than we can find positions for'.[42] 'We have more than sufficient musicians to go around and meet all requirements', Trevelyan wrote to his British counterpart on another occasion, 'always admitting the fact that, the same as in all other callings, there is always room on top, and there is always a large

---

[39] See, for example, Hoffman, 'Workers and Players', p. 3; Steinweis, *Art, Ideology and Economics in Nazi Germany*, p. 15; Kater, *Different Drummers*, p.27; Arthur, 'Industrial Relations', 348–349; Dümling, 'Uncovering Traces', p. 227.

[40] General Secretary MUA to General Secretary MU, 18 August 1927. NBAC MUA E156/2/4(i). There are no statistics available for the number of foreign musicians active in Australia in the early 1930s to compare with those given for Germany by Steinweis, *Art, Ideology and Economics in Nazi Germany*, p. 15.

[41] General Secretary MUA to General Secretary MU, 9 November 1925. NBAC MUA E156/2/4(i).

[42] General Secretary MUA to General Secretary MU, 7 March 1924. NBAC MUA E156/2/4(i).

number of, what I might term, average performers disengaged'.[43] Out of this conundrum arose the ongoing conflict, in this chapter of Australian music history, between the Musicians' Union and entrepreneurs over standards and supply, and the Union's steadfast argument that 'any influx of professional musicians from other countries would be prejudicial to the interests of ... the Australian ... musician'.[44] Most areas of the profession were identified as susceptible to competition from foreign musicians: theatre, light, and symphony orchestras, nightclubs and bands for social dancing.[45]

Developing a defensive strategy

Discussion at Federal Conferences through the 1930s and early 1940s largely continued in the general terms that were established in the 1920s, concerning either strategies to obtain legislative protection against the perceived 'influx' of foreign musicians into Australia, to discourage entrepreneurs from engaging specific foreign musicians, and to expand or vary internal procedures for processing (rejecting) applications for membership by unnaturalised resident foreigners. It should be noted that the matter of foreign musicians was only one of the issues dealt with over the several days of a Federal Conference. It was, however, a persistent one, paradoxically kept alive by the licensing system for entrepreneurs desirous of importing foreign musicians as attractions, introduced by the government in response to Union pressure in 1928, as the Minister of Home and Territories had reserved his right to 'consider each case on its merits'.[46] Accordingly it was not long before the importation of foreign musicians, driven by commercial competitiveness between prospective employers and changing fashions in popular music, was once again an issue.[47] Additional pressures were created by the entry into the entrepreneurial field of the Australian Broadcasting Commission, with its insistent attempts to import 'key instrumentalists' to supplement numbers and standards in its various ensembles.

---

[43] General Secretary MUA to General Secretary MU, 22 October 1928. NBAC MUA E156/2/4(i).
[44] General Secretary MUA to General Secretary MU, 7 March 1924. NBAC MUA E156/2/4(i).
[45] See, for example, MUA President to Harold Holt, Minister for Labour and National Services, 12 December 1951. NBAC MUA Z401, Box 5.
[46] Assistant Secretary, Home and Territories Department to MUA General Secretary, 3 September, 1928. NBAC MUA E156/2/6(ii) (each case).
[47] Such, for example, as the fashion for hot or sweet swing, or 'the growth of public interest in jazz'—swing and jazz being inherently imported genres. See Bruce Johnson and John Whiteoak, 'Jazz', in Whiteoak and Scott-Maxwell (eds), *Currency Companion to Music and Dance in Australia*, especially pp. 376–377.

Though Union officials persistently lobbied government on a range of issues including protective legislation, and negotiated preferential awards with entrepreneurs, the MUA was most immediately effective in controlling admission to membership, whether through formally registered rules or through resolutions ratified at district or federal level but not formally registered as rules. Three specific determinations affected the handling of applications from foreign musicians; their use in rejecting John Kay's application was particularly scrutinised during the hearing of his appeal. The first, a resolution linking membership to naturalisation, was added to federal policy in 1928.[48] Implicit in this resolution was the idea that an unnaturalised applicant would not work in the music profession while fulfilling the mandatory qualifying five-year residency requirement. The second was the above-mentioned amendment to the rule governing processing of applications, duly registered by the Industrial Registrar in August 1935, which required all applications from unnaturalised musicians to be voted on by each of the district components of Federal Council. The third was added to MUA policy in November 1940, when delegates to the Federal Conference resolved to adopt and apply regulation 5 of the National Security Supplementary Regulations, No. 213 of 1940 (introduced in September 1940), under which the committee of any club or association was authorised, its constitution notwithstanding, to suspend or cancel membership of any person who 'is or has been a subject of a country with which His Majesty is at war'.[49] This last resolution was used to justify the rejection of John Kay's application (see below). As in government policy generally, no distinction was made between Jewish and other German-speaking nationals.

Of these three determinations, only the rule registered in 1935 had legal status; the other two, though endorsed by the Union's federal conference, were no more than 'guiding principles' intended to drive best practice but unsupported by actual rules.[50] There are two points to be noted about the 1935 rule. First, it is quite clear from the files that General Secretary Trevelyan's purpose in proposing the 1935 amendment was to dismantle the blanket embargo against the admission of foreign musicians that had been in place since 1929. Trevelyan had been moved by the story of one Lazar

---

[48] The Victoria District resolved, 12 January 1928, that 'no foreigners [sic] be admitted as a member of this district unless and until such foreigner has become a naturalised British subject'. NSW District Minute Book 1926–1930, p. 143. NBAC MUA T7/1/8.
[49] Minutes of Federal Conference, November 1940, p. 6. NBAC MUA E156/6/5.
[50] General Secretary to Federal Council, 2 November 1934. NBAC MUA E156/2/2(xx) '1938–48'.

Sverdloff, a highly qualified Russian Jewish refugee musician who arrived in Australia in 1934, and wished to set a mechanism in place whereby individual cases could be assessed more sympathetically.[51] Unfortunately, Trevelyan died in August 1935, and his hard-line colleagues on the MUA Executive realised the rule's exclusionary potential instead. The 1935 amendment was specifically presented to members as part of the Union's efforts to 'oppose in every possible way the importation of musicians, and to safeguard the interests of members'.[52] Secondly, in the case of a trade union such as the MUA that was registered under Australian arbitration law, a rule was not binding until registered by the Industrial Registrar of the Court of Conciliation and Arbitration. The obligations and powers of the Registrar in considering a rule for registration were clearly prescribed. It was his task to adjudicate the rule's compliance with the terms of the Act, in intent and in wording. He did not adjudicate the use or potential misuse of the rule, and in fact the court in some cases decided that there were no grounds for disallowing a rule which 'though proper in itself' might be applied 'harshly or tyrannically'.[53] Democracy and autonomy were delicately balanced in the relations between the law and the unions within the arbitration system.

The MUA and the Weintraubs

Throughout its public and political campaigns of the 1920s and into the early 1930s, the MUA maintained a distinction between the importation of groups under contract—which it opposed—and individual musicians who entered the labour market in free and equal competition with local musicians—which it professed to tolerate, if not encourage. For example, members of an MUA deputation protesting the importation of a Canadian band to the Minister for the Interior in April 1937 stated that 'no exception was taken to individual artists coming here'.[54]

---

[51] On 5 October 1934, Trevelyan wrote to his colleagues on Federal Council, 'Hitler's action in Germany has driven many estimable people out against their will and their position must be extremely difficult. Can we not make some gesture of sympathy?' NBAC MUA E156/2/2 (xx), '1938–48'. For Sverdloff, see NBAC MUA E156/2/2(xx) '1938–48'. A partial account of the Union's treatment of Sverdloff may be found in Arthur, '"Ban the Talkies!"', pp. 55–56.

[52] Secretary's Report, NSW District, November 1935. Minute Book No. 12, NBAC MUA T7/1/10.

[53] *Commonwealth Arbitration Reports*, Misc. 61 of 1953, Harry Pole challenge to the rules, 1953. NBAC MUA T7/15/8.

[54] Minister for the Interior (T. Paterson) to Attorney-General, 6 April 1937. NAA A432, 1937/383.

As has been noted, the Weintraubs initially entered the country as imported contracted musicians, a class to which the MUA was uncompromisingly opposed. However, the Weintraubs came back from New Zealand as freelance individuals (albeit in a group), and as such were hypothetically acceptable to the Union under the above distinction. As reported in the music journals of the time, the band had obtained the engagement at Prince's in open competition with eligible Australian bands. The distinction was, however, more apparent than real. The official view of the Union, wrote NSW Secretary Frank Kitson in his report to the NSW District in November 1936, was 'that all importations are undesirable and should be discouraged whilst we have so many capable orchestral and dance musicians resident in Australia unemployed. This applies to foreign and British musicians'.[55] Paradoxically, then, the fact that the band had entered into active competition with MUA members for the Prince's job now became a matter of objection by the Union.[56]

There is no record in the files that the Musicians' Union directly opposed the importation of the Weintraubs (nor indeed that it was consulted). But from the moment of the band's appointment to Prince's (December 1938), it became a highly visible symbol of the generic problem—of contracted imports who decided to stay, of refugees, of foreigners taking the best jobs from local musicians—and the target of Kitson's unwavering resistance, as Union spokesperson.[57] By chance, the band's engagement at Prince's coincided with the intensification of migration applications in the aftermath of *Kristallnacht* (November 1938) and the subsequent polarisation of Australian opinion around the refugee question. Opinion was also polarised within the Union movement. Paul Bartrop notes that on 18 November the New South Wales Trades and Labour Council 'departed from its usual policy of opposition to immigration in order to pass a resolution which called on the government not only to admit Jewish refugees from Germany, but to accept financial responsibility for doing so'.[58] The NSW District of the MUA, however, had already 'closed its ranks to foreigners' in August

---

[55] NBAC MUA 7/1/10.
[56] Secretary's Report, NSW District, February 1939. NBAC MUA T7/1/10.
[57] On the Weintraubs as exemplary, see Secretary's Report, NSW District, May 1940, NBAC NUA T7/1/10: 'Representations have again been made to the Minister for the Interior to prohibit foreign musicians coming to Australia, particularly in regard to stage acts. The danger of members of such acts remaining in Australia in competition with local musicians outside the sphere of stage acts was emphasised and the example of "The Weintraubs" was quoted'.
[58] Bartrop, *Australia and the Holocaust*, p. 97.

1938, reaffirming that decision in a statement to *Tempo*, in which Kitson explained that 'Even when naturalised, the Musicians' Union would probably prohibit them [foreigners] from joining the Union while there are so few jobs to go around'.[59]

Prince's management (J.C. Bendrodt) acceded to Union pressure to the extent of appointing a second, all-Australian band for dancing in addition to the Weintraubs, thus limiting the Union's ability to continue to oppose the latter band's appointment, either in public statements or with government. However, in November 1938, with the arrangements for Prince's strongly rumoured in the music press, a circular letter was sent from the Union to all principal employers of musicians throughout the Commonwealth requesting that 'any work available in Australia should be the prerogative of Australians'.[60] Timing and context suggest clear links to the Weintraubs and to Prince's; wording links 'foreigners' to 'exiled Jews'. 'The policy of the Union is to refuse foreigners admission to our ranks', the NSW Secretary reported to his district in February 1939. Not surprisingly, the band's attempts to regularise its professional situation by joining the Union were unsuccessful. An application in February 1939 was refused in April; a second application in November was again refused, though there is no evidence that either of these applications were voted on by the constituents of Federal Council, as per the 1935 rule. It is worth noting that in May 1939, the New South Wales Trades and Labour Council recommended the admission of European refugees in Australia to membership of its constituent unions.[61] Far from adopting or even referring to this recommendation, Kitson reported to Federal Conference in November 1939 that a favourable reply had been received from a number of the entrepreneurs to the circular letter of the previous November (1938) urging preference for Australian musicians. By that time the Union had begun to recover membership numbers,[62] and to gain strength from organising new opportunities offered by live broadcasting (with the Australian Broadcasting Commission as a major employer of musicians) and social dancing.

---

[59] Minutes of the NSW committee 5 August 1938. NBAC MUA T7/1/10: 'Embargo on Foreign Musicians', *Tempo*, September–October 1938, p. 1.

[60] Secretary's Report, NSW District, February 1939, p 2. NBAC MUA T7/1/10. The letter was sent out in November 1938 (Minutes of Federal Conference, NBAC MUA E156/6/4) as reported in *Australian Music Maker and Dance Band News*, 1 November 1938, p. 4.

[61] *Sydney Morning Herald*, 6 May 1939, cited in Bartrop, *Australia and the Holocaust*, p. 176.

[62] Lamble to Kitson, 26 July 1939, gave the total financial membership as 3,170. NBAC MUA E156/2/2(ib).

In general, the trade journals took a generous attitude towards the Weintraubs and their troubles with the Musicians' Union. Unlike the Union, the profession at large seems to have been appreciative of the band's musicianship, largely endorsing Snider and Deans's original claim that there was no other combination like the Weintraubs in Australia.[63] In the opinion of one commentator, the band's ability to play all styles and types of music, plus the musicians' remarkable ability to 'double' on different instruments, made them 'one of the finest small bands in Australia'.[64] Of the band's 'Union troubles', *Tempo* observed,

> that Union trouble before they become naturalised is just one big bugbear, but, as Meredith said, 'Hurdles are made for those who cannot fly' and the Weintraubs have been flying for 15 years so far.[65]

And again:

> Being foreigners, they were not allowed to join the Musicians' Union and consequently were unable to accept many jobs offered them. They have now applied for naturalization. In due course it will come, and with it a multitude of new work.[66]

Further support came from government. When Kitson contacted the Department of the Interior to protest Kay's and Graff's applications for permanent residency,[67] the reporting officer, A.R. Peters, head of the Immigration Branch, noted in his memorandum of 19 October 1939:

> Mr Graff and Mr Kay are both men of superior class in their profession, and the only difficulty standing in the way of granting permanent admission is the objection raised by the Musicians' Union of Australia to the permanent admission of alien musicians who are likely to play in dance bands or orchestras. Several members of the 'Weintraubs' were granted permission to remain permanently before the protest came in from the Union and it would be unsatisfactory to break up the combination by not allowing Messrs. Graff and Kay to continue with the troupe.[68]

---

[63] *Tempo*, December 1939–January 1940, p. 2.
[64] *Australian Music Maker and Dance Band News*, March 1940, p. 4. This generous tribute has added poignancy as being the last such published comment I have found in the music magazines before the Weintraubs disappeared as a collectivity from their pages.
[65] 'Who are the Weintraubs?', *Tempo*, December 1938–January 1939, p. 8.
[66] *Tempo*, December 1939–January 1940, p. 2.
[67] Kitson to H.S. Foll, 24 May 1939. NAA A444, 1952/16/2762.
[68] A434, 1944/3/690.

Paul Bartrop has described Peters as 'efficient, able, and seemingly incorruptible, and there was no one who knew as much about the workings of Australian immigration policy. Between 1933 and 1945 this knowledge was more often than not employed so as to deny, rather than assist, the entry of Jewish refugees to Australia',[69]—but not, however, in this case.

Getting rid of the Germans

Once war was declared in September 1939, the parameters of engagement changed as control of aliens passed from the Minister for the Interior to the Department of Defence. The circumstances of war and the involvement of the military authorities, with their very different values and concerns, altered the ways in which the MUA's rejection of the Weintraubs was understood by those army officers who were responsible for domestic security, particularly when read in conjunction with the (unproven) accusation that the band had been engaged in espionage on behalf of the German Government while touring in Russia. There is no indication that any Union official was aware of the denunciation. However, on 15 September 1939, Kitson wrote to Senator Foll, Minister for the Interior, requesting information about the nationality of the six musicians employed at Prince's.[70] The minister's reply of 29 September 1939 was read to the meeting of the NSW District Committee on 6 October 1939, whereupon the meeting determined that the secretary should 'endeavour to terminate the employment of the Weintraubs, particularly in the case of the three Germans'.[71] Kitson reported to Federal Conference in November 1939 that he was working to discourage the management of Prince's from continuing to employ the Weintraubs. Letters were sent to the Department of Information and the Returned Sailors' and Soldiers' Imperial League of Australia protesting the continued employment of the Weintraubs (at Prince's and on radio),[72] and their renewed application for Union membership was again refused, despite their efforts to conciliate Union concerns. On behalf of the

---

[69] Bartrop, *Australia and the Holocaust*, see caption to photograph between pp. 144 and 145.
[70] NBAC MUA Z401, Box 5, 'Letters to State and Federal Parliamentarians'.
[71] See NBAC MUA Z401, Box 5 for the Minister's letter and T7/1/10. NSW District Minutes, 6 October 1939.
[72] Minutes of Federal Conference, 1939, fourth day, pp. 5–6, NBAC MUA E156/6/4; NSW District Minutes, 29 December 1939, NBAC MUA T7/1/10. At the meeting of 9 February 1940, the District Secretary reported on a conversation with the Department, in which he was informed that the Department could do nothing about the Weintraubs, 'it being more a matter of government policy than one controlled by regulation'. NSW District Minutes, 9 February 1940. NBAC MUA T7/1/10.

musicians, Horst Graff undertook that they would 'never work individually but only as in our present combination'. Graff also suggested 'If your present rules forbid you to accept alien members, we would be very glad to become associate members until such time as our status allows us to achieve full membership'.[73] At this time, Kitson contacted a different branch of government, forwarding the Weintraubs' letter of application and advice of the Union's rejection to Major W.J.R. Scott of Military Intelligence, expressing his hope that it might be of assistance in 'curtailing their employment while we have competent Britishers capable of carrying out the same work'.[74] The two letters became part of the Crown Solicitor's brief for opposing Stefan Weintraub's application for release from internment, though the transcripts do not show that any use was made of them.[75]

J.C. Bendrodt (of Prince's) withstood Kitson's approaches and extended the band's engagement until April 1940.[76] But in the event, the whole situation was radically changed when, in June 1940, three of the musicians were interned and, as has been noted both by film script-writer Jörg Süssenbach and Dümling,[77] the band known as the Weintraubs Syncopators dissolved, at least under that name. What is not correct is Dümling's suggestion that the musicians 'got no more engagements', as is shown in Chapters Three and Five.

The John Kay summons

By 1944, John Kay and Leo Weiss were the only members of the original group of seven musicians still involved professionally in music in Australia. Kay had made no effort to rejoin Mannie Fisher's 'Midnight Sextette' at Prince's after his release from internment;[78] after an eight-month hiatus, he found full-time employment as head of the musical arrangements

---

[73] NSW District Minutes, 5 December 1939. NBAC MUA T7/1/10. Letter, Horst Graff to Frank Kitson, 23 November 1939. NAA MP529/2, WEINTRAUB/S.
[74] Kitson to Major Scott, 29 November 1939. NAA MP529/2, WEINTRAUB/S.
[75] NAA MP529/2, WEINTRAUB/S (brief); NAA MP529/3, TRIBUNAL 1/WEINTRAUB (transcript).
[76] Kitson report to Federal Conference, November 1939, NBAC MUA E156/6/4, p. 6; John K. Kaiser to Department of the Interior, 6 September 1939, NAA A434, 1944/3/690.
[77] For Dümling, see 'Uncovering Traces', p. 228.
[78] As was recounted in Chapter Three, three of the original six musicians—the Frischer brothers and Leo Weiss—formed a new group at Prince's that continued until the Frischers were drafted into the army in August 1943. Three musicians (two Australians and a Canadian), resigned from the NSW District of the Union in order to play with the non-Union survivors of the Weintraubs group, as was reported to Federal Conference on 17 November 1941. See Minutes p. 8. NBAC MUA E156/6/5.

department with the Colgate-Palmolive Radio Unit 'writing musical arrangements and supervising the other arrangers for all music necessary for the broadcasts conducted by this company'.[79] Entrepreneurial by nature, he had had his own outfit in Berlin before joining the Weintraubs, and had begun to develop his independent music ventures before his internment. On 16 March 1944 John Kay formally applied to become a member of the MUA, using the official membership application form. Kitson, acting unilaterally and against the requirements of the Federal Union's 1935 rule for the processing of applications by non-naturalised musicians, rejected the application. He gave as his reason, for both rejection and his handling of the matter, that Kay's was a 'repetition of a previous application which was dealt with by the Federal Council in November 1939' (the reference here is to the collective application by the Weintraubs mentioned above). On 27 June, Kitson advised General Secretary Lamble that Kay had taken action under the NSW State Act to compel his admission.[80] Only then did Lamble, in accordance with federal rules, submit Kay's membership request to the vote of all districts.[81] The application was rejected on the grounds that 'our rules do not permit of the admission of foreigners to membership'.[82]

Kay lodged his 'summons to show cause' with the Industrial Commission of NSW under section 115 of the state's *Industrial Arbitration Act* 1940–43,[83] which allowed the Commission to resolve any dispute as to the character of the applicant or the reasonableness of the Union's admission fee and rules, and gave it the power to direct any alteration deemed necessary 'to bring [the Union] into conformity with what [the Commission] declares to be

---

[79] For a complete transcript of the tribunal hearing, see 'Kay v. Musicians' Union of Australia', pp. 645–663. Many details of Kay's career emerge in presentation of evidence and cross-examination, see, for example, pp. 646–650.

[80] Kitson to W.H.S. Lamble, 27 June 1944. NBAC MUA E156/2/3 (vb), 'John Kay'.

[81] W.H.S. Lamble to all districts, 27 June 1944. NBAC MUA E156/2/3 (vb), 'John Kay'. Five of the six states canvassed opposed the application. The Tasmanian District however, responded positively, observing that, 'they consider his having been in Australia for six and a half years entitles him to become a member. It will also be in the best interests of the Union to accept him'. Secretary, Tasmanian District to Lamble, 5 July 1944. NBAC MUA E156/2/3(vb), 'John Kay'. Not for the only time, the moderate voice of Tasmania was overruled.

[82] Letter tendered to the NSW Commission (transcript p. 646), and cited in Kinsella's judgment at p. 342. The complete text of the judgment may be found in *The Industrial Arbitration Reports, New South Wales 1944*, Vol. XLIII, 1944 (Sydney: Government Printer, 1946), pp. 341–348.

[83] Industrial relations legislation in NSW, as in the Commonwealth, evolved over decades. The *Industrial Arbitration Act* 1940 replaced the 1912 Act.

reasonable in the circumstances' and for such alterations to be binding. As was made clear during the hearing, the judge was not empowered to direct the Union to admit Kay, but only to rule on his eligibility for membership under the terms of the Act, which provided for the admission to a union of 'all persons who are, by the nature of their occupation or employment, of the class of which a trade union is constituted and who are not of generally bad character ... so long as they comply with the rules of the union'.[84] Kitson advised Lamble that 'as the decision will effect [sic] future applicants and the federal body, I have briefed Counsel to defend it'.[85] Kay was also represented by counsel.

The Union gave four grounds for its rejection of Kay's application: (1) that the applicant was not working as an instrumentalist but as an arranger and had therefore not established that he was by profession or employment of the class embraced by the Union; (2) that the applicant was an enemy alien and thus not entitled to the aid of any of the King's Courts;[86] (3) that the Union was entitled lawfully, under paragraph 5 of the National Security (Supplementary) Regulations, to exclude him from membership; and (4) that the application, as submitted, was invalid as it did not tender the subscription fee.[87]

Mr Justice E.P. Kinsella addressed each of these points in turn in making his ruling on Kay's eligibility for membership. He determined that Kay was, in fact, an instrumentalist; that, since his claim to Peruvian nationality was not proven, he was an enemy alien, but that the fact of his registration as such in Australia, whereby he disclosed himself to the Executive Government and was permitted to remain in the country, conferred on him the right, shared with friendly aliens and British subjects, to approach the tribunal for 'such relief as he deems he is entitled to';[88] and that the words in paragraph 5 of the National Security (Supplementary) Regulations had no application to trade unions. The judge dismissed the issue of the fee as trivial. On the Union's grounds for refusing Kay's application, namely that he 'happened to be by birth a foreigner', the judge declared:

---

[84] The reference to persons of bad character echoes exclusions under the *Immigration Restriction Act* of 1901. For the same reason, official reports on applications for permanent residency include an assessment of 'character'.

[85] Kitson to Lamble, 27 June 1944. NBAC MUA E156/2/3(vb) 'John Kay'.

[86] The Union's categorisation of Kay as an enemy alien ignores the fact that the Union was advised on 20 September 1939 that Kay was a Peruvian. Letter, H.S. Foll to Secretary, MUA. NAA A434, 1944/3/690.

[87] For summary, see Kinsella judgment, 'Kay v. Musicians' Union of Australia', p. 343.

[88] Kinsella judgment, p. 346. While there is extended discussion in the transcript of the validity of Kay's claim to Peruvian nationality, his Jewishness is never mentioned.

It is not within my province to discuss the social or ethical aspects of the union's attitude, nor the results which might follow if all unions should adopt the same policy towards persons coming to this State from other countries. I am concerned only to determine the rights and obligations of the parties according to the existing law.[89]

The NSW District of the MUA, it must be remembered, was a distinct entity, registered independently of the federal body of the Union for the purposes of handling intra-state industrial matters, and having its own rules. By bringing his complaint against the Union in the NSW Industrial Commission, Kay had essentially appealed against the refusal of the *district* to admit him as a member, even though his application had been handled under federal rules. This being so, the judge compared the statement in the Union's letter to Kay with the constitution and rules of the NSW District (Numbers 18, 19 and 26), which set out the district's conditions of eligibility for members, and included a special provision for the admission of unnaturalised foreigners. Kinsella found that the Union's rejection of Kay's application was not supported by the rules of the district and pronounced his ruling accordingly: 'I declare that Ned John Kurt Kaiser (known as Kay) is entitled to be admitted to membership of the Musicians' Union of Australia, New South Wales District, and to remain a member thereof and to enjoy all advantages of membership so long as he shall comply with the rules of the union'.[90] Kay reapplied immediately and was admitted to membership of the NSW District.[91]

Union reception of the judgment and its consequences

The John Kay summons and the judgment received extensive coverage in the press, not least because the hearing coincided with a public controversy linked to a report on the ABC's symphony orchestras by visiting American conductor Eugene Ormandy.[92] The debate over the Ormandy report and

---

[89] Kinsella judgment, p. 347.
[90] Kinsella judgment, pp. 347–348.
[91] Subsequent to the Kinsella judgment, the complexities of Federal versus District membership were explained to the Union in H.H. Hoare's 'Opinion re Branch Membership', 22 September 1944. The Union solicitor, while supporting Justice Kinsella's rulings and reasoning, made it clear that the judge did not and could not order that Kay be admitted as a member of the federal organisation. H.H. Hoare, 'Opinion on Branch Membership', 22 September 1944, p. 5. NBAC MUA E156/2/3(vb) 'John Kay'.
[92] For reports of the hearing and the Kinsella judgment, see *Sun*, 8 and 9 August 1944; *Daily Mirror*, 8 and 9 August 1944; *Daily Telegraph*, 9 and 10 August 1944 (together

the outcome of the Kay challenge run concurrently in the Sydney papers of August 1944. The two issues are specifically linked in Kitson's response, published in *Truth* on 13 August 1944. Among other recommendations, Ormandy noted that in order for Australia to develop ensembles of quality, it was necessary to import first-class players capable of taking key positions in the orchestras, emphasising that in America forty years earlier virtually all orchestral musicians had been foreign-born. Without naming the Union directly, Ormandy referred to the consequences of its exclusionist policy. 'I have learned that quite a few artists who were forced to leave their homeland have sought refuge in your wonderful country', he wrote,

> Many former members of great orchestras in Europe are now in this country, and do not have the opportunity to give of their talents. No country can afford to waste artistic resources in this way. Some of these people have been forced to take up other professions in order to have the minimum necessities of living. This I consider a short sighted action because it is doing great music and Australian culture a serious disservice.[93]

Ormandy urged Australia to take advantage of the redistribution of musical talents throughout the world that had occurred because of world developments. The ABC concurred. The MUA did not.

Kitson, ever the strategist, immediately addressed the question of how the Kinsella judgment was to be accommodated polemically and administratively, without compromising or modifying the Union's position on foreign musicians. The propaganda aspect was dealt with relatively swiftly. In his published rejoinder, Kitson simply exploited the publicity value of the fact that Kay was earning £25 per week in his job while 258 of the MUA's 958 NSW members were in uniform, observing that 'the mere mention of money and opportunity in the offing has attracted the interest of foreign musicians like flies to the honey pot'. The administrative situation was more difficult, since the judgment challenged the criteria on

---

with report on the Ormandy recommendations); *Sydney Morning Herald*, 10 August 1944; *Tempo*, June [sic] 1944. For Kitson's rejoinder, see *Truth*, 13 August 1944. The Ormandy report may be found at NAA SP613/1, 6/12/8, Report on Orchestras, all states—Eugene Ormandy [Box 20]. Clippings reporting the two events are found in 'Press cuttings 1938–52', MUA NBAC Z401, Box 13 and across various files, including John Kay's security file A6126, 1236.

[93] Eugene Ormandy to Deputy Prime Minister Francis Forde, 11 July 1944, p. 2. NAA SP613/1, 6/12/8.

which the MUA was excluding its foreign applicants, at least within the NSW District. The legal opinion commissioned from the Union's solicitors identified the problem: that although the federal body had incorporated a number of special rules regarding foreign musicians, the NSW District, with its separate constitution and an older set of rules that were binding under the state system, had never taken steps to register any federal amendments.[94] The problem was inherent in the arbitration system, resulting from the dual registration of unions that necessarily operated concurrently at a state and federal level under Australian arbitration law.[95] The result in this case was a critical anomaly between the rules of the state district and those of the federal organisation[96] which the Union dealt with by coralling the NSW District within the organisation. Members admitted in NSW were no longer assumed automatically to be members of the federal body (of which the NSW District was a part).[97]

The Kinsella opinion continued to influence MUA policy towards foreign applicants for at least another decade. For example, an internal exchange between district and federal secretaries in 1953 referenced the Kay judgment:

> As you are aware, the NSW State Union is compelled by the law to admit applicants who, briefly, are musicians and are not of general bad character. We had not accepted members who were not eligible for Federal membership until the Kay Kaiser case (now John Sydney Kay). We discourage and delay applications as far as we are able.[98]

The Union, including the NSW District, continued to deny applications on the basis of naturalisation—overtly, in the case of the federal body, since its rules were not affected by the judgment; covertly in the case of the NSW District, since its rules had been enforced.

---

[94] Hoare, 'Opinion re Branch Membership', p 4. NBAC MUA E156/2/3(vb) 'John Kay'.
[95] See Cockburn and Yerbury, 'The Federal/State Framework of Australian Industrial Relations', pp. 52–84 and especially pp. 61–64.
[96] Transcript, 'Kay v. Musicians' Union of Australia', p. 653.
[97] General Secretary to Mrs E. Anthony, 24 August 1948, NBAC MUA E156/2/3(v), '1945–50', or General Secretary to George Kraus, 20 March 1952, NBAC MUA E156/2/3(v), '1950-52'. This largely affected an individual's ability to work in another state and was particularly onerous for musicians employed by the ABC.
[98] 'Secretary' (Mr V. Massey) to C. Wheatland, 12 May 1953, NBAC MUA E156/6/17. Files on foreign applicants show that they were all rejected. NBAC MUA E156/2/3(v) (three files, 1945–55).

How much did membership matter?

One question that occurred during the John Kay hearing and that also presents itself generally is this: How much did it matter to the early history of the Weintraubs that the musicians could not become members of the MUA? Clearly the fact that they were not unionists did not prevent J.C. Bendrodt from hiring them for Prince's, described as one of the most desirable musical jobs in the country at the time;[99] similarly, Union counsel argued that John Kay had managed to secure a plum job with the Colgate-Palmolive Radio Unit without benefit of membership.

Kay argued convincingly that, as a non-Unionist, his musical activities were circumscribed; his ability legitimately to employ or work with unionists would have been an ongoing difficulty. For example, in 1942 the Union threatened to 'instruct the orchestra not to play under [Heinrich] Krips' baton', if entrepreneur Frank Tait employed Krips, an émigré and non-unionist, as conductor.[100] While it is true that internment, not the MUA, was responsible for breaking up the Weintraubs, files document at least three occasions on which the Union's rejection of the band's applications for membership is clearly linked to key decisions by military intelligence and other government agencies. So, for example, the report on Horst Graff's financial situation in the context of his application to bring his parents and brother to Australia, dated April 1939, includes the comment, 'The Weintraubs orchestra can only get specialised employment as members are not and cannot become members of the Profl. Musicians Union'.[101] The application was refused and Graff's parents, Hermann and Friderika, perished. Secondly, the musicians' failure to achieve membership is given as one of the reasons supporting the case for Weintraub's internment.[102] Finally, in a document dated 21 August 1943 supporting the assignment of

---

[99] Kitson to District Secretaries, 1 December 1938. NBAC MUA E156/2/2(ic).
[100] Lamble to Kitson, 10 March 1942. The Krips veto was not new. See Kitson to Lamble, 3 May 1940. Both NBAC MUA E156/2/2(ib). Curiously, the *Australian Dictionary of Biography* entry on Krips states that he 'soon found work in the music industry' after arriving in Australia in November 1938. In fact, though admitted to the country as a musician, he had to wait from 1939 until he was naturalised in 1944 before being admitted to the Union, a waste of time reported with some bitterness in a portrait interview in *The New Citizen*, 15 May 1948, p. 7. And see Zaiga Sudrabs, 'Krips, Henry Joseph (1912–1987)', *Australian Dictionary of Biography*, Volume 17, (2007), pp. 640–641.
[101] Hand-written comment added to the inter-departmental CIB report by D.R.B. Mitchell, 17 April 1939. NAA ST1223/1, N22597.
[102] Undated, unsigned report from MPI Section, Police Headquarters, Sydney. NAA MP529/2, WEINTRAUB/S.

Stefan Weintraub to the 'Security Service Black List "A"', we read 'Here [in Australia] they commenced playing at Prince's Cabaret ... and there, despite various efforts by the responsible authorities [the Union?] to have them deported, some of the troupe still remain'.[103] On the balance of credibility, Kitson, as an elected officer of a registered organisation entrusted with the regulation of a trade/profession, carried more weight than did a band of alien musicians who, individually and collectively, were the objects of suspicion of the security services. While Kitson, as a union official, could be seen to be part of what Robert Gellately calls 'the apparatus of surveillance and control',[104] motivated by an altruistic concern for the well-being and advancement of his membership, the musicians appeared variously as shifty and unreliable and worse.[105]

In their study of 'Individual Rights and the Law in Australian Industrial Relations', Richard Mitchell and Stuart Rosewarne have pointed out a fundamental inconsistency that prevails in situations of economic conflict, namely, 'that one set of freedoms must be sacrificed to another'.[106] In the situation of the late 1930s we have on the one hand the Union's obligation to seek, secure and protect preferential employment for its members; on the other the ethical question of the migrant musicians' right to work in their chosen profession—a right acknowledged by spokesmen within the profession at large and within society generally. In the John Kay hearing, Justice Kinsella is reported as having said 'It would be extraordinary if aliens allowed to enter Australia were condemned to starve because unions would not accept them'.[107] In 1949 Abram Landa, ALP Member for Bondi in the NSW Parliament, refugee advocate and John Kay's solicitor, wanted the Union's anti-foreign regulations declared illegal.[108] Kim Rubenstein has written of 'notions of exclusion being more important than inclusion in determining membership of the Australian community'.[109] By withholding

---

[103] Recommendation dated 21 August 1943. NAA A367, C38143.
[104] Gellately, 'Denunciation as a Subject of Historical Research', p. 18.
[105] Suspicion attached to all members of the band from the moment of the Russian espionage allegation, September 1939. Comments to this effect occur across the named NAA files and recur throughout this narrative. To some extent this assessment was influenced by suspicions attaching to the profession of 'musician' and to the itinerant nature of the band's lifestyle before arriving in Australia.
[106] Mitchell and Rosewarne, 'Individual Rights and the Law', p. 190.
[107] *Daily Telegraph*, 9 August 1944. Press cuttings 1938–52, MUA NBAC Z401, Box 13.
[108] *Daily Telegraph*, 14 January 1949. Press cuttings 1938–52, MUA NBAC Z401, Box 13.
[109] Rubenstein, 'An Unequal Membership', p. 146.

membership from foreign musicians, the Musicians' Union sought to isolate them as a pariah group within the profession, disadvantaged by the Union's legislative ability to negotiate preferential employment for unionists under the awards in many though not all situations, and to enforce prohibitions against members working with non-members.

To what degree, then, is it feasible to sustain even the limited comparison between the Musicians' Union of Australia and the *Reichsmusikkammer* proposed by Dümling? Fundamentally, the validity of the comparison rests on the extent to which the exclusionist policies of each organisation were driven by State-sponsored racist ideologies, and the ultimate objectives of those ideologies. I have noted the ironies inherent in the fact that it was their exclusion from work in Germany in the early years of the Third Reich that set this group of musicians on the journey that brought them to Australia[110] and that, once here, they encountered such determined opposition from the MUA. Yet it is the varied experience of the members of the group that enables us to approach some of the complexities involved in the comparison that Dümling suggests.

When the MUA formally adopted the White Australia policy into its rules in 1923 it accepted that policy's core categories of admissible (European) and non-admissible (non-European) immigrants. 'Coloured' musicians were excluded without exception. Both groups implicated in the evolution of the Union's pre-Second World War exclusionary policy towards foreigners were 'low status' European groups—Italians and Central-European Jews[111]—but I believe this is coincidental, driven more by historical circumstance and opportunistic prejudice than a specifically targeted racist ideology. This is not to say that individual unionists did not hold racist or even antisemitic views. However, the fact that the MUA worked equally strenuously to exclude bands from England, to prevent the entry of musicians under contract from Commonwealth countries, and designated British musicians as a special (albeit privileged) group within the foreigner class, suggests that the primary objective of at least this part

---

[110] John Kay's account of the circumstances in which the band left Germany links both 'foreigners' and 'Jews' as constituting the 'racial reasons' why the band could not obtain further employment and was dismissed from existing contracts after the elections at the beginning of March 1933. Undated statement [1945?]. NAA A6126, 1236, doc. 64.

[111] For negative stereotyping of Jewish refugees, see Markus, 'Jewish Migration', pp. 20–21; Rutland, *Edge of the Diaspora*, pp. 188–192 and Hilary Rubinstein, *The Jews in Australia: A Thematic History Volume One 1788–1945* (Port Melbourne: William Heinemann Australia, 1991), especially Chapter 3, 'Inter-War Immigration and Australian Jewish Communal Responses, 1918–1945' (pp. 145–233).

of the Union's 'ban' against foreigners was protectionism, irrespective of the organisation's lip service to the principles of the country's restrictive immigration act. Nonetheless, the formal inclusion of a statement of allegiance to the principles of White Australia, and the rules and resolutions that flowed from it in the closing years of the 1920s, signalled a turning point in the Federal Union's attitude towards foreign musicians, enabling the development of a binary opposition of the kind that provides 'a building block for ideas of inequality'.[112]

The MUA was not an instrument of government and, as I have shown, its attempts to position itself in an instrumental relationship to government were largely unsuccessful. Indeed, by virtue of the Union's official registration under the Commonwealth and State arbitration systems, government acted through the industrial tribunals as a regulatory body overseeing the development, articulation and application of Union rules, including membership rules. Kitson was unsuccessful in persuading management or government to take any steps against the Weintraubs, whether dismissal or deportation. Indeed, in the case of John Kay's appeal, the machinery of government supported him—an enemy alien and a Jew—against the Union. As was clearly shown by the John Kay judgment, the Union's exclusion of individual foreigners from membership was not always supported by its rules. The rules of the NSW District included provisions for the admission of foreign members and many of the provisions introduced by the federal body of the Union to exclude or delay the admission of foreigners—for example, the requirement for naturalisation—were similarly not reflected in the rules as registered and were thus open to challenge and remedy. The early career of the Weintraubs demonstrates clearly that the Union's efforts to segregate resident foreign musicians from the mainstream of musical life were neither wholly successful nor supported by the profession at large. Even in cases where the Union was more effective in frustrating the careers of some refugee musicians (and it was), the moment an individual was naturalised, he (or she) could demand admission. Naturalisation, unlike Aryan status under the Third Reich, could be and was acquired.

There is no question that the MUA's hard-line pursuit of unnaturalised resident musicians caused enormous hardship and loss of profession for many individuals and was a breach of the concept of the 'right to work'. Nor was every situation open to remedy. Stefan Weintraub's appeal to the civic authorities (the police) in 1941 against the collusion of interests that

---

[112] Markus, *Australian Race Relations*, p. 6.

was attempting to keep him out of employment as a musician following his release from internment was unsuccessful. Frank Kitson's public 'outing' of Stefan Weintraub as a decorated German First World War veteran (*Truth*, 16 November 1941) is a shameful incident, and not one to be justified as an industrial relations strategy since its purpose was clearly to humiliate and discredit Weintraub as an individual. The Union's most extreme positions were enunciated in the press, as MUA mouthpiece Frank Kitson sought to give his opinions leverage by his appeal to current prejudicial concerns, and to create mythic slogans out of appropriations of popular vocabulary.[113] In general, in its interactions with officials of the government or the industrial courts, the MUA's positions and rhetoric were tempered by the provisions of the law, though supported by the prevailing ideologies of race and gender that the law embodied.

The RMK was, from its establishment by the Reich Cabinet in September 1933, an instrument for the articulation and execution of the state's cultural ideology, under the direct political control of Goebbels' Ministry of Propaganda.[114] It was also a theatre in which the vested interests and personal rivalries of the Nazi leadership were acted out. Even the notion of 'protection' is challenging in the context of Third Reich cultural policy. It was not a 'benign' objective—the protection of German musicians—which the RMK shared with unions in other countries at this time, since it also worked against many German nationals. The exclusionist policies of the RMK, unlike those of the MUA, were primarily directed inwards and their end objective was *ausmerzen* [to eradicate];[115] the basis for expulsion was the notion of 'reliability and fitness' or 'aptitude'. As Alan Steinweis writes, 'From the standpoint of National Socialist ideology, the eradication of the unhealthy went hand in hand with the promotion and "care" of the healthy'.[116] Aryan ancestry was the basis for reliability and 'foreigners', by

---

[113] A good example would be the MUA's alliance with the extreme nationalist rhetoric of William Hughes in public debate over Italian migration in 1928, mentioned in Chapter Two.

[114] Erik Levi (*Music in the Third Reich*, p. 32) writes that from late 1937, as a unified policy for the Chamber developed, the relationship between the Ministry and the RMK was spelled out publicly, 'In future, it was the Ministry which would direct the policy, and the RMK that would effect its implementation'. On the RMK as an instrument of cultural regulation by the State, see Steinweis, *Art, Ideology and Economics in Nazi Germany*, p. 1.

[115] See Eva Weissweiler, *Ausgemerzt! Das Lexikon der Juden in der Musik und seine mörderischen Folgen* (Köln: Dittrich-Verlag, 1999).

[116] Steinweis, *Art, Ideology and Economics in Nazi Germany*, p. 103. Levi, too, writes that contemporary propaganda about the RMK tended to echo Goebbels' 'utopian and protective view', in accordance with which, however, 'membership of the RMK was

definition, were those 'for whom "cultural activity in the services of German cultural policy" could not be expected'.[117] From as early as November 1933, foreign musicians were subject to the same regulations as those that governed the professional life of native-born German musicians, including the requirement to prove 'Aryan' status.[118] Regulations were enforced with the assistance of the police (who often used physical violence to remove non-member musicians from performance venues), the civil service and the judiciary.[119] As against the democratic, self-governing structure of the Australian trade unions, the 'authoritarian framework of the chamber system, [was] structured ... according to the Nazi *Führerprinzip*'.[120]

It is true that the RMK had social, economic and professional objectives in addition to its better-known purge and censorship activities. However, according to Steinweis, the goals of the Chamber's exclusion policy, 'especially with regard to Jews, remained clearly in view at all times ... The exclusion of Jews and other supposed enemy groups from the culture chambers was integral to the Third Reich's improvised but purposeful program of racial and political persecution'.[121] While there is no doubt that Australia's restrictive immigration policy had problematic features, as did MUA ideology in the 1930s and 1940s, it is not possible to say that discrimination of any colour is discrimination of every colour. Whereas the Union's leadership cohort used its appeals to nationalistic slogans like 'Australia for the Australians' to rationalise its protectionist agenda, the RMK bureaucracy used its protectionist policies to implement the state's ultimately murderous program of cultural purging.[122]

Finally, then, there is the question of how much it mattered to the MUA that the Weintraubs were Jewish, an issue of fundamental importance to both German and foreign musicians excluded from the RMK on racial grounds. Dümling wrote, 'Given that aspect, the Musicians' Union of Australia was no less restrictive than the Reichs Music Chamber in Germany, which protected German musicians only'.[123] Since the RMK explicitly discriminated

---

confined to those deemed to be racially and politically "reliable"'. *Music in the Third Reich*, p. 28.
[117] Steinweis, *Art, Ideology and Economics in Nazi Germany*, pp. 158, 108–109.
[118] Kater, *Different Drummers*, p. 37.
[119] Steinweis, *Art, Ideology and Economics in Nazi Germany*, p. 45.
[120] Ibid., p. 49. A diagrammatic representation of the structure of the RMK may be found in Levi, *Music in the Third Reich*, p. 25.
[121] Steinweis, *Art, Ideology and Economics in Nazi Germany*, p. 175.
[122] Ibid., p. 107: 'The founding of the *Kulturkammer* was the next major step in the creeping institutionalization of this cultural purge'.
[123] 'Uncovering Traces', p. 227.

against Jewish members, this statement at once raises the question: were German Jews not Germans? It is noteworthy in this context that the MUA leadership's wartime attacks on individual members of the Weintraubs, as in the case of Stefan Weintraub mentioned above, centred on the musicians' nationality (or on the 'formative years' argument in the case of the non-Germans[124]), rather than on race or ethnicity. The fact that they were Jewish is rarely mentioned. Nor is 'Jewishness' a significant element in the Union's efforts to resist pressures from the Australian Broadcasting Commission to import key instrumentalists from overseas or to make use of those European musicians who made their way independently to this country as refugees in the 1930s and 1940s. It is this latter struggle with the ABC over so-called 'nationality quotas', I believe, that provides the context in which the Union's attitude towards foreign musicians in the 1930s and 1940s is to be properly understood.

---

[124] The 'formative years' idea was articulated in a memo from the Secretary of the Army to the Secretary of the Department of Defence on 4 March 1942, and referred to the doubtful security status of 'any person who spent his formative years in an enemy country'. Paul R. Bartrop, 'Enemy Aliens or Stateless Persons?', p. 276 and n. 25.

Chapter Five

BREACHING THE PROFESSION

Foreign Musicians and the Postwar Australian Music Industry,
a Postscript

In August 1946, the New South Wales District of the MUA published a complete list of its members, in order to assist them in observing the rule that unionists should not play with non-unionists. The list included four former members of the Weintraubs: the Frischer [sic] brothers Adolph and Emanuel, Cyril Schulvater and Leo Weiss. Stefan Weintraub, Horst Graff and John Kay were not listed, though Kay had, according to the Union, 'forced admission through the courts'. Kay's name, so the Union assured his solicitor, was left out inadvertently and appeared in the revised 1949 list.[1] All the listed non-British members had been naturalised by 1946.

At the beginning of the year, Leo Weiss had taken a new combination into Prince's Restaurant as the main dance orchestra replacing Craig Crawford's, the all-Australian band appointed to Prince's alongside the Weintraubs in 1938. Weiss, who was naturalised in November 1945 and changed his name to Leo White in June 1947, continued to lead a highly successful orchestra under his own name at Prince's until December 1951 when, ironically, it was replaced by a (short-lived) 'European combo'.[2] White's orchestra, voted

---

[1] NBAC MUA Z401, Box 2 (1946 list); E156/7/5, booklet 1 (1949 list); M. Ricketts (Kitson's secretary) to General Secretary, 4 June 1951 ('forced admission'), NBAC MUA E156/2/2(iii); Minutes of Federal Conference 1945, pp. 7–8, NBAC MUA E156/6/6 (left out inadvertently). Because of ongoing difficulties of proof of his claim to Peruvian nationality, Kay's naturalisation was not confirmed until January 1947. NAA A435, 1946/4/1792.

[2] *Tempo*, August 1945, p. 3, *Music Maker*, 21 January 1946, p. 14 (new band in Prince's); NAA A435, 1947/4/2710 (name change); *Tempo*, April 1952, p. 1 ('new European combo'); *Music Maker* January 1952 ('incoming band of "New Australians"'). A

the best nightclub band by *Tempo* in 1948, also included Ady Fisher (double bass and vocals) and, briefly, Mannie (June-August 1945).[3] Cyril Schulvater joined Goossens' revamped Sydney Symphony Orchestra as a cellist in 1946. John Kay, though still working as an arranger for the Colgate-Palmolive Radio Unit, had founded his Mercury Theatre with Peter Finch, and was sponsoring the Saturday afternoon performances of the Theatre for Children.

It would appear that the Weintraubs' 'union troubles' had, as *Tempo* predicted before the war, largely been resolved—though where possible Kitson's opposition continued to the last moment. Ady and Mannie Frischer, for example, had been naturalised in November 1943 and January 1944 respectively. In December 1943, following the appearance of Ady's obligatory advertisement of intent to apply for naturalisation in the Sydney newspapers, Kitson wrote to the Minister for the Interior, J.S. Collings, to enquire as to the brothers' naturalisation status, adding provocatively, 'I would appreciate it also if you would inform me if it is customary to grant naturalisation to persons born in countries with which we are at war'. The minister declined to engage with the latter issue.[4]

The MUA entered the postwar years with its ideal of a complete embargo on foreign musicians, originally articulated in 1929, as the ongoing primary goal of policy. The general operational principles remained constant, at least in the short term. Union officials continued to discourage, delay and deny applications from individual immigrant musicians by insisting on naturalisation as a condition of eligibility.[5] In accordance with the 1935 (federal) rule, applications were circulated to all six districts of the Union for voting, but none was successful until the middle of 1953. The implied link between citizenship (through naturalisation) and membership in the

---

resume of White's career, including his radio work, may be found in *Radio Call*, 27 February 1952.

[3] *Tempo* June 1945 p.7 and August 1945, p.3 (Frischers at Prince's); NAA SP613, 6/1/7, Parts 1 and 2, Sydney Symphony Orchestra—personnel (1943–48; 1949–56), Sametz, *Play On! 60 Years of Music-making with the Sydney Symphony Orchestra* (Sydney: ABC Enterprises, 1992), p. 359 (Schulvater); SLNSW MLMSS 7164X, 'Sydney John Kay—Scrapbooks concerning the Mercury Theatre, 1940s–1950s', *Music Maker*, December 1948, p. 18 (John Kay).

[4] Kitson to J.S. Collings 21 December 1943 and the Minister's reply, 28 January 1944. NAA A659, 1943/1/248.

[5] For example, W.H.S. Lamble (henceforth 'General Secretary') to H.G. Willis, 16 January 1949: 'To become eligible to be a member of the Musicians Union of Australia the applicant must have obtained a certificate of British Naturalisation'. NBAC MUA E156/2/3(ii).

standard letter of rejection not only lent the decision a semblance of official weight, but discouraged appeals on the part of applicants whose grasp of the language and conventions of their new country was uncertain. In consequence of the Kinsella judgment in the John Kay case, the Union had to be more circumspect in New South Wales, but officials exploited anomalies arising from the fact that the same application form was used for both federal and state entities, and that while the state was obliged to admit foreign applicants if they fulfilled other membership criteria, the federal body was not.[6]

The Union also continued to lobby government for protection and to question the admission of particular immigrant musicians. As early as its annual conference of November 1945, the Union had considered the possibility that the government would institute some form of immigration after the war, and that foreign musicians might be amongst those admitted to Australia. The conference resolved

> that representations be made to appropriate Governmental ministers to protect Australian musicians against any flooding of the market by foreign musicians. In the event of immigration being permitted or encouraged, steps be taken to ensure work for both the Australian and foreign musician.[7]

Communications with the government began at once. But immigration numbers were initially small, even though for the first time the government was sponsoring assisted migration by non-British Europeans in addition to assisted and free British migration and limited Jewish migration under the Close Relatives Scheme. Shipping shortages drastically curtailed an agreement with the International Refugee Organisation to settle at least 12,000 displaced persons a year from camps in Europe. Andrew Markus notes that in the period August–December 1947, only 840 of the anticipated 4,000 immigrants arrived; a further 856 reached Australia in the first quarter of 1948.[8] Union approaches were appropriately cautious. Writing to the Minister for Immigration on 2 December 1946, the MUA's General Secretary was sympathetic:

---

[6] See, for example, General Secretary to George Kraus, 20 March 1952. NBAC MUA E156/2/3(v), '1950-52'. A seemingly random list of foreign musicians admitted to the NSW District between 1947 and 1953 may be found at NBAC MUA Z401, Box 2, 'Annual returns'.
[7] Minutes of Annual Conference, 1945, pp. 23–24. NBAC MUA E156/6/6.
[8] Markus, 'Labour and Immigration 1946-9', p. 82.

At the Annual Conference of the Musicians' Union of Australia held in Hobart on 7 November last, concern was expressed at the number of foreign musicians who were entering the Commonwealth. While we entertain the deepest sympathy with the peoples of countries that have been ravaged by war and who have been rendered homeless and stateless, we respectfully point out that the field of employment for musicians in Australia is very limited compared with that of other countries. We urge, therefore, that musicians should not be permitted to enter Australia in greater numbers than the market is able to absorb, because we believe that preference of employment should be available to British born persons in their own land.[9]

As actual applications began to arrive in numbers, from 1946, the Union stepped up its campaign, characteristically arguing policy issues on the basis of individual cases. Accordingly, in April 1948, the General Secretary wrote to the Secretary of the Department of Immigration to enquire on what basis a list of ten musicians, all unsuccessful applicants for Union membership, had obtained permits to enter the country, enabling them to 'compete in a field of employment whose scope is so very limited?'[10] The list included two Polish-Jewish musicians, Mathys Wisnia and Samuel Helfgott, both classically trained orchestral violinists. At the time of application in January 1948, 32-year old Wisnia, a survivor of six years in concentration camps, had been in Australia for ten months, and 38-year old Helfgott for two weeks. Helfgott, who had 'taken refuge' through the war in central Asia, claimed prior experience as a member of the Broadcasting Symphony Orchestra in Stettin.[11] The departmental secretary replied that Wisnia and Helfgott had been allowed to enter the Commonwealth 'on humanitarian grounds in view of the fact that they had suffered persecution during the war years', noting that 'their occupations were not taken into consideration under the policy then in force, and in fact were not stated on the application forms'.[12] Humanitarian concerns clearly did not extend to ensuring that survivors, once allowed into the

---

[9] NBAC MUA E156/2/6(iii).
[10] General Secretary MUA to Secretary, Department of Immigration, 9 April 1948. NAA A444, 1952/16/2762.
[11] NBAC MUA E156/2/2(xx), '1938-48'. Helfgott was admitted under the Close Relatives scheme, NAA A261, 1946/1973. For Wisnia, see NAA A12508, 56/460, WISNIA, Mathys and B78, 1952/WISNIA M. For the MUA applications, see E156/2/2(xx), '1938-48'.
[12] T.H.E. Heyes, Secretary, Department of Immigration, to General Secretary, 6 July 1948. NAA A444, 1952/16/2762.

country, could obtain employment in the profession of their choice, nor were Union attitudes softened by the revelation of personal suffering. The Union was not exceptional in this regard. Scholars have noted that 'the extensive exposure in Australia of the atrocities perpetrated against the Jews of Europe was not translated into sympathy for the survivors'.[13] It has also been noted that negative prewar attitudes, particularly towards Jewish refugees, persisted in the immediate postwar period.[14] This general trend was exacerbated within the Musicians' Union by the entrenched ideologies of long-serving officials.

In the same letter, however, the secretary assured the Musicians' Union that, in consequence of its representations and based on a ministerial directive of February 1947, 'applications for the admission into Australia of alien musicians other than concert artists are refused except in very special circumstances'.[15] The exclusion of musicians was secret: 'You will appreciate', the secretary wrote, 'that no publicity can be given to the fact that any restriction is placed on the admission of alien musicians as, if it became widely known, musicians who apply for permission to enter the Commonwealth would be likely to suppress information as to their true occupation'. Again, this was not the only secret deal in operation at the time. Andrew Markus has shown that, although the Australian Government's agreement (of July 1947) with the International Refugee Organisation stipulated that there was to be no discrimination in the selection process on the basis of race or religion, secret instructions were issued that 'only Baltic (read "Nordic" or "Aryan") persons were to be selected'.[16] Jewish survivor musicians were thus doubly disadvantaged, though in general the Union made no distinction between the various classes of foreign musicians who came to Australia at this time, whether Jewish, non-Jewish DPs or, more problematically, British.

---

[13] Blakeney, *Australia and the Jewish Refugees*, p.292. Blakeney argues his case for this assertion, as reflected in public opinion (see pp. 292–300) and anti-refugee sentiments among parliamentarians (pp. 300–304). Compare also Markus, 'Jewish Migration', p. 26: 'It seems that the revelation of near genocide in Europe did nothing or very little to soften attitudes in the general community'.

[14] Blakeney, *Australia and the Jewish Refugees*, p.293. For the prewar analogy, see also Bartrop, *Australia and the Holocaust*, p.179, citing *Westralian Judean*, 1 May 1939, p. 2: 'The cry from suffering humanity overseas must not deafen us to the cry from distressed workers in this country …'

[15] NAA A444, 1952/16/2762. An unsigned internal memorandum, dated 14 February 1950, was 'submitted for direction as to whether this policy is to be continued', but see the correspondence with the Minister for Labour and National Service, Harold Holt, below.

[16] Markus, 'Jewish Migration', p. 29.

The Union, the ABC and the nationality quotas

Despite these assurances, the decade and a half from 1945 found the Union increasingly at odds philosophically with the government's immigration agenda, and industrially with the ABC's expansionist objectives for its symphony orchestras. In 1948 the Union's intransigence on the issue of foreign musicians brought it into open conflict with Eugene Goossens, conductor of the Sydney Symphony Orchestra (SSO), the first of the ABC's permanent orchestral units to be reconstructed postwar. Goossens had taken up his position as permanent conductor of the SSO in July 1947, announcing his intention of transforming his new orchestra 'into one of the world's greatest—in two years'.[17] It very quickly became apparent that Goossens' ambition for the orchestra necessitated the importation or engagement of European musicians. This was not a new debate. A-class radio stations had been nationalised under the auspices of the Australian Broadcasting Commission in 1932, and by 1936 the ABC had established studio orchestras for radio and concert work in all capital cities, supplemented by other musical ensembles including a military band and a dance band. Although it was not until 1946 that the ABC looked to expand its studio orchestras into concert symphony orchestras, the Commission was already emerging, in the 1930s, as a major employer of musicians across a range of musical styles.[18]

Throughout the 1930s and into the 1940s, the ABC regularly invited its visiting conductors to submit reports on the state of its ensembles and suggest ways in which standards could be improved. Celebrity conductors like Hamilton Harty (1934), Malcolm Sargent (1936), Georg Schnéevoigt (1937 and 1940), Georg Szell (1938 and 1939), Antal Dorati (1940), Thomas Beecham (1941) and Eugene Ormandy (1944) were all asked to comment on the standard of orchestral playing in Australia, and all recommended the importation of key players from overseas or suggested that the Commission take advantage of European musicians of quality who were already in the country as refugees. Sargent, for example, found Australian double bass players to be dreadful; he also had concerns about the general standard of horn players, oboists and bassoonists, as did Harty and Schnéevoigt.[19] Dorati, who assessed the strengths and weaknesses

---

[17] Buzacott, *The Rite of Spring*, p. 210.
[18] A.H. Forbes, 'Australian Broadcasting Corporation (ABC)', in Warren Bebbington (ed.,) *The Oxford Companion to Australian* Music (Melbourne: Oxford University Press, 1997), pp. 32–33.
[19] Buzacott, *The Rite of Spring*, p.85; Sametz, *Play On!*, p. 55.

of each section of the orchestras, identified a dearth of woodwind and brass players: 'No one studies these instruments, no one teaches them', he observed. Despite sustained pressure, the Union remained adamant that its members could supply all that was needed, given the right opportunities; the ABC argued that they could not. Dorati commented that the MUA 'protects its members as individuals only and leaves musicianship completely outside of its policy'.[20] The Union countered by claiming that 'The inclusion of Foreigners, many of whom speak English very indifferently, generally means the displacement of an Australian. This does not make for peace in the industry'.[21]

In May 1937, Charles Moses, General Manager of the ABC, had begun negotiations with the Postmaster-General (the minister responsible for the ABC) and the MUA to implement recommendations in the reports provided by Harty, Sargent and Schnéevoigt by importing competent players of certain 'key' instruments felt to be lacking in Australia. The instruments in question were the oboe, bassoon and French horn.[22] At that time, Cabinet was happy to endorse the Union's view that 'with careful selection and proper training, the material is available in Australia to meet the Commission's needs'.[23] The Union also rejected the request. The matter of importations persisted, however, until, in February 1940, the MUA agreed to the importation of four front-rank instrumentalists 'under certain conditions'.[24] Negotiations began to engage the musicians, but were placed in abeyance due to the international situation. In 1946, however, the Commission's right to import four key instrumentalists— oboe, bassoon, string bass or French horn—was written into the Award agreement with the MUA.[25] Importations were permitted on condition that they should not have the effect of displacing a musician already employed

---

[20] Antal Dorati 'General report on the orchestral position in Australia, 2 September 1940, p. "B"'. NAA SP1558/2, 750.
[21] Undated document [1949?], 'Explanatory statement of grounds on which the claims [are] set out in the memorial against the Australian Broadcasting Commission in respect of orchestral musicians'. NBAC MUA E156/9/1, folder pt. 2.
[22] C.J.A. Moses to Postmaster-General, 24 May 1937. NAA SP1558/2, 741.
[23] Postmaster-General to ABC Chairman (W.J. Cleary), 2 June 1937. NAA SP1558/2, 741.
[24] W.G. James to Moses, 21 February 1940. NAA SP1558/2, 741.
[25] *Commonwealth Arbitration Reports* 57, 1946 (Sydney: Law Book Co. of Australasia), 205. Music historians have yet to make the imaginative use of arbitration transcripts, reports and judgments that social historians have done. See, for example, Mark Hearn, 'Sifting the Evidence: Labour History and the Transcripts of Industrial Arbitration Proceedings', *Labour History* 93 (2007), pp. 3–13.

by the Commission, that they should be natural-born or naturalised British musicians and that they should immediately join the Union.[26] On the issue of the Commission's employment of foreign musicians, however, the Union remained unyielding.

In the five years between 1946 and 1951, the ABC established permanent professional orchestras in six cities.[27] In so doing, it was specifically implementing the report undertaken by visiting Hungarian-American conductor Eugene Ormandy in 1944. Ormandy, like most of his colleagues including Goossens, linked the expansion of Australia's orchestral culture to the importation or deployment of European musicians in key sectional leadership positions.[28] More than that, Ormandy premised his recommendations on the assumption that this would happen as, in his opinion, 'the existing pool of talent is limited'. Accordingly, from the middle of 1948, the Union began to receive applications from resident, unnaturalised foreign-born musicians, who had received offers of employment either from the ABC or from Goossens himself, acting in his double role as director of the NSW State Conservatorium and conductor of the Sydney Symphony Orchestra.[29] Following extended discussion of the development of Australian orchestras at its 1948 Federal Conference, Council reaffirmed the Union's intention to 'resist as far as it is able the entry into Australia of any foreign musician'.[30] A noisy public debate followed Kitson's announcement of the Union's new membership criteria:

> Mr Kitson said that the union aimed at maintaining a membership consisting of 90 percent Australians and 10 percent British people who had lived here for 10 years ... The council would not approve further applications [from overseas musicians].[31]

---

[26] Sametz discusses these early importations, their successes and failures. *Play On!*, pp. 109–112.

[27] For a recent study of this topic, see Kenneth Morgan, 'Cultural Advance: the Formation of Australia's Permanent Orchestras, 1944–1951', *Musicology Australia* 33/1 (July 2011), pp. 69–93.

[28] Buzacott, *The Rite of Spring*, pp. 188–189, 195. For the Ormandy report, see Eugene Ormandy to the Right Hon. F.M. Forde, Minister for the Army in the Curtin government, 11 July 1944. NAA SP613/1, 6/12/8. Forde released the report to the press within a month of receiving it, opening issues raised to public discussion. Sametz, *Play On!*, p. 93.

[29] See, for example, NBAC MUA E156/2/3(v) ('1945–50'; '1950–52'; '1953–55'); NAA SP613, 6/1/7, PART 2 (1949–56).

[30] General Secretary to Graeme Bell, 1 July 1949. NBAC MUA E156/2/3(ii).

[31] *Sydney Morning Herald*, 13 January 1949. Kitson's announcement and various responses from within the profession (including Goossens) were reported in various Sydney newspapers between December 1948 and January 1949. Clippings occupy

I can find no evidence that this resolution was incorporated into the 1949 revision of the Union's Constitution and Rules. However, vestiges of the principle survive in the binding agreement for nationality quotas that was ratified with the ABC in November 1951. The Commission's orchestras were to comprise 80 percent Australian-born musicians; half of the remaining 20 percent should be British.[32] The quota idea was not new: the notion that orchestras should not include a greater percentage of foreigners than 10 percent was, together with the general object of keeping orchestras British, added to the federal rules in 1927.[33] In 1956 the rules were amended to include the specific quota requirements as negotiated with the ABC.[34]

By insisting on the naturalisation requirement and obliging the ABC to ascertain the availability of any Australian or British musician of the requisite standard before appointing a foreign-born musician, even under the nationality quota, the Musicians' Union was able, at least until the late 1950s, to frustrate ongoing efforts to introduce high-quality immigrant professionals into the symphony orchestras. But the ABC persisted. Under the terms of the nationality quota agreement, the Union was not allowed to withhold district membership from an immigrant musician who, after due process and within the terms of the quota, was found to be the best applicant for an orchestral position. The situation in New South Wales was also different because of the John Kay judgment. Although foreign musicians were still excluded from the federal Union, a small number of unnaturalised immigrant musicians, including Samuel Helfgott, were able to join the Commission's symphony orchestras especially in New South Wales and Queensland, where districts were constituted as separate entities. The list of SSO personnel from 1953 published by Sametz includes the names of six musicians, in addition to Helfgott, whose initial applications for membership were rejected by the Union, but who were admitted to membership of the New South Wales District: violinists Bela Dekany, Klara Korda and Peter

---

some ten pages of the Union's scrapbook NBAC MUA Z401, Box 12, 'Press cuttings 1938-52'.

[32] Moses to Lamble, 15 November 1951. Moses' letter also set out definitions and exceptions. Correspondence between the Union and the ABC re. negotiation of the Nationality Quotas is at NBAC MUA E156/2/3(va).

[33] Rules 1929, p. 14. NBAC MUA N93/478.

[34] A new rule expressing the Union's idea of acceptable quotas (at least 70 percent Australian, not more than 20 percent British-born and 10 percent foreign-born) was proposed and registered in 1949. Minutes of Annual Conference, 14 November 1949, p. 2. NBAC MUA E 156/6/7. For correspondence about this rule change see NBAC MUA Z391/73 'Rules 1948-49'; Amendments 1956, Z401, Box 3.

Figure 25. 'I'm no Kreisler but I'm an Aussie …'
John Frith's cartoon is one of the more benevolent newspaper representations of the ongoing conflict between Eugene Goossens and the MUA following the Union's announcement of draconian quota requirements for foreign-born musicians, early in 1949. *Sydney Morning Herald*, 18 January 1949, p. 2.
NBAC MUA Z401 Box 13.Reproduced with permission NBAC.

Abraham; principal violist Robert Pikler; principal cellist Hans George (formerly Gyors) and bass player George Kraus(z).[35] Five years earlier Krausz had flirted with deportation by joining the SSO:

> George Krausz was granted permission to enter Australia from Singapore in 1947 for the purposes of studying music at the Conservatorium of Sydney [of which Goossens was then Director]. However, in view of the fact that he has been playing with the Sydney Symphony Orchestra it has been decided that unless he ceases to accept employment and

---

[35] Sametz, *Play On!*, p. 359. Pikler was the subject of a particularly vigorous oppositional campaign by the Union. See NAA SP613, 6/1/7, Part 2 (January 1949–1956). The orchestra also included Guido Gervasoni, one of the Italians who came in the 1920s.

does not confine himself to the study of music at the Conservatorium, he will have to leave the Commonwealth.[36]

Five foreign-born musicians remained in the SSO in 1956.[37]

It is not yet clear to me how these immigrant musicians came to secure positions in the SSO and whether, as in other documented cases, it was necessary for the ABC to establish that no Australian musician of equivalent skill was available or willing to take each job. Hans Gyors, for example, arrived in Australia on 9 January 1951, was auditioned in early February, and given a ranking of B plus to A with a recommendation that he could be offered a trial engagement, despite the inevitable difficulty with the Union.[38] It is possible that Goossens recruited in the European camps or the local migrant hostels; he certainly attended one well-publicised event, a performance of *Tosca* at the Bathurst Immigration Centre in July 1950.[39] Even if immigrants were not brought to Australia as musicians and were contracted to the government in other occupations, their musical skills were frequently lauded in the press.[40] Historians have noted Calwell's awareness—and conscious exploitation—of the propaganda value of positive publicity about his immigrants; according to Kunz, Calwell 'fought xenophobia with publicity'.[41]

Two features of immigrant membership of Goossens' SSO in 1953 are worth noting. The first is that five of the seven musicians under discussion were Hungarian and all were string players. The preponderance of Hungarians is reflective of more general postwar trends among immigrant musicians. Hungarians constitute the largest national group within the circa 275 applicants considered by the MUA's Federal Council over a

---

[36] T.H.E. Heyes, Secretary [Department of Immigration] to General Secretary MUA, 4 March 1949. NAA A444, 1952/16/2762. Correspondence concerning Kraus's application for membership of the federal union is at NBAC MUA E156/2/3(v), '1950–52'.

[37] Minutes of Annual Conference 1956, Item 65, NBAC MUA N93/2A.

[38] NAA ST2238/1, GYORS HANS; NBAC MUA E156/2/3(v), '1950–52'.

[39] 'Company of New Australians to Stage Opera Tonight', *Sydney Morning Herald*, 6 July 1950, p. 2.

[40] For example, 'Talented Migrant Musicians', *Argus*, 23 September 1949, p. 3. Such immigrants (including, in this instance, violinist Geza Bachmann, who performed at the annual Citizenship Convention in 1951 and had joined the SSO by 1954), were noted to be 'straining at the leash of their two-year contract with the Federal Government to get back into the world of music'. *Sydney Morning Herald*, 6 July 1950, p. 2.

[41] See, for example, episode two of the documentary film *Immigration Nation: The Secret History of Us* (SBS/Madman, 2011); Kunz, *Displaced Persons*, p. 14.

twelve-year period from 1945 to 1957. Forty-six applications from Hungarian musicians were received over this time, and while this cohort is sufficiently numerous to support certain observations, it is almost certainly not complete. It does not, for example, include an application from Tommy Tycho, a Jewish Hungarian who immigrated in 1951 and is perhaps the best-known musician from this national group. George Pikler is another well-known absentee.

The ratio of women to men—two out of forty-six—is also reflective of the proportions in the larger set. The various Hungarian vintages identified by Kunz are apparent in the musician groupings: the first postwar arrivals were predominantly Jewish and well-educated musically; that is, classically trained. Among the later vintages, starting with the 'Fifty-sixers' (refugees from the 1956 Hungarian Revolution), Kunz noted a high proportion of young people, factory workers and tradesmen.[42] Among the musicians, one can observe a swing away from full-time professional musicians, predominantly string players and pianists most likely to be engaged in orchestral work or teaching, to light-music players who were liable to combine casual work (at parties or dances and in cafés) with another occupation. Some but not all of the postwar arrivals were contracted immigrants. The significant number of Hungarians in the SSO also mirrors the demographic concentration of Hungarian immigrants in Sydney noted by Kunz.

The presence of two foreigners as sectional leaders in the SSO, in fulfilment of Ormandy's recommendations and Goossens' plan, also highlights a significant point of divergence between Union and (in this instance) the ABC. Arthur Calwell, Minister for Immigration and chief advocate for mass immigration postwar, believed that the way to protect Australian working conditions was to urge immigrants to join trade unions; in fact they were required to do so in cases where membership was compulsory.[43] However, in selling its postwar immigration program to the union movement, the government pledged that immigrant workers were not to be introduced into occupations where Australian workers were available, nor to displace Australian workers. DPs were to come in at the bottom end of the labour market, taking jobs that were least attractive to Australian workers, thus affording the latter the opportunity for upward

---

[42] Egon F. Kunz, *The Hungarians in Australia* (Melbourne: AE Press, 1985), pp. 82–83.
[43] Ann-Mari Jordens, *Redefining Australians: Immigration, Citizenship & National Identity* (Sydney: Hale & Iremonger, 1995), p. 29 and note 12; Markus, 'Labour and Immigration 1946–9', p. 88 (required to join).

mobility.⁴⁴ Not so in the case of the musicians, who came in at the top. As early as 1938, the ABC recognised that displacement was inevitable if, in open competition, the work of refugee musicians was judged to be of higher calibre.⁴⁵

The fact that a handful of gifted individuals survived the Union obstacle course to find a place in the profession and make their mark on Australia's musical life was due in part to the determined advocacy of Charles Moses, then Chairman of the ABC. While seeking to honour his commitment to the Union of ensuring the Australian character of the ABC orchestras, and constrained as he was by the Commission's position as a government instrumentality and a party to the Awards of the Court of Conciliation and Arbitration, Moses nonetheless also sought to secure the best performers available and fought resolutely for the engagement of individual high-quality, foreign-born musicians. Cases in point were (Czech) oboist Jiri Tancibudek and (Hungarian) clarinetist Gabor Revesz (later Reeves). Regarding the appointment of Tancibudek, Goossens deplored 'the narrow-minded policy of the Union in restricting (and/or forbidding) the admission of high-class overseas artists (performers) into Australian [orchestras?]'.⁴⁶

The numbers of such musicians should not, however, be exaggerated. In July 1951, while negotiating the nationality quotas with Moses, the MUA undertook an audit of foreign-born musicians in ABC state orchestras. Tasmania declared three foreign-born members, one of whom was English; South Australia registered two naturalised Italians, and three English. Out of a total of fifty in the Queensland Symphony Orchestra, thirty-eight were Australian-born, eight were born within the British Empire and resident in Australia for ten years and four were foreigners. Of the latter, three were resident in Australia for more than twenty years and naturalised and the fourth was Gabor Reeves.⁴⁷ Reeves' appointment was vigorously contested and unsuccessfully obstructed by the Union;⁴⁸ he went on to become one of the country's most respected clarinetists.

---

44 Markus, 'Labour and Immigration 1946–9', p. 88 (not to be introduced or displace); p. 90, and citing *Sydney Morning Herald*, 18 June 1949 (least attractive employment).
45 Memo, W G James to the General Manager [ABC], 5 December 1938. NAA SP1558/2, 741.
46 Eugene Goossens to Charles Moses, 2 June 1955. NAA SP613, 6/1/7, PART 2 (1949–56).
47 Tasmanian District to General Secretary 7 July 1951 and South Australian District to General Secretary 7 July 1951, both NBAC MUA E156/2/3(va), '1948–55'; Queensland District to General Secretary, 16 July 1951. NBAC MUA E156/2/3(va).
48 General Secretary to ABC, 29 May 1951. NBAC MUA E156/2/3(va), '1948–55'.

The definitions of 'Australian-born' for the purpose of calculating the orchestral quota deserve some scrutiny as indicative of Union attitudes at the time. As agreed in 1951, these included the following categories: musicians born in Australia or born of Australian parents; musicians employed in the Commission's orchestras as at 1 July 1948 who had been employed continuously from that time (this allowed the inclusion of some long-serving, foreign-born musicians); musicians who became or would become resident in Australia at the age of twelve or under, were educated in Australia and completed ten years of service as a member of one of the Commission's permanent units; musicians of British birth who completed fifteen years' service; musicians who were naturalised Australians and completed twenty years' service.[49] The fact that the Victorian orchestra's 1954 tally of foreign musicians included George Dreyfus demonstrates the rigidity of these definitions if literally applied: Dreyfus arrived in Australia at the age of eleven, was educated in Melbourne and naturalised, but failed to make the count of ten years' service as a Commission employee.[50]

The last of these definitions, echoing as it does the Union's use of the naturalisation requirement as a barrier to membership, and clearly conceived as a means of further limiting the numbers of foreign-born musicians in Australian orchestras, was to be the cause of unjust treatment of individuals, of discomfort to the ABC as a Commonwealth semi-government instrumentality out of step with official immigration policy, and of the eventual demise of the nationality quota accord as a whole. Charles Moses articulated the difficulty in his letter to the General Secretary, 31 October 1955. Citing a recent letter from the Secretary of the Department of Immigration, Moses wrote,

> their treatment (ie that of certain foreign-born orchestral players) is opposed to the wording of their Certificate of Naturalisation that the holder has 'to all intents and purposes the status of a natural-born British subject'. The Minister is, of course, anxious to ensure that once an alien is naturalised he shall not be subjected to any form of discrimination and should enjoy to the full all the privileges which the Naturalisation Certificate confers upon him as a British subject.[51]

---

[49] Charles Moses to General Secretary, 15 November 1951. NBAC MUA E156/2/3(va).
[50] See internal memo, 'Nationality Quotas—Victorian Symphony Orchestra', 15 June 1954. NAA B2114, 6/7/4.
[51] NBAC MUA E156/2/3(ii), 'Letters General Secretary MUA to ABC, August–November 1955'.

BREACHING THE PROFESSION

Figure 26. Is he an Aussie?
A. Stuart Peterson caricatures ongoing Union insistence on preference for Australian musicians in the *Sun*, 28 January 1949.

Press cuttings 1938–52, MUA NBAC Z401 Box 13.
Reproduced with permission NBAC.

Moses expressed himself as anxious to avoid any overt discrimination against naturalised foreign players that might result in the Commission having to defend publicly the precise terms of its agreement with the Union. Perhaps coincidentally, Moses' letter followed closely upon the dispute between the Union and the ABC over the status of violinist Frederick Kramer.

Friedrich Kramer came to Australia from Austria in 1938. He auditioned at once and successfully for a place in the Melbourne Symphony Orchestra (MSO) but the Union withheld membership until he was naturalised, an event for which he waited seven years. He was then immediately engaged as a casual by the MSO and, when the orchestra became a subsidised government instrumentality in 1949, was taken on as a permanent member. He played for six years with the MSO then, having relocated to Sydney, for two and a half with the SSO. However, in 1954, because the Union would not agree to release his name from the foreign quota and because the SSO needed to reduce the number of foreign players by one in the off-season, Kramer was dismissed. Nor could he get his position back when it was offered because the Union refused his appeal to be classified as an Australian. Reporting this victory, the hard-line secretary of the NSW District of the Union observed that 'New South Wales feels the quota contract has justified itself in this matter. The position has been filled by a young Australian named Ritchie, who is a very good player and the reports are more than favourable'.[52]

Immigrant musicians in the immigrant scene

Not every immigrant musician who came to Australia in the years immediately following the Second World War wanted to play in the nation's symphony orchestras. A tiny few (perhaps two out of forty-two) from the next largest national group of postwar applicants, the Dutch, for example, are identifiably classical orchestral musicians. Equally or more concerning to the Union was the alleged infiltration of the dance and nightclub and café scenes, with immigrant musicians working in partnership with immigrant management.[53] Orchestral musicians could not work without union membership; other musicians could. Musical skill, not being language dependent, is in that category that Egon Kunz characterises as 'highly transferable'.[54] Moreover, this kind of work could be combined with different day-time work; the scene was notoriously difficult to regulate.

Following the change of government in December 1949 (from a Labor government under Ben Chifley to Robert Menzies' Liberals), the Union renewed its representations to government with a deputation to the Prime

---

[52] V. Massey (Secretary, NSW District) to Lamble, 15 December 1954. The Kramer correspondence is at NBAC MUA E156/2/6(va).
[53] F. Kitson to Lamble, 4 August 1951. NBAC MUA E156/2/2(xiii).
[54] Kunz, 'Australian Professional Attitudes and the Immigrant Professional', p. 5.

Minister.⁵⁵ By 1951, the Union was obliged to reiterate its request for exclusion at the point of selection, protesting 'a few of the many cases where Australians are the victims of foreign infiltration' to the Liberal government's Minister for Labour and National Service, Harold Holt. Holt's response was less than reassuring:

> While I am personally aware that among the migrants who have come to this country, and particularly among the Displaced Persons, there are many very gifted musicians and artists, none of the migrants in relation to whom the Commonwealth exercised selection controls were brought to this country because they were musicians. Attainments in the arts have never been the subject of enquiry because the whole basis of selection has been fitness for particular employment. That rule will continue to govern selection in future.⁵⁶

Holt seemed to think that the presence of such musicians could only be a benefit, and expressed the hope that the chances of gifted young Australian-born musicians travelling abroad should not be 'jeopardised by foreign countries taking the attitude that seems to characterise your approach'.

In an impassioned reply that dismissed as irrelevant Holt's reference to gifted young Australians, the MUA President identified 'the migrant player of modern or jazz music' as the greater present threat to the livelihood of the Australian musician. The trade magazines expressed a reasonably generous attitude. They were generally supportive editorially of the idea that 'if a man is brought to this country as a migrant, he cannot legally be denied the right to work at his profession'; they also acknowledged that European musicians possessed attributes and skills that Australian musicians did not have, particularly in the field of café entertainment. 'The European musicians have been brought up in the café music atmosphere', wrote the editor of *Tempo* in October 1951,

> —they like playing it—and they have learned to make the customer feel that they are pleased to play what he wants—not, as so often happens

---

55 See Minutes of Annual Conference 1950, p. 5. NBAC MUA E156/6/7. The deputation was reported in the *Herald*, and *Telegraph* 21 January 1948. Press cuttings 1938–52, NBAC MUA Z401, Box 13.
56 General Secretary to Harold Holt, 14 August 1951 (request for exclusion); Harold Holt to General Secretary, 10 September 1951 (Holt's response). Both NBAC MUA E156/2/6(iii). President to Harold Holt, 12 December 1951 (greater threat). NBAC MUA Z401, box 5.

here, that they are annoyed at his temerity in interfering with the musicians' selection of numbers.[57]

Even so, by 1952, the editorials were expressing concern that New Australians were taking Australian jobs; *Tempo* noted 'There are at least six complete New Australian dance orchestras playing in clubs throughout Sydney and suburbs right now'. The issue was no longer one of 'the acceptance of one or two classical players into symphony aggregations', but of entire New Australian dance bands competing for the limited work available. *Tempo*, acknowledging the reality that the foreign-born musician was 'here to stay', expressed the view that New Australians working in the nightclub scene 'ought to join the Union' and advocated compromise: 'a set number of immigrant musicians to be admitted to the union each year'.[58] Inverting *Tempo*'s generous assessment of the effectiveness of European musicians, the Union asserted that

> The housing of migrants in camps has encouraged the formation of small groups, ill equipped musically, but well rehearsed as Show men. They provide themselves with an array of instruments, satin shirts, ribbons and Mexican hats. Thus equipped they secure employment, where they intermingle with patrons and exploit their 'difference of manner and speech'.[59]

The Union saw the commitment to two years' indentured labour as no deterrent: 'they are in a position to wait on and augment their income from Seasonal work'.

In the 1920s, Union rhetoric had found an echo in the uninhibited pro-British, anti-foreign oratory of politicians like W. M. Hughes and, through him, a conduit of political pressure that resulted in the licensing agreement of 1928. Apart from the fact that the postwar immigration program enjoyed a broad base of bipartisan support, Holt's position was different: as early as 1945, during the government's immigration debate, he had identified the attitude of the Australian people towards immigrants as the most important issue to be addressed, noting their 'curiously

---

[57] 'Editorial', *Tempo*, September 1951, p. 4.
[58] 'Editorial', *Tempo*, October 1951, p. 4 (right to work; attributes and skills); Editorial 'A Grave Problem', *Tempo*, January 1952, p. 1 (New Australian bands; a set number); *Tempo* April 1953, p. 4 (ought to join the Union).
[59] President to Harold Holt, 12 December 1951; ibid., (seasonal work). NBAC MUA Z401, box 5. The letter was written by Victor Massey, Kitson's equally hard-line successor as Secretary of the NSW District. The Union's efforts were reported in *Tempo*'s January 1952 Editorial.

intolerant attitude' as something he found difficult to understand.[60] Holt's response must also be seen in relation to the responsibility, assigned to the Department of Immigration under the 1948 *Nationality and Citizenship Act*, 'for facilitating the immigrant's compliance with the expectation that those granted permanent entry would become "absorbed" into the national community' by becoming a citizen.[61]

To some extent it was true, as the Union's executive claimed, that full-time employment prospects for musicians were limited in Australia, a country of some seven million people at the end of the Second World War. Addressing the employment issue in 1948, General Secretary Lamble enumerated other employment possibilities:

> Apart from the Australian Broadcasting Commission there are only four legitimate theatres carrying orchestras ranging between 18 and 20, and perhaps half a dozen picture houses with small bands, in Australia. We have a membership of about 4,000, most of whom, apart from those in the above orchestras, depend on casual work. The supply is obviously much in excess of the demand.[62]

Paradoxically, however, the very numbers involved in the postwar migration program and its character led to an increase in the demand for musical services. Although free and assisted British migrants were the largest ethnic element in the settler intake until 1953, the concentration of national 'vintages' in the mass resettlement scheme produced a diversification of 'musical tastes, preferences and practices embedded in social life ... and a range of nationally distinctive popular entertainment genres were performed by musicians within communities'.[63] Various examples permeate the Union files: of a foreign musician running his own dances, of the presence

---

[60] Patricia Anne Bernadette Jenkings, 'Australian Political Elites and Citizenship Education for "New Australians" 1945–1960' (PhD thesis, University of Sydney, 2001), p. 43, quoting *Federal Parliamentary Debates*, 29 August 1945, pp. 4998–4999.
[61] Jordens, *Redefining Australians*, p. 5.
[62] General Secretary to Mr J. Cheatle, 6 October 1948. NBAC MUA E156/2/3(ii). Nor should one overestimate the potential for employment that was offered by the ABC at this time. According to a letter from the Postmaster General to MUA General Secretary Lamble, the Commission had permanent places for 374 musicians and choristers by June 1954. Postmaster General to General Secretary MUA, 3 June 1954. NBAC MUA E156/2/3(ii).
[63] For British numbers, see A. James Hammerton and Alistair Thomson, *Ten Pound Poms: Australia's Invisible Migrants* (Manchester: Manchester University Press, 2005), Table 1, p. 32. The term 'vintages' is from Kunz, *Displaced Persons*, p. 23 *passim*, and see his table summary of nationalities, p. 43. For diversification of musical tastes, see Graeme Smith, 'Public Multicultural Music and the Australian State', *Music & Politics* III/2

of Latvian bands in the café scene, of Russian musicians from Shanghai working casually playing for weddings, parties and other social events, or in cafés.[64] Nor was this activity confined within communities. In his volume on the Hungarians in the Australian Ethnic Heritage Series, Egon Kunz puts forward the large claim that 'multiculturalism in Australia's broadcasting began with [Geza] Bachman's "Golden Melodies"', a program that began and ended with the 'famous melody of the Hungarian gypsy song "Only One Girl"'.[65] From the 1930s onwards Hungarian—and other immigrant—musicians were identified with gypsy orchestras for broadcasting purposes; classically trained immigrant artists performed and recorded this national music.[66] Karoly Szenassy complained that the ABC forced him to play gypsy music instead of giving him the concert engagements he desired.[67] Szenassy left for America in 1948 where, among other things, he founded a gypsy violin ensemble.

The movement of multicultural music into the public sphere is a complex story spanning successive decades, but Graeme Smith asserts that 'the process began with political moves to accommodate the social changes resulting from Australia's postwar migration'.[68] From the early 1950s one may detect the beginning of an ethnically-based sector in the music industry with immigrant musicians of the same national background working together by preference, servicing the social needs of their own communities. It could be argued that Richard Goldner's Musica Viva ensemble, comprised of (and largely supported by) immigrants in its early years, was born of his and their exclusion from the mainstream profession as much as from Goldner's wish to compensate for the lack of a certain kind of chamber music performance.

Dismantling policy: rewriting the rules 1949–60

By 1954, Union recalcitrance placed it significantly at odds with the thrust of federal government policy, as enacted symbolically in the *Nationality and*

(Summer 2009), [p.2]. At http://www.music.ucsb.edu/projects/musicandpolitics/past.html, accessed September 2010.

[64] Kitson to Lamble, 27 January 1951 (foreigner running own dances); Kitson to Lamble 4 August 1951 (Latvian bands). Both NBAC MUA E156/2/2(xiii). Boris Usiskin was one of the Russian musicians who finally forced change. See E156/2/3(v) '1953–55'.

[65] Kunz, *The Hungarians in Australia*, p. 110.

[66] Mark Richards, 'Hungarian traditions,' in Whiteoak and Scott-Maxwell (eds), *Currency Companion to Music and Dance*, p. 320.

[67] 'No "Welcome" Sign for Gifted Musician', *Sunday Telegraph* 13 (?) February 1949. NAA SP767/1, KAROLY SZENASSY (BOX 4).

[68] Smith, 'Public Multicultural Music', [pp. 1–2].

Citizenship Act of 1948 and expressed in annual citizenship conventions and naturalisation ceremonies. The success of the immigration program, and of its underpinning assimilation philosophy, rested on the wholehearted acceptance of the newcomers by the Australian public and the removal of legal differences between native-born Australians and those who assumed Australian citizenship through naturalisation.[69] The creation of a new status of Australian citizenship by the 1948 Act was an important step towards the slow development of 'a notion of citizenship based on equality of rights rather than on British culture and ethnicity'.[70]

My research has shown that the development of the Union's exclusionist policy towards foreign musicians was linked to the revision and consolidation of the rules for the federal body through the 1920s. Similarly, in the late 1940s and through the 1950s, the dismantling of exclusionary aspects of policy was accompanied by and expressed through revision of the federal rules. But whereas the rewriting of the rules in the 1920s was supported by a broad consensus within Council, the changes of the 1950s were not. Internal ideological differences are reflected in discussions at annual conferences and in comments on applications from unnaturalised individual musicians. Only the deaths of long-serving hard-line officials such as Kitson (NSW Secretary and Federal President, died November 1951), W.H. Lamble (General Secretary, Victorian Secretary, died 1956) and Victor Massey (NSW Secretary after Kitson, and Acting General Secretary after Lamble, died 1957) allowed more moderate voices within the Union executive to prevail.

On several occasions from 1947 onwards, the Tasmanian District secretary had expressed the view that it was better to 'admit a certain number of foreigners from time to time', noting with unease Calwell's comments that he would compel the Union to accept migrants, and urging that the Union could 'handle these people much better in the Union than outside our ranks'.[71] At this time, engaged as it was with the question of the ABC's nationality quotas and its quest for legislative protection from the newly

---

[69] Jenkings, 'Australian Political Elites', pp. 151, 161.
[70] Jordens, *Redefining Australia*, p. 7. For a nuanced discussion of the philosophical and legislative approaches to citizenship (as exclusive or inclusive) in relation to the 1948 Act, see Rubenstein, 'An Unequal Membership', pp. 145–162.
[71] B.A. McCann (Secretary, Tasmanian District) to General Secretary: 15 May 1947 ('from time to time'), NBAC MUA E156/2/2(xx), '1938–48'; 24 January 1949 (Calwell comment), 4 August 1949 ('handle better in Union', both NBAC MUA E156/2/3(v), '1945–50'. Tasmania supported the admission of both Samuel Helfgott and Mathys Wisnia.

elected Liberal government, Council responded to such urgings by writing the quota requirements into the rules, and reaffirming its naturalisation requirement (though not as a registered rule). The number of applications received intensified in the early 1950s, but all were routinely rejected until June 1953.[72] That 1953 was a pivotal year is reflected in the Union's annual conference when, after considerable debate of the issue, Federal Council passed two apparently contradictory resolutions: the one affirming the policy of discouraging the admission of foreigners, the second proposing that 'when a District recommends the admission of any applicant for membership, all other sections of the Federal Council agree to the admission unless a good reason can be advanced for its rejection'.[73] A list of foreign applications followed, all of whom were admitted, though several of these individuals had applied unsuccessfully before.

What were the reasons for the change? Most immediately, the pressure of numbers: 170,000 refugees (or displaced persons) arrived in Australia between 1947 and 1953; c.16,300 Jewish survivors between 1946 and 1954; a total of 1,253,083 settler arrivals in the decade from 1949 to 1959.[74] Union files record a consequently higher number of applications from immigrant musicians. General Secretary Wheatland's letter to Massey of 16 June 1953 provides a summary of changed industrial circumstances:

> It appears that quite a few of these [unsuccessful] applicants are seeking legal advice, and it is strange that they seem unaware of the recent amendment to the Arbitration Act; but if this is so, it will not be long before it is realised that they can force the issue. I, therefore, think that the policy suggested by Victoria of admitting highly qualified applicants is the safest course at the moment, and it would show that we are not excluding all foreigners, but are accepting those whom we think would, to some extent, be an asset to the organisation. If something like this is not done, I am afraid we will be forced, before long, to accept all applicants.[75]

NSW opposed the selective admission of any foreigners:

---

[72] NBAC MUA E156/2/3(v), '1953–55'.
[73] Minutes of Annual Conference 1953, item 52. NBAC MUA E156/6/9.
[74] For the numbers, see Markus, 'Labour and Immigration 1946–9', p. 83; Rutland, *Edge of the Diaspora*, Appendix 1, p.405; Charles Price, 'Postwar Immigration, 1947–98', *Journal of Population Research* 15/2 (1998), p. 122.
[75] C.M. Wheatland (Secretary, Victorian District) to Massey, 16 June 1953. NBAC MUA E156/2/3 (v), '1953–55'.

> Frankly we feel if any foreign applicant is rejected, they all should be … We are no more meeting the provisions of the Arbitration Act by admitting only 50% of applicants than by admitting none … [76]

Membership application files for the period 1953–55 chart the disintegration of a unanimous policy. Russian clarinetist Eugene Danilov applied on 14 October 1952 while waiting on naturalisation and after being in Australia for one year.[77] He declared himself to be well-known among New Australians as a band leader and wished to employ registered musicians. His marriage to an Australian singer confirmed his bona fides as a prospective citizen. His application was rejected, but he gathered support from the Victoria District, reapplied, and was admitted in January 1953. Solicitors representing another Russian applicant, Boris Leoned Usiskin, cited the Danilov case among their other arguments against their client's rejection:

> Our client informs us that in the exercise of their discretion the Council has already admitted to membership his friend Mr Eugene Danilov … who is not yet naturalised and arrived to this country subsequently to our client.[78]

Another applicant, one Rudolf Schwarz, warned of intended legal action. He forwarded a clipping from the February 1953 issue of the newspaper *The New Citizen*, which cited a statement prepared by the Department of Labour and National Service advising that New Australians were encouraged to become members of unions.[79] Victoria proposed and instituted an audition process to identify 'highly qualified applicants', and some few (including Danilov) were admitted under this system.[80] Once exceptions were made, the walls were breached.

---

[76] Massey to Lamble, 5 April 1954. NBAC MUA E156/2/3(v), '1953–55'.

[77] See NBAC MUA E156/2/3(v), '1953–55' for this and other internal correspondence about Danilov, December 1952–February 1953.

[78] A.R. Pritchard to General Secretary, 1 June 1953. NBAC MUA E156/2/3 (v), '1953–55'. Usiskin first applied in September 1950. NBAC MUA E156/2/3(v), '1950–52'.

[79] He referred to a recent court case in NSW in which 'the Union' [unnamed, the MUA?] was ordered to issue a New Australian with a membership card. Rudolf Schwarz to General Secretary, 1 March 1953. E156/2/3 (v), '1950–52'. This Schwarz is not to be confused with the Austrian conductor of the same name who emigrated to England after the war and made a career and reputation there.

[80] General Secretary to Federal Council, 29 December 1952 and 2 April 1954. NBAC MUA E156/2/3(v), '1953–55'.

District responses were not unitary or always predictable, but it was rare for an application to be rejected after the 1953 Conference. This is not to imply that internal resistance was at an end. In sending forward applications from foreigners the NSW District did not, as a matter of policy, add any recommendation. It mostly voted in favour of their admittance, though Massey continued to protest the new procedure, asserting that 'the fact that foreign applicants must await a decision from all districts on their application fosters a belief that admittance is not "routine"'.[81] South Australia then refused to vote in favour of any application forwarded without recommendation by NSW, in compliance with the resolution of the 1953 Conference. When districts did not respond at all, or voted against an applicant, the basis of acceptance became the 'majority vote'. Procedure was followed but the issue had lost its bite. Between late 1955 and early 1956, more applications were lodged than over the entire previous three decades from unnaturalised immigrant musicians who had been in the country from a few days to fifteen years (in one case), with an average stay of between three and seven years. Many more formerly unsuccessful applicants reapplied. Applicants now mostly used the application form. The heart-rending details that were often recounted in personal letters are missing, but the answers provided to questions on the form are a rich source of comparative data: length of time in Australia, route taken, current occupation, previous professional experience as musicians and union membership, and instrument/s played in relation to nationality. The rule change on the voting mechanism was registered in 1958, and decision-making authority returned to the districts.[82]

The issue of the ABC nationality quotas continued to attract intermittent public criticism from visiting and local musicians—as, for example, by Isaac Stern in August 1954. The ABC was asked to restrain the public expression of such opinions.[83] Change, when it came, was once again precipitated by individuals. In 1959 the unaffiliated West Australian Musicians' Union

---

[81] General Secretary to District Secretaries, 3 April 1956, NBAC MUA E156/3/6; M. Ricketts (for Massey) to Wheatland, 28 August 1957. NBAC MUA Z391/73, '1958–61'.

[82] For the decision re the rule change, see Item 25 of the Minutes of the 1957 Annual Conference, NBAC MUA N93/3; for the rule registration, see Z391/73, 'Rules 1958–61'.

[83] Stern's criticism appeared in the Melbourne *Sun*, 17 August 1954. For the Union response, see Minutes of Federal Conference 1954, Items 89 and 90 (NBAC MUA E156/6/10), and General Secretary to Federal Council, 19 August 1954 (NBAC MUA E156/2/6(va), 'Isaac Stern Criticism'). For the ABC asked to restrain, see Lamble to Moses, 27 July 1955. NBAC MUA E156/2/3(ii).

auditioned a foreign-born cellist for a position in the ABC's WA Symphony Orchestra. As his engagement would have resulted in the ABC exceeding its quota for this orchestra, the secretary of the WA Union expressed his viewpoint on behalf of the Union:

> An Englishman who elects to take an Australian domicile should be reckoned as an Australian for the purposes of employment. A foreign-born player, who has been naturalised, should also be considered to be an Australian. The Union makes no distinction against either of the above classes of player.[84]

On the strength of this statement, Charles Moses wrote to the General Secretary declaring the ABC's intention of likewise making no distinction between musicians of Australian, British or foreign birth once Australian citizenship was established. Moses recommended that the Union endorse his position, since it complied with the stated policy of the federal government, that 'upon naturalisation, a New Australian should not be subject to any disadvantage either culturally or industrially in comparison with the natural born Australian'.[85] The issue was hotly debated at that year's Federal Conference and the WA secretary was sanctioned, but when the Union declined to accept Moses' proposal, he responded in July 1960 by cancelling the ABC's commitment to the nationality quotas, citing continual pressure from the Immigration Department:

> This will in no way affect our intention to maintain the essential Australian character of our orchestras. We feel, however, that discrimination against foreign born musicians, particularly those who have become naturalised Australians, is not in the national interest and cannot be supported.[86]

Other discriminatory rules were challenged by reference to an argument that 'when migrants are invited to Australia, they should have full

---

[84] For the WA matter, see Wheatland to C.S.L. Vickery, Secretary WA Musicians' Union, 6 January 1960. Z391, box 34, '1960', 'Quotas in ABC orchestras'. The affiliation of the WA Musicians' Union was discussed at a Special Conference in February 1955 (item 22), (NBAC MUA N93/1); the issue was still unresolved in 1959 (NBAC MUA N93/5). Western Australia is not listed as a State branch on the Union's current website. See http://www.musicians.asn.au/, accessed September 2010.

[85] Charles Moses to Wheatland, 4 November 1959. Z391 box 34, '1959'. The letter was read into the minutes of the 1959 Federal Conference. NBAC MUA N93/5.

[86] Minutes of Annual Conference 1960, item 36, NBAC MUA N93/6; Charles Moses to Wheatland, 7 July 1960, NBAC MUA Z391, box 34, '1960'.

citizenship rights'.⁸⁷ In the early months of 1960, the higher entrance fee charged to immigrants before and after naturalisation drew criticism from the Immigration Department and other migrant-advocate bodies (such as the Good Neighbour Council of NSW).⁸⁸ The last barrier to fall was the Union's commitment to uphold the principles of the White Australia policy. This clause was withdrawn from the rules on a recommendation from the Queensland District, following a visit from a Maori band who 'protested bitterly against racist discrimination' in May 1961. The secretary gave as the reason for the deletion that 'the words are most provocative and not in the interests of members as a whole'.⁸⁹ These rule changes were registered on 12 July 1961.

The decade of the 1950s has been described as one of 'complexity, frustration and transition'.⁹⁰ While the government and its agencies affirmed their intent to preserve the British character of Australian society, the success of the postwar immigration program was nonetheless dependent on the social and economic absorption of non-British migrants into Australian society. Following the 1948 *Nationality and Citizenship Act*, Australian citizenship became a status that allowed 'all Australians, whether of British or non-British background, to have membership of Australian society including all the legal and political responsibilities and privileges accompanying such status'.⁹¹ Jenkings identifies the Act as an important step towards the success of nation-building emanating from postwar immigration. Dutton describes its significance as more rhetorical than administrative, 'since legislation underpinning political rights and social benefits continued to specify British subjects, rather than Australian citizens, as the category of eligibility into the 1970s'. Nonetheless, the symbolic value of the acquisition of Australian citizenship was captured in the citizenship ceremony, the 'key moment in the

---

87 Wheatland to District Secretaries, 27 May 1960. NBAC MUA Z391/73, 'Rules 1958–61'.
88 On the fee, see General Secretary to George Kraus, 25 March 1952. NBAC MUA E156/2/3 (v) '1950–52'. On protest, see M.S. Watts, Executive Secretary, Good Neighbour Council of NSW to H. Souter, ACTU, 18 May 1960. NBAC MUA Z391/73, 'Rules 1958–61'. The alteration was registered in July 1961.
89 A. Robinson, Secretary, Queensland District to Wheatland, 24 May 1960 (Queensland objection); Wheatland to District Secretaries, 17 June 1960 (reason for change). Both NBAC MUA Z391/73, 'Rules 1958–61'.
90 Jenkings, 'Australian Political Elites', p. 2, citing Nicholas Brown.
91 Ibid., p.52.

process of assimilation' that 'signified the alien's crossing of the boundaries of citizenship'. Naturalisation, that critical impediment to Union membership, was presented as the gateway to full citizenship, with all its rights and obligations.[92]

According to Jordens, the government's objective was that all those granted permanent residence in Australia would become citizens through naturalisation. Jordens writes in particular of the Department of Immigration's development of an understanding of the psychological disincentives to compliance with that objective created by procedural unfairness, claiming that such non-compliance on the part of migrants was a powerful spur to governmental administrative reform.[93] Long-serving, ageing MUA officials embodied and articulated a prewar philosophy that aimed to preserve an imagined professional community by the application of rules, regulations and resolutions that discriminated against those who were not seen to be part of that imagining. The Union's journey through the decade of the 1950s mirrors the nation's transition to a society where all the citizenry, irrespective of birthplace, participated equally in the civic community and the equal treatment of its members was required by legislation.[94] The Union's 'rule' that none but British subjects might be admitted to membership and its requirement that unnaturalised musicians should not work as such made it almost impossible for immigrant musicians to enter legitimately into full participation in Australian community life in their chosen profession, at least during their five-year qualifying residency period. Musical skills do not survive extended periods of neglect. The extent to which this exclusionary device also acted as a disincentive to these musicians in making larger decisions about their commitment to Australian citizenship would require a more detailed analysis of available evidence than is possible within the frame of this study. However, it is worth noting that, complementing a trend within the youthful musician population at large, a number of those foreign-born musicians in the SSO in 1953 had left the orchestra, and in some cases the country, for various

---

[92] David Dutton, *Citizenship in Australia: A Guide to Commonwealth Government Records*, National Archives Research Guide No. 10 (Canberra: NAA, 1999), p. 15 ('category of eligibility'); David Dutton, *One of Us? A Century of Australian Citizenship* (Sydney: University of New South Wales Press, 2002), p. 17 ('key moment'; 'crossing of the boundaries'). Dutton points out that it was not until 1973 that naturalised citizens enjoyed full equality with the natural-born (*One of Us?*, p. 13), but the history of naturalisation lies outside the scope of this discussion.
[93] Jordens, *Redefining Australians*, p. xi.
[94] Ibid., p. 1.

reasons by the end of the 1950s: Dekany, Krausz, Pikler and Hans Gyors (George). As these musicians went on to make noteworthy reputations overseas—Dekany, for example, was concert master of the BBC Symphony Orchestra from 1969, taught at the Guildhall School of Music and Drama and recorded extensively with his own string quartet—Australia's short-term gain was clearly a long-term loss.[95]

There is no doubt that Union protectionism grew out of a legitimate desire to secure the best possible employment conditions for its members. However, given that the provision of an adequate supply of musicians of quality was seen to be one of the key issues for the implementation of what Buzacott calls Ormandy's 'resource-heavy' vision for Australian orchestral development,[96] it is hard to escape the conclusion that the Union's insistence on 'Australian jobs for Australian workers' was to the detriment of our pursuit of cultural excellence, at least in this field. Australia in the 1950s was a land of limited opportunity musically speaking, although Richard Goldner, a prewar Austrian Jewish refugee best remembered as one of the founders of Musica Viva, referred bitterly to what he called '"Australia's ingenious conspiracy" to get rid of its best people'.[97] As for the Union, its refusal to confer equal benefits even on naturalised members, as expressed in the definitions imposed on the ABC through the nationality quota, signalled the extent to which its philosophy eventually diverged from national policy. In the end, it was this divergence that precipitated the dismantling of forty-year old discriminatory procedures.

---

[95] Carole Rosen, Goossens' biographer, commented wryly on Goossens' attitude towards brilliant young Australian musicians (like Barry Tuckwell and Charles Mackerras), whom he encouraged to go abroad rather than stay in Australia to play in his orchestra. Carole Rosen, *The Goossens: A Musical Century* (London: Andre Deutsch, 1993), p. 279.
[96] Buzacott, *The Rite of Spring*, p. 189.
[97] 'How Australia Lost a Devoted Musician', *Sydney Morning Herald*, 7 August 1972, p. 11.

PART THREE

THE ENCOUNTER WITH THE STATE

INTRODUCTION

War was declared in Australia at 8.45 pm on Sunday 3 September 1939, half an hour after the British Prime Minister had announced that his country was at war with Germany. In Sydney, a number of events coincided on the following day. The manager of Prince's, J.C. Bendrodt, wrote a letter to the Secretary to the Minister of the Department of the Interior on behalf of the Weintraubs, attesting to their pro-British, anti-Nazi sentiments. John Kaiser married his long-term fiancée, Gertrude (née Pfund), a German national, not Jewish, who had travelled with him in and from Europe. Earlier that same day, in a series of night and pre-dawn raids, police patrols working under the direction of military intelligence had rounded up a large number of enemy aliens—mainly but not exclusively known or suspected Nazi sympathisers—in Sydney and other centres in New South Wales. The raids were reported in the *Sydney Morning Herald* of 5 September.[1]

It was a nervous time. Public debate continued around the issue of internment: some of those arrested in the first days of the war were quickly released; some were re-interned. Arrests continued as a domestic policy on the matter took shape. In this context, Frank Kitson wrote to the Minister for the Interior on the question of the nationality of the Weintraubs.[2] The minister's reply, when it came, was measured. He set out the facts but drew no conclusion from them, although in fact, from now on and for the duration of the war, nationality was to be a crucial factor in determining the fate of individuals.

Of the German nationals in the band, only Stefan Weintraub and Leo Weiss had permanent residency when war broke out. Of the other musicians, John Kaiser/Kay and Horst Graff were still under temporary permits. Kaiser (as he was known officially during the war years) reapplied for permanent residency on 6 September. He and Graff had already applied unsuccessfully

---

[1] 'Many Aliens Detained. Swift Move by Police', *Sydney Morning Herald*, 5 September 1939, p. 11; NAA A434, 1944/3/690 (Bendrodt letter); Certificate 13053/1939, NSW Registry of Births Deaths and Marriages (Kaiser marriage). Stefan Weintraub married a week later, on 11 September. See his application for naturalisation, February 1944. NAA A435, 1946/4/988 and certificate 13113/1939, NSW Registry of Births Deaths and Marriages.

[2] Kitson to Senator H.S. Foll, 15 September 1939. NAA A434, 1944/3/690.

in February 1939, in Graff's case, mustering support from the editor of the Sydney *Sun*. But despite the fact that the musicians were sympathetically assessed by A.R. Peters, Head of the Immigration Branch of the Department of the Interior, as was noted in Chapter Four, their applications were deferred out of consideration of the MUA's objections 'to the permanent admission of musicians who are likely to play in dance bands or orchestras'.[3] The two men were given permission to remain in Australia for a further six months (to 27 April 1940), pending a further review.[4] Kaiser reapplied in May 1940. Unfortunately for him, control of aliens became a matter for the defence authorities with the outbreak of war and an additional clause had been added to the routine enquiries as to the applicant's financial position, employment, income and character, namely, 'whether the military authorities have any objection to his permanent admission to Australia'. On 26 June, 1940, the Sydney Inspector of the Commonwealth Investigation Branch informed his director in Canberra that Kaiser had been interned.[5]

The musicians had become subjects of interest to the security services on 11 September 1939, when officers at No 10 Police Station in Paddington recorded the first of the two confidential statements made by William Muir Augustus Erskine Buchan, in which he claimed to have knowledge of incriminating events in Russia involving the Weintraubs. Exactly how he came by this knowledge was not at first clear. He implied that he had been in Leningrad, Russia, at the same time as the Weintraubs had been performing there (1937).[6] Later, he amended this claim and alleged that he had received his information about the troupe from Soviet officials with whom he had become friendly while in Russia on business for his firm, an American company with headquarters in Shanghai. Buchan alleged that the Russian secret police had arrested two members of the troupe on a charge of espionage involving the possession and sale of the plans of the Kronstadt naval base, that one of the women travelling with the musicians had taken responsibility for the offence and had been tried and sentenced, whereupon the other members of the troupe had been banished from the country. Interviewed again by the local police, he declared that he had been present at the trial and that the band was also present. Although he claimed to know the names of several of the members of the ensemble and their addresses, he

---

[3] A.R. Peters, 'Memorandum', 19 October 1939. NAA A434, 1944/3/690.
[4] Secretary, Department of the Interior to Kaiser, 24 October 1939. NAA A434, 1944/3/690.
[5] D.R.B. Mitchell, to Director CIB, 26 June 1940. NAA A434, 1944/3/690.
[6] The date was wrong, the first of several errors of fact in Buchan's statements. The Weintraubs left Russia at the beginning of November 1936.

PART THREE: INTRODUCTION

supplied only two: Stefan Weintraub and Horst Graff, both of whom lived in neighbouring streets in Potts Point.[7]

It is not clear, from surviving documents, how Buchan came to make his first statement to the police. Perhaps coincidentally, however, one of the files in which it was placed begins with an anonymous complaint about a noisy party in a flat occupied by Germans in Macleay Street, Potts Point, a reportable offence once war was declared, and one to which police routinely responded by making exhaustive neighbourhood enquiries. In this case, though nothing conclusive came from their investigation, it established that Stefan Weintraub lived in the same apartment building in Macleay Street. Obliged, as in all such cases, to probe the reliability of their informant, the police found Buchan's character, credentials and patriotic motivation to be above reproach, though in point of fact his statement was progressively, though immaterially, shown to contain a number of half truths, anomalies and inaccuracies. Not only was he British-born, but he had seen service in the last war, and had again offered his services to the Australian forces. The musicians, on the other hand, were less than impressive in their responses to police questioning about events in Russia. The police reports concluded with a damning summary of the group's credibility:

> In view of these facts we are of the opinion that these troup [sic] of artists with their wives are subjects which cannot be looked upon without a grave doubt as to their bona fides.[8]

The local police officers who took Buchan's statement reported it at once to the Military Police Intelligence Section (MPI) at Police Headquarters, Sydney. MPI, established even before war was declared in order to form a line of defence against espionage, was modelled on the British MI5. A military intelligence section, charged with the exclusive authority for making investigations of aliens, suspected enemy agents, suspect persons or organisations, was located at Police Headquarters in Sydney (and in other capital cities throughout the Commonwealth). Manned by specially selected officers acting in concert with military, naval and police authorities, the section was assisted by personnel from Police Special Squad (those officers who dealt with betting and liquor) under the cloak of their normal police

---

[7] NAA MP529/2, WEINTRAUB/S. The documents are dated 11 and 29 September 1939.
[8] Summary comment by reporting police officers, letter from No 10 Police Station, Paddington, to Inspector Keefe, Special Squad, 29 September 1939. NAA MP529/2, WEINTRAUB/S.

duties.⁹ According to Andrew Moore, MPI evolved out of a civilian subgroup set up in 1935, linked to both the New South Wales police and the Commonwealth Military Intelligence. The section was established in New South Wales because the headquarters of the Communist Party of Australia was in Sydney and trade union militancy was more strongly organised there.¹⁰ Inspectors Keefe and Watkins were in charge of the Police Section and Major William John Rendell Scott of the Military Section.

Investigating officers reported in the first instance to Inspector Keefe. For the most part, Major Scott is a shadowy presence in the Weintraubs' files—partly because security documents routinely passed from hand to hand and could be initialled by a number of otherwise unidentified individuals. I have only found two documents addressed directly to Scott and none of his replies. One is the letter from Frank Kitson advising that the Weintraubs' application for MUA membership of November 1939 had been rejected and forwarding a copy of the letter of application, with its references to a forthcoming increase in radio work, in the hope that it 'may be of assistance to you in curtailing their employment whilst we have competent Britishers capable of carrying out the same work'.¹¹ Exactly how the letter might be helpful or how the Weintraubs' employment might be curtailed is unspecified. The other is a request for an interview on behalf of her husband, recently interned, from Margery Minna (Margot) Graff on 9 June 1940.¹² It is unclear whether she ever met Major Scott, as her follow-up letter is addressed to the Officer in Charge, Internment Department. Scott was, however, the known recipient of secret reports on other, denounced, and subsequently interned German-Jewish refugees.¹³

---

9   W.J. MacKay to the Premier of NSW, 9 May 1939. SRNSW A39-1230. The letter also outlined other details of organisation, jurisdiction and cost. See also C. D. Coulthard-Clark, 'Australia's War-Time Security Service', *Defence Force Journal* 16 (May/June 1979), p. 23.
10 Moore, '"... When the Caretaker's Busy Taking Care"?', p. 50; Frank Cain, 'Australian Intelligence Organisations and the Law: A Brief History', *University of New South Wales Law Journal* 27/2 (2004), p. 300. This is not the first instance where evidence suggests that the fact that the musicians settled in Sydney had a bearing on their treatment. Guyatt, for example, alleges that the national security regulations concerning aliens were administered more oppressively in NSW than in Victoria. Guyatt, 'A Study of the Attitude to Jews and of the Jewish Stereotype in Eastern Australia', p. 88 and n. 180.
11 Kitson to Scott, 29 November 1939 enclosing Horst Graff's letter of application to the MUA of 23 November 1939. ST1233/1, N19220.
12 Margot Graff to Major Scott, 9 June, and to Officer in Charge, Internment Department, 10 June 1940 (5-page handwritten personal dossier and history). C123, 10381.
13 See, for example, secret reports forwarded to Major Scott, 19 September 1939 in the dossier of Erich Gerhard Warschauer. MP529/2, WARSCHAUER/GE. Warschauer was arrested that day.

PART THREE: INTRODUCTION

As the incident of the party and the following investigation coincided with the requirement for non-British residents to register with and report regularly to their local police station, alien inquiry reports (internal ref.: file No I/2259/19) were prepared for each of the six members of the Weintraubs' band as employed at Prince's. Comprising a brief biographical summary and a response to the Russian allegations, these reports were then also forwarded from Police Headquarters to MPI, where Inspector Keefe, the receiving officer, concluded that 'there is insufficient evidence to warrant any drastic action at present', although 'suspicions are entertained in regard to these people'—a decision that possibly reflected the efforts of the Military Board, at that time, to find a way of dealing with those enemy aliens—refugees or long-term residents—who were known to be no longer in sympathy with their country of origin.[14] Based on Keefe's recommendation to Scott, dossiers were established for each of the current members of the band, one at least of whom (Ady Fisher) had not been in Russia, and for others (Cyril and Ernest Schulvater) who had been in Russia but were not then or no longer in the band. A second round of interviews with each of the musicians was carried out by local police and reports were filed. These (internal ref.: file No I. 3306/177) contained a more detailed summary of the band's movements before arriving in Australia and of the individuals' local associates.

Buchan disappears from the narrative almost at once. The impact of his allegations, however, can hardly be underestimated. Though they were never proved nor disproved, suspicions aroused by Buchan's statements weave their way through the files like Chinese whispers, gathering certainty, framing the state's case for internment or release, and providing a focal point of reference for undermining the credibility of individuals and their families in matters such as naturalisation, security classifications, army service—in fact, in all dealings with the state until the end of the war.[15] Technically only those members of the Weintraubs who were German nationals by birth were rightfully to be classified as 'enemy aliens;' the others were aliens but not enemy aliens. In terms of official suspicion, the Buchan allegations ensured that the whole group was smeared by association, irrespective of niceties of classification. The issue of the musicians' credibility was further

---

[14] Inspector Keefe to Major Scott, 4 October 1939. NAA MP529/2, Copy of dossier—S. Weintraub; Department of Defence Military Board memorandum, Control of Aliens—Instruction No 4, 15 September 1939. NAA MP729/6, 65/401/79, Control of Aliens—Independent Tribunals.

[15] A study of the permutations of the components of Buchan's statements through many repetitions would be a fascinating one in itself.

complicated, in the cases of non-German nationals, by the continuing suspicion, set out in a memo from the Secretary of the Army to the Secretary of the Department of Defence on 4 March 1942, of the doubtful security status of 'any person who spent his formative years in an enemy country',[16] which all the musicians had.

In Chapter Six, I examine the circumstances surrounding the Buchan denunciation with a view to understanding its impact and consequences. In the case of the musicians, my research involved two lines of enquiry. First, since the band's tour of Russia was central to Buchan's denunciation and to the individual musicians' subsequent treatment by the Australian authorities, I needed to ask what could be known about the band's activities in Russia and about the two women—Schulvater's mother and Mannie Fisher's wife—whose fates are central to the story. Secondly, it is very apparent that the effectiveness of Buchan's statements was very much linked to official perceptions of his credibility as a witness. A comparison with other internee files shows that the police investigated citizen reports and complaints quite dispassionately and usually gave careful consideration to the motivation of the person initiating the report.[17] In the case of Buchan, however, reporting officers seem to have taken his credentials and motives at face value. But who, in fact, was William Buchan? Why was he in Australia? And what is one to make of the synchronicity that he was allegedly in Russia, possibly in Shanghai and then in Sydney at the same time as the musicians?[18]

Approaching the more general question of why Buchan's statements proved to be so damaging involves consideration of the particular historical moment and of the heightening of prevailing ideologies that accompanied the declaration of war. Given the perceived urgencies of the wartime situation, the police, and even more so the military, were solicitous of and receptive to information from the public. Andrew Moore cites files as indicating that in late 1939 and early 1940, the New South Wales military police intelligence unit was inundated with unsolicited reports from members of the

---

[16] Bartrop, 'Enemy Aliens or Stateless Persons?', p. 276 and n. 25. This argument was used to reject Emanuel Frischer's application for naturalisation. Deputy Director of Security for NSW to Director-General of Security, Canberra, 22 October 1942. NAA C123, 1211.

[17] This is in marked contrast to the wartime situation in Germany, where Robert Gellately asserts the Gestapo paid little attention to motivation. Gellately, 'Denunciations and Nazi Germany', p. 234.

[18] In addressing these questions I have been aided by the genealogical search skills of my colleague Douglas Hermann who, among other information about Buchan, located his son, David Buchan, in Victoria, Canada.

PART THREE: INTRODUCTION

public regarding alleged acts of espionage. If, as Moore suggests, a 'Military Intelligence report later recognised [that] the fear of a substantial "fifth column" was more significant and debilitating than treachery itself',[19] what gave the Buchan charges their enduring credibility in the eyes of Australian security agencies? Serendipitously, residence location may be of significance here. It is worth noting that a number of the musicians—Weintraub, Graff, Kaiser and Weiss—were living in Potts Point, a suburb of Sydney with a view of the Harbour. Paul Bartrop draws attention to the anxiety caused among local residents by alleged congregations of refugees in particular areas, while Joy Guyatt identifies Potts Point as a suburb of publicly expressed concern.[20] An editorial in the Sydney *Sun*, 15 January 1939, claimed that refugees had 'taken over' Potts Point: 'The very isolation that everyone wishes to avoid has happened under our own noses'.[21] Was it coincidental that Buchan, too, was living in an apartment in Potts Point?

By May 1940, the *Sydney Morning Herald* reported that hundreds of letters were reaching the authorities every day, in response to appeals from federal government ministers, and the Post-Master General in particular, for information about possible fifth columnists.[22] All reports were acknowledged and checked, the paper reported, and even though most were found to be of little value or relevance, none were neglected. The appeal for information may have been made in the interests of national security, but responses were not always high-minded, as citizens used the opportunity provided by official distrust of (particularly) enemy aliens to vent more personal grievances. Letters denouncing individuals are referred to by Margaret Bevege and Andrew Moore. Moore is dismissive, characterising his examples as 'mainly spite and tittle-tattle', since the motivation is clearly venal, and nothing more than a hysterical response to a spy scare of massive proportions. Bevege acknowledges that the climate was one of high anxiety and notes that 'much of this general public unease was based on prejudice and jealousy'.[23] Her analysis of about one hundred investigation reports of citizen complaints,

---

[19] Moore, "' ... When the Caretaker's Busy Taking Care"?' p. 55 and p. 267, n. 37.
[20] Bartrop, *Australia and the Holocaust*, p. 177; Guyatt, 'A Study of the Attitude to Jews and of the Jewish Stereotype in Eastern Australia', pp. 39, 81.
[21] Cited in Rutland, *Edge of the Diaspora*, pp. 190-191 and n. 74.
[22] 'Enemy Aliens at Large. Internments Suggested', *Sydney Morning Herald*, 29 May 1940, p. 15.
[23] Moore, "' ... When the Caretaker's Busy Taking Care"?', p.55; Bevege, *Behind Barbed Wire*, p. 79, 81-82 (response of police). An examination of the correspondence with the Premier's Department (State Record Office, NSW, Special Bundle File 41-1486, 'Activities of Enemy Aliens, 1916–41') on which Moore based his assessment confirms the venal motivation of most letters received.

however, concentrates on the measured response of the police. As has been found in studies of other situations, denouncers 'took advantage of the state's means of coercion for selfish purposes ... They rendered a service to the state—by providing the police with information—and the state rendered a service to them—by settling a conflict or removing one of the parties involved'.[24]

One question raised by scholars of international practices of denunciation such as Fitzpatrick and Gellately is this: what did the citizens expect to happen to the people they denounced? In the Australian wartime context, the answer to this question is unequivocal: internment. The application by the intelligence services of the principle 'that [in] cases of doubt the benefit should be given to national interests rather than to the individual'[25] resulted in the incarceration of a number of people on the basis of a citizen denunciation, even in cases where the investigating police recommended against it. In Chapter Seven I will look at the link between denunciation and internment in the case of a small number of German and Austrian Jewish men—including Horst Graff and Stefan Weintraub—who fortuitously came to constitute a group by virtue of their objections to being interned together with Nazi sympathisers in Tatura from August 1940. This cohort has been studied by Konrad Kwiet.[26] Twenty-five years ago, when Kwiet's research was undertaken, he was unable to access the dossiers of the internees.[27] These files are now open (in some cases 'with exception'), thus facilitating a close analysis not only of the role of denunciation, but of its effect in shaping the official response. Comparison enables me to identify elements that are specific and distinctive to the Buchan denunciation, both in the way it is recorded in and across the files, and in the way its allegations were used against the individuals concerned.

Recently, historians of internment have opened a conceptual space in their discussions in which denunciation as a wartime social activity might be

---

[24] Gellately 'Denunciations and Nazi Germany', p. 235.
[25] Klaus Neumann, *In the Interest of National Security*, p. 17 and n. 16. Though this principle was set down for the guidance of the Aliens Appeals Tribunals, its application may be clearly seen in the files under examination here.
[26] Konrad Kwiet, '"Be Patient and Reasonable!" The Internment of German-Jewish Refugees in Australia', in Konrad Kwiet and John A. Moses (eds) *Australian Journal of Politics and History* 31/1 (Special Issue: *On Being a German-Jewish Refugee in Australia*) (1985): pp. 61–77, especially pp. 64–9.
[27] Ibid., p. 68. NAA file statistics show that determinations governing access to many of the individual internee files were made after Kwiet's research was published. He did not, for example, have access to arrest and detention chronologies in the MP1103/1 and MP1103/2 series, now available online.

considered, and its impact and effectiveness evaluated.²⁸ Usually discussion of this particular issue is linked to specific periods in the war: the early months of 1940, for example, when Hitler's apparently effortless European conquests created high levels of public disquiet around the possibility of a locally active fifth column, or following Pearl Harbour in early 1942, when the Japanese military threat to mainland Australia became very real. First, scholars have shown how government policy at such times was shaped as much by a wish to appease and mollify public sentiment as to secure public safety. Secondly, by focusing attention on the actual experience of internment using the methodology of case histories, scholarly narratives have begun to accommodate recognition of denunciation as a catalyst of a particular official response.²⁹

Expressions of public concern occur along a continuum that includes at one extreme letters to the editors of newspapers and petitions addressed to government ministers or the Prime Minister, usually protesting 'the menace of the Enemy Alien' in Australia and advocating universal internment of all enemy foreign nationals, without exception.³⁰ Ilma M. O'Brien provides several examples of such generic petitions: from the Korong Vale Soldiers' Welfare Committee, the Executive of the Constitutional Association of New South Wales, the Housewives' Association of NSW, the Feminist

---

28   See, for example, David Henderson, 'Academic Aliens: The University of Sydney during the Second World War', in Joan Beaumont, Ilma Martinuzzi O'Brien and Matthew Trinca (eds), *Under Suspicion: Citizenship and Internment in Australia during the Second World War* (Canberra: National Museum of Australia Press, 2008), pp. 84–92; O'Brien, Ilma Martinuzzi. 'Citizenship, Rights and Emergency Powers in Second World War Australia', *Australian Journal of Politics and History* 53/2 (2007): pp. 207–222; Neumann, *In the Interest of National Security*, Chapter Two.

29   Klaus Neumann's study of civilian internment during the Second World War lists appeasement of public opinion as one of three factors determining the establishment of internment camps, while Kwiet establishes, but does not elucidate, a direct link between denunciation and the internment of individuals. Neumann, *In the Interest of National Security*, p. 7; Kwiet, '"Be Patient and Reasonable!"', p. 66. Writing of the prewar period, Paul Bartrop (*Australia and the Holocaust*, pp. 48, 55–56) refers to 'letters of protest from concerned citizens' expressing opposition to Jewish migration, sent to the Department of the Interior in quantity from late 1938 when the refugee presence was established, and flags the importance of understanding the relationship between public opinion expressed in this particular semi-private way and the official response of policy makers.

30   One such petition, issued by the Diggers Association Queensland, is reproduced in Neumann, *In the Interest of National Security*, p. 9. Files containing unsolicited letters from the public to various government departments are listed in Dutton, *Citizenship in Australia*, p. 68. Examples viewed online suggest that these are largely of the generic kind concerning the desirability of universal internment. A digital copy of one file identified by Dutton (p. 68, MP508/1, 115/703/553) may be viewed at http://naa12.naa.gov.au/scripts/ItemDetail.asp?M=0&B=376046, accessed 26 August 2007.

Club of NSW and the Arts Club.[31] At the other extreme, however, occur the denunciations made by one individual against another (or a group, as in the case of the Weintraubs). Since, even in the face of public pressure, the government maintained its commitment to a selective policy based on case by case assessment, security dossiers on interned individuals preserve a range of materials relating to those individuals, including denunciations where these occurred. Despite the availability of documentation, however, only David Henderson has given serious consideration to the effects and consequences of denunciations of individuals by other individuals, in his study of two academics from the University of Sydney, both of whom were born in Australia of German parents.[32]

The prevailing assessment is that wartime denunciations were fed by general anti-alien attitudes and xenophobia—specifically anti-German feelings that persisted from the First World War[33] and, after Italy entered the war, anti-Italian feelings originating in the large-scale migration of the 1920s—which enabled individuals to take advantage of the high level of official receptiveness and voice local animosities or expunge personal grievances.[34] It is assumed that similar anti-alien feelings guided the recommendations made by military intelligence. The negative effect of the application of ill-defined concepts like 'liable to cause disaffection' or 'reasonably suspect' on the evaluations of probable culpability of the person denounced are postulated,[35] though sources quoted show clearly that, despite the large volume of such complaints received, only a small percentage ever led anywhere.[36] Henderson concludes that, in giving consideration to outlandish claims, in validating the wildest rumours and gossip, the country crossed a moral line.[37] But is this really the case? Was the situation so predictably uniform in its outcomes?

---

[31] O'Brien, 'Citizenship, Rights and Emergency Powers', p. 211.
[32] David Henderson, 'The Internment of Germans in Second World War Australia: An Exploration in History and Memory' (PhD thesis, La Trobe University, 2009), Chapter 6.
[33] See ibid., pp. 47–50, for discussion of what the German Consul General Dr Rudolf Asmis called 'a psychosis against Germany' in Australia in the 1930s.
[34] Such, for example, as the idea that foreigners were making money while loyal Australians were off fighting for the country. O'Brien, 'Citizenship, Rights and Emergency Powers', p. 212. The settling of everyday grievances against neighbours, co-workers and so forth is noted by Fitzpatrick ('Introduction V. Denunciation in Comparative Perspective: An Overview', in Fitzpatrick and Gellately (eds), *Accusatory Practices: Denunciation in Modern European History 1789–1989* [Chicago and London: Chicago University Press, 1997], p. 17) as a common motivation.
[35] O'Brien, 'Citizenship, Rights and Emergency Powers', p. 220.
[36] Henderson, 'The Internment of Germans in Second World War Australia', p. 132: 'only about one percent'.
[37] Ibid., p. 142.

PART THREE: INTRODUCTION

It is likely that a denunciation of an enemy national brought that person to the attention of officials of the security services and that such attention was particularly disadvantageous in the wartime environment. So, for example, writing in November 1940, an unidentified Major of General Staff Intelligence, Eastern Command, observed that the Weintraubs had been 'made notorious by suspected espionage in Russia, prior to arriving in Australia'.[38] My account emphasises the damage caused to the Weintraubs by the Buchan allegations, statements in which a kernel of truth was surrounded and embellished by a counterpoint of supposition, with the whole being incapable of proof. But other citizen reports and statements about the musicians were not similarly or uniformly injurious. The question that remains is that of whether the damage caused by Buchan's unproven charges was more or less profound than that experienced by other, mainly German or Austrian Jewish refugees whose internment was similarly linked to unproven allegations or assertions of fifth column activities.

Klaus Neumann has written that internment 'could justifiably be perceived as the nation's dark underside during World War II',[39] referencing the psychological damage incurred by some internees. Other historians have adopted a language of outrage in discussing aspects of the internment regime. O'Brien, for example, deplores the violation of citizen rights that accompanied the internment of naturalised British subjects of enemy origin, or of people who, despite being born in Australia, had parents born in enemy countries.[40] Scholars of Australian Jewish history have questioned how the Australian Government could possibly have thought that those who entered the country as refugees from Nazism could pose the same threat as German Nazis, or Nazi sympathisers or agents.[41] As early as 1943, introducing his government's revision of aliens control regulations, Arthur Calwell acknowledged that there had been 'obvious injustices' in the implementation of internment policy.[42] Nonetheless, and by comparison with repressive contemporaneous detention regimes in other countries, as Christine Winter writes, 'the internment of enemy aliens in Australia during the Second World War appears to have been, despite the deprivation

---

[38] Internal Memo, November 1940. NAA C123/1, 1213.
[39] Neumann, *In the Interest of National Security*, p. 86.
[40] O'Brien, 'Citizenship, Rights and Emergency Powers'.
[41] See for example Bartrop's detailed exploration of how this came about in his 'Enemy Aliens or Stateless Persons?'.
[42] Arthur A. Calwell M.P., introduction to N.W. Lamidey's 'Report upon some Aspects of Alien Control in Australia during Time of War', 1947, in Noel Lamidey, *Aliens Control in Australia 1939–46* (Sydney: Noel Lamidey, 1974), [Part 1], p. 2.

of the freedom of the internees, a model of national and international procedures'.[43] Internees were safe, at liberty to organise the internal affairs of the camps and had avenues of complaint (to so-called Official Visitors[44]) and appeal open to them. As Felix Werder, a *Dunera* detainee, observed in a recent publication, 'It was all very unpleasant, unjust, even unethical, but by comparison not half as bad as being in a concentration camp, bombed out, or dying on the Stalingrad front of frost-bite'.[45] As far as the Jewish internees were concerned, however, Australia was slow to implement Article 9 of the Geneva Convention (1929), which stated 'Belligerents shall, so far as possible, avoid assembling in a single camp prisoners of different races or nationalities'. Jewish internees sent to Tatura in 1940, including Graff and Weintraub, were incarcerated in the same compound as known Nazis—a lack of differentiation which in itself was the cause of great distress for men who 'came to Australia to escape from these fiendish people only to be imprisoned with them on the outbreak of war'.[46] The Australians' tolerance of internal Nazi governance of Tatura 1 is examined in Chapter Seven.

Neumann has also written that there was no single representative internment experience: 'As the internees themselves had often little in common, and as the reasons for their internment differed, so did their experiences of the camps'.[47] I have an elderly friend who, as a young married woman, was transferred from Singapore to Tatura in September 1940, together with her husband and baby.[48] She, a German Jew who was entirely innocent of any offence against national security, will not hear a word against the Australians. She accepts that internment was a necessary consequence of being at war: people had husbands and sons who were fighting and dying; these were desperate times. Her only concern was that Hitler should not win. There is no doubt that her resolutely optimistic and resilient temperament and her

---

[43] Christine Winter, 'Neutral Intermediaries? The Role of the Swiss Government in Looking after Internees during the Second World War'. In Joan Beaumont *et al.* (eds), *Under Suspicion*, p. 53.
[44] 'Members of each State's Supreme Court who were appointed by the Australian Government to visit all camps once a month'. Ibid., p. 53. Winter notes that internees were also visited by members of the International Committee of the Red Cross. Swiss consuls represented the German government in visiting German nationals, but Jewish internees addressed themselves to the Australian appointees.
[45] Ken Inglis, 'From Berlin to the Bush', *The Monthly*, August 2010, p. 53.
[46] Sheila Warschauer to Hon. E.J. Harrison, MP, September 1940. NAA MP529/2 WARSCHAUER/GE.
[47] *In the Interest of National Security*, p. 86.
[48] Her's was the baby mentioned by Bartrop, 'Incompatible with Security: Enemy Alien Internees from Singapore in Australia, 1940–45'. *Journal of the Australian Jewish Historical Society* XII, Part 1 (November 1993), p. 153.

PART THREE: INTRODUCTION

duty of care towards her child shaped her internment experience. She was also in the family camp, and insulated from some of the political complexities to be found in other compounds. For the Jewish internees at Tatura 1, that exposure negatively defined their internment experience. There is cruel irony in the fact that Stefan Weintraub was unexpectedly made vulnerable to hostile Nazi elements in Tatura 1 having avoided that confrontation in Germany. Moreover, Weintraub's subsequent behaviour certainly endorses the view that internees who were not formally cleared of obscure charges of subversion or disloyalty sometimes carried that stigma into their civilian life.[49] The events of the European war may have been far away, but even in remote Australia, the war claimed its casualties.

As was noted in the Introduction to Part One, the approach taken in Part Three is different from that taken in Part Two, as is dictated by the different thematic content. First, the chronological frame is narrower. Whereas the narrative in Part Two traversed a long half century from circa 1918 to circa 1960, Part Three is telescoped almost exactly within the six-year period of the European war, September 1939–July 1945. As they affected my subject musicians, the events considered occupy an even smaller timeframe, from September 1939 to September 1941. As was also explained in the Introduction to Part One, the focus in Part Three has shifted from the formation of policy to the implementation and impact on individuals of policy decisions. This shift reflects the relative exhaustiveness of secondary literature around wartime management of aliens and internment policy in Australia.

Creating a file biography

The preparation of dossiers was a major project of the investigative and intelligence agencies. Coulthard-Clark reveals that by 1941 the MPI section in New South Wales had assembled dossiers on 'more than 12,000 people and firms', while Moore alleges that, over four years to 1940, Major Scott's group (civilian and military) had assembled dossiers on 30,000 aliens, of whom 3000 were identified as potentially dangerous. Detailed information on thousands of individuals was instantly available, though the plethora of agencies resulted in strong inter-departmental conflicts and rivalries over access to records and a lack of a consistent philosophy.[50]

---

[49] O'Brien, 'Citizenship, Rights and Emergency Powers', p. 216.
[50] Coulthard-Clark, 'Australia's War-Time Security Service', p. 23; Moore, '" ... When the Caretaker's Busy Taking Care"?', p. 54; Frank Cain, *The Origins of Political Surveillance in Australia* (Sydney, Melbourne: Angus & Robertson Publishers, 1983),

My primary source of information about the wartime experiences of the musicians and associated individuals are the named files held in the NAA, a detailed list of which is included in the bibliography. The composition and focus of individual files is largely determined by the administrative responsibility of the creating agency and there is often more or less duplication of material, as documents were copied and lodged across files, which may overlap and interconnect chronologically. Dedicated composite dossiers were created in the case of individuals kept under surveillance by government and military security agencies, but security investigation reports also appear in files concerning issues such as applications for naturalisation, military service records, or applications for the admission of friends and relatives to Australia. Personal revisions of self-identification can be inferred from autobiographical documents such as letters of appeal for release from internment, or applications for alien reclassification (for example, from enemy to refugee alien, to Jew and to Stateless person). My discussion is thus focused more or less in the public domain, though internment files may also contain occasional copies of intercepted private correspondence. In addition to the security files, there are other 'single issue' subject files, some reflecting wartime concerns and regulations, others to do with ongoing national bureaucracy.

The auto/biographical portraits that emerge from the NAA files share some features of what Rom Harré characterises as 'file-selves', that is, 'selves or accounts and histories of selves that are documented in bureaucratic files labeled with the person's name'.[51] The sometimes quite detailed autobiographical accounts that are found in applications, letters, statements and submissions from the file subjects themselves are complemented and modified by the analyses, commentaries, investigations, solicited (official) and unsolicited (citizen) reports and agency cross-referencing that formed part of the official surveillance of so-called aliens. As Harré makes clear, 'file-selves' differ in essential ways from other types of narrative selves, though they are not discrete categories. First of all, the assemblage of documents in the file is controlled by a principle of selection that is imposed by the bureaucratic file-master, not the subject, and is mostly subjected to an analysis that is relative to some abstract moral order (in this case, to a perceived threat to national security or an idealised notion of citizenship). The person in file-self mode does not have agency: s/he cannot 'produce a tactical lie, extemporise or

---

pp. 279–81 (rivalries).
[51] Cited in Fitzpatrick, 'Becoming Soviet', p. 14 and n. 32.

PART THREE: INTRODUCTION

elaborate, nor can a file-self correct mistakes in the corpus of information'.[52] File-selves are not reflexive: they cannot be accessed at will by the subject and are thus impervious to self-reconstruction. Finally, they may be read selectively: the reader may look for salient documents without regard for the bulk of the file. Thus, 'a person's fate hinges on a very small selection from the available file material'.[53] There is certainly evidence of selective reading and extrapolation in the official treatment of the Weintraubs musicians' files.

Assembling a narrative from this source demands a clear understanding of the purpose of each file and of the underlying principle of selection. For example, NAA MP529/2, WEINTRAUB/S, recorded by the Deputy Crown Solicitor's Office, Victoria, is a copy of selected documents from Stefan Weintraub's security dossier No 1212, setting out the substance of the army's case against him as based on the two 1939 Buchan statements and accompanying police reports (which are included in full). This file provided the basis for Weintraub's cross-examination at his Appeals Tribunal hearing by the solicitor representing the Minister of State for the Army. No copy of the Buchan report was included in the complementary dossier that briefed the Crown Solicitor for Graff's tribunal appeal, so that only passing reference was made to the Russian affair in Graff's interrogation. Although this latter fact was noted by the army analyst, this did not prevent him from drawing negative conclusions.[54]

The first task in reading the files for the purpose of compiling a narrative is one of consolidation. Biographical information about individual musicians before they arrived in Australia and details of the band's travels between leaving Berlin in February 1933 and arriving in Australia in July 1937, particularly the critical period spent in Russia, are spread across a number of files. The entire internment process from arrest to release including, for Graff and Weintraub, the hearing of their appeals for release, can be reconstructed from disparate files.[55] Consistency and inconsistency have

---

52   Rom Harré, *Personal Being: A Theory for Individual Psychology* (Oxford: Basil Blackwell, 1983), p. 70.
53   Ideas in this paragraph are paraphrased from Harré, pp. 69–71, as cited in Fitzpatrick, 'Becoming Soviet'.
54   NAA C123, 1213, document dated 25 August 1941, p. 5: 'Perusal of the evidence in the two cases, indicate beyond doubt that it was decided that neither of the two, nor their wives, were to admit any knowledge of the Russian affair beyond heresay and that they were only apprised of the happening after their arrival in Japan' [grammar and spelling as in the original].
55   Arrest warrants (dated 5 June 1940) and initial internee reports (NAA C123/1, 1213 [Horst GRAFF]; A1626, 197 [John Kurt KAISER] [Volume 1], docs 32 and 33); registers of internment (NAA MP1103/1) and summaries of the personal details of

different values according to the purpose for which the files are being read. The search for and resolution of inconsistencies, for example, is not just a matter of ascertaining facts with maximum possible accuracy, but of reading the psychological narrative that emerges from the counterpoint of converging voices, even though it is not a counterpoint in which all parts may be heard by all participants. On one side of the narrative, subjects are completely exposed; on the other side, respondents are protected by secrecy and anonymity.

From the official perspective, inconsistency was linked to credibility. The officer who analysed the transcript of Graff's appeal for release from internment, cross-checked his and Weintraub's answers to common questions, where these were put, looked for contradictions and differences and based his recommendation on his reading of them.[56] Inconsistencies or apparent contradictions sometimes result from observable 'disorders' of the discourse: a failure of language or cultural understanding between musicians and officials or even a fairly obvious malfunction of memory, especially in relatively stressful situations. Official encounters with the musicians yield several examples of inability to understand or explain unfamiliar cultural conventions: for example, the discussion of Horst Graff's attendance at a *Technische Hochshule*, rendered as 'Technical High School' (which it is not) in his tribunal transcript may not in itself have been consequential, but nonetheless reinforced the conclusion that he was a liar.[57] Within the biographical narratives that emerge from the files, however, discrepancies

---

internees (MP1103/2); Kaiser's application for release (NAA SP1048/7, S56/1/1041); Weintraub's application to lodge an objection (NAA MP529/8, WEINTRAUB/S); copies of dossiers prepared as briefing for the solicitor representing the Minister of State for the Army (NAA MP529/2, WEINTRAUB/S and MP529/2, GRAFF/H, [some sections of the latter file are sealed, but the dossier may be found in the back section of NAA C123/1, 1213]); and transcripts of Weintraub's and Graff's hearings (NAA MP529/3, TRIBUNAL 1/WEINTRAUB [copied as C329/P1, 997]; C329/P1, 402 [Graff]). Part of the army's assessment of Weintraub's evidence may be found in NAA ST1233/1, N19220 (internal memo dated 23 August 1941, page 1 only [the remainder is sealed under the terms of the *Archives Act 1983*]) and the whole assessment of Graff's transcript (5-page internal memo from Captain G.H.V. Newman, Intelligence Section (I.b), Eastern Command, 25 August 1941, in NAA C123/1, 1213). The Tribunal's report to G.O.C. Eastern Command, on objections submitted by Graff, dated 11 August 1941, is preserved in NAA C123/1, 1213.

[56] As the transcript of the Army analysis of Weintraub's transcript is sealed in the file, I cannot tell if the same approach was applied in his case, though it seems likely, given the recommendation. Needless to say, neither Graff nor Weintraub was aware that their responses were being compared.

[57] NAA C329, 402, transcript of hearing pp. 14–15; NAA C123, 1213, document dated 35 August 1941, pp. 3–4. For the idea of discourses as 'disordered', see Ruth Wodak, *Disorders of Discourse* (London: Longman, 1996), p. 2.

PART THREE: INTRODUCTION

may also be read as resulting from an individual's desire for distance from problematic personalities or situations, particularly as relationships disintegrated. For example, John Kay, once released from internment, quickly took steps to distance himself from his fellow internees. Later, at their hearings before the Aliens Tribunal for release from their internment, Graff and Weintraub similarly attempted to distance themselves from Cyril Schulvater; unfortunately, they succeeded only in further discrediting themselves. The distancing purpose, whether conscious or unconscious, is clearly self-preserving; how, then, does motivation affect the constructed narrative?

Chapter Six

'NO SHADOW OF DOUBT'

The Impact and Consequences of the Buchan Denunciation

Apart from the two Buchan statements, there are thirteen other clearly identifiable citizen reports involving the Weintraubs across seven of the NAA files examined. Each one was investigated and police findings were written up. Internal memoranda beginning 'A report/complaint has been received …', assumed to have originated with a public source where an alternative internal source is not clearly identified, are included in this count. Except in the case of the Buchan allegations, which spill across the range of files, most citizen reports are concentrated in the investigative files (including the enquiries that followed applications for naturalisation).

There is only one clear case of seemingly disinterested reporting of what appears potentially to be suspicious behaviour, concerning a request made by Cyril Schulvater to have mail addressed to the informant's home under a false name.[1] Two or perhaps four could be attributed to a generalised anti-alien sentiment, and two of these (one of which also recommends internment for all the persons complained about) could be described in normal times as 'tittle-tattle', being mainly concerned with the comings and goings of foreign neighbours. The wives attracted their share of attention: Gertrud Weintraub and Hildegard Frischer (Ady's wife) were followed around for some days after an anonymous informer accused Mrs Frischer of anti-Jewish, anti-British remarks. The surveillance yielded nothing of interest.[2] Five examples might

---

[1] Statement by Eugene Francis Caulfield, Ashfield, 20 June 1940, reported at Ashfield Police Station, 19 June 1940. Schulvater wanted to use the name of Phil Caulfield. NAA C123, 1210.
[2] Unsigned memo, 30 September 1941 and unsigned report on surveillance, 9 October 1941. NAA C123, 16027.

be attributed to professional jealousy or rivalry and are specifically linked to the musicians' employment at Prince's (and Romano's) either before, after or during the internment of Weintraub, Graff and Kaiser, and are aimed at having the musicians dismissed.[3] One of the latter, 'Looking for spies?' from February 1942, is illustrated (see Figure 23 on p. 111).[4] Out of a total of eight (more than 50 percent) where motivation is venal or 'affective' (to use one of Gellately's categories), two examples are classic instances of the patriotic motive being used to cover far more banal and less noble motives. The investigation of a complaint of suspicious behaviour brought against Ernest Schulvater (Cyril's brother) by his landlady, for example, revealed that her true motive was her desire to get rid of him as her tenant because she found his violin practice annoying. Investigating officers dismissed her complaint as groundless.[5] Cyril Schulvater's jilted fiancée accused him of anti-British, pro-Japanese sentiments, producing a superficially incriminating photograph that showed Schulvater apparently giving a Nazi salute under a Japanese theatre from which a swastika flag was hanging. Revenge was implied to be her motive.[6] In other instances, anticipated outcomes, whether stated or unstated, are only obliquely linked to motivation. Only two specifically mention internment as a desired objective. Five of the reports are anonymous, four complaints are presented anonymously by the reporting officer but the source is clearly known; and four informants are named. Confidentiality is frequently requested in cases where the complainant is identified—most spectacularly by William Buchan. None, however, had the wide-ranging impact of the Buchan statements. Why was this so?

With knowledge in hindsight of the outcomes of Nazi antisemitic racial policies, it seems absurd that the Weintraubs Syncopators, as Jews and refugees by circumstance, should have been suspected of spying for the German Government. But prevailing ideologies affected the perception of the reliability of the denouncer—a British citizen and First World War veteran—

---

[3] Gellately, 'Denunciation as a Subject of Historical Research', p. 24, identifies getting rid of competitors as a classic motivation for affective denunciation.
[4] The same document is reproduced in Klaus Neumann's internment study *In the Interest of National Security*, p. 20. Neumann's caption notes that 'Unfounded allegations were responsible for the internment of Weintraub and other members of the band in June 1940', but he does not elaborate further.
[5] Report, Sergeant D.E. Priestly to Officer in Charge, F.S.P. Section, 30 September 1941. NAA C123, 1210.
[6] Police report, 31 January 1942 and MPI report, 11 March 1942. NAA C123, 1210. Edzia Fisher offers an explanation of the photograph in the film *Weintraubs Syncopators: bis ans andere Ende der Welt*: the Japanese sponsors hung the flag as a courtesy to their German visitors.

and the denounced—aliens who, when interviewed, appeared as conniving, defensive and ultimately untrustworthy. Moreover, the involvement of the military in matters of internal security, a particular feature of wartime Australia, brought different values to the assessment of possible threats to that security, affected as it was by the external events of the war. Concerns over the European experience of fifth column activity among false refugees and a series of convoluted theories of the possible motivations of even legitimate refugees[7] created an atmosphere of deep suspicion in which any suggestion of subversive activity brought a heavy-handed response. A convergence of ideologies and circumstances provided the setting for the Buchan denunciation and a context for an explanation of its longevity and effects.

Citizens and aliens in wartime Australia

The philosophical background

Denunciation is situated at a point of contact between the citizenry and the state. In the condition of heightened patriotism that prevailed on the home front in Australia during wartime, most citizens sought to align themselves, at least overtly, with the values of the state, that is, to be 'system loyal' (to use Gellately's second category).[8] In order to understand the philosophical positioning of the Australian community at this time one must scrutinise official attitudes towards citizenship in the years leading up to and including the Second World War, with their corollaries of allegiance, loyalty and trust. These are best understood in relation to Australia's origins as a British colony and later constitution as a member of

---

[7] Such, for example, as the idea that a person might be hostile to the regime in power but not wish to see the country completely defeated (Dutton, '"Mere Passion and Prejudice": The Allegiance and Nationality of Aliens in Commonwealth Government Policy, 1914–57', in David Day (ed.), *Australian Identities* [Melbourne: Australian Scholarly Publishing, 1998], p. 105); or that, even if hostile to the regime, a person might wish to store up credits against a possible German victory (Bartrop, 'Enemy Aliens?', p. 274 and n. 16, quoting an Army Memorandum on 'Refugees: Internment, Fifth Columnists', October 1940). The idea that the presence of family in a hostile country or the possession of financial assets in that country might make a refugee vulnerable to pressure from its government was another recurrent fear (Bartrop, ibid.; Dutton '"Mere Passion and Prejudice"', p. 98). See also 'Control of Aliens—Instruction No. 4', Comments by Brigadier G. Manchester, 3 July 1940: 'We know enough of German methods to convince us that the German authorities would not scruple to threaten the relatives in Germany in order to secure obedience from the refugee in Australia'. NAA MP729/6, 65/401/79.

[8] The concepts of 'affective' and 'system loyal' denunciations are Reinhart Mann's, cited in Robert Gellately, *Backing Hitler, Consent and Coercion in Nazi Germany* (New York: Oxford University Press, 2001), pp. 136-137; see also 'Denunciation as a Subject of Historical Research', p. 23.

the Commonwealth. At Federation in 1901, 'British subject' remained the only civic status; no legal category of native-born Australian citizenship yet existed.[9] Persons who were not British subjects were aliens. A category of 'alien', or non-citizen, was thus inherent in Australia's constitutional definition of citizenship, giving rise to the *Immigration Restriction Act 1901* (the so-called 'White Australia' Policy) which, while specifically aimed at excluding migrants of non-European origin also fed 'the intense nationalist desire to keep Australia 98 per cent British',[10] and enshrined wartime Prime Minister John Curtin's view of Australia as 'forever the home of the descendants of those people who came here in peace in order to establish in the South Seas an outpost of the British race'.[11] 'We are Britain "beyond the seas",' stated the Editorial in the Melbourne *Argus* on 6 June 1940, as Germany launched its attack against France, the allies retreated from Dunkirk, and Britain braced itself for possible invasion. Inherently pro-British, a deep suspicion of 'foreigners' was ingrained in government thinking about citizenship, mainly because, it was feared, such persons would retain allegiance to foreign powers, and thus threaten social cohesiveness and undermine national security. Australian citizenship was, as Joan Beaumont observes, positioned within a wider framework of 'imperial citizenship'; 'membership of the Empire ultimately transcended and was superior to membership of the nation'.[12] Within this imperial framework, citizenship and nationality, though often used interchangeably, came to embody different symbolisms.[13]

David Dutton has written that '[w]hen war broke out in September 1939 the association of allegiance and nationality again became immediately evident in policy'.[14] As far as the Security Service was concerned, 'a person born and bred in Germany, of German parents, will never be anything but a German at heart'.[15] The argument linking allegiance to national origin was particularly vexatious to Jewish aliens of German and Austrian nationality seeking to demonstrate their allegiance to Australia as their country of

---

[9] Dutton, *Citizenship in Australia*, p. 13; *One of Us?*, p. 10 ff.
[10] Turnbull, *Safe Haven: Records of the Jewish Experience in Australia*, National Archives Research Guide No. 12 (Canberra: NAA, 1999), p. 16. Turnbull (p. 12, n. 11) cites Humphrey McQueen's speculation that the Act of 1901 was in part a reaction to a rumoured influx of Russian Jews.
[11] Quoted in 'Abolition of the "White Australia" Policy', Department of Immigration Fact Sheet No 8, /www.immi.gov.au/facts)
[12] Beaumont, 'Introduction', in Beaumont *et al.* (eds) *Under Suspicion*, p. 5.
[13] O'Brien, 'Citizenship, Rights and Emergency Powers', p. 210.
[14] Dutton, '"Mere Passion and Prejudice"', p. 101.
[15] Cited in David Dutton, *One of Us?*, p. 98 and n. 35.

refuge. For '[a]llegiance to one's nation-state of origin was perceived as a sign of moral rectitude and proper conduct;' even when the country of origin was in conflict with the British Empire, such behaviour remained within the bounds of respectability. Conversely, 'to oppose the policies of the state to which one owed allegiance ... was to be open to the accusation of disloyalty' and worse.[16] MP Archie Cameron articulated the dilemma in opposing the right of 'enemy aliens' to appeal against their internment, 'I know that when my country is engaged in a life and death struggle with Germany and Italy any man of German or Italian birth is an enemy alien. If he is friendly to this country, then he must be a traitor to his own, and I do not think it is our part to encourage treason'.[17] Such conundrums characterised official thinking about German and Austrian refugees. As early as 1937, Bishop Venn Pilcher, speaking of the plight of Jewish refugee doctors, pointed out that they had been persecuted in Germany because they were *not* Germans and were now persecuted in Australia on the ground that they *were*.[18] In the early years of the war, Jewish internees were generally classified first by nationality as derived from birthplace;[19] this derivation was the source of the problems around John Kay's claim to Peruvian nationality, since he was born in Leipzig. Jewishness was a matter of religion, not nationality.

The First World War had altered official attitudes towards the incorporation of aliens, particularly Europeans, who had been 'reconceptualised during the war in close relation to subversion and disloyalty'.[20] Only a generation separated the First World War from the Second, and inherent attitudes of suspicion, especially of Germans, persisted in the national consciousness. Economic pressures resulting from the Great Depression of the early 1930s deepened suspicion into a fear that 'foreigners' would take employment from Australians. For these reasons, for half a century following the First World War the government also emphasised assimilation as

---

[16] David Dutton, 'The Commonwealth Investigation Branch and the Political Construction of the Australian Citizenry, 1920–40', *Labour History* 75 (November 1998), p. 158.
[17] Speech in the House of Representatives, 2 April 1941, cited in Dutton, '"Mere Passion and Prejudice"', p. 103 and n. 23.
[18] *Sydney Morning Herald*, 7 December 1939, cited in Hooper, 'Australian Reaction to German Persecution of the Jews', p. 121. See also Dutton, citing Arthur Calwell, *One of Us?*, p. 99.
[19] Drawing on her analysis of the NAA MP1103/1 forms, O'Brien has concluded that Australian officials were 'careless' in noting the legal nationality of individuals, particularly those born in Australia of foreign ancestry ('Citizenship, Rights and Emergency Powers', p. 214). Jewish individuals were sometimes noted as such, or as refugees, but not consistently. Internees Service and Casualty Forms (NAA MP1103/1), used to record the movements of Jewish internees, are universally stamped as 'German' or 'Austrian'.
[20] Dutton, *Citizenship in Australia*, p. 47.

the goal of a successful immigration policy, namely 'the incorporation of strangers into the national citizenry, such that they were indistinguishable and unrecognisable from the wider population'.[21] Any private behaviours that worked against this goal—whether congregating rather than dispersing, preferencing relationships within a national group rather than with Australians, preserving identifiably foreign characteristics such as the language or cultural practices of the country of origin—were viewed as inappropriate. Achieving inconspicuousness was the ideal and conspicuous foreignness was discouraged. Such an aspiration immediately made the Weintraubs vulnerable once war was declared since, as has been noted, conspicuous foreignness, their European elegance and suavity—'so not-Australian'—was an essential part of the band's appeal, and their high-profile engagement at a classy Sydney restaurant invited negative comment. As Bartrop has noted, since the majority of prewar refugees had settled in Sydney, it was Sydney's newspapers that 'bore the brunt of public opinion battles over the "enemy alien" issue, particularly in June and July 1940'.[22]

The legislative framework

David Dutton has written that much more attention was devoted by government to the presence, conduct and control of aliens in the years between the First World War and the 1950s (when the national immigration policies came under review), than to the meaning of citizenship.[23] However, 'no legal machinery existed in Australia for the control of aliens until 23rd August 1939', when a number of Statutory Rules were passed under the *Defence Act*. With the declaration of war on 1 September, a *National Security Act* embodying new rules was passed (on 9 September, with retrospectivity to 25 August). This Act gave the Governor-General (titular Vice-Regal head of state), the power to 'make regulations for securing the public safety'.[24] The first statutory regulations in pursuance of this act came into effect on 13 September 1939. Two aspects of the National Security (Aliens Control) Regulations are of particular relevance here. First, the regulations divided the citizenry into administrative classes according to the perceived threat

---

[21] Ibid.
[22] Bartrop, *Australia and the Holocaust*, p. 198. The phrase 'so not Australian' is from my 2004 conversation with Edzia Fisher.
[23] Dutton, *Citizenship in Australia*, p. 59.
[24] For a comprehensive discussion of Australia's wartime Aliens Control and related security legislation, including the problematic features of definitions as affecting Jewish refugees, and for the chronology of the government's revision and modification of its policy as the war progressed, see Bartrop, 'Enemy Aliens or Stateless Persons?' pp. 270–280 and especially p. 270.

they afforded to homeland security, namely, British subjects on the one hand, 'aliens' and 'enemy aliens' on the other. (Naturalised British subjects were in a special class too.) Aliens were 'not entitled to all the political and other rights, powers and privileges to which a natural-born British subject was entitled'.[25] Thus, in a climate of high public anxiety about national security, a group of people—so-called 'enemy aliens' (including German and Austrian Jewish refugees)—were isolated and made vulnerable by definitions that set them apart as subject to different legal norms from the rest of the community. Secondly, all aliens were required to register and were subjected to restrictions governing travel, rights of work, residency and ownership (of real estate and other property such as radios, telephones and cars). Regulations were highly invasive of social and personal lives: attitudes, political opinions and social behaviour could legitimately be the subject of investigation by police or military security intelligence agencies. Breaches of the regulations could be and were prosecuted with vigour in the courts. 'You cannot wear kid gloves in wartime', said Mr Sheridan, Stipendiary Magistrate of the General Summons Court, Sydney in sentencing four aliens who had changed their addresses without permission: 'Aliens who infringe these regulations leave themselves open to the suggestion that they are not all that they would appear'.[26] Finally, regulations provided the legal framework for the internment regime. Prime Minister Menzies, who was not insensible of the tension between individual and state rights embedded in the Regulations, determined that internment was to be restricted 'to the narrowest limits consistent with public safety and public sentiment'.[27]

Perhaps unintentionally, the Aliens Control Regulations also went some way towards creating a culture in which information could be routinely gathered from what O'Brien calls 'informers and field operatives who were often local police and returned soldiers'.[28] Some regulations could only be enforced if loyal citizens were willing to inform. For example, the MPI alien investigation proforma questionnaire requires the provision of references by friends of British nationality (Q. 17, 18), the gathering of information about associates (Q 19) and the interrogation of 'reliable neighbours' about an alien's

---

[25] Nonja Peters, 'From Aliens to Austr(aliens): A Look at Immigration and Internment Policies', paper presented to the seminar *From Curtin to Coombs: War and Peace in Australia*, Curtin Institute of Technology, March 2003, http://john.curtin.edu.au/events/seminar2003_peters (accessed December 2004).
[26] 'Aliens Sent to Gaol. Law Not Complied With. Internment Recommended', *Sydney Morning Herald* 6 June 1940, p. 11.
[27] Cited in Beaumont, 'Introduction', in Beaumont *et al.* (eds), *Under Suspicion*, p. 2 and n. 4.
[28] O'Brien, 'Citizenship, Rights and Emergency Powers', p. 213.

general conduct and behaviour in the home—such as keeping late hours or holding parties attended by foreigners (Q 37, 38)—or the expression of anti-British or subversive utterances (Q40). The form scrutinises ownership of prohibited items (Q 29), financial assets (Q 26, 27) and licenses the searching of premises for 'subversive items' (Q 30, 31).[29] Although no specific law was passed that required citizens to inform, it is very clear from the NAA files that information was welcomed and acted upon. An unsigned internal memorandum in Horst Graff's security file, written in response to one such unsolicited report of potentially 'suspicious behaviour', states the official position unambiguously: 'any information concerning a German is welcome insofar as it concerns any suspicious activities'.[30]

The reporting of 'suspicious behaviour' lent itself to abuse. Henderson deplores the fact that 'after June 1940, even the slightest suspicion could result in internment', and that in the heightened atmosphere of those critical months, 'rumours and gossip were treated seriously'—even though he records earlier that only about one percent of the complaints received ever led anywhere.[31] To a large extent the problem was systemic. As Gellately observes, 'Systems that are hungry for information about wrongdoing, open themselves to manipulation by denouncers'.[32]

Flashback: the Russian tours, 1935–1936

However much the details were reviewed and debated—and ultimately never proven—Buchan's statement was taken to establish beyond a doubt that 'something had happened in Russia'. Since the band's tour of Russia is central to Buchan's denunciation and to the individual musicians' subsequent treatment by the Australian authorities, we need to ask what can be known about the band's activities in Russia. In May 1935 the Weintraubs, already on tour in Czechoslovakia, started a fifty-day tour of Russia with engagements in Moscow and Leningrad. While in Moscow, the band's manager Heinz Barger negotiated an extension of the contract with GOMEZ for a further twelve months (from 9 July 1935 to 8 July 1936); according to John Kay,

---

[29] Gellately, 'Denunciations and Nazi Germany', pp. 229–230, observes that a high level of control of the details of a person's social and personal life and a willingness of the authorities to respond are key prerequisites for a flourishing practice of denunciation.
[30] Unsigned internal memorandum, dated 9 December [1942]. NAA C123/1, 1213.
[31] Henderson, 'The Internment of Germans in Second World War Australia', p. 132 (complaints), pp. 140–141 (rumours and gossip).
[32] Gellately, 'Denunciation as a Subject of Historical Research', p. 24.

the tour began in Moscow on 9 August.³³ In the early months of 1936 the musicians interrupted the Russian tour for holidays and concerts in Sweden, Hungary and Romania, returning to Russia in May. NAA files show that they left Russia on 1 November 1936, and started a 6-month tour of Japan, Korea and Manchukuo.

Further details emerged from the initial police enquiries. Emanuel Frischer had married Lidia (aka Jeanette or Jeanna) Gluszkow on 4 July 1936 at Rostow, after knowing her for only a few weeks. In his second statement (29 September 1939), Buchan alleged that he had received information that Frischer's wife had been arrested and sentenced to five years' imprisonment. Interviewed by police, Ernest Schulvater added that she had been charged with treason. The truth of these allegations was never established and Schulvater later said he did not know why Frischer's wife had been arrested.³⁴ What is clear is that she was not allowed to leave Russia with the band when it moved on to Japan, that Frischer returned to Poland from Japan between March and May of 1937 to try and secure a visa for her, that he saw her briefly while passing through Moscow on transit visas but heard from her for the last time in December 1937. After that he was unable to trace her or find out what had happened to her.³⁵ Frischer's missing wife played a large part in his subsequent engagement with the Australian authorities.

The trial referred to by Buchan did not concern Frischer's wife, but Schulvater's mother. Cyril's brother Ernest was finally invited to make a deposition concerning the Russian events on 5 July 1945, by which time official government enquiries had proved fruitless.³⁶ John Kay, Stefan Weintraub and Horst Graff also testified to their memory of Mrs Schulvater's

---

33 The contracts with the GOMEZ agency, setting out terms, conditions and salary, may be found in the Bestand Weintraubs Syncopators, AdKB Item 269. Frederick Starr, who acknowledges his debt to jazz historian H.J.P. Bergmeier for information on the Weintraubs in Russia, quotes a Russian source from August 1935. *Red and Hot: The Fate of Jazz in the Soviet Union 1917–1980* (New York: Oxford University Press, 1983), p.335, n. 43. See also John Kay's summary of the Russian itinerary, NAA A1626, 1236, doc. 65 [1945?]

34 For Schulvater, see undated MPI report [possibly 1 June 1940], and statement 5 July 1945. Both NAA C123, 1211. For details of the marriage see Abram Landa to Secretary, Department of Foreign Affairs, 25 October 1944. NAA A989, 1944/480/20.

35 See, for example, Emanuel Frischer to Inspector, CIB, 6 October 1942. NAA C123, 1211.

36 Government enquiries are documented in NAA A989, 1943/235/4/19. Ernest Schulvater's statement is copied across several security files, but see NAA C123, 1211. Ernest and his Russian wife Antonia [Antonina] arrived in Australia on 31 July 1939. NAA K269, 31 JUL 1939 MORETON BAY, 'Incoming passenger list to Fremantle …'.

arrest at the same time.[37] Ernest Schulvater stated that he had gone to Russia in 1935, played saxophone with Sid Barton's band at the European Hotel in Leningrad for about a year, then in other orchestras (Dutch, Czech and French). His mother came at the end of 1935 or early 1936. She was arrested at Leningrad railway station (he thought in January 1936) carrying 18,000 roubles and various foreign currencies.[38] The NAA file summary continues, '[Cyril] Schulvater [interviewed in 1939] stated that the money belonged to his brother Ernest, and himself'. However, in his 1945 statement, Ernest Schulvater admitted that his mother was selling items of foreign clothing to Russians, and changing Russian money for English, but claimed she did not know these activities were a breach of any regulation as she did not speak Russian. In the documentary film discussed in Chapter One, stage manager Fritz Goldner jokes that the band members were smuggling large amounts of foreign currency (concealed under brown paper in an old alarm clock and the back of the Schulvater's cello) as they left the USSR, apparently ignoring the warning stamped in Weiss's passport 'not permitted to take foreign currency out (of USSR)'. At least some of the musicians were clearly sailing close to the wind, a speculation to some extent supported by the behaviour, particularly of the Schulvaters, later in Australia, where Cyril was convicted for running a common gaming house and selling sly grog at his business in Liverpool Street, and Ernest was arrested and charged for selling contraband cigarettes.[39]

The handling of money was certainly a problem for the musicians in Russia. On the one hand they were earning fabulous salaries. John Kay recounted how the band's Russian tour came about because its 'enormous salary became uneconomical for the Moscow organisation [GOMEZ] so we were compelled to transfer the contract to Gofilegt State Philharmony and Vaudeville Trust in Tiflis, Georgia ... [which] sent us, after completion of the Leningrad contract [September–December 1935] on a concert tour through approximately 30 different Russian cities'.[40] On the other hand, the band was

---

[37] A joint statement by Graff and Weintraub, dated 7 July 1945, may be found in NAA C123, 1213. Kay's several statements relating to the events of the Russian tour are in NAA A6126, 1236, docs 60–65, only one of which is dated 21 June 1945.

[38] NAA A989, 1943/235/4/19, summary dated 24 January 1944. Sheila Fitzpatrick, *Everyday Stalinism. Ordinary Life in Extraordinary Times: Soviet Russia in the 1930s* (New York: Oxford University Press, 1999), p. 53, identifies railway stations as a site for black-market activity.

[39] Police reports dated 29 September 1939 (for Cyril) and 19 January 1943 (for Ernest). NAA C123, 1210. See also *Sydney Morning Herald*, 6 December 1938 p. 14 for an account of Cyril's appearance at Burwood Court.

[40] This and the following John Kay quotes are from NAA A6126, 1236, doc. 62.

paid in Russian rubles and their contract specifically stated that the Russian agency was not to be asked to transfer rubles into foreign currencies. As Kay explained, 'There was no legal possibility of purchasing foreign values from the Russian State Bank and no money could be transferred outside the Soviet Union'. According to Kay, the trip to Romania was undertaken specifically 'to dispose of valuables like fur coats etc, which we were legally permitted to export from Russia, [thus] transferring part of our earnings outside of Russia ...' The contract with Gofilegt, cancelling and replacing the earlier contract with GOMEZ, was for twelve months from 20 December 1935.[41] Gertrud Weintraub, interviewed by police in her husband's absence in September 1939, stated that the band had to leave Russia while there were still seven months of the contract left to run because of the trouble over Mrs Schulvater. But Stefan Weintraub insisted, when interrogated extensively on this point at his Aliens Tribunal hearing in March 1941, that they had not fulfilled the Russian contract because they had secured the contract for Japan, and that the Russian contract allowed them to take up engagements in other countries (which they had done). John Kay offered yet another explanation: that the contract with Gofilegt had nine months to run when the musicians left, but they thought to return in 1937 to complete it. The authorities favoured Mrs Weintraub's account.[42]

As early as 1939, both Cyril Schulvater and Gertrud Weintraub proffered the suggestion that Mrs Schulvater was arrested for selling contraband.[43] Mrs Schulvater's trial took place in Leningrad two months after her arrest and she was given a two-year sentence (less the two months she had already spent in custody). After an unsuccessful appeal, she was sent to a prison camp at Karaganda in Central Russia. Her son Ernest waited for her until 1938 but she was not released at the end of her sentence. A letter subsequently received from the German embassy in Russia confirmed that she had completed her term of imprisonment on 13 May 1939 and been repatriated to Lublin, Poland. A message from Jenny Schulvater to her sons, dated 11 December 1941 and forwarded by the German Red Cross, Berlin, was written from 11 Grodzka Street, a building that housed the Jewish Orphanage called Ochronka until 24 March 1942, when it was liquidated by the Germans.[44]

---

41   AdKB Item 272.
42   NAA MP529/2, WEINTRAUB/S (for Gertrud Weintraub); NAA C329, 997 (Objection 156 of 1941), pp. 7–8 (for the Stefan Weintraub transcript); NAA A1626, 1236, doc. 62 (for John Kay).
43   Police report, 28 September 1939, NAA MP529/2, WEINTRAUB/S (Gertrud Weintraub); police report, 29 September 1939, NAA C123/1, 1210 (Cyril Schulvater).
44   NAA C123, 1211. I am grateful to Doug Hermann for identifying the address in Lublin.

The most detailed chronology of the band's Russian tour is that reconstructed from his diaries and notes by John Kay in 1945,⁴⁵ the main purpose of which was to show the Australian authorities that the band had not been in Leningrad at the time of Mrs Schulvater's arrest or subsequent trial, and hence had no direct knowledge of or involvement in those events. Establishing conclusive dates for the arrest and trial has not been possible with information available to date. John Kay, in one of his statements to the police, states that the musicians found out about the arrest while in the Caucasus. Weintraub and Graff recalled that Cyril Schulvater showed them a telegram from Moscow (where Ernest was playing in a band at the Hotel Metropole) when they were in Stalingrad. Putting together dates derived from these two locations, it seems likely that Mrs Schulvater was arrested in the second half of 1936, between July and October.⁴⁶ Police enquiries linked to the second Buchan statement (29 September 1939) affirmed the arrest as October 1936, but their source is not stated. Kay believed that her trial was in 1937, after the band had left the country. This date would make sense of Weintraub's and Graff's remark that Cyril left necessary instructions for the trial with his brother, and that Cyril told them the result of the trial when in Japan. It also lends credence to Buchan's date of 1937, but problematises his assertion that the band was present at the trial, though he may have (wrongly) associated Ernest Schulvater, who was present, with the Weintraubs.

Who was William Muir Augustus Erskine Buchan?

Australian military intelligence created its own certainties out of the evident confusions and contradictions of the various accounts of the Weintraubs' Russian experiences, giving preference to versions that reinforced the charge that the band had been involved in espionage and consequently expelled from the country. Critical to the long-term impact of Buchan's allegations was the official perception of his personal credibility and the assumption that his motivation was what Gellately (after Mann) calls 'system loyal'—that is, disinterested and concerned only with the preservation of the integrity of the system.⁴⁷ It should be noted that Buchan does not speak in his own voice; his charges are recorded in and enhanced by the detached tones of the reporting police officers.

---

45   NAA A1626, 1236, doc. 65.
46   The Weintraubs were in Leningrad on 21 September 1935, in Stalingrad from 5 to 18 October 1936 and undertook the second part of their tour of the Caucasus region between July and October 1936.
47   Gellately, 'Denunciation as a Subject of Historical Research', p. 23 and n. 8.

Figure 27. William Muir Augustus Erskine Buchan, Shanghai, 1929

Reproduced with permission of David Buchan from his personal collection.

William Muir Augustus Erskine Buchan was born in London on 8 February 1900 and received air force training in Britain during the First World War.[48] From the early 1920s he began travelling to China and Japan. He registered with the British Consulate General in Shanghai on 27 June 1927 and served with the Shanghai Fire Brigade from 1927 to 1932. The firm of Burkhardt, Buchan & Co, based in Shanghai, was closely associated with the local branch of a Soviet enterprise known as Exporthleb. In April 1933, G.J. Burkhardt, the firm's Swiss principal partner and Buchan's brother-in-law, committed suicide; the company was liquidated in November.[49] Soon

---

[48] Much of the information on William Buchan and his family in the following section comes from documents supplied by Buchan's son David (see Bibliography).

[49] Report made by D.S. Tcheremshansky, Special Branch, Shanghai Municipal Police, 18 April 1936. SMP Special Operations Branch files are held at the University of Oregon. See online *Guide to Scholarly Resources Microfilm Edition of the Shanghai Municipal Police Files 1894–1949* (Wilmington, Delaware: SR Scholarly Resources Inc., n.d.). At http://

after, William Buchan and his brother Reginald re-established the company as 'Burkhardt, Buchan & Co (1934) Ltd'. Presumably this is the 'American company' Buchan mentioned to the Australian police, though his designation hardly reflects the full range of its commercial interests (see below).

An unsigned memorandum on the subject of R.S. and W.M. Buchan, by the Special Branch of the Shanghai Municipal Police (SMP), 18 April 1936, noted of the company,

> It is reported that the Buchan brothers possess only a very limited capital but that their firm is financed by the government of the U.S.S.R. in order to be able to transact certain business through the medium of a British firm on certain occasions when it is not convenient for a Soviet owned concern to act directly.[50]

The company continued to deal in various imports from the USSR through 1935 and 1936—machinery, motor trucks, chemicals, paper—but ceased operation in the summer of 1936, with the brothers heavily in debt. Accordingly they left Shanghai for Manila in June 1936, allegedly to escape their many creditors.[51] SMP Special Branch noted that William Buchan made a trip to the USSR in 1936: one of the brothers had claimed in conversation 'recently' that he was to be decorated with the Order of the Red Star (a military decoration) for services rendered in connection with the promotion of Soviet trade in South China. It was also noted that the family's rooms (at 27 The Bund) were used as 'a place of rendezvous' by their various friends, 'including Soviet employees and agents'.[52]

Shanghai police did not share the Australians' good opinion of William Buchan. At the time of the brothers' brief return visit to Shanghai in January 1937, a reporting officer observed

> Despite the fact that they held positions of trust during their association with Messrs. Burkhardt, Buchan & Co (1934) Ltd., the two brothers are regarded in well informed local circles as being thorough paced

---

libweb.uoregon.edu/ec/e-asia/read/shanghaicops.pdf, accessed September 2010. My copies are from David Buchan. See also *Shanghai Times*, 29 November 1933 (Burkhardt suicide) and *North China Daily News*, 16 December 1934 (liquidation).

[50] Report made by D.S.Tcheremshansky, Special Branch, Shanghai Municipal Police, 18 April 1936. The same allegation is paraphrased in the Special Branch Memorandum on R.S. Buchan and W.M. Buchan, 27 January 1937.

[51] D.S. Pitts, SMP Special Branch Report, 18 April 1936. An account of a court case against the two brothers for undischarged debt appeared in the *North China Daily News*, 19 May 1936.

[52] D.S. Tcheremshansky, SMP Special Branch Report, 18 April 1936 (Red Star claim, 1936 visit, and rendezvous).

rascals who owe money right and left to the extent of several thousands of dollars.[53]

Various members of the Buchan family attracted suspicion as moving in a fast set among Shanghai's emigré communities. As a city divided into independently governed foreign concessions, prewar Shanghai was unique: 'the sixth largest city in the world, the greatest commercial enterpôt in the Far East and a magnet for foreign, particularly British, investment'. It was also, according to Bernard Wasserstein's account, the intelligence capital of the Far East—'a killing-field of brutal economic competition, ideological struggle and murderous political intrigue'.[54] The administrative conditions of prewar Shanghai, particularly its division into separate police jurisdictions, created a distinctive milieu in which, according to Wasserstein, trade, vice, criminal and quasi-political activity on behalf of local or foreign powers, flourished.[55]

Reginald Buchan is described in one police report as 'a shady character who associated with quite a number of suspicious persons';[56] in 1934 he unsuccessfully attempted a large-scale insurance swindle in Shanghai. Evelyn Buchan, sister of William and Reginald and widow of G.J. Burkhardt, subsequently married a Spaniard named Oleaga who was implicated in the disappearance of a large sum of money from the Manila firm that employed him. She later co-habited with an American citizen of French descent [Hilaire du Berrier] who, amongst other activities, worked as an agent for the Japanese Intelligence Service.[57] Writing about Evelyn's activities and associates, Wasserstein notes that the municipal police regarded her as politically suspect: 'They watched her movements and reported that she "attempts to peddle information to various consular authorities in Shanghai"'.[58] Wasserstein provides a vivid assessment of Evelyn and her cohorts:

> "Count" du Berrier [Evelyn's current de facto partner], Evelyn Oleaga, her daughter "Countess" Victoria Lea ... all formed part of a meretriciously smart, if dangerous circle in which lack of respectability was redeemed by liberal spending of large amounts of (sometimes nonexistent) money, in which life histories and titles were fabricated, and

---

[53] D.S. Pitts, SMP Special Branch Report, 26 January 1937.
[54] Bernard Wasserstein, *Secret War in Shanghai: Treachery, Subversion and Collaboration in the Second World War* (London: Profile Books 1998), pp. 1, 3.
[55] Ibid., pp. 7–8.
[56] D.S. Pitts, SMP Special Branch Report, 31 December 1934.
[57] D.S. Young, SMP Special Branch Report, 7 April 1941.
[58] Wasserstein, *Secret War in Shanghai*, Chapter 3, pp. 72–73 and n. 65.

political and sexual loyalties were commodities for sale to the highest bidder.[59]

William Buchan himself is included in the British Foreign Office's Indexes to 'Green' or Secret Papers, 1940, as a suspected Soviet agent in Shanghai,[60] though this may simply reflect his firm's association with Russian commercial interests.

According to his son, Buchan was active on behalf of the British American Tobacco Corporation, and of a South African tobacco enterprise.[61] He also acted as agent for Mitsubishi Heavy Industries in China; a Japanese admiral and representatives of Mitsubishi attended his wedding in Shanghai on 11 November 1941.[62] In 1946 William Buchan was arrested for the theft and black-marketeering of more than 4000 packages purchased with money from the Red Cross and intended for prisoners of war. Buchan was acting as supervisor for their distribution after a period of internment in the Lunghua Camp.[63]

A fragment of evidence places Reginald Buchan in Australia in January 1939, acting as representative of the Asia Investment Company.[64] This company was established by a Belgian financier Serge Wittouck, based in Hong Kong and Manila, who in 1940 attempted to secure an oil concession in East Timor, in competition with Australian interests. An Australian Cabinet briefing paper assessed Wittouck as 'an adventurer open to the highest bidder'—in this case, it was feared, the Japanese.[65]

---

[59] Wasserstein, *Secret War in Shanghai*, p. 73.
[60] *Indexes to the 'Green' or Secret Papers among the General Correspondence of the Foreign Office, 1940*. Nendeln/Liechtenstein: Kraus-Thomson, 1972, p. 44: File F1806/7/61.
[61] Email from David Buchan, 25 May 2010.
[62] Email from David Buchan, 27 September 2010.
[63] *Berkeley Daily Gazette*, 22 March 1946. At http://news.google.com:80/newspapers?nid=1970&dat=19460322&id=5EkyAAAAIBAJ&sjid=OeQFAAAAIBAJ&pg=5552,6269387, accessed July 2010.
[64] Australian Government, Department of Foreign Affairs and Trade Historical Publications No. 12: Mr W.M. Hughes, Minister for External Affairs, to Lt Col W.R. Hodgson, Secretary of Department of External Affairs, 26 January 1939. At http://www.info.dfat.gov.au/info/historical/HistDocs.nsf/vVolume/78D25556D0CFCD49CA256D3B0079E50F, accessed September 2010. Another fragment, even more intriguing though inconclusive in itself, has one 'R. Buchan' arriving in Fremantle from Singapore, along with the musicians and their companions, on the Gorgon, 14 July 1937. 'Gorgon from Singapore', *The West Australian*, 15 July 1937, p. 15.
[65] Australian Government, Department of Foreign Affairs and Trade Historical Publications No. 98: Cabinet Submission by Sir Henry Gullett, Minister for External Affairs, 13 March 1940. At http://www.info.dfat.gov.au/info/historical/HistDocs.nsf/%28LookupVolNoNumber%29/3~98, accessed September 2010. Thanks to Douglas Hermann for discovering this connection.

Something of Buchan's activities and family and business milieu begins to emerge from behind the veil of strict confidentiality he requested and obtained from Australian police. His reason for visiting Australia and the dates of his visit remain unknown, however, as do his motives in making his reports on the Weintraubs. It is possible that Buchan could have encountered the musicians in Russia in 1936, though unlikely that they met at Mrs Schulvater's trial. They could also have been in Shanghai at the same time; John Kay's passport shows a visa for entry to Shanghai from 19 May 1937, where the band remained for about a month.[66] The musicians travelled on together, via Manila (transit only between 20 and 23 June) and Singapore (27–28 June) to Australia. Comments in the Australian police reports suggest that Buchan knew the musicians and their wives reasonably well. For example, he recommended that Horst Graff not be interviewed in the presence of his wife, 'as she is known to be a shrewd and cunning woman'[67] and he claimed intimate knowledge of the musicians' local associates. Uncharacteristically, the police did not investigate Buchan's connection with the musicians.

It would be inappropriate to draw conclusions about William Buchan from the behaviour of his siblings, Reginald and Evelyn, though it is clear that the family lived and operated closely together. But it is apparent that he, and they, moved in a social setting in which financial opportunism and the peddling of information were acceptable behaviours, and the obligations of national allegiance were flexibly interpreted. The evidence from Shanghai suggests that Buchan was probably less reliable and certainly less scrupulous than the musicians. In falling so completely for Buchan's story, and for the image of nationalistic integrity he projected, the Australian police and military assessors seem to have succumbed to that very threat they were so fearful off with regard to the fifth column: that of failing to distinguish between the genuine patriot and the convincing con-artist.

The impact of the Buchan denunciation

One reason why public letter-writing in wartime Australia was linked specifically to the objective of internment during the Second World War was that the government did not introduce a policy of universal internment;

---

[66] See also Mannie Fisher's list of countries visited, including 'China' from May 1937 - June 1937. NAA A659, 1943/1/248.

[67] Statement of 11 September 1939. NAA MP529/2, WEINTRAUB/S. As Margot Graff was British, she was also unlikely to fall foul of any misunderstandings of language, as some alien suspects clearly did.

Prime Minister Menzies advocated a more selective approach than had prevailed during the First World War, and thus opened the door to a flow of denunciations about individuals or groups whom other members of the public wished to see taken off the streets. NAA Fact Sheet 59 notes that, 'From the beginning of the war, the Australian authorities were inundated with letters and petitions calling for the immediate and indefinite imprisonment of all enemy aliens'. However, until June 1940, the government followed a narrow policy of detention, with membership of the NSDAP as a central criterion.[68] But as the public—and the military—became increasingly nervous following German victories in Scandinavia, Holland, Belgium and France, this selective policy came under pressure.

Kay Saunders describes internment procedures as more reflective of Allied defeats on the battlefields than a fair assessment of individual cases.[69] The arrest of Kaiser, Weintraub and Graff on 6 June 1940 clearly supports her assertion. On this day, the *Sydney Morning Herald* carried simultaneous reports of heavy German bombing in central France and of the arrest of a large number of aliens in Sydney, an area under the control of Eastern Command. State police, working in cooperation with military intelligence, carried out a series of night raids during which officers in groups of three called their listed suspects from their beds—in the case of Weintraub and Graff, at 4 and 4.30 am respectively—and, after searching their homes, took them to metropolitan jails.[70] The roundup was described as the result of nine months of meticulous investigation, was driven by and intended to allay public concern over the European experience of fifth column activity, and targeted predominantly German nationals living in Sydney's eastern suburbs either close to or overlooking the entrance to Sydney Harbour, a highly sensitive military target.[71] Graff, Kaiser and Weintraub were all living in Potts Point, as was Leo Weiss, another of the German nationals in the band. As reported by the *Sydney Morning Herald*, the New South Wales Government was particularly active in agitating for action on internment of enemy aliens.[72] Premier Alexander Mair's views were critiqued in the editorial of the *Sydney Morning Herald* of 24 July 1940, following a deputation of churchmen who waited on the Minister for the Interior,

---

[68] Winter, 'The Long Arm of the Third Reich: Internment of New Guinea Germans in Tatura', *Journal of Pacific History* 38/1 (2003), p. 86 n. 5.
[69] Saunders, 'A Difficult Reconciliation', p. 114.
[70] *Sydney Morning Herald*, 6 June 1940 p. 9.
[71] Bevege, *Behind Barbed Wire*, p. 55.
[72] 'Enemy Aliens at Large', *Sydney Morning Herald*, 28 June 1940, p. 8.

Figure 28. The internees
Composite of three passport pictures showing, clockwise from top left, Stefan Weintraub (National Archives of Australia: A435, 1946/4/988), Horst Graff (National Archives of Australia: A435, 1945/4/4668) and John Kurt Kaiser, whose Peruvian passport was issued in Zurich (1934?) (National Archives of Australia A435, 1946/4/1792).

All reproduced with permission, NAA.

Senator Foll, to seek assistance in 'remedying the oppressive treatment of refugees in New South Wales'. Mair (United Australia Party) considered that all enemy aliens should be interned and that the obligation should be on them to prove their loyalty to Australia and not on the Commonwealth to disprove it.⁷³ It is probably relevant to his hard-line position that both his sons were enlisted in the second Australian Imperial Force.

The standard warrants as issued for the arrest of Kaiser and Graff, were signed by Lieutenant General V.A.H. Sturdee, the General Officer Commanding, Eastern Command, a man described by Bevege as 'rocklike in his own loyalty [who] lacked sympathy for enemy aliens and refugees. He was of the opinion that the only really effective way of dealing with enemy aliens was to intern every one; he suggested that a start be made by interning all those who had arrived in the last two years'.⁷⁴ No reasons were given to individuals for their arrest, no formal charges were laid, no preliminary hearings took place and detention was for an indeterminate length of time.⁷⁵ Nonetheless and paradoxically, procedures were highly legalistic. So, for example, because of the special circumstances attaching to John Kaiser's claim to Peruvian nationality, a ministerial order was sought to make his internment 'watertight from a legal point of view' and a summary of the case was provided for the benefit of the minister.⁷⁶ The document reiterates elements of Buchan's first allegation, still unproven, but now presented as if it were hard fact and as the main reason why the musicians were on the list for the arrests of 6 June.

Documents outlining the MPI case for interning Graff and Weintraub are also preserved in the files. Some of the reasons for Graff's arrest were generic and included that his 'German-born parents reside in Berlin' (having relatives in Germany was seen as a potential pressure point for blackmail by the Gestapo), that he was of military age, and his address. Other reasons were specific to the Weintraubs as a group (the recurring Buchan espionage allegations); still others related to Graff's behaviour as an individual and included, among other recorded misdemeanours, his belligerent attitude towards police and expressed disdain for regulations on the occasion of the issue of the permits for travel to Canberra for the Lady Gowrie function in

---

73   *Sydney Morning Herald*, 24 July 1940, p. 10. The deputation took place on Monday 22 July 1940. See also Peter Ewer and Peter Spearritt, 'Mair, Alexander (1889–1969)', *Australian Dictionary of Biography* 10 (1986), pp. 385–386.
74   For the comment on Sturdee, see *Behind Barbed Wire*, pp 67–68 and n. 60. See also James Wood, 'Sturdee, Sir Vernon Ashton Hobart (1890–1966)', *Australian Dictionary of Biography* 16 (2002), pp 340–342. For warrants see A6126, 197, doc. 32 (Kaiser) and C123, 1213 (Horst Graff).
75   Saunders, 'A Difficult Reconciliation', p. 115. The warrant provided for the person named to be detained 'in such place, under such conditions and for such period as the Minister, or person so authorised determines'.
76   Application for Ministerial Order, n.d. [October 1940?] NAA SP1048/7, S56/1/1041 [box S64].

April 1940, discussed in Chapter Seven below. His wife's ability to speak German, which she denied, is noted. Most damningly, reference is made to an article in *Smith's Weekly* paper, on 23 May 1940, 'commenting on the non-internment of this person [and] purporting to have proof of his Nazi affiliations'. Membership of the Nazi Party was regarded as prima facie grounds for internment.[77] The complementary document about Weintraub embroiders the Buchan espionage claim: now the troupe was 'banished from Russia'.[78]

Two specific allegations are worthy of note. The first was Buchan's assertion that the Weintraubs associated with employees of the known Nazi firm of Hardt & Co, a declared enemy firm with Nazi directors which did not employ any Germans unless they were true Nazi sympathisers.[79] Bevege notes that the managing-director of the company, Herbert E. Hardt, had been the economic advisor to the Nazi Party in Australia and that when he was recalled (to Germany) the doctrinaire Captain Georg Kollat promptly dismissed all employees of Jewish extraction. Secondly, the MPI report stated that 'this band has been refused admission to the Musicians' Union on two occasions, after they had made written application'. With no reason given for this refusal, the context makes it seem like a judgment of the band's integrity. In the undated application [possibly October 1940] for a ministerial order pertaining to the internment of John Kurt Kaiser (John Kay) referred to above, officers of General Staff Intelligence, Eastern Command restated that in planning the operation of 6 June, the State Committee had recommended that the whole band should be interned, on the basis of the Buchan allegations, but legalities around nationality prevented such an action.[80]

The internment records for Kaiser, Graff and Weintraub held by the NAA do not detail the first stages of their detention. However, Bevege has described how the internees went from their local police cells to Darlinghurst jail, then to Long Bay—a series of shocks for men who considered themselves, in her view, as 'either upright citizens of a worthy enemy or twice-victimised

---

[77] MPI report, 1 June 1940. NAA C123, 1213; Bevege, *Behind Barbed Wire*, p. 13 (Nazi party membership). I have been unable to locate the *Smith's Weekly* report. Like the Sydney *Bulletin*, *Smith's Weekly* was known for publishing (mainly satirical) anti-semitic representations, particularly of those it characterised as 'bad Jews' (Bartrop, *Australia and the Holocaust*, p.15), though this comment seems to have a harder accusatory edge.

[78] Undated, unsigned report from MPI Section, Police Headquarters, Sydney. NAA MP529/2, WEINTRAUB/S.

[79] Bevege, *Behind Barbed Wire*, pp. 22, 55–56 (Hardt; dismissed Jewish employees).

[80] NAA SP1048/7, S56/1/1041.

refugees'.[81] They were thus initially handled by the New South Wales Prisons Service and incarcerated with common law criminals in conditions judged to be 'contrary to the provisions of the Geneva Convention'.[82] John Kaiser's first letter protesting his arrest is written from Long Bay prison on [10?] June 1940 and clearly reflects his shock and dismay. Addressing himself to the Military Investigation Department, Victoria Barracks, he opens by asserting his Peruvian nationality[83] and affirms his pro-British and anti-German sentiments. Kaiser appears from preserved documents to have had a good facility in the English language. He writes eloquently and, after the first shock passed, with a cool head, focusing in subsequent communications on the legality of his detention and his right, as a neutral alien, to access to an appeal process. He was interned, he alleged incorrectly, under Regulation 20 of the National Security Act of 1939 as an enemy alien which, as a Peruvian national, he was not. The Military Board of Eastern Command, on reviewing the facts of his case including his nationality claim, nonetheless recommended that his detention be continued under Regulations 25 or 26 of the National Security (General) Regulations, irrespective of the question of nationality.[84] On 10 June, together with Graff and Weintraub, Kaiser was transferred to the internment centre at the Orange Showgrounds—the rough, provisional nature of which, vividly described in the 'New South Wales' section of a pamphlet entitled 'Chronicle of German Internment Camps in Australia', was another shock for the internees.[85]

---

[81] Bevege, *Behind Barbed Wire*, pp. 56–57. For internment see NAA Series MP 1103/1: PWN1261 (Horst Graff), PWN1273 (Ned John Kurt Kaiser) and PWN1297 (Stefan Weintraub). For John Kaiser's letter see NAA A6126, 197, doc. 36.

[82] His Honour Judge Davidson to Vernon Treatt, MLA, 23 July 1940: 'Such treatment of internees is contrary to the provisions of the Geneva Convention and one would think of decent humanity ...' State Record Office, NSW, Bundle 41-1486.

[83] Kaiser's German born grandfather lived in Peru where his father was born; Kaiser travelled on a Peruvian passport and was never recognised as German by the German authorities. NAA A6126, 197, doc. 36.

[84] A letter from the K.G. Wybrow, Secretary to the Advisory Committee, Crown Solicitor's Office of the Commonwealth of Australia to the Commanding Officer, Intelligence Section General Staff, 30 October 1940, established that this was a matter of some importance to the internee since, 'if the detention order was made under [Regulation 20], Kaiser had no right of appeal [as an enemy alien] to the Advisory Committee' for a review of his detention. NAA SP1048/7, S56/1/1041. The matter did not proceed (memo 21 November 1940), perhaps due to the intervention of the Consul for Peru. See also NAA A 6126, Item 197.

[85] This Chronicle, a record of the internment of German nationals from the beginning of the war to 15 December 1940, was written by two Tatura 1 German internees as a Christmas gift to Nazi inmates. Smuggled out of the camp when its owner was released, a copy was discovered in a lavatory of the London Club Hotel in Sydney, and excerpts

Kaiser was released relatively quickly, by wartime standards, on 19 November 1940, following interventions by the Consul of Peru. Graff and Weintraub, both German nationals, were sent on to Tatura, in country Victoria, on 28 August. Like Kaiser, but less successfully, at least at first, Weintraub and Graff wrote letters to the camp commandant requesting a reassessment of their cases. Since, like all internees, they did not know why they had been arrested but seemed to have grasped that the onus of proof rested with them, they could only protest their innocence: as victims of Nazism unable to return to Germany, as willing patriots for the British cause constrained by circumstance from a full expression of their loyalty. Documents show clearly that Weintraub was quite unaware of the Buchan charges; in his letter to the camp commandant at Orange, 22 July 1940, he writes, 'The reason for my internment is completely unknown to me and I presume that only jealous competitors could have made false accusations against me'.[86] Graff, too, was perplexed, claiming that 'All the years since my marriage [to an English woman] I tried to eliminate every German characteristics [sic] in myself and to blot out the German language, to assimilate as quickly as possible to the country of my choice, Australia'.[87] Letters of support for Graff from Venn Pilcher (the Anglican Bishop Coadjutor of Sydney and a known refugee advocate who frequently spoke for the release of internees[88]) and the Australian Jewish Welfare Society were to no avail, and although his case was reviewed on 27 August, it was decided that he should be kept in internment. Files suggest that the provision of references and petitions on behalf of internees was a well-established, if ineffectual, procedure before the establishment of the appeals tribunals. Weintraub appears to have had no advocates.

In November 1940, however, the government reviewed its policy on internment with a view to developing a strategy for hearing appeals from enemy alien internees, and assessing and releasing back into the community those deemed not to be a threat; the War Cabinet decided to allow enemy aliens interned in Australia the right to appeal to tribunals. Almost

---

were translated for military intelligence in March 1941. The translation may be found at NAA MP508/1, 255/711/59. The German original is in AAJUS, Max Joseph papers, Box 3. For conditions at Orange, see also Bevege, *Behind Barbed Wire*, p. 57.

[86] NAA ST1233/1, N19220.

[87] Horst Graff to the Camp Commandant at Tatura, 12 November 1940. NAA C123/1, 1213. It is ironic that Graff was clearly perceived as quintessentially German by many observers.

[88] As Chairman of the Inter-Church Committee for Aid to Refugees, see Hilary Rubinstein, *The Jews in Australia*, p. 177. For Pilcher's efforts on behalf of refugee internees, see NAA MP508/1, 255/702/529.

immediately, Weintraub and Graff lodged their request for the right to present an objection to their internment. Delays occurred, but they were eventually successful in achieving a hearing. Files identified for Weintraub and Graff record the entire process, though not completely for each. First Graff and then Weintraub appeared before Aliens Tribunal No. 1 in Melbourne in March 1941. Mr Justice T.S. Clyne chaired the tribunal, assisted by members Dr T.C. Brennan and Mr E.R. Stafford. Mr Alec Masel appeared for both objectors;[89] Mr D.I. Menzies, instructed by the Crown Solicitor, appeared for the Minister of State for the Army.[90] Bevege observes that the use of judges and lawyers in the tribunal system meant that the legal system was second only to the military in its involvement with internment procedures.[91] It was an uneasy partnership. For whereas on the one hand, the tribunal hearing had an appearance of being a judicial process, and indeed was legal to the extent that the tribunals were constituted under the National Security Act and were understood to be a wartime phenomenon,[92] in fact the hearings entailed procedures that sat contrary to established procedures of the British justice system. For one thing, national security policy, as articulated by the army, placed the onus of proof with the objector (the 'accused'), the basic premise of British justice being that the onus of proof rests with the Crown.[93] While the objector's evidence was 'sworn', the military was able to introduce evidence and reports that were unsworn, presented anonymously with no scrutiny of their motivation and with no material witnesses appearing in the court to be cross-examined.[94]

[89] Bevege, *Behind Barbed Wire*, p. 39 notes that some objectors were able to hire senior counsel to represent them. I have not yet established how Alec Masel came to represent both Graff and Weintraub except to note that he was, in 1941, Honorary Solicitor to the Australian Jewish Welfare Society and the Society was active on behalf of Jewish refugee internees (see NAA MP508/1, 255/730/143 [Jewish refugee internees]). For Masel, see Rodney Benjamin, *'A Serious Influx of Jews': A History of Jewish Welfare in Victoria* (St Leonards, NSW: Allen & Unwin, 1998), p. 388.

[90] Two transcripts of Weintraub's hearing are preserved: NAA MP529/3, TRIBUNAL 1/ WEINTRAUB (as held by the Crown Solicitor's Office, Melbourne) and NAA C329/ P1, 997 (as held by Security Service, New South Wales), the latter presumably the basis of Army Intelligence's assessment.

[91] Bevege, *Behind Barbed Wire*, p. 39.

[92] Bevege, *Behind Barbed Wire*, p. 40.

[93] This idea of the burden of proof being with the alien is set out in Army Headquarters Alien Control Instruction No 13, par. 2 Quoted in MP729/6, 29/401/273, 1940, 'Memo on Refugees, Internment: Fifth Columnists', internal memo from Military Security dated 18 July 1940. The item (barcode 389041) is available online at the NAA website. It is discussed in Bartrop, 'Enemy Aliens', p. 274. For the comparison with British justice, see Bevege, *Behind Barbed Wire*, p. 39.

[94] Some of these concerns were expressed by Mr Justice Cleland in a frequently quoted passage in a letter to Minister for the Army, 23 December 1941, NAA MP742,

The objector was expected to convince the tribunal of his or her 'loyalty', but not in relation to specific charges. The resulting confusion and distress is apparent in the letters of appeal forwarded by internees to respective camp commandants and other army officials. Stefan Weintraub's letter to the Commanding Officer, Intelligence Section, Eastern Command, 14 September 1940, for example, includes the statement 'I am interned now for more than 3 months. The reason for it is absolutely unknown to me. I only presume that untrue denunciations of jealous competitors—because I had some success with my work—could have been the motive for my internment. What have I done that I have to go through all this and that I cannot find a corner in the world where I am welcome?'[95]

Saunders charges that 'in official procedures the hazy concept of "disloyalty" was all too readily and tragically confused with "subversive activities"'.[96] In fact the difference between the two is profound: despite the powerful, socially constructed values that attach to 'loyalty', especially in wartime, it is not a legal category; specific subversive activities—which might include sedition, sabotage, treason, or aiding and abetting the enemy—on the other hand constitute a most serious offence against the state. It was an impossible situation for both objectors and adjudicators. As South Australia's Mr Justice Cleland observed of the tribunal hearings, 'I understand that the onus of satisfying the [presiding] Committee that any person detained is loyal lies upon the person detained and the more general and indefinite the charge against him is, the more difficult it is for him to satisfy the Committee'.[97] The result, for Weintraub and Graff at any rate, was a situation of ambiguity and paradox of which uncertainty, not certainty, was the outcome.

There is another way to look at the purpose of these appeal tribunals, though it is not one that substantially challenges the legitimacy of the unease that participants and scholars have expressed about their functioning. The tribunals emerged over time out of a desire to find a way of separating out and according sympathetic treatment to 'enemy aliens who, having left

---

255/2/814. (Cited, for example, in Saunders, 'A Difficult Reconciliation', p. 115 and Bevege, *Behind Barbed Wire*, pp. 40–41.) There is no record, in that file at least, of the Minister's response.

[95] NAA MP529/2, WEINTRAUB/S.
[96] Kay Saunders (with Helen Taylor), 'The Enemy Within? The Process of Internment of Enemy Aliens, 1939–45', in *War on the Homefront: State Intervention in Queensland 1938–1948* (St Lucia: University of Queensland Press, 1993), p. 36.
[97] E.E. Clelland to the Minister for the Army, 23 December 1940. NAA MP742, 255/2/814.

their own country on political, racial or religious grounds, or having been in this country for many years, are known to have lost sympathy with the country of their origin'.[98] The need for this differentiation was recognised by the Military Board of the Department of Defence as early as 15 September 1939. The difficulty was to find an administrative mechanism that would enable such persons to be identified and assessed with certainty, given the lack of supporting evidence and the difficulties of proof. If, for example, a German-Jewish refugee claimed, as several did, to have been incarcerated and mistreated in Buchenwald concentration camp after *Kristallnacht*, what material evidence could he produce to support his claim, and how could it be evaluated given the knowledge base of the time?[99] Prospective procedures also had to accord with British wartime practice and with the provisions of the National Security Regulations already in force. Early proposals for special forms and exemptions or appeals committees were found to be unworkable.

It is clear from the files that the army had a very different view of the tribunals than did the presiding judges. In fact, Brigadier Manchester (Commandant, 6th Military District) opposed the use of 'legal gentlemen' for the purpose of classifying enemy aliens for exactly this reason:

> It is felt that the classification must, for safety, be on a broader basis than that of a purely legal nature and that the direct evidence which might be necessary to satisfy the legal mind may NOT in many cases be forthcoming, yet suspicion may be strong enough to warrant a higher degree of potential danger than the definite evidence would indicate.[100]

Manchester believed that the classification of aliens should remain in the hands of the Intelligence Corps since, in his view, 'all aliens, nationals of enemy countries and/or countries dominated by the enemy, must be considered as potentially dangerous to internal security'. It was fortunate for local Jewish internees that his recommendation did not prevail.

In 1941, Douglas Ian Menzies (cousin to the Prime Minister) was acting as Secretary to the Defence Committee and Chiefs of Staff Committee,

---

[98] 'Control of Aliens—Instruction No. 4', Military Board, Department of Defence, 15 September 1939. NAA MP729/6, 65/401/79, Control of Aliens Independent Tribunals.
[99] This question came up at the hearing for Max Flesch (both his ill-treatment and the reasons for his release). NAA MP529/3, TRIBUNAL 1/FLESCH.
[100] Brigadier Manchester to Headquarters, Southern Command, re Control of Aliens Instruction No 4, 3 July 1940. NAA MP729/6, 65/401/79, Control of Aliens Independent Tribunals. Bevege, *Behind Barbed Wire*, p. 40, maintains that these differences became marked as cases progressed.

in which role he was responsible for 'formulating submissions to the War Cabinet and Advisory War Council'. He therefore not only represented the army through his cross-examination of individuals at the tribunal hearings, but by his involvement in the process itself. In his biographical entry in the *Australian Dictionary of Biography*, Menzies is described as 'one of the leading advocates of his generation'.[101] Though his interrogations of Graff and Weintraub were rigorous, he was not always unsympathetic (see Chapter Seven). A wider reading of tribunal transcripts shows that his function was to establish, given the above-mentioned difficulties of proof, 'whether they [the alleged Jewish refugees] are to be trusted or not'.[102] If the goal of the interrogations at the tribunal hearings was not to prove innocence in the accepted legal sense, but to establish the trustworthiness of the objector (as the internee appellant was called), then the thrust of the questioning of Graff and Weintraub by Masel and Menzies makes more sense, as indeed do the army assessments. Masel led the objector through his story; Menzies interrogated the problematic features of that story and the alien's claim to be believed; the army assessor evaluated the result. Whether such an objective is legitimate or achievable or whether it was even clearly articulated are other questions. The system was flawed; its confusions are mirrored in other aspects of the implementation of policy, as are considered in Chapter Seven. Nonetheless, a large number of the local Jewish internees were eventually released following appeal.

The inadequacies of the tribunal system in regard to the gathering and presentation of evidence, impacted on Menzies' ability to fulfil his role as much as on the other participants. His interrogations were entirely based on dossiers prepared by the security services. File MP529/2, WEINTRAUB/S, recorded by the Deputy Crown Solicitor's Office, Victoria, is a copy of selected documents from Weintraub's security dossier No 1212, setting out the substance of the army's case against Weintraub as based on the two 1939 Buchan statements and accompanying police reports (which are included in full).[103] After briefly questioning Weintraub about the timing of

---

[101] John M. Williams, 'Menzies, Sir Douglas Ian (1907–1974)', *Australian Dictionary of Biography* (2000), pp 351–353.

[102] Lieutenant General V.A.H. Sturdee to Secretary, Military Board, re Control of Aliens—Instruction No 4, 27 June 1940. NAA MP729/6, 65/401/79, Control of Aliens Independent Tribunals.

[103] The dossier also includes Weintraub's requests for a review of his internment, dated respectively 17 June, 10 July, 22 July, n.d. [before August 1940] (from Orange) and 14 September 1940 (from Tatura), and the Army's review report recommending that he not be released, dated 23 October 1940.

his marriage, Menzies immediately initiated a discussion of the incidents of the Russian tour. His questions are very clearly based on the details of the Buchan allegation, for while they benefit from clarifications elicited by subsequent police investigations, they also reflect the initial statement's mistakes (for example, about the date of the band's Russian tour) and its wilder insinuations (that the members of the band held multiple passports).[104] At no stage is Buchan's name mentioned, nor is the fact of his having made the statement, and of course Buchan himself, the principal hostile witness and source of the most damaging charges against the objector, does not present for cross-examination. By assuming the facts of the statement to be true, and presenting them as truth, the lawyer is able to severely test the credibility of the witness, who is of course unable to show that they are untrue. The aggressive style of exhaustive questioning that Menzies brought to this and other internee interrogations picked up on inconsistencies or failures of memory to confuse the objector and make his testimony appear unreliable. How well the internee coped with his cross-examination depended greatly on his English language proficiency.

The last two pages of the transcript and the final stages of Weintraub's interrogation are directly concerned with his relationship with Cyril Schulvater, whose mother was central to the Russian allegations as the one arrested by Russian police, put on trial and jailed. It is at this point that the irresolvable paradox of Weintraub's situation becomes clear. Here is a man who has not been accused of anything specific, but yet bears the onus of proof (whether he knows this or not is unclear). Having presented those arguments that seem to him to demonstrate his commitment to the British cause, he is confronted with a set of allegations, unsworn and unexamined by the tribunal, about a series of events in Russia about which he may or may not have had knowledge but about which he can prove nothing. One option available to him was to distance himself from the events, firstly by disclaiming knowledge of them, secondly by disavowing intimacy with those most closely implicated—in this case from Cyril Schulvater, a person who had left the band after its New Zealand tour three years earlier. Unfortunately, in attempting to do this, Weintraub involved himself in a number of apparent contradictions and what could be made to seem like a betrayal. First, he alleged that Schulvater had only been an average musician and that, although he had been a member of the band for eight or nine years,

---

[104] Which was true. What is not acknowledged is that band members obtained alternate passports from sympathetic embassies when they were unable to obtain renewals of their German passports.

the other musicians were 'glad to get rid of him'. While Weintraub was at pains to explain that Schulvater liked him better than he (Weintraub) liked Schulvater, his denial of any friendly feelings towards a man who had been his close associate for so many years and who, so the tribunal was informed, had offered Weintraub employment after his release from internment, did not sit well with an attempt to establish a capacity for undivided loyalty.[105] Schulvater actually offered to act as Weintraub's financial guarantor which, being British by birth (South African) he could do.

One problematic feature of the tribunal system was that the transcripts of the hearings were subject to assessment by the army's intelligence officers operating independently of the tribunal and able to make contrary recommendations. In the case of Graff and Weintraub this produced a further anomaly, as Graff's wife explained to him in her letter of 1 September 1940:

> It seems that your case is not being judged singly but collectively, i.e. the 3 Weintraubs [Graff, Weintraub, Kaiser/Kay], therefore, what silly misdemeanour one does reflects on the other two.

She identified the two issues affecting Graff's likelihood of release: 'No. 1 is Weintraubs. No. 2 is Russia'.[106] Comparison thus became the basis of the assessment of each musician's evidence, though the manner in which this evidence was collected did not change.

Army Intelligence subsequently (and secretly) reviewed the transcripts of both Graff's and Weintraub's hearings; its opposition to the tribunal's recommendation for release was based in part on an unfavourable comparison of their testimony,[107] which deduced collusion over an alleged lack of frankness about the 'Russian affair' and used discrepancies in their expressed attitude towards Schulvater to support negative conclusions. The assessor, Captain G.H.V. Newman, wrote:

> It is also worthy of note that both objector [Horst Graff] and Weintraub, when questioned, expressed dislike of Schulvater, but it might also be noted that, whereas Weintraub said that Schulvater, who was not up to the musical standard of the other members of the troupe, left

---

[105] NAA MP529/2, WEINTRAUB/S, dated 9.8.40, and addressed to 'To whom it may concern'. It is not clear from the file how this letter came to be written.
[106] Margot Graff to Horst Graff at Tatura, 1 September 1940. NAA C123, 10381.
[107] Pages following the first page of the assessment of Weintraub's tribunal transcript by Army Intelligence are suppressed in the NAA file. However, the Army's recommendation is summarised in the 'Security Service Black List, List 'A'', 23 August 1943, attached to a rejection of Weintraub's application for naturalisation. NAA A367, C38143.

voluntarily, objector, obviously to add color to his story regarding their non-association with the happening, stated that Schulvater was *ejected* from the troupe because they did not like him.[108]

Newman concluded 'there appears to be no shadow of doubt that the Band was to some extent involved in the happening in Russia and objector's statement regarding the rumours of espionage indicates that Mr Buchan's statement to that effect is not without foundation'. Introducing elements that were completely extraneous to the evidence offered at the hearing, Newman observed that the musicians' wives had also been able to supply information, thus further corroborating Buchan's account. The tribunal had, however, made a positive recommendation for the release of both men; unlike Newmann, presiding members were persuaded of the musicians' claims to be hostile to Nazi Germany and accepted their assurances that they 'would not do anything prejudicial to the interests of Australia or the Empire'.[109] The tribunal's assessment prevailed and both men were paroled in early September.[110]

It is worth pausing here briefly to look at Captain G.H.V. Newman. His is a name that recurs across the Weintraubs' and other files. As quoted by O'Brien, he was a man of firm, even prejudiced opinions. For example, in commenting on the work of the Aliens Classification Committee, he wrote of the Italians, 'So far as Italians are concerned naturalisation means nothing and generally speaking has been used by them solely as a means of obtaining the rights and privileges of a British citizen while they are resident in the British Empire'. 'Jewish refugees' as a group also attracted his attention; together with Italians, they were carrying on business apparently undisturbed by the war, 'largely making money at the expense of our own nationals who are fighting to protect their country'.[111] As military assessor, the potential impact of his bias on those individuals whose transcripts passed over his desk was profound; in the case of Weintraub and Graff, however, his view that they should not be released did not prevail, though Weintraub continued to be regarded 'with the deepest suspicion' by the intelligence services. Unbeknownst to him, the

---

[108] Captain G.H.V. Newman, précis of case of Horst Graff, 25 August 1941, p. 5. NAA C123, 1213.

[109] See for example, the Tribunal's recommendations for Graff's release, in its report to G.O.C. Eastern Command, 11 August 1941. NAA C123/1, 1213.

[110] The tribunal reports to Eastern Command recommending release may be found at C123, 1213 (re Horst Graff, 11 August 1941) and ST1233, N19220 (re Stefan Weintraub, 23 August 1941).

[111] O'Brien, 'Citizenship, Rights and Emergency Powers', pp. 210 (Italians), 212 (making money).

Security Service, acting under new government principles introduced after March 1943 to allow reclassification of aliens 'according to the degree of doubt that might reasonably attach to their loyalty', reviewed his dossier and gave him an 'A' (the most doubtful) categorisation on its Black List,[112] offering as its substantive proof, Buchan's still unsubstantiated Russian allegations (now stated as fact), plus the army's assessment of Weintraub's responses to questioning at the Aliens Tribunal hearing, which it characterised as 'misleading, evasive, inaccurate and inconclusive'. John Kay also received a 'Black List level 'A' security classification on the basis of Buchan's allegations, but also in part because of ongoing uncertainties as to the genuineness of his claim to Peruvian nationality.[113] Weintraub's 'Black list level A' security status was not to be revised until after the end of the European war.

In spite of the State Committee's recommendation of 'internment of the whole of the members of the Band', only three of the six were arrested in June 1940. The Frischer brothers, as Poles and friendly aliens, were not liable for internment. The reason why Leo Weiss was not interned is unknown, since his security file has not been located. The Frischers remained at Prince's until they enlisted, the ultimate proof of allegiance, in August 1943. Although security objections to their naturalisation and mobilisation were withdrawn, the shadow of suspicion lingered. On 23 February an application by the Superintendent of Concert Parties ([LHQ] HQ NSW L of C Area) was forwarded to 'G' Staff (Intelligence) HQ NSW L of C Area, requesting permission to transfer the brothers to the 2 Australian Division Concert Party, 'as they are outstanding musicians'. Referred back to the Security Service for screening, the Deputy Director of Security (NSW) advised that

> Prior to and shortly after arrival in the Commonwealth, N464208 Pte. FRISCHER E. was a member of a group of persons concerning whom inquiries are at present being made outside the Commonwealth. Until the result of these inquiries is known, this Service is unable to

---

[112] Document dated 21 August 1943. NAA A367/C38143. For a full discussion of the Aliens Classification and Advisory Committee's recommendations and details of the categories, see David Dutton '"Mere Passion and Prejudice"', pp. 104–106. For the full report, see Lamidey, *Aliens Control in Australia 1939–46*, Part 2: Aliens Classification and Advisory Committee Interim Report, Canberra March 1943. Dossiers continued to be reviewed by the Security Services, even when the subject had been 'cleared' by the tribunal. See report dated November 1944 in C123/1, 1213 (Horst Graff).

[113] NAA A6126, 1236, doc. 15 (21 August 1943). See also docs 114–116, esp. 114, 'Personal Particulars Sheet (P.P.S.)'. Weintraub's wife Gertrud received a 'B' classification, since 'suspicion attaches to her as certain members of the Orchestra were charged with espionage in the Soviet [sic] and finally all were deported'. Internal memorandum, Security Service, Sydney, 21 August 1943. NAA A367, C72133.

say that E. FRISCHER is without suspicion and it is felt that for the present, and until the inquiries are completed, FRISCHER should not be employed in a capacity that would involve service in a forward area.

Of N464017 Pte. A. Frischer, utterly blameless in the Russian affair as he had not been there, the memo states that 'he is not adversely recorded here, but any suspicion which might eventually attach to his brother might also concern him' and thus he too should not go to a forward area. A further internal memo from the Deputy Director of Security (NSW), 15 August 1944, perpetuates the same conundrum: 'Though nothing concrete against subject [Emanuel Frischer], as a member of "Weintraub's Band" for many years, an element of suspicion must attach pending information to clarify'. At the same time the memo records yet another contradictory recommendation: 'not now considered as Security risk'.[114]

Late in 1943, the Australian Security Service concluded a three-year investigation into John Kay's claim to Peruvian nationality, during the process of which Kay 'offered to give any information that he possessed regarding the WEINTRAUBS'.[115] Before accepting Kay's offer, officials determined to contact the Australian Legation in Russia in an attempt to determine the truth of Buchan's espionage allegations. Following exhaustive enquiries and based on advice received from the Australian legation in Moscow in December 1944, it was concluded that 'No information has been forthcoming and we believe none [is] likely to be'.[116] With the end of the European war, the musicians were invited to make their statements, a decision was made to accept their version of what happened in Russia and this matter, which had caused so much grief to the individuals implicated, was simply dropped.[117]

In her essay 'Signals from Below', a study of denunciation in the Soviet Union in the 1930s, Sheila Fitzpatrick writes, 'Denunciations are never written in a vacuum … People write the kind of denunciations they think are likely to be heard and acted upon by authority… they denounce offenses

---

[114] NAA C123, 1211. Documents dated 23 February, 8 and 9 March, 15 August and 15 December 1944. The abbreviations unpack as [Land headquarters], Headquarters, NSW Lines of Communication Area [Boronia Park].
[115] Internal memorandum dated 19 November 1943. NAA A989, 1943/235/4/19.
[116] Cablegram from Australian Legation, Moscow, to Security Service, 10 December 1944. NAA A989, 1943/235/4/19.
[117] Report, Deputy Director of Security, NSW, to Acting Inspector, CIB, on Leo Weiss's application for naturalisation, 13 July 1945. NAA A435, 1947/4/2710.

that authority condemns and punishes'.[118] It is easy, then, to see why, in a wartime setting, Buchan's accusation that the Weintraubs were engaged in espionage would have elicited a strong response from the Australian military authorities. But it seems highly unlikely that the charge was true. Why then, did he make it? This fundamental question remains unanswered.

Much of the discussion of denunciation in the Australian literature focuses on its absurdity and its single objective of internment; often, it becomes one more element in a critique of the internment regime. Apart from Henderson's chapter and article on the two Sydney academics referred to earlier, little attention is given to the impact of these 'accusatory letters' (the phrase is Fitzpatrick's). But denunciation fed into a complex of ideologies, uncertainties, paranoia and legitimate fears, with profound and often damaging effects for the individuals concerned. The fact that Buchan's allegations could never satisfactorily be either proved or disproved gave them great weight at a time when the operation of a principle of 'reasonable doubt' carried such consequences and the military was obsessed with establishing 'proofs' for refugee aliens. Prejudice informed the official response: Buchan's credentials were never interrogated, though documents suggest they might well have been. Certainty was attributed to the idea that 'something had happened in Russia' because the alleged perpetrators, who had probably not been involved in the events that did occur, could therefore not remember them convincingly or consistently.

In its Interim Report, submitted to H.V. Evatt in his role of Attorney-General in John Curtin's Labor government in 1943, the Aliens Classification and Advisory Committee addressed the very issue of the appeals tribunals' reliance on citizen reports and the 'very real and positive danger' this reliance represented. While affirming its commitment to the principle that 'where there is a conflict between the needs of the nation and the interest of an individual ... the welfare of the nation must come first', the committee nevertheless expressed its concern

> to see that the existence of Security mechanism does not give encouragement to secret delation, and that persons resident in this country are not exposed to injury by spiteful persons whose malicious talk and idle gossip is recorded as confidential, and, whilst relied on as a ground for repressive action against the person concerned is by reason of a pledge of confidence, not capable of being divulged or made available to a Tribunal hearing an objection.

---

[118] Fitzpatrick, 'Signals from Below' in *Tear Off the Masks!*, p. 237.

Citing Article 9 of the Sankey Declaration of the Rights of Man,[119] the committee recommended against the continued use of security dossiers as secret evidence against objectors: 'a dossier is merely a memorandum for administrative use; it shall not be used as evidence without proper confirmation in open court'.[120] The use of the word 'delation' is noteworthy. It comes from the French, and denotes the distinction, also in earlier English usage, between 'bad (treacherous/self-interested) denunciation [*délation*]' and 'good (public-spirited) denunciation [*dénonciation*]'.[121] In the case of the Weintraubs, however, as has been shown, the damaging effects of Buchan's denunciations were not so quickly undone.

---

[119] A charter prepared in 1940, under the Chairmanship of Lord Sankey, and originally drafted for discussion by H. G. Wells. At http://www.voting.ukscientists.com/sankey.html, accessed September 2010.
[120] Lamidey, *Aliens Control in Australia, 1939–46*, Part 2: p. 17.
[121] See Sheila Fitzpatrick, 'Introduction: VI. Discourses of Denunciation', in Fitzpatrick and Gellately (eds), *Accusatory Practices*, pp. 17–18.

Chapter Seven

'I CANNOT FIND A CORNER IN THE WORLD WHERE I AM WELCOME'[1]

The Internment Experience of Stefan Weintraub and Horst Graff (June 1940 – September 1941)

Historian Joan Beaumont has written that 'the story of internment is … important for what it tells us about the ambiguous construction of Australian citizenship in the mid-twentieth century'.[2] Lacking a formal definition of citizenship, Australians were classified as 'British subjects', a status which could be acquired either by birth or naturalisation. As Beaumont points out, however, citizenship also had 'a number of other, more subjective dimensions'.[3] It is these more subjective ideas of what constituted a good and loyal citizen that shaped official assessments of the Buchan denunciation of the Weintraubs, of unfavourable reports of other enemy nationals including Jewish refugees, and of the plausibility of denouncer and denounced.

Citizenship, loyalty, and the question of military service

Both Dutton and Beaumont have noted that a willingness to undertake military service is at the core of twentieth-century Australian notions of allegiance and citizenship.[4] With regard to refugees, Beaumont discusses the Australian Government's initially negative position on military service by aliens, even when the latter were eager or willing to serve. The matter can,

---

[1] Stefan Weintraub to Officer in Charge, Intelligence Section, Victoria Barracks, Sydney, 14 September 1940. NAA MP529/2, WEINTRAUB/S.
[2] Joan Beaumont, 'Introduction', in Beaumont *et al.* (eds), *Under Suspicion*, p. 4.
[3] Ibid., p. 5.
[4] Dutton, *One of Us?*, p. 124; Beaumont, 'Introduction', pp. 5–6.

however, be looked at from a different angle. One question on the army's internee questionnaire (NAA MP1103/2) concerns a statement of prior war service. This may be a consequence of the same form being used for internees and prisoners of war, though the information is reproduced across other documents.[5] But service in the German forces during the First World War was a further marker of a possible conflict of loyalties, especially for those who, like Stefan Weintraub, had been decorated for their service.

The matter of German military service was confusing enough for highly assimilated European Jews themselves. Martin Gilbert quotes the recollections of one Jewish refugee who, describing his father's efforts to obtain enough money for food by sweeping the streets in Aschaffenburg, commented 'What humiliation for a man ... who had fought for Germany in the First World War and won the Iron Cross'. Michael Abrahams-Sprod tells how another refugee, crossing the German-French border at Strasbourg in late 1938 en route for Canada and Australia, took his Iron Cross from his pocket and threw it into the Rhine.[6] Within Germany, military service in the First World War was an important benchmark for members of the Nazi Party.[7] For Jewish First World War veterans, ownership of an Iron Cross brought with it short-term benefits under the Nazi regime. Despite the Law on the Admission to the Legal Profession disallowing the admission of Jews to the bar (7 April 1933), for example, Jewish lawyer Max Flesch was allowed to continue practicing (until the end of November 1938) in consideration of his war service.[8] Later, exemptions for veterans included delayed ghettoisation and deportation, or removal to the 'model' camp at Theresienstadt.[9] In Australia, a country that one generation earlier

---

[5] For example, in the Army's précis of the Weintraub case in response to the recommendation for his release by the Aliens Tribunal, 23 August 1941. NAA ST 1233/1, N19220. It is not clear from this (incomplete) document how his military service was viewed by the assessing officer.

[6] Martin Gilbert, *Kristallnacht: Prelude to Disaster* (London: HarperPress, 2006), p. 253; Michael Abrahams-Sprod, "Australien! Wo ist den das?" The Migration Experience of Jewish Refugees from Nazi Germany', *Australian Journal of Jewish Studies* 17 (2004): p. 19.

[7] Henderson, 'The Internment of Germans', p. 58. In the early 1920s the Nazi Party recruited former First World War soldiers.

[8] NAA MP529/3, TRIBUNAL1/FLESCH, transcript of evidence of objection, pp. 2–3, 13. The first anti-Jewish laws for public officials and members of the legal profession contained a clause exempting veterans from dismissal.

[9] Gilbert, *Kristallnacht*, pp. 256, 258; Randolph L. Braham, *The Politics of Genocide: the Holocaust in Hungary* (Detroit: Wayne State University Press, 2000), p. 102; Wannsee protocols, at http://remember.org/wannsee.html, accessed August 2010. A large number of the medals (first and second class) were issued: one site gives the figures of 218,000 First Class and 5,200,000 Second Class awards. http://www.theaerodrome.com/medals/germany/prussia_ic.php, accessed August 2010.

had suffered 60,000 soldiers killed and around 90,000 more permanently disabled in the conflict,[10] the issue of aliens' war service was certainly likely to cause public disaffection and provide the military with reasonable grounds for suspicion. In this context, the internment of enemy nationals 'of military age' takes on a different significance. Any refugee born before 1900 was likely to have served, since conscription was standard policy in prewar Germany; younger refugees had fathers who would have served.

Historians have tended to view Australia's prewar refugee policy through the prism of the Holocaust: how much was known, why more refugees were not accepted and so forth. But the *reception* of individual refugees needs also to be considered in the context of the devastating aftermath of the First World War. Ken Inglis has written, 'If we count as family a person's parents, children, siblings, aunts and uncles and cousins, then every second Australian family was bereaved by the war'.[11] He provides some stark statistics in support of this claim. One in five of the 330, 770 who enlisted was killed; two out of every three Australians in uniform died or were wounded. The proportion of casualties to embarkations was 68.5 percent, a higher percentage even than the British army's 52.5 percent, because Australians were almost all sent to battlefields. Despite the place occupied by Gallipoli in the national mythology, three out of every four Australians killed died fighting the Germans in France or Belgium.[12] Inglis further points out that 80 percent of the AIF (Australian Imperial Force) were unmarried; one might say that almost a whole generation of potential husbands and fathers was killed or maimed. If the women these men might have married were in their twenties in 1918, they were in their forties in 1939, a fact that may go some way to explain the anguish and outrage that shows through in some citizen protests against 'enemy aliens' remaining at large during the Second World War.[13]

Australians were still living with the effects of the First World War when the Second World War broke out. Marina Larsson, who has studied the impact on the nation of those who returned wounded, her 'shattered Anzacs', notes that 'At the outbreak of the Second World War, over 77,000

---

[10] Ken Inglis, *Sacred Places. War Memorials in the Australian Landscape* (Melbourne: The Miegunyah Press, 1998); Marina Larsson, *Shattered Anzacs: Living with the Scars of War* (Sydney: UNSW Press, 2009).
[11] Inglis, *Sacred Places*, p. 97.
[12] Ibid., pp. 91–92; p. 92 (two out of three) and p. 97 (80 percent unmarried).
[13] For example, Mary Isaacs' statement against Kurt Herweg, 29 July 1940: 'I had six brothers fighting in the Great War and really I don't know why these people are allowed to be at large … ' NAA MP529/2, HERWEG/K.

veterans of the First AIF were still living with a war disability. Three were dying each day from their wounds'.[14] Larsson argues eloquently that war wounds were family wounds. It would be a mistake to underestimate the extent and depth of feeling that attached to such experiences of grief, loss and suffering. We are not speaking here simply of xenophobia but of a profound, complex and widespread national trauma, albeit one that has been obscured by more dominant, collective national mythologies of the Great War.[15]

Larsson notes that 'most injuries did not involve missing body parts, but took the form of invisible damage to organs, bones, muscles and other bodily systems'. For example, soldiers experienced respiratory problems due to exposure to poisonous gas.[16] Jewish internee Herbert Smolka, an engineer, was identified as a commissioned officer who, during the First World War, was responsible for the release of poisonous gas on allied troops.[17] With the coming of the Third Reich, his Austrian non-Jewish wife divorced him, his mother committed suicide and their property in Germany was confiscated. But how was his plea for special treatment as a Jew to be understood by people who could not yet see that Jewish Germans were also victims? Is it surprising that, in the circumstance of another war, Australians closed ranks against a group of people who, two decades earlier, had literally, not hypothetically, been 'the enemy'? Is it any wonder that fifth column anxieties took such hold?

Denunciation and frame conflict

It is generally acknowledged in the literature that internment policy was very fluid, since it took shape as a series of responses to the unfolding events of the war.[18] Accordingly, it is possible to scan the files and find quotations to support a variety of interpretations: from Bevege's widely viewed as uncritical account of internment as 'a mostly justified response to a genuine alien threat',[19] to the 'revisionist' view of writers such as Saunders and O'Brien, who have critiqued the treatment of naturalised internees or

---

[14] Larsson, *Shattered Anzacs*, pp. 18–19 and nn. 7, 8.
[15] That this trauma is unrecognised is one of Larsson's central theses. *Shattered Anzacs*, pp. 22, 265.
[16] Ibid., p. 19.
[17] See the police report, 10 September 1939, in NAA MP509/2, SCHMOLKA/HD. In February 1940 he offered his expertise to the Allied cause.
[18] Bevege is one historian who stresses the fluidity of internment policy.
[19] Dutton, *One of Us?*, p. 97.

those native-born of foreign ancestry, and emphasised the underlying role of xenophobia, racism and Anglo-Australian chauvinism.[20]

On the question of the unjust internment of German and Austrian Jewish refugees, I would like to argue the importance of frame conflict, hinging on the issue of military service during the First World War.[21] An example is provided by the dossier of one of the Tatura 1 Jewish internees. Nineteen-year-old Peter Wolff was a German-Jewish pastry cook who arrived in Fremantle on 21 March 1939. On 26 October 1940, Wolff was reported to army headquarters as having made statements of a disloyal nature to other passengers on the ship from Western Australia to Sydney. He was alleged to have said, 'I am a German. My father is a German, and he fought for Germany in the last war'. Questioned by police, Wolff gave a rather different account of the incident. He claimed that in conversation with another passenger he answered 'yes' to a series of questions: 'Are you a German? Is your father German? Did he fight in the last war?' As a Jew fleeing into exile, Wolff may well have continued, as did many highly assimilated German Jews who fought for the Kaiser and thought of themselves first of all as Germans, 'This being so, why are we being persecuted?' His interlocutor, however, had a different response: 'His questioner then got agitated and said, "I fought in the last war and lost two brothers there"'.

Wolff's internment was based on the reports of this shipboard conversation.[22] But one can clearly see, first how it was misrepresented, and then how it was misunderstood, a misunderstanding that arose out of mutually incompatible conceptual frames, or intractable interpretations of the same set of events. Bevege quotes the responses of the commanding officers of the administrative Commands to the suggestion that, in order to separate refugees from other German nationals, independent tribunals might be set up. Lieutenant General V.A.H. Sturdee of Eastern Command, who signed the arrest warrants for Weintraub and Graff, was quite clear. He responded

---

20 Saunders, 'A Difficult Reconciliation', pp. 136–137; O'Brien, 'Citizenship, Rights and Emergency Powers'.

21 Donald A. Schön, an American theorist who developed the concept of 'frame conflict', defined it as 'arising when "several different stories about the same situation" are constructed; "each story is internally coherent and compelling in its own terms but different from and perhaps incompatible with all the others"'. Cited at http://books.google.com/books?id=QiJRvuXA_VcC&pg=PA296&lpg=PA296&dq=arising+when+se-veral+diff, accessed September 2010. The idea of 'frame conflict' as occurring when worlds of knowledge and interest collide with one another is also discussed by Wodak, *Disorders of Discourse*, p. 2.

22 See Wolff's letter [to the Camp Commandant] from Orange, 22 July 1940 and Sergeant 3C Paramatta to Inspector Keefe, 2 April 1940. NAA MP529/2, WOLFF/KP.

that '"the only really effective way of dealing with enemy aliens" was to intern them all before "setting up a tribunal to review the cases of internees who consider that they can submit proof that they are traitors to their own country"'.[23] Read in the context of the whole document in which it appears, Sturdee's remark is quite startling—a sudden eruption of apparent prejudice in what is otherwise a measured, if critical, assessment of the viability of appeals tribunals for this class of internees, a continuation of an internal discussion that had been proceeding since September 1939. His remark does not show any great degree of understanding of or sympathy for the true status of the refugees but, although it references circumstances specifically related to the internees' Jewishness, it is not antisemitic. Sturdee is a First World War veteran and a professional soldier in a position of command who is applying the (inflexible) precepts of the military code to a group of men, some of whom were formerly soldiers, who claimed to have changed allegiance.

Internment and the German and Austrian Jewish refugees

The ambivalent position of the prewar German and Austrian Jewish refugees within the general population of the recipient countries has been well canvassed in the literature. Central to the discussion about Jewish refugees in Australia is a consideration of how Jews fitted within the country's racial discourse and, specifically, of the presumed link between the construction of Jews as a race and their nationality.[24] On this point, Dutton observes that 'Although the racial category of Jewishness was distinct from any particular nationality, the nationality of Jews remained significant'.[25] The presentation of prewar Jewish immigrants as refugees was also problematic, once war was declared, as I have mentioned before. Writing more dispassionately than some Jewish historians of the period, Joan Beaumont remarks that '[d]espite their apparent claim on sympathy they were still considered a security risk, in that they might be subverted through pressure being brought to bear on the families they left behind'.[26] Bartrop notes the irony that it was their very status as refugees that made

---

[23] Lieutenant General V.A.H. Sturdee to Secretary to the Military Board, 27 June 1940. NAA MP729/6, 65/401/79. Cited in Bevege *Behind Barbed Wire*, p. 92.
[24] See for example, Stratton, 'The Colour of Jews: Jews, Race and the White Australia Policy', *Journal of Australian Studies* 20/50–51 (1996), pp. 51–65.
[25] Dutton, *One of Us?*, p. 54.
[26] Beaumont, 'Introduction', pp. 3–4.

the refugees suspect, especially after the invasions of Scandinavia and the Low Countries implicated false refugees in fifth column activities.[27]

Much has been made of the apparent injustice of interning German and Austrian Jewish refugees. But were they always and in every case passive victims of an unjust policy? Christine Winter proposes her study of the internment in Tatura 1 of German nationals (including both Australian-born citizens with foreign parents and citizens by naturalisation) as undermining those 'discourses of the great wrong done to harmless civilians swept up in Australian hysteria and deprived of their freedom for no good reason'.[28] The idea that internees may have contributed to their own detention is not a proposition that is ever applied to German/Austrian Jewish refugees in this country, but is it an idea that has any traction?

Let us reconsider the example of the Weintraubs Syncopators. The Buchan statements were made over two weeks in September 1939, by which time a first mass roundup of German nationals had occurred, mainly, but not exclusively, known NSDAP members or sympathisers. David Henderson writes that 'before dawn had even broken on the first day of the war, 257 people were behind bars'.[29] Given the weight that was later to be attached to Buchan's charges against the Weintraubs, it is notable that Inspector Keefe, of MPI section, concluded on 4 October 1939 that 'there is insufficient evidence to warrant any drastic action at present'.[30] Eight months later, the self-same Buchan allegations were to serve as the basis of the security services' decision to intern Kaiser, Graff and Weintraub. What, other than the fortunes of war, had occurred during this time to bring about this change of opinion? Did the musicians themselves cause disaffection? I believe the answer is yes.

The Lady Gowrie incident (April 1940)

In Chapter Three above, I recounted how, in April 1940, as part of their activities in aid of the Australian war effort, the Weintraubs donated their services to a garden party at Government House in Canberra and a ball at the Hotel Canberra in aid of Her Excellency The Lady Gowrie's War

---

[27] Bartrop, 'Enemy Aliens or Stateless Persons?', p. 274.
[28] Winter, 'The Long Arm of the Third Reich', p. 87. This point is also raised by Henderson, 'The Internment of Germans', p. 10.
[29] Henderson, ibid., p. 108, and citing the *Argus*, 5 September 1939, p. 2.
[30] Memo, Inspector W.J. Keefe to Major Scott, 4 October 1939. NAA MP529/2, WEINTRAUB/S.

Funds.³¹ In the earlier discussion I focused on the Musicians' Union's response to the Weintraubs' patriotic undertakings in general and the Lady Gowrie events in particular. The focus here is different. As registered enemy aliens, the Weintraubs were not free to travel from Sydney to Canberra without permits from the Aliens Registration Office. Permits had to be applied for, screened by military police intelligence (since the administration of alien registration matters was vested in the Department of the Army), issued personally to and signed for by the individual applicants. The transactions with the musicians over the issuing of permits to travel were reported by request in comprehensive detail across a number of files,³² in itself a significant fact.

Ostensibly the point of conflict was over timing: issuing of permits was handled through local police stations during normal office hours (9 am to 5 pm); the Weintraubs were engaged to play at Prince's during the day and were not free until after 5 pm. Actually the conflict was one of representation: the Weintraubs saw themselves as celebrity volunteers whose efforts were endorsed in this case by Vice-Regal patronage, none of which moved the police officers with whom they were directly dealing and who observed and reported those dealings, nor the MP and army intelligence officers who reviewed and decided the case. From an official point of view the musicians were one thing only: 'aliens'. Their behaviour and attitude were the focal points of official interest.

Graff handled the initial negotiations with the police and the story begins in his security dossier, NAA C123/1, 1213. It is documented with great attention to details of timing, dialogue, procedure and attitude. On 15 April 1940, an internal memo from Lieutenant Strack [Military Police Intelligence Section] to Major Powell, advised that:

> At 1440 hours a large, well-dressed German Gentleman bounced into the office and announced in a loud voice that he was the leader of the Weintraubs, and gave me to understand that he must have a permit to travel immediately for himself and band to Canberra on Saturday next, where the Band would be playing for charity at some function in which Lady Gowrie is interested. He made it clear that his call was merely a matter of form, and seemed a little disturbed that he could not have the

---

31   Horst Graff to Department of Military Intelligence, Sydney, 17 April 1940. NAA C123/1, 1213.
32   NAA C123/1, 1213 (Horst Graff); NAA ST1233/1, N19220 (Stefan Weintraub); NAA MP529/2, WEINTRAUB/S (copy of dossier of Stefan Weintraub); NAA MP529/2, GRAFF/H, (copy of dossier of Horst Graff).

whole permit instantly. I advised him to go away, and suggested that he return with a letter setting out the facts and a list containing the names of his Band.

The language is loaded with implicit judgments about Graff's attitude: he 'bounced' into the office, he spoke in a loud voice, he did not request information, he 'gave the officer to understand' what he wanted, he wanted the permits instantly and he made it clear that his call was a mere matter of form, perhaps the most damaging insinuation, as it implied a disregard for the regulations. The officer continued with a resume of other incidents recorded in Graff's file, some small in themselves, but cumulatively damaging and of course ending with reference to the Buchan espionage allegations. He concludes, 'In the circumstances, the desirability of this man and his Band playing at what is probably a patriotic function seems very much open to question', and asks for direction.

His irritation notwithstanding, Graff wrote his letter (17 April 1940) providing the necessary details while Strack's memorandum circulated among the officers of army intelligence, collecting file comments, one of which reads:

> It is strongly recommended that this application be refused. It is highly improbable that Lady Gowrie can know what sort of people these are and there is no justification for them being allowed to play at a patriotic function.[33]

Despite this opposition, permission was granted, permits were prepared and left for collection with the Station Sergeant at the ARO, Darlinghurst Police Station, and Graff was notified that they were available. Graff made two telephone calls in the afternoon of 19 April, attempting to find out how to apply for and collect the permits. Both are recorded. His manner towards the police was belligerent. During the second call, to the Aliens Registration Office, 'Graff became abusive and finally stated he couldn't be bothered about permits'.[34]

Stefan Weintraub's file, ST1233/1, N19220, contains a full report by two officers of the No 3 Police Station at Darlinghurst, describing the events of the afternoon of 19 April, including phone calls (with dialogue), and continuing with a description of behaviour and conversation that ensued when the musicians—with the exception of the two Frischer brothers—collected their permits. Matters did not improve:

---

33   Internal memorandum from P[?]P [Major Powell?], 16 April 1940. NAA C123/1, 1213.
34   Internal memo from MKS [Lieutenant Strack], 19 April 1940. NAA C123/1, 1213.

Throughout the time they were in this Office signing their permits, they took up a very dominating attitude and conversed amongst themselves about all the bother they had been put to and one stated 'To think we are doing all this for charity'. From their demeanour they gave the impression that we were under an obligation to them and were anything but courteous.

Challenged by the officer over his offensive behaviour on the phone and advised that the officer intended to report the matter, Graff backed down, apologised and the two men shook hands. At the same time, the officer noted an apparent anomaly between information provided by some members of the band on their permits as to their birthplaces, and information recorded at the Aliens Registration Office as to their nationalities.[35]

The Weintraubs travelled to Canberra and fulfilled their obligation to report to the Police on arriving and departing, and on returning to Sydney. But there was a further difficulty at the Ball in the evening on 20 April. The report of the incident, in which at least one member of the band ('comprised of enemy aliens') was subjected to some rough treatment, is filed in Stefan Weintraub's dossier, NAA MP529/2, WEINTRAUB/S, based on a word of mouth report, given to Lieutenant Strack's wife by Mr Jennings MHR and forwarded first to MPI, then from MPI to the Director of the CIB in Canberra on 8 May 1940.[36] The dispute concerned the musicians' apparent refusal to stop playing at midnight, as was required in a public venue on a Saturday night. The inferences surrounding this event were to have damaging consequences. Graff's comment on the permits was reproduced in the document recommending his internment; comprehensive summaries of reports appear in the briefing dossiers for the solicitor instructed to argue against Weintraub's and Graff's appeals for release from internment.

This incident makes very clear that the Weintraubs did not at first understand or know how to deal with the change that occurred in their situation once war was declared. They had come to Australia as celebrities and, in

---

[35] The individuals in question were Kaiser and the Frischer brothers. Debates over perceived ambiguities of their nationality were to become a major issue for all three individuals.

[36] Correspondence preserved in the AdKB (Item 116) suggests that the incident is open to another interpretation, but the details are not clear. Letter, Phyllis Parkinson to Horst Graff, 29 April 1940: 'As for the final incident at the Ball itself—words fail me. And I can only say Thank You from the bottom of my heart to one and all of you for the way in which you carried it off'. For her part, Lady Gowrie expressed her gratitude to the musicians 'for helping us as you did'.

Figure 29: Bad timing?
The publicity photograph that accompanies the Weintraubs' seasonal greetings in the *Australian Music Maker and Dance Band News*, January 1940, faithfully projects the group's comedic personae, but perhaps misjudges the public mood of the anxious early days of 1940.

Magazine held in the Mitchell Library, State Library of New South Wales, reproduced with permission.

spite of opposition from the Musicians' Union, had obtained employment at the top of their profession while apparently gaining permission to remain in the country speedily and with ease. The introduction of the alien control regulations had not affected their employment at Prince's, since they were not in a proscribed or high security occupation and, although the Buchan allegations had invited close official scrutiny, these were not publicly known. The band's contract with AWA's Rinso Melody Riddles radio program was, however, terminated 'on patriotic grounds' at the wish of the sponsor from November 1939. Graff protested unsuccessfully the mix of nationalities within the group, the refugee status of the German nationals, and the fact that the musicians were in Australia with the government's permission.[37] An undated draft request to renounce German citizenship, probably from 1940 and preserved in the Bestand Weintraubs Syncopators of the AdKB, states that the musicians' label as 'enemy aliens' was causing some problems—for example, at soldier entertainments. It is in the detail of the Gowrie affair, however, that one sees most clearly that it is pivotal, exemplifying an emerging discrepancy between the musicians' collective self-representation as helpful celebrities and official perceptions of them as troublesome foreign (or 'enemy') nationals. It was a clash of background beliefs in which the musicians could only lose.[38] To this point, their public personas and their popularity had hinged on the appeal of their 'foreignness'. They did not perceive that that very element, combined with their nationality and the lack of public differentiation between German Jews and other types of German nationals, aroused oppositional views of their patriotic service among more conservative social elements, particularly as the war situation deteriorated in the early months of 1940. Nor did they understand how their arrogant behaviour towards local police officers contributed to an unfavourable assessment of their attitude and ultimately towards the decision that some of them at least should be interned.

'Arrogance' was a quality stereotypically attributed to German Jews in wartime Australia.[39] Writing to the Secretary of the Military Board concerning a citizen description of another German-Jewish internee, the reporting officer observed, 'While a report … that "Warschauer is a typical fair-haired German from Munich and of arrogant nature" may not be of tangible value, it is in keeping with the disdain with which many such enemy aliens regard British subjects'.[40] Micro details such as this are revealing of the background beliefs that shaped attitudes towards the

---

[37] AdKB Item 138 for correspondence re Melody Riddles; item 105 for draft to renounce German citizenship.

[38] For the importance of 'background beliefs', see Gellately, 'Denunciations and Nazi Germany', p. 237.

[39] See Blakeney, *Australia and the Jewish Refugees*, p. 223, citing *Australian Jewish Herald*, 21 March 1940.

[40] Report on internee, Lieutenant-General, Eastern Command, to Secretary to the Military Board, November 1940. NAA MP529/2, WARSCHAUER/GE.

refugee internees and inhibited understanding of their position. These beliefs come out of the immediate past of the First World War and cannot be measured by reference to our knowledge of what was to follow.

Tatura 1, the 'Nazi camp'

As mentioned in Chapter Six, Graff, Weintraub and Kay were initially detained in Long Bay Jail after their arrest on 6 June, then in makeshift accommodation in the showground at Orange. Graff and Weintraub were relocated to the war's first purpose-built internment camp at Tatura at the end of August 1940; Kay was sent to Hay at the beginning of November, from where he was paroled on 19 November. Possibly because he was able to argue successfully that he had been erroneously detained by focusing on the legalities of his case, Kay appears to have suffered no ill-effects from the potential stigma of internment and re-entered civilian life without difficulty.[41] Professionally and personally, he quickly took steps to distance himself from his fellow internees. In a letter to Weintraub and Graff of 29 January 1941, he writes of how, in relation to his efforts to 'further the speedy conclusion of your cases, and simultaneously have your rehabilitation and release effected, I have been advised by Lieutenant East of the Military Intelligence Dep., that any interference from my side would only complicate your cases and possibly delay your deliberation'.[42] While protesting his faith in their integrity and in the absence of proof of any 'subversive activities', he absolves himself from further involvement. A man of diverse talents, as previous discussions have shown, Kay found casual employment with the Hansen-Rubensohn advertising agency on his release[43] and had assumed a full-time position as arranger for the Colgate-

---

[41] Confidence seems to have been one of his personal attributes; under 'other distinguishing characteristics' on his Personal Particulars Sheet [n.d. 1946?] an unnamed official has noted 'Dark and swarthy with an abundance of confidence'. NAA 6126, 197, doc. 249. The sobriquet 'dark and swarthy', with its implicit reference to skin colour, has a more sinister connotation. In relation to Australian selection procedures, Andrew Markus writes of a potential immigrant, 'As late as 1964 an English-born resident in Australia was prevented from sponsoring his twin brother when it was found that the latter was "swarthy and dark"'. *Australian Race Relations*, p. 168 and n. 46. Perhaps an association of skin colour with moral superiority underpinned the MUA General Secretary's description of the intended father-in-law of an Italian applicant as a 'white man'. W.H.S. Lamble, memorandum [June 1929]. Resolutions of Federal Council, NBAC MUA E156/6/15.

[42] NAA file ST 1233/1, N19220.

[43] Letter from the agency, 8? February 1941. NAA A6126, 197, doc. 128. The Colgate-Palmolive date may be inferred from the Statutory Declaration accompanying his application for naturalisation, 12 January 1946. NAA A435, 1946/4/1792.

Palmolive Radio Unit by the middle of 1941. In *Music Maker*, 21 April 1941, Kay issued a public disclaimer: 'Multi-instrument man John Kay (late of the Weintraubs) has requested us to point out that although he spent some years in Germany, he is NOT a German and that actually he was born in Peru and is a Peruvian citizen'.[44] The distancing purpose, whether conscious or unconscious is self-preserving; as Erwin Goffman writes, '[i]n general the tendency for a stigma to spread from the stigmatized individual to his close connections provides a reason why such relations tend either to be avoided or to be terminated, where existing'.[45]

In Tatura, Graff and Weintraub joined a small group of Jewish refugees, some of whom had also been transferred from Orange at the end of August, in Camp 1. According to Christine Winter, Camp 1 at Tatura ('Tatura 1') was an aberration within the many internment and POW camps in Australia (though not if viewed as part of what Winter calls 'a worldwide German internment camp policy').[46] With the apparent endorsement of the German Government, as relayed through the conduit provided by envoys of the Swiss protecting power, Tatura 1 was allowed to develop as the national camp for *Reichstreue*, that is, internees who were openly supportive of and loyal to Hitler's New Germany and the doctrines of National Socialism. The camp thus included known members of the local branch of the NSDAP and was known as the 'Nazi Camp'. By the middle of June 1940, Tatura 1 housed 319 Germans (including fifteen German nationals from New Guinea [Lutheran missionary personnel] and a few German anti-Nazis) and 114 Italians.[47] As Australian camp authorities allowed the management of the camp, in all matters but security, to rest with 'officials' elected from within the internee population, internal leadership positions were essentially occupied by Nazis. Nazi memorabilia—including photographs of Hitler and swastika emblems and flags—was permitted on open display, the Hitler salute was given and key events in the Nazi calendar (such as Hitler's birthday or the anniversary of *Kristallnacht*) were

---

[44] *Music Maker*, p. 55.
[45] Goffman, *Stigma*, p. 43.
[46] By which she presumably means German policy on the internment of its nationals worldwide. Winter, 'The Long Arm of the Third Reich', p. 87.
[47] Memo for the Hon Mr Justice Gavan Duffy, 15 June 1940. MP508/1, 255/7125/94. For the Templers (New Guinea internees), see Samuel Koehne, 'Refusing to Leave: Perceptions of German National Identity During Internment in Australia, 1941–45', in Beaumont *et al.* (eds), *Under Suspicion*, pp. 67–83. Early in 1941 Max Joseph identified approximately thirty political refugees and non-Nazis (non-communists) in addition to about twenty Jews. Undated draft, Box 3, File 9, AAJUS.

'I CANNOT FIND A CORNER IN THE WORLD'

celebrated.[48] Periodic efforts were made to regulate these activities but with limited effectiveness, since the Australians were unwilling to compromise good relations within the camp and between internees and guards. Winter describes the outcome: 'With a core group of dedicated National Socialists concentrated in one camp and the backing of the German Reich, National Socialism flourished in Tatura 1. Initially, the Commander of the Tatura internment camps … and his subordinates tried to keep the Nazi rule under control. In this endeavour they had little success'.[49]

The names, activities, organisational hierarchy, complaints and political sentiments of the patriotic German majority in Tatura 1 in the period between June and December 1940 are documented in Part II of the mimeographed pamphlet, *Chronik der Deutschen Internierungslager in Australien* (translated as Chronicle of German Internment Camps in Australia), mentioned in Chapter Six. The loyalties of the group were unambiguously expressed:

> Wherever and under what conditions those Germans who are still Germans have spent the past months in Australia, they have taken part with proud hearts in the magnificent achievements of the Homeland in military, political, diplomatic and economic spheres. They have celebrated and admired the victories, particularly the convincing defeat of France. The great deeds in the air, on land and on sea, they have accompanied with their best wishes for future successes, which will bring victory and peace … [and so on] …Heil Hitler![50]

Scholars have put forward various answers to the not unreasonable question of why it was that the Australian camp authorities tolerated such displays. Koehne postulates that, with the preservation of order as their primary concern, the Australian camp administrators were not overly

---

[48] Winter, 'The Long Arm of the Third Reich', pp. 90–91, 98 and n. 62; Samuel P. Koehne, '"Disturbance in D Compound": The Question of Control in Australian Internment Camps During World War II', *Melbourne Historical Journal* 34 (2006), p. 72; 'Refusing to Leave', pp. 74–75. See also Konrad Kwiet, 'Max Joseph. Lebensweg eines Deutsch-Jüdischen Emigranten', in Rainer Erb and Manfred Schmidt, *Antisemitismus und Judische Geschichte* (Berlin: WAB, 1987), p. 236.

[49] Winter, 'The Long Arm of the Third Reich', p. 90.

[50] This translation of an extract from the introduction, by Lieutenant W. Young I.O., is at MP508/1, 255/711/59 ('Chronicle of German Internment Camps in Australia'). The same extract, signed in the original by G. Neumann and F. Müller at Tatura, Christmas 1940 (*Chronik*, p. 3), is cited in Lurline and Arthur Knee, *Marched In. Seven Internment and Prisoner of War Camps in the Tatura Area during World War 2* (Tatura: Lurline & Arthur Knee, 2008), p. 22.

disturbed by the politics of internees and indeed found it easier to cooperate with an already established 'command' system such as the German Nazis appeared to offer.[51] Koehne's studies have also shown a bias of preference by the Australian camp administration for the German internees, whom they valued as '"helpful", efficient, co-operative, and willing to help maintain order'.[52] Christine Winter notes, however, that the Australian Government's acquiescence was in part the result of concerns for the reciprocal treatment of Australian prisoners of war in Europe.

Profiling the Jewish internees in Tatura 1

Konrad Kwiet cites a letter from the Minister of the Army to the Consul for Switzerland (protecting power of the German internees) in March 1940 in which the minister stated that 'every internee held at present is regarded as potentially dangerous'.[53] Tribunals set up in the United Kingdom had roughly classified German nationals (including Jews) into categories 'A', 'B' and 'C'. Category 'A' included those considered hostile, or whose conduct or character had been such as to make it undesirable to allow them to remain at large. Two hundred and fifty-one of these 'A' category internees were included in the group of circa 2500 mainly German and Austrian Jewish men notoriously dispatched from England to Australia in July 1940 on board the ship *Dunera*. Ninety men in this group of 251 were believed by supervising officers on the voyage to be 'of a dangerous type' and were segregated at Tatura Internment Camp No.1 at about the same time as Weintraub and Graff arrived, in late August 1940.[54] Based on her reading of these and other sources, Christine Winter asserts that the Australian authorities viewed Tatura 1 as the camp for dangerous internees and that the small number of Jews interned in Tatura 1 were there because they, too, were deemed to be 'of a dangerous type'.[55] The actual number of Jewish internees in Tatura 1 from late 1940 through 1941 varies, in the different items of correspondence preserved in the Max Joseph papers, between seventeen and twenty-seven. In December 1940, however, a letter was

---

[51] Winter details the *Lagerordnungsdienst* hierarchy that prevailed in Tatura 1 in 'The Long Arm of the Reich', p. 92. Koehne describes the LODI as 'an internal system of discipline patterned on a Nazi model'. 'Refusing to Leave', p. 71.
[52] Koehne, '"Disturbance in D Compound"', p. 86. For reciprocity, see Winter's 'Neutral Intermediaries?', pp. 53 and 62.
[53] Kwiet, '"Be Patient and Reasonable"', p. 64 and n. 20. No file source is given.
[54] For the *Dunera* segregation and assessment see Minute Paper, Secretary to the Military Board, Department of the Army, n.d. [January 1941?]. MP508/1, 255/715/140.
[55] Winter, 'The Long Arm of the Third Reich', pp. 88, 89 and n. 14.

sent to the Hon. P.C. Spender, Minister for the Army, thanking him for implementing the new regulations that would allow for the establishment of appeals tribunals. The letter was signed by twenty-five Jewish internees from Internment Camp 1A, Tatura, the group that had unsuccessfully applied to be segregated from the Nazi inmates, as recounted by Kwiet.[56] My discussion will be based around the twenty-five signatories to that letter to the minister.

In what sense could these individuals be viewed as dangerous? Of the group of twenty-five, twenty-three were German, one Austrian and one Polish. Twelve were married, twelve were single, one had been divorced by his non-Jewish wife (presumably in accordance with the Nuremberg decrees); the (non-Jewish) wife of one had remained in Germany. To the question of 'religion', three answered Protestant but had Jewish parents; six left the answer blank, the remainder wrote 'Jewish'. Eleven of the twenty-five were born before 1900 and of these all but two had served in either the German or Austro-Hungarian army during the First World War; three had received the Iron Cross or other decorations. Two of the others had done postwar military training. A range of professions, trades and occupations were represented within the group, some of which—like engineers, electricians and mechanics—were of more potential concern to the security services than others—like musicians or philosophers.[57] The youngest of the group was 19, the oldest 54.

Three of the group had been arrested previously on 4 September 1939 but released within a few days; a fourth, arrested on 19 September, was detained for a month. Of the whole group, eleven (including Graff and Weintraub) were in the round up on 6 June 1940, the remainder were detained between 7 June and 10 October 1940. Of the group arrested on 6 June, eleven were transferred to Orange on 15 June and nineteen to Tatura on 29–30 August. Two were already in Tatura and four more came in October. One had arrived in Australia on the *Dunera*. Two members of the group were released on parole by the end of December 1940. The other twenty-three all lodged objections against their internment and were heard before appeals tribunals in Melbourne and Sydney. Of these, fourteen were released on the recommendation of the tribunal after periods of between one and a half and circa six months (the latter in the case of Weintraub

---

[56] Letter dated 3 December 1940. Max Joseph Collection Box 3, File 9, Archive of Australian Judaica, University of Sydney [AAJUS].
[57] Data in this and the following paragraphs are from two series NAA MP1103/1 and NAA MP1103/2, both available online.

and Graff). The nine remaining internees were transferred from Tatura to Loveday, where they were further detained, in two cases until as late as April and May 1944.

Briefing dossiers prepared for the solicitor representing the Minister for the Army at the appeals tribunals (MP529/2 series) are available for twenty-one of the group, of which I have read the nineteen held in the NAA Melbourne office. All the files read started from or contained citizen reports alleging anti-British statements or demonstrated pro-Nazi sympathies attached to conversations overheard, social activities or associates, ownership of prohibited items or assertions without foundation. The statements were made by neighbours or co-workers who claimed some acquaintance with the person accused and could be said to reflect, at a local and personal level, a prevailing general public anti-alien sentiment, some of it held over from the First World War.[58]

The effects of denunciation

David Henderson has written powerfully that fear of the fifth column in the early months of 1940 resulted in a subtle shift of emphasis from an internment policy based on perceived issues of national security, to one based on concerns for public sentiment, a shift that 'precipitated a moral compromise on the home front that gave credibility to the wildest denunciations and rumours'. He continues,

> And although many denunciations were often couched in the rhetoric of national security, Germans, and later Italians could be denounced for more mundane and personal reasons: conflicts between neighbours, friendships gone wrong or for financial gain.[59]

In the dossiers under analysis here, there is certainly evidence of venal motivation on the part of the denouncers in some cases; other examples support the idea that Australian employees did not wish to work with enemy aliens. But do such examples signal a moral compromise on the part of the whole nation? In considering the question of whether the Australian public might have been more sympathetic towards the particular situation of German and Austrian Jewish refugees at this particular time, Paul Bartrop notes that after January 1940 and for the remainder of that year, 'there was

---

[58] Denunciation was not confined to the German/Austrian Jews, as is shown by Henderson's study, 'Academic Aliens: The University of Sydney during the Second World War'.
[59] Henderson, 'The Internment of Germans', pp. 142–143.

scant news published in Australian newspapers on anti-Jewish measures in Europe ... Where European Jews were mentioned at all in Australian papers, it was usually in regard to their status in Australia as "enemy aliens" and, as such, as potential fifth columnists or spies'.[60] Understanding was certainly slow to follow knowledge, at both macro and micro levels. To give a single example from Horst Graff's evidence before the Appeals Tribunal: Captain G.H.V. Newman, of Eastern Command's intelligence section, in writing his assessment, commented:

> He [Graff] was unable to furnish any information as to the treatment of his parents, who are still in Germany, merely stating ... that every Jew in Germany is ill-treated. Had their treatment been such as he would infer, it is reasonable to assume that they would have done as so many other Jews had—left Germany.[61]

Assuming, that is, that they could have found somewhere to go. In fact, Graff applied, unsuccessfully, to bring his parents and brother to Australia in February 1939. As I have noted in Chapter Four, his application failed because, as non-members of the MUA, the Weintraubs Orchestra was assessed as only able to get 'specialised work' and therefore (implicitly) Graff was judged unable to support his family.[62] Twist and twist about, individuals suffered.

I have not sighted documents (such as warrants) that might elucidate specific reasons for the arrest of individuals in this group other than my subject musicians, although the dossiers in the MP529/2 series that are the basis of the present discussion contain the substance of the army's case against the person concerned. Citizen reports may be said to represent grounds for general disaffection; specific issues emerged from the ensuing investigations. These included 'genuine' wartime concerns such as ownership of motor vehicles or other breaches, large and small, of the Aliens Control Regulations, or employment in a high-risk occupation. Other assessments involved more subjective judgments: one internee, for example was found to possess high levels of intelligence and organisational skills (as manifest in his successful business), which made him a hypothetical security risk.[63]

---

[60] Bartrop, *Australia and the Holocaust*, p. 198.
[61] Document dated 25 August 1941, p. 4. C123, 1213.
[62] NAA A261, 1939/769 (for application) and NAA ST1223/1, N22597 (for negative assessment).
[63] MPI report recommending internment of Max Joseph, 24 August 1940. NAA MP529/2, JOSEPH/MAX.

However, if the war situation allowed the development of a culture of denunciation, it also accommodated a counter-culture of advocacy on behalf of refugee internees. Files contain letters of support and endorsement from individuals who (like the denouncers) were neighbours, fellow employees and acquaintances, as well as from publicly recognised refugee advocates like Bishop Venn Pilcher or Mrs Harris (Rieke) Cohen.[64] The difference lies in the response. It can clearly be shown that where doubt was seen to exist, the application of the benefit of the doubt in favour of the nation resulted in the internment of denounced enemy aliens. Positive references, usually written in support of appeals for release after the subject was interned, produced no immediate result. Offers of sponsorship by organisations like the Jewish Welfare Society were likewise of little effectiveness in altering the army's decisions about individual internees:

> Sponsoring by the Jewish Welfare Society or kindred organisation would form part of any well-organised background for the introduction of enemy agents as refugees. This does not suggest that such Society would be a party to the scheme, but, from its public utterances and policy, there can be little doubt that it gives insufficient regard to the fact that the country is in a state of war. Acceptance of responsibility for internees, however good the sponsor, can be of little value if sabotage does result …[65]

The tenor and character of the denunciations in these dossiers show quite clearly what is distinctive about the Buchan allegations against the Weintraubs. The context of the latter was international, and could neither be proved nor disproved nor even properly evaluated by reference to local sources. Since the musicians' recall of the events was not consistent— either because they were not involved and so did not remember, as they asserted, or because they were fabricating their responses to questioning, as the assessing officers maintained—suspicions mounted. Another distinguishing feature is the comprehensiveness of documentation of the Buchan statements. There is no masking of the Buchan documents in any of the relevant files. Masking, usually to protect confidentiality under

---

[64] For Rieke Cohen, see Suzanne D. Rutland, 'Cohen, Rieke (1887–1964)', *Australian Dictionary of Biography* 13 (1993), pp. 457–458.

[65] Report on internee Gerhard Erich Warschauer, Lieutenant-General Eastern Command to Secretary to the Military Board, November 1940. NAA MP5092/2, WARSCHAUER/GE. Advocacy by the Jewish Welfare Society assumed greater importance for a group that was otherwise without backing of a nation state or protecting power.

'I CANNOT FIND A CORNER IN THE WORLD'

Section 33 of the Archives Act of 1983, is widespread in other dossiers: denunciation statements are sealed inside envelopes which in general are removed from the files before issue. I was only able to make the above comparison because the issuing librarian forgot to remove the envelopes from the files I requested. Each envelope had a photocopy of at least some of the enclosed pages stuck to the front, which I could then read, though the names of denouncers were routinely blacked out. Since in many cases the substance of the charges and their motivation were discredited by investigating police officers, it is an oddity of NAA access policy that the identity of denouncers is protected while that of the denounced is not, as Paul Bartrop has noted in another context.[66]

Experiencing internment

As documented in the files, the responses of Jewish internees to their encounter with Nazi-administered *Lagersordnungsdienst* in Tatura 1 fell into two broad categories. The first reflects their perplexity with the circumstances of their internment, the absence of information about the charges against them or the likelihood of their release. Ernst Flegenheimer's solicitors articulated his concerns on his behalf:

> The Internee ... has a very strong dislike to being interned with the very men whose persecution in Germany he fled from as he is a Jew ... you can well imagine the mental and physical effects of confinement on a man who does not know what there is against him in Australia, who is just held indefinitely and is given to understand that he is liable to be deported to a country where he is immediately again liable to arrest and sentence of death for actions contrary to Nazi principles, while here, he is regarded evidently, as a supporter of those principles.[67]

These sentiments found an echo in many letters written by or on behalf of the Jewish internees, including Stefan Weintraub's *cri de coeur* quoted at the head of this chapter, 'What have I done that I have to go through all this and that I cannot find a corner in the world where I am welcome?'[68] Lacking other

---

[66] Bartrop, 'Incompatible with Security', p. 160. Oftentimes details of the denunciations can be inferred from the tribunal transcripts if, as in many cases, the denunciations formed the basis of the interrogations.
[67] Samuelson and Ewing to Intelligence Section, General Staff, Sydney, 11 September 1940. NAA MP529/2, FLEGENHEIMER/E.
[68] The sentiment is repeated in his two letters of 14 September 1940, to Commanding Officer, Tatura Internment Camp and to the Officer in Charge, Intelligence Service,

explanations, many of the Jewish internees attributed their detainment to malicious gossip and rumour—in Weintraub's case to 'untrue denunciations of jealous competitors'—and expressed their consternation that decisions could be 'influenced by entirely private squabbles and interests'.[69]

High levels of psychological stress resulted from close confinement with people overtly sympathetic to Nazi ideology including its antisemitic racial attitudes, particularly for those inmates who had already experienced mistreatment in concentration camps in Germany following the *Kristallnacht* pogrom in November 1938. In one of his many letters to the camp's Official Visitors pleading the case for complete segregation of the Jewish (and anti-Nazi) internees, Max Joseph described their daily situation:

> [O]n January 30th of this year ... in the celebration of the anniversary of Hitler's accession to power, the official speaker insulted the Jewish people [in German] in the harshest way and availed himself of all the most abusive language so well-known from the 'Stuermer'[70] and such antisemitic Nazi-papers. These insults represent the link in a long chain of inconveniences and incidents of smaller and larger importance. Smaller incidents had occurred continuously and will always remain unavoidable as we are forced to live together with the Nazis and meet them wherever we are going, e.g. at the wash-house, at the mess-rooms, at the kitchen, at the hospital, and so on ... [71]

As has been recounted by Kwiet, segregation was not implemented until October 1941, and then not completely.[72]

Despite the fact that Jewish internees were given separate sleeping quarters[73] and the two groups worked out a *modus vivendi*, incidents such as that described by Joseph placed the so-called 'truce' under constant strain.

Victoria Barracks. NAA MP529/2, WEINTRAUB/S.

[69] Heinz A. Bernhard to Commandant, IC Tatura, 18 November 1940. NAA MP529/2, BERNHARD/HA.

[70] *Der Stürmer* (literally, 'The Stormer') was the vehemently antisemitic weekly Nazi newspaper published by Julius Streicher from 1923 to the end of the Second World War in 1945.

[71] Max Joseph to Justices Gavan Duffy and Norman O'Bryan, 8 February 1941. Max Joseph collection File 9, Box 3, AAJUS.

[72] Kwiet, '"Be patient and Reasonable"', p. 68. The final incentive for segregation was probably the riot between Jewish and Nazi internees that took place in D compound at Tatura in September 1941. See Koehne '"Disturbance in D Compound"'; Paul R. Bartrop, 'Incompatible with Security', 159–162.

[73] Extract from transcript of evidence by Max Flesch, 6 February 1941. NAA C123/1, 1213.

'I CANNOT FIND A CORNER IN THE WORLD'

According to Joseph, physical violence was not at issue. But a dossier relating to Weintraub's application for naturalisation contains an extract from a statement made by one Edmund Campion (alias Thomas Campion and Tom Ackroyd) to Constable F.C. Krahe of Newcastle Police, alleging that he had heard Nazi elements within Tatura 1 'plotting to assault WEINTRAUBB [sic] and destroy certain musical instruments'. Described as a witness of doubtful credibility known to police as an ex-internee with a criminal record, Campion nonetheless claimed 'that the Nazi Party in the camp had formed a Gestapo Service and its members were used to intimidate and assault any member of the camp who had earned the displeasure of the Party'.[74] An internal report on Erich Goldfeld states that 'at the present time [he] is the subject of extreme hatred and vicious attacks by the Nazis in Tatura'.[75] Goldfeld elaborated on his internment experience during his tribunal hearing:

> It is mental torture to be interned with deadly enemies of the Jews; they call you bloody Jews and they use other expressions. They make pictures on the blackboard of Jews, caricatures. They often do that ...[76]

Campion named several of the 'strong arm members of the Gestapo', a group known in the camp as the 'Holy Ghost'.

A degree of ambiguity attaches to the issue of segregation. For while the Official Visitors recommended it, the Jewish internees petitioned for it, and the authorities claimed that financial constraints prevented its implementation, the close association of Jews and Nazi sympathisers became a subject for enquiry at the aliens appeal tribunals. Objectors were regularly asked to comment (inform?) on 'the views and sympathies' of other men who were in the camp at the same time, and the information was copied across to other files.[77]

---

[74] The document from which the extract was taken is not named, addressed or dated; the section relating to Weintraub has clearly been copied across from another source. NAA A367, C38143. For Campion, a British internee of known Fascist sympathies who was interned in October 1940, see MP1103/2, PWN 1429.

[75] Memo signed 'J.M'. to Captain Tyrell, 23 September 1940. NAA MP529/2, GOLD FELD/E. It is very likely that the Australian guards would not have been aware of verbal abuse between groups within the camp if they were speaking German. Eric Goldfeld stated at his tribunal hearing that he had not been speaking English during the last seven months (that is, of his internment). NAA MP529/3, GOLDFELD/E, transcript, p. 21.

[76] NAA MP529/3, GOLDFELD/E, transcript, p. 21.

[77] See, for example, the report by Dr V. Stadler on a number of internees including Horst Graff, 27 February 1942. A promise was given that the source would not be divulged. NAA C123/1, 1213. See also NAA MP529/3 FLESCH/M, transcript p. 8; NAA

Appealing release

Frame conflict was very evident between the competing narratives put forward in the hearings before the Aliens Tribunals: on the one hand, the testimony of the objectors (which could not be proved), on the other, the interrogation of the solicitor representing the Minister for the Army. As the briefing dossiers clearly show, the army's case was often shaped by citizen reports and denunciations which could not be scrutinised, but whose substance was validated by the duty of the cross-examining solicitor 'to put to the witness anything that he thought material in the dossier'.[78] As previously discussed in Chapter Six, the flaws in the system were apparent to those who implemented it. Of the reliance on citizen reports, Justice Cleland observed,

> [on the one hand] the Committee has before it, the oath of a person detained subject to cross examination, and on the other, the unsworn efforts of more or less anonymous individuals (always described as 'a particularly reliable agent') and some of these reports may be personally malicious, probably honest [sic], and sometimes, no doubt, inspired by patriotic hysteria.[79]

Tribunal members deplored the fact that hearings were held out of the state in which the objector was resident, and that the policy of the military authorities was not to incur the expense of bringing character or other witnesses across to testify.[80]

At the end of his chapter on the appeals process, Henderson quotes Herbert Evatt, Attorney-General and Minister for External Affairs in the Curtin Labor government who said, when addressing the Parliament in 1946, 'that reading the transcripts of the Committees and Tribunals "one has a feeling of utter despair at the lack of not only humanity but also

---

WEINTRAUB/S, transcript pp. 11–12; NAA GOLDFELD/E, transcript pp. 19–20. The Flesch report then appears in Graff's file, as noted above, and in Weintraub's, NAA ST1233/1, N19220.

[78] NAA MP529/3, GOLDFELD/E, transcript p. 21.

[79] As also mentioned in Chapter Six, this comment is cited by several scholars including Bevege, *Behind Barbed Wire*, pp. 40–41, Saunders, 'A Difficult Reconciliation', p. 115 and Henderson, 'The Internment of Germans', p. 155. It is the kind of comment that invites repetition. The comment as it occurs in the document, a letter from Justice Clelland to the Minister for the Army, 23 December 1940 (NAA MP742/1, 255/2/814, Advisory Committees & Aliens Tribunals—Clerical Assistance), is very odd though clearly deeply felt. The rest of the letter and indeed the whole file concerns administrative issues, principally the payment of tribunal officials and support personnel. There is no record, in this file at least, of the Minister's response.

[80] NAA MP529/3, FLESCH/M, transcript, p. 16.

common sense'".⁸¹ Henderson goes on to conclude that 'neither the Menzies government, nor Evatt's own party, recognised this at the time'. Evatt's comment is powerful, but seductively misleading: by 1946 the world had a better understanding of what had happened to the Jews of Europe during the war years than Australians did in 1941. What appears to be at issue with this group of (predominantly) German-Jewish internees is not so much what was known about the treatment of the Jews in Hitler's Germany, but how this was understood, and the extent to which that understanding could explain or validate the refugees' professed shift of allegiance, especially in the case of men who had served Germany's patriotic cause in the First World War.⁸² If Jewish objectors themselves could testify that, at least until November 1938, they believed 'it was impossible that such a regime could last', that they 'thought Hitler would disappear', how could the Australians understand their insistence that they could not or would not go back to Germany, that the break with the fatherland was absolute?⁸³ Ruth Wodak has written that 'disorders of discourse' result from 'gaps between distinct and insufficiently coincident cognitive worlds'; that is, oral exchanges that produce confusion, misunderstanding and non-understanding instead of clarity, comprehension and concord.⁸⁴ It may be that Evatt was responding to the abundant examples of disordered discourse that are provided by tribunal transcripts, though this disorder is not always apparent to the same degree. The appearance of disorder depended on two factors: the vigour with which the solicitor for the Minister for the Army prosecuted a hostile counter interrogation, and the objector's English language proficiency. So, for example, there is a high degree of disorder in Menzies' interrogation of Horst Graff, resulting from the former's pursuit of inconsistencies in Graff's statements about events in his personal life (his education, marriage date and so forth), but a low degree in Menzies' interrogation of Max Flesch, another of the Tatura 1 Jewish internees. In the latter case, Menzies believed that the denunciation on the basis of which Flesch had been interned was without substance and stated as much to the tribunal.⁸⁵

---

81   Henderson, 'The Internment of Germans', Chapter 7 and esp. p. 168 and n. 615.
82   See, for example, NAA MP529/3, GINSBURG/W, transcript, p. 7; MP529/3, FLESCH/M, transcript, p. 3.
83   NAA MP529/3, FLESCH/M, transcript, pp. 3, 11–12; GOLDFELD/E, transcript, p. 12. These examples could be repeated.
84   Wodak, *Disorders of Discourse*, pp. 2–3.
85   Of Flesch, interned on the basis of a report from a member of staff in the office where he worked as an articled clerk, Douglas Menzies remarked at the conclusion of the hearing, 'we know nothing against this man'. NAA MP529/3 FLESCH/M.

In relation to the question of the unsuccessful requests for segregation by Jewish internees, Winter observes that, in the reciprocal world of international internment policy, people without the backing of a nation-state 'fell through the cracks'.[86] However, all inmates had access to Official Visitors, who relayed their requests and monitored their health and well-being. Jewish internees had Australian Visitors; Max Joseph corresponded with Justices Gavan Duffy and Norman O'Bryan, both justices of the Supreme Court of Victoria.[87] Within the camps, and eventually within the wider administrative context, complaints and appeals were heard and addressed, though it is striking that while the non-Jewish German internees in Tatura 1 complained about every imaginable aspect of their detention, the Jewish internees routinely only advanced one issue: the need for segregation. Accordingly, Jewish voices are muted in the surviving record while German voices are clamorous and loud. Though deprived of their liberty, inmates were treated with reasonable kindliness by the Australians—to the extent that, as noted, even NSDAP sympathisers were permitted to express their political views freely within Tatura 1. Motivations can be scrutinised and criticised, but the reality is that internees enjoyed a degree of freedom within the camps, were partially self-governing, well-fed and given access to medical care and recreational activities, though the removal of New South Wales internees to a Victorian location made family visits difficult.

Various reforms accompanied the change of government in 1941: a revision of aliens control regulations, the formal appeals mechanism, new refugee classifications and a national security organisation with a coordinated policy approach under the authority of the Attorney-General. Under John Curtin's Labor government, control of enemy aliens was transferred from the Department of the Army to the Attorney-General's Department; the new classification system allowed Weintraub, Graff and other members of the Jewish group from Tatura 1 to be reclassified as 'refugee aliens', though subject to further categorisation on the basis of their perceived security status. The worst excesses of previous policy were reigned in relatively quickly: internment was no longer to be based

---

[86] Email from Christine Winter, 22 August 2010.
[87] O'Bryan also acted as legal adviser to the Minister for the Army during the Second World War. For Duffy, see Charles Francis, 'Duffy, Sir Charles Leonard Gavan (1882–1961)', *Australian Dictionary of Biography* 8 (1981), pp. 351–352. For O'Bryan, see J. McI. Young, 'O'Bryan, Sir Norman John (1894–1968)', *Australian Dictionary of Biography* 15 (2000), p. 513. For Visitors reports see the NAA series MP508/1, 255/715/[…].

solely on origin or nationality and internment ideology became one of prevention, not punishment. Dutton claims that the Curtin government's different attitudes were the reflection of a movement from 'a conception of nationalist conflict to one of ideological conflict [which] reduced the relevance of nationality to perceived political action'. Curtin saw the war as a 'philosophic war'.[88] Calwell's postwar immigration program also involved a revision of the earlier view that allegiance and national origin were immutably linked, 'to allow for allegiance to be genuinely acquired through assimilation'.[89]

Among all the historians of internment it is Joan Beaumont who in my view has made the most balanced assessment. '[T]his total war', she wrote, 'presented individuals and governments across the globe with choices of the most profound moral complexity'.[90] It may well be that Calwell, writing in 1947[?] with an eye to his postwar immigration program, offered his own apology to the innocent victims of internment:

> When passions are let loose by war it happens all too often that foreigners, whether or not of enemy origin, and even locally born persons bearing foreign names, become the objects of denunciation and persecution ... from the fall of France in June 1940 onwards a good deal of avoidable misery was caused by some of the actions taken in connection with the control of aliens. In the nature of things, this may have been inevitable, for war as the democracies wage it is largely an affair of improvisation, and in urgent situations which demand prompt and effective action, there is little time to weigh the niceties of human rights.[91]

Coda

Coincidentally, as I first worked on this internment chapter, Radio National's Encounter program of 19 September 2010 included an interview with Reverend Elizabeth Warschauer, Uniting Church minister in Tenant Creek. She spoke most affectingly of her father's experience of internment to illustrate her idea that an individual's painful experiences, 'the wounds and difficult times', can provide opportunities for them to understand and

---

[88] Dutton, *One of Us?*, p. 99.
[89] Ibid., p. 102.
[90] Beaumont, 'Introduction', in Beaumont *et al.* (eds), *Under Suspicion*, p. 7.
[91] Calwell, 'Introduction', in Lamidey *Aliens Control in Australia*, [Part 1], p. 2.

connect in a deeper way with other people's issues. Erich Warschauer, one of the group of twenty-five Jewish internees in Tatura 1, was interned for three years, 'because he was German, not because he was Jewish'. He had been working as an engineer at the White Bay Power House in a position considered as of vital importance for potential sabotage. Denounced as unreliable by a fellow worker, Warschauer was arrested on 19 September 1939. Released on 28 October, he was arrested again on 15 June 1940. Warschauer's wife, a New Zealander, wrote powerfully and with eloquent passion—even if ineffectually—on behalf of her husband, protesting the injustice of his internment with Nazi sympathisers and the unkindness of his transfer to another state. Nonetheless, Warschauer's appeal in March 1941 was unsuccessful, and he was transferred to Loveday in January 1942, finally being released on 5 July 1943, more than three years after his second arrest. 'That was very difficult', said his daughter, 'but my father on release, in the middle of the war, embraced Australia. Australia was his country and he experienced Australia embracing him after it had sought to reject him completely'. For Elizabeth Warschauer, her father's journey from rejection to acceptance was redemptive and gave her an understanding of her Aboriginal congregants' feeling for land, and their experience of dispossession. I long to know how it was for others—but that, too, is a story for another time.

PART FOUR

CONCLUSION

Chapter Eight

CLAIMS TO BE JEWISH

In this concluding chapter I return to the question of how much it mattered, in Australia in the period under consideration, to the Weintraubs themselves and to others, that they were Jewish. This is the question that has threaded its way through my discussion of the two rather disparate, though sometimes connected themes of this book.

Two propositions may be seen to have framed the discussion. The first comes from an interview in one of the Australian music trade magazines, shortly after their arrival, in which the musicians denied emphatically that their decision to leave Germany had had anything to do with the current political situation. 'This is quite ridiculous,' the reader was informed, 'as long before any change of regime was contemplated in Germany, this band was touring Europe'. The second comes from Captain G.H.V. Newman's assessment of the testimony presented at Horst Graff's tribunal appeal against his internment, in which Newman wrote of Graff, 'Objector is undoubtedly a Jew and is undoubtedly clever enough to make such capital as he could from that fact, and from the common belief that Jews have been persecuted in Germany in recent years'.[1] In relation to the musicians themselves, the narrative of this book is situated between these two points on a continuum from denial to redefinition, from an assumed identity as celebrities to an assigned identity as victims of persecution, but the journey from one point to the other was not the same for every member of the group.

Obviously 'being Jewish' was the catalyst for the musicians' experience of expulsion and exile. In Berlin, the musicians were embedded in Weimar

---

[1] James Lucas, 'Played Around the World: Story of the Weintraubs', *Australian Music Maker and Dance Band News*, 1 November 1937, p. 19; NAA C123, 1213, document dated 25 August 1941, p. 4.

cabaret, a milieu that the Reich's Minister of Propaganda Joseph Goebbels considered to be 'a cesspool of "decadent", "Bolshevik" and "Jewish" culture', with the area around the Kurfürstendamm as the centre of Jewish corruption.² That leading roles in Weimar culture were played by Jews was not lost on the antisemites of the Third Reich, who viewed Weimar's experimentation and novelty as signalling 'moral and aesthetic decay'. As imitators of American jazz, the Weintraubs invited further opprobrium. For while Weimar's progressive spirits saw the essence of modernism in jazz, the conservative elements that came to dominate the Third Reich's cultural policies saw 'Negro' jazz as 'a potent symbol of cultural decay'. Thus 'a link was forged between racially inferior blacks and Jews'.³

But was there something specifically Jewish about the art that Jewish cabaret artists and musicians created and performed for their audiences, the art that the Weintraubs subsequently brought to Australia? Peter Jelavich, answering this question in the affirmative, posits that the Jewish culture of joke-telling was probably a response to the difficulties of assimilation; their prominence in the field of cabaret is linked to the fact that, despite nominal civic equality, advancement in the traditional institutions of higher culture and education was blocked to Jews. Moreover, coming as they did from lower middle-class backgrounds, Jewish entertainers did not have family links to German-language 'high' culture, hence their prominence in popular entertainment fields. But this is a question that is not so easy to answer in this particular case, for the Weintraubs were *re*-creative artists, and Jelavich also asserts that 'it was primarily as composers and writers of lyrics that Jews shaped and sustained the cabaret movement in both the Imperial and Weimar eras'.⁴ Adaptability was a key to the Weintraubs' success in their various touring environments. Their art was imitative, as their clients required; their individuality rested on their musical skills and the visual impact of their clowning. Satirical skits and parody were certainly markers of such Weimar institutions as the Kabarett der Komiker (KadeKo), where the Weintraubs also performed their stage routine.⁵ As anarchic musical gagsters they sit in a long tradition that includes Jack

---

2   Jelavich, *Berlin Cabaret*, pp. 230, 202.
3   Kater, *Different Drummers*, pp. 20-23.
4   Peter Jelavich, 'Kabarett', in *Europäische Traditionen—Enzyklopädie jüdischer Kulturen*, ed. Dan Diner (Leipzig:Simon Dubnow Institut für jüdische Geschichte und Kultur an der Universität Leipzig, volume 3, forthcoming); 'Performing High and Low: Jews in Theater, Cabaret, Revue, and Film', in Emily Bilsky (ed.), *Berlin Metropolis: Jews and the New Culture, 1890–1918*, (New York: The Jewish Museum, 1999), pp. 212, 224.
5   Bergmeier, *The Weintraub Story*, p. 13.

Benny, Victor Borge and today's comedians Aleksey Igudesman and Hyung-ki Joo. (The fact that the last-named derives some mileage from describing himself as a Korean 'Joo' says something in itself of the role of Jewish musical comedians in this tradition.)

This kind of musical comedy has certain characteristics, one of which is subversion of the dominant musical tropes of classical or popular music. In the German context, Hitler deplored such subversion as a specifically Jewish attribute:

> Culturally, [the Jews'] activity consists in bowdlerizing art, literature, and the theatre, holding the expressions of national sentiment up to scorn, overturning concepts of the sublime and beautiful, the worthy and the good...[6]

The Third Reich's views on its 'Jewish problem' were well reported in Australia: German Consul-General Rudolf Asmis writing in 1933 and Sir David Rivett in January 1937 both identified the degradation and demoralisation of theatrical life in Berlin as the direct result of the disproportionate influence of so-called 'night club Jews', a degenerate class aligned with communist Jews in eroding the health of the body politic.[7] In January 1939, as the Weintraubs were establishing themselves as a specialty entertainment at Prince's, the Sydney *Bulletin* editorialised on the government's proposed quotas for Jewish refugee immigrants, of which it was not in favour. The writer felt that Germany was likely to try and encumber Australia with the worst, not the best, Jewish types, and concluded 'Two classes that should be ruled out from the beginning are (1) night club Jews and (2) Communist Jews'.[8] One thing to notice about the Weintraubs, then, is that although the group made no secret of its association with the leading personalities of Weimar culture—in cabaret, theatre and film—this classic antisemitic association of Jewish Weimar with moral and cultural degeneracy was never used against them, even by the Musicians' Union, which characteristically adopted the prevailing anti-foreigner rhetoric

---

6   Cited in translation from *Mein Kampf* in Steven T. Katz, '1918 and After: The Role of Racial Antisemitism in the Nazi Analysis of the Weimar Republic', in Sander L. Gilman and Steven Katz (eds), *Anti-Semitism in Times of Crisis* ([New York]: New York University Press, 1991), p. 244.
7   'Germany's Defence', Letter to the Editor from Rudolf Asmis, *Sydney Morning Herald*, 21 July 1933 p. 8 (cited in Hooper, 'Australian Reactions to German Persecution of the Jews', p. 14); Sir David Rivett, 'Germany Today', *Argus*, 9 January 1937, p. 19 (cited in Blakeney, *Australia and the Jewish Refugees*, p. 72).
8   'The Fifteen Thousand Refugees', *The Bulletin*, 18 January 1939, p. 13 (cited in Blakeney, *Australia and the Jewish Refugees*, p. 73).

to prosecute its own oppositional agendas. What was straightforward in definition and consequences in Germany was a more complicated affair in Australia.

Why Australia?

In her essay on Leon Samuel Snider in the *Australian Dictionary of Biography*, Rosslyn Finn claims that the fact that the Weintraubs were Jewish influenced Leon Snider's decision to bring the band to Australia in 1937. Finn writes:

> Increasing anti-semitism in Europe prompted him and others to lobby the Commonwealth government to permit the immigration of central Europeans, many with professional qualifications ... Snider negotiated contracts to assist Jewish musicians, among them the Weintraub Syncopators who settled in Sydney in 1939 and later played at Prince's Restaurant.[9]

Be that as it may—and I have not found any documents that would either directly support or contradict Finn's claim—the Weintraubs, fortuitously, were not part of the wave of Jewish emigration that followed the *Anschluss* in March 1938 and, more particularly, the *Kristallnacht* pogrom in Germany in November 1938, events that placed such pressure on Australia's capacity and desire to absorb large numbers of Jewish refugees. The musicians arrived in July 1937, and did not present as potential immigrants. My discussion does not, therefore, involve a consideration of the efforts of the Australian Government to restrict Jewish immigrant numbers, nor of the ideologies that underpinned those efforts. My study is primarily concerned with the reception of the musicians once they had arrived in Australia.

The Weintraubs entered the country under contract to employers who, in their turn, had negotiated a license with the government that required them, among other things, to ensure that the musicians left Australia at the conclusion of their contract. That the Weintraubs' departure for New Zealand was accepted as fulfilment of that part of the contract and that they were permitted to re-enter Australia in May 1938, at the conclusion of their New Zealand tour, is witness to the government's relatively benign view of the group as professional musicians (again, not Jewish refugees),

---

[9] Rosslyn Finn, 'Snider, Leon Samuel (1896–1965)', *Australian Dictionary of Biography* 16 (2002), pp 278–279.

Figure 30. Tony Hudson's cartoon drawing of the Weintraubs Syncopators [1937?]

This undated, unattributed drawing, by Sydney cartoonist Tony Hudson [1937?] was used as promotion during the Weintraub's New Zealand tour, 1938, and published in *MAN*, February 1939, p. 112. Despite elements of stereotyping in the cartoon, the musicians' 'Jewishness' was not a factor in their professional reception.

State Library of New South Wales MLMSS 7164X. Scrapbooks concerning the Mercury Theatre, 1940s–1950s [Sydney John Kay], with permission.

despite persistent and adverse representations from the Musicians' Union. The musicians displayed mixed responses to the idea of Australia as a refuge. Weintraub, Goldner and Emanuel Frischer quickly made application to remain permanently in this country. At the same time, Horst Graff, acting as manager for the band, attempted (unsuccessfully) to secure ongoing engagements in South East Asia that would presumably have taken at least some of the musicians on further journeys.

As far as the musicians themselves were concerned, I would argue that an acknowledgement of Jewishness was to a certain extent forced upon some of them, though not all, by the circumstances of the war. If endogamy—that is, marriage within a particular group in accordance with custom or law—is one the markers of Jewish self-identification,[10] it is worth noting that all the musicians who were married either on or soon after their arrival in Australia had non-Jewish wives. In the case of Weintraub and Graff, interned as they were in the Nazi camp at Tatura, their claim to be Jewish came initially through their inclusion in Max Joseph's group of Jewish internees, was defined religiously and associated with their request for segregated accommodation, and arose from their desire to define themselves against other German nationals.[11] To some extent Captain Newman's assessment of Graff's claim to be Jewish was correct: it was opportunistic insofar as it constituted the only possible basis for Graff's appeal for release from internment. Consequential claims to be refugees and stateless followed as responses to official changes in aliens classification categories: the new classification of 'refugee alien' that was gazetted in February 1942, and the more comprehensive definitions that were finally introduced in 1944.[12] As a refugee alien, Leo Weiss was thus able to apply successfully for naturalisation in 1944. Weintraub, with his 'A' security classification was not so lucky; although he was the first of the group to achieve permanent residency, Weintraub had to wait for the end of the war to be naturalised. In support of his 1944 application, Weintraub provided a letter from the Chief Minister of the Great Synagogue who testified that Weintraub was 'a member of the Jewish faith'.[13] However true or necessary the Rabbi's testimonial might be, I find it hard not to see it as symbolising Weintraub's final surrender of agency in terms of his self-definition.

Much of the discussion of defining moments in the Weintraubs' early Australian experience involves differing perceptions of identity, and the conflicts and misunderstandings that arose from the discrepancies between the musicians' self-representations and the designations that were ascribed to them. These discrepancies became much more critical once war was declared. At a certain level, official Australian perceptions of the musicians as Jewish were characterised by one feature: lack of differentiation. As I

---

[10] Stratton, 'The Colour of Jews', pp. 56–57.
[11] A vote was taken on how the Tatura group should be constituted, and Max Joseph's suggestion won: 'Nur Juden der Religion nach (Volljuden) [Only Jews who practice religion (full Jews)]'. See handwritten minutes of the 'Meeting of the Jewish Group of Camp 1A', 27 February 1941. AAJUS, Max Joseph papers, Box 3, file 9.
[12] Bartrop, 'Enemy Aliens or Stateless Persons?', pp. 275, 277–278.
[13] Rabbi Dr I Porush to Secretary, Department of the Interior, 11 April 1944. NAA A435, 1946/4/988.

have shown, the Musicians' Union made no distinction between Jewish refugees in the 1930s (or postwar survivor immigrants) and other classes of foreigners whose entry into the music profession the Union opposed for almost half a century. The Weintraubs offended the Union not because they were Jewish, but because, as foreigners and non-members, they routinely flouted Union rules and were rewarded for doing so. Punishment of members for infringements of the rules was an important element in the internal management of the Union; one could see Kitson's 'outing' of Weintraub at Romano's as a form of retribution. For their part, the security services made no distinction, at least in the early stages of the war, between German and Austrian Jews and other German or Austrian nationals. As the subjects of Buchan's charge of espionage, the German nationals in the group fell victim, at a time of national crisis, to a kind of double jeopardy. It was not that either group—Union or security services—was ignorant of the fact that German Jews were being persecuted, but each had its own reasons for discounting ideas of special treatment. The Union argued shortage of employment opportunities, the security services argued the necessities of war, administrative logistics, practical difficulties and cost. Whatever the opinion of individual officials might have been, it is hard to see that policy was driven by antisemitism in either case. On the contrary, I have attempted to show that attitudes affecting the reception of Jewish musicians or the early wartime treatment of Jewish refugee aliens were shaped by historical experiences of earlier origin.

What 'destroyed' the Weintraubs?

According to Bonnie Weintraub, interviewed in the documentary film discussed in Chapter One, 'war destroyed the Weintraubs'. The commentary of the film is more specific: once Weintraub, Kay and Graff were interned in June 1940, the Weintraubs ceased to exist. Once again, however, the situation was more complex than these assertions might suggest. For one thing, changes of personnel were a feature of the band from its inception; indeed movements of personnel between one group and another are characteristic of this part of the commercial music industry. That being said, I have no doubt that Weintraub in particular was driven out of the music profession by the relentless apparent vendetta of the MUA's Frank Kitson. One should not downplay the damaging effects of Weintraub's wartime experiences, which gave Frank Kitson his final and most effective weapon. It has been argued that the whole experience of exile and emigration involved quite difficult remakings of identity, in particular for German Jews for whom 'a successful German and Jewish symbiosis' was a marker.[14] For Stefan Weintraub the rupturing effect was cumulative. Already fractured by expulsion, as a Jew, from the German *Volksgemeinschaft* (a situation replicated through chance in Tatura 1), he then found himself publicly vilified, as a German, as he attempted to rejoin his profession at Romano's in 1941. Even in this supposedly safe haven 'at the other end of the world', the war cost Weintraub his career and his marriage; for him, as for some of the others, these sufferings were added to the more profound losses that followed revelations of the Holocaust in Europe. It is no wonder that, as an old man, Weintraub retreated into his dreams.

Why 'silences and secrets'?

I visited Mannie Fisher in 2004, shortly before he died. When I arranged the appointment, his wife neglected to tell me that he had had a stroke, was completely paralysed and could not speak. My introduction to him came as a very great shock, so much so that I decided not to make oral history a part of my research. In any case, the other musicians had died, or so I thought.

I can now see that that encounter was highly symbolic. When later, quite by chance, I met Mannie's son Michael, I quickly realised that Mannie had never spoken about the Weintraubs' Australian wartime experience in any detail, an impression confirmed by the Shoah Foundation interviews with both Mannie and Ady Fisher. I also realised that I not only knew things about Mannie that his son did not know, but things that Mannie himself would probably not have known: confidential exchanges between government officials concerning his lost Russian wife, for example, reports on his security status and so forth. Similarly, Dorothy Graff, Horst's second cousin, knew nothing about Horst's 'troubles': his internment, his tribunal interrogation, Australia's unwitting complicity in his parents' fates, the incident at Romano's. To some degree, then, my narrative tells the secret story of the Weintraubs Syncopators' early Australian experience, addressing the silences that fell across these families as they frequently fell across other Jewish families affected by the Holocaust. There is always an ethical question attached to a researcher's right to break into such silences and reveal secrets, but the material I have used comes from the public record, much of it now available online.

---

14   Abrahams-Sprod, "'Australien! Wo ist den das?'", p. 21.

Serendipity played its role in the survival of these records. It is remarkable that the Buchan denunciations are documented without restriction across a range of files when the identities of other, far less consequential 'denouncers' are protected by legislation—though the identities of their subjects are not. It was my good fortune that an issuing librarian forgot to remove masked material completely from a number of internees' dossiers. It is noteworthy that comprehensive records of the Musicians' Union of Australia have been preserved and that they turned out to be such a rich, untapped resource. It is paradoxical that an extensive collection of the band's Australian business papers found their way back to Berlin, courtesy of one Frau Myrle Geleynse, and that Henry Barger's widow decided to follow suit with her gift of the earlier European materials.[15]

At the end of the war and with no possibility of proof forthcoming, the whole Russian espionage charge against the musicians was simply dropped. No apology was made, no compensation was offered. Contemplating the Weintraubs' story, one is left with perhaps the bleakest and most painful question of all: what was it all for? I am reminded of a poem I read some time ago in a Melbourne train. It went like this,

> *down under*
>
> *how do narrow minds grow*
>
> *beneath such wide skies?*[16]

At the time, I was struck by the resonances with aspects of the Weintraubs' Australian experience, and I still am. However, even as I think these gloomy thoughts, I also remind myself that hard-line attitudes towards this group of individuals were not endorsed at every level of Australian society, or government, or bureaucracy: if the Weintraubs had opponents and detractors they also had supporters and advocates. It was a matter of which view prevailed at any given moment, and why.

---

[15] This information is from the records of the AdKB.
[16] The poem, by Danielle Johnston, was featured in the first Moving Galleries exhibition in Melbourne in 2006 and is reproduced here with her permission.

BIBLIOGRAPHY

Part One: Primary Sources
*Digital files

NAA Named Files (Weintraubs Syncopators and Associates)

A261 Application forms (culled from other file series) for admission of relatives or friends to Australia (Form 40). Recorded by: (1953–1961) Department of Immigration, Central Office.

Fisher, Mannie (1946) A261, 1946/1366
Frischer, Adolf (1938) A261, 1938/758
Frischer, Emanuel (1938) A261, 1938/759
Goldner, Fritz (1938) A261, 1938/849
Goldner, Fritz (1946) A261, 1946/1719
Graff, Horst (1939) A261, 1939/769
*Kaiser, Ned John Kurt (1945) A261, 1945/702
Weintraub, Stefan (1946) A261, 1946/5086
Weiss, Leo (1946) A261, 1946/5093

A367 Correspondence files, single number series with 'C' prefix, 1927–1953. Recorded by: (1919–1946) Commonwealth Investigation Branch.

*Frischer, Adolf (1939–1943) A367/1, C46730
Weintraub, Gertrude [sic] Irene (1942–1945) A367, C72133 (Copies of all material held in A 659, 1942/1/1313)
Weintraub, Max and Elly (1942–1945) A367, C62279
Weintraub, Stephan [sic] (1943–1944) A367, C38143

A434 Correspondence files, Class 3 (Non British European Migrants) Recorded by: (Jan–April 1939) Department of the Interior [I], Central Administration; (April 1939 – July 1945) Department of the Interior [II], Central Office; (July 1945 – Dec 1950) Department of Immigration, Central Office.

Weintraub, Gertrude (1946–1947) A434, 1946/3/2962
Weiss, Leo (1937–1939) A434, 1946/3/7299

A435 Class 4 correspondence files relating to naturalisation. Recorded by: (1939–1945) Department of the Interior [II], Central Office; (1945–1950) Department of Immigration, Central Office.

Goldner, Camilla (1944–1945) A435, 1944/4/4138
Goldner, Fritz (1943–1946) A435, 1945/4/3315
Graff, Horst (1944–1946) A435, 1945/4/4668
*Kaiser, Ned John Kurt [aka John Kay] (1945–1946) A435, 1946/4/1792
Weintraub, Max (1944–1946) A435, 1945/4/4635
Weintraub, Stefan (1942–1946) A435, 1946/4/988
*Weiss, Leo (1942) A435, 1947/4/2710

A440 Correspondence files, multiple number series, class 12 (Migrants D–G) (1 Jan 1904 – 31 Dec 1995). Recorded by: (1 Jan 1951 – 31 Dec 1952) Department of Immigration, Central Office.

Frischer, Salomon (1944–1946) A440, 1951/12/7766

A659 Correspondence files, class 1 (general, passports). Recorded by: (26 Apr 1939 – 31 Dec 1945) Department of the Interior [II], Central Office.

Frischer, A. (1943–1944) A659, 1943/1/4539
Frischer, E. (1942–1944) A659, 1943/1/248
Graff, M. (1940–1942) A659, 1942/1/2610
Weintraub, Gertrud [sic] Irene B. (1942–1943) A659, 1942/1/1313

A714 Books of duplicate certificates of naturalization A(1) [individual persons] series. Recorded by (26 Apr 1939–13 Jul 1945) Department of the Interior [II], Central Office; (13 Jul 1945–6 Mar 1956) Department of Immigration, Central Office.

Frischer, Adolf (1943–1957) A714, 16/7726
Frischer, Emanuel (1943–1957) A714, 16/7786

A989 Correspondence files, multiple number series with year prefix. Recorded by: (Dec 1942 – Jan 1945) Department of External Affairs, Central Office.

*Defence Subversive Activities "The Weintraubs Orchestra" (1943–1944) A989, 1943/235/4/19
Frischer (Fisher), Mr Emanuel (1944) [Enquiries regarding whereabouts of wife] A989, 1944/480/20

A997 Applications for Permit to enter Australia, Form 47 (with Form 7a). Recorded by: (Jan 1945 – 31 Dec 1956) Department of Immigration, Central Office.

Weintraub, Max and Elly (1945) A997, 1945/706

BIBLIOGRAPHY

A1066 Correspondence files, multiple number series with year and letter prefixes. Recorded by: (Jan–Dec 1945) Department of External Affairs [II], Central Office.

Frischer, Emanuel (1945) A1066/4, IC45/23/2/18

A1067 Correspondence files, multiple number series with year and letter prefixes. Recorded by: (1 Jan – 31 Dec 1946) Department of External Affairs [II], Central Office.

Bergmann, G (1946) A1067/IC46/3/80
Kaiser, Mrs G (1946) A1067, IC46/68/2/4

A12217 Alien land transfer files, single number with L [Land] prefix. Recorded by: (1 Jan 1940 – 8 Aug 1946) Investigation Branch, Central Office, Melbourne and Canberra.

Kaiser, Gertie (16 Jan – 22 Feb 1946) A12217, L11469

A12508 Personal Statement and Declaration by alien passengers entering Australia (Forms A42). Recorded by: (1937–1939) Department of the Interior [I], Central Administration; (1939–1945) Department of the Interior [II], Central Office.

Bergmann, G (1937) A12508, 57/21
*Frischer, Adolf, (1938) A12508, 50/652
Frischer, Emanuel (1937) A12508, 50/650
*Frischer, Emanuel (1938) A12508, 50/653
Frischer, Salomon and Feigel (1939) A12508, 50/651
Goldner, Camilla (1939) A12508, 21/1557
Goldner, Fritz (1937) A12508, 5/52
*Graff, Horst (1938) A12508, 21/1616
*Kaiser, John Kurt (1937) A12508, 48/2
Paris, Antoinette (1937) A12508, 31/3846
Pfund, Gerty Margarete (1937) A12508, 21/3288
Pfund, Richard (1937) A12508, 21/3289
*Weintraub, Stefan (1937) A12508, 21/4571
*Weintraub, Stefan (1938) A12508, 21/4574
Weiss, Josef (1939) A12508, 21/4582
*Weiss, Leo (1937–1938) A12508, 21/4604
Wise, Gordon Freddy (1937) A12508, 2/9746

A1336 Applications for Literary and Dramatic Copyright (with exhibits). Recorded by: (inter alia), (1930–1969) Copyright Office [III].

Kaiser, John Kurt trading as Microphone Music Publishers (applicant): 'The Elixir of Life', dramatic work, 24 December 1939. A1336/1, 33888.
Kay, Sydney John as author, together with Iris Oakley Mason and James Hallett Saunders, Herbert Walter Marks, Rex Shaw, Wilbur Patey Sampson, William

Henry Lewis and Kurt Herweg. Incidental Music, Australian Record Libraries, 3 February 1948. A1336/1, 45668.

Weiss, Leo (Allan Martin), 'I Shall Never Forgive You', 13 July 1944. A1336/1, 40053.

Weiss (White), Leo and R L Breen (author), 'I'll Always See You (As You Looked Last Night)' and 'Sleep Baby Sleep', 25 November 1945. A1336/1, 42190.

Weiss (White), Leo and R L Breen (author), 'A Mooning in the Moonlight', 27 September 1945. A1336, 41949.

A1337 Applications for Registration of a Design. Recorded by (inter alia): Designs Office (1907–1992)

A1337, 27654 (1949) Application for registration of design by Cyril Schulvater for Portable cocktail cabinet

A1539 Correspondence files, annual single number with 'W' (War) infix. Recorded by: (1939–1950) Department of Trade and Customs, Central Office.

Weintraub, Stefan (1940) A1539, 1940/W/6864

A6126 Microfilm copies of personal and subject files (CRS A6119 and CRS A6122). Recorded by: (1 Jan 1960) Australian Security Intelligence Organisation, Central Office.

Kaiser, John Kurt (volume 1) (1939–1955) A6126, 197
Kaiser, John Kurt (volume 2) (1942–1957) A6126, 1236

B884 Citizen's Military Forces Personnel Dossiers, 1939–1947. Recorded by: (1940–1947), 2 Echelon, Army Headquarters.

*Frischer, Adolf (1939–1948) B884, N464017
Frischer, Emanuel (1939–1948) B884, N464028
Goldner, Fritz (1939–1948) B884, Q272891

BP242/1 Correspondence files relating to national security, single number series with Q (Queensland) prefix. Recorded by (Jan 1924 – Mar 1942) Investigation Branch, Queensland: (17 Mar 1942 – 15 Dec 1945) Security Service, Queensland; (15 Dec 1945 – 8 Aug 1946) Investigation Branch, Queensland.

Goldner, Fritz (1938–1949) BP242/1, Q15366

BP25/1 Alien registration papers, alphabetical series by country of citizenship. Recorded by: (01 Jan 1939 – 06 Dec 1945) Collector of Customs, Brisbane, Queensland; (6 Dec 1945 – 31 Dec 1966) Department of Immigration, Queensland Branch.

*Goldner, John Johann (1949) BP25/1, GOLDNER J J AUSTRIAN

BIBLIOGRAPHY

C100 Radio Archives Library recordings, radio audio production material. Recorded by: (01 Jan 1973 – 01 Jul 1983) Australian Broadcasting Commission, Head Office.

Weintraub, Stefan (1979) Interview, C100, 80/7/353 M

C123 World War II security investigation dossiers, single number series. Recorded by: (1941–1945) Commonwealth Security Service, New South Wales.

Frischer, Adolf (1941–1944) C123, 16027
*Frischer, Emanuel/Mannie FISHER (1939–1945) C123, 1211 [Security Service, New South Wales, dossier] [box 7]
Graff, Horst (1939–1945) C123, 1213 [Security Service, New South Wales, dossier] [Box 7]
*Graff, Margery Minna (1940–1945) C123, 10381
Kaiser, Gerty (Peruvian) (1940–1942) C123, 19959 [Box 578]
Schulvater, Ernest and Cyril (1939–1945) C123, 1210 [Security Service, New South Wales, dossier] [Box 7]

C329 Transcripts of internees' appeals before the Aliens Control Tribunals and Advisory Committees. Recorded by: (1939–1942), NSW Police, Military Police Intelligence Section (unregistered); (1941–1945), Security Service, New South Wales.

Graff, Horst (1941) C329, 402 [Box 13]
Weintraub, Stefan (1941) C329, 997 [Box 31]

C422 Dossiers on Jews resident in Australia compiled by the German Consulate. Recorded by: (1 Jan 1943 – 15 Dec 1945) Security Service, New South Wales.

Weiss, Leo [Israel], (1939) C422, 58

J25 Case files, annual single number series [Queensland]. Recorded by: (1 Jan 1946 – 12 Jun 1974) Department of Immigration, Queensland Branch.

Goldner, John (1955) J25, 1955/5374

K269 Inward passenger manifests for ships and aircraft arriving at Fremantle, Perth Airport and Western Australian outports, chronological series. Recorded by: Collector of Customs, Western Australia.

K269/4, 'Incoming passenger list "Gorgon" arrived Fremantle' from Singapore, 14.7.1937.
K269, 10 MAY 1938 LARGS BAY, Adolf and Hildegard Frischer, arrived Melbourne from Port Said.
K269, 31 JUL 1939 MORETON BAY, Ernest and Antonina [sic] Schulvater, arrived Sydney from Southampton.

MP529/2 Dossiers of German internees who lodged objections to detention under National Security (Aliens Control) Regulations. Recorded by (1939–1941) Deputy Crown Solicitor's Office, Victoria.

Graff, Horst (1939–1941) MP529/2, GRAFF/H
Weintraub, Stefan (1939–1940) MP529/2, WEINTRAUB/S

MP529/3 Aliens Tribunal transcripts of evidence of objections against internment under Regulation 26 of the National Security (General) Regulations. Recorded by: (22 Jan 1941 – 20 Aug 1942), Deputy Crown Solicitor's Office, Victoria.

Graff, Horst (1941) MP529/3 TRIBUNAL 1/GRAFF
Weintraub, Stefan (1941) M529/3, TRIBUNAL 1/WEINTRAUB

MP529/8 Applications by enemy aliens for leave to submit objections against detention orders made under National Security (Aliens Control) Regulations. Recorded by: (22 Jan 1941 – 20 Aug 1942), Deputy Crown Solicitor's Office, Victoria.

Weintraub, Stefan (1940) MP529/8, WEINTRAUB/S

MP1103/1 Registers containing 'Service and Casualty' forms (a 112) of enemy prisoners of war and internees held in camps in Australia. Recorded by: (1939–1947) Prisoners of War Information Bureau (also known as Prisoners of War and Internees Information Bureau)— Directorate of Prisoners of War and Internees.

*Graff, Horst (1940–1941) MP1103/1, PWN1261.
*Kaiser, Ned John Kurt (1940) MP1103/1, PWN1273
*Weintraub, Elly (1940–1942), MP1103/1, ZF35547
*Weintraub, Max (1940–1942) MP1103/1, Z35548
*Weintraub, Stefan (1940–1941) MP1103/1, PWN1297

MP1103/2 Dossiers containing reports on Internees and Prisoners of War held in Australian camps, single number series with alphabetical prefix.

*Graff, Horst (1939–1945) MP1103/2, PWN1261
*Kaiser, Ned John Kurt (1939–1945) MP1103/2, 1273
*Weintraub, Elly (1939–1945), MP1103/2, ZF35547
*Weintraub, Max (1939–1945) MP1103/2, Z35548
*Weintraub, Stefan (1939–1945) MP1103/2, PWN1297

PP246/4 Personal Statement and Declaration forms, alphabetical order within nationality. Recorded by: (1924–1946) Investigation Branch, Western Australia.

Frischer, Emanuel (1937) PP246/4, POLISH/FRISCHER E
Goldner, Fritz (1937) PP246/4, AUSTRIAN/GOLDNERF
Graff, Horst (1937) PP246/4, GERMAN/GRAFF H
Kaiser, John Kurt (1938) PP246/4, SOUTH AMERICAN/KAISER J K

BIBLIOGRAPHY

Weintraub, Stefan (1937) PP246/4, GERMAN/WEINTRAUB S
Weiss, Leo (1937) PP246/4, GERMAN/WEISS L
Wise, Gordon Freddy (1937) PP246/4, AMERICAN/WISE G F

SP11/2 Applications for registration (aliens registration files). Recorded by: 01 Jan 1939 - 31 Dec 1947, Collector of Customs, Sydney.

SP11/2, SWEDISH/WEINTRAUB G I (1943) [title page only]

SP11/5 Applications for registration (aliens registration files) (forms A1, B1 and C), alphabetical series—naturalised. Recorded by: (01 Jan 1940 – 01 Nov 1945) Collector of Customs, Sydney; (01 Nov 1945 – 31 Dec 1947) Department of Immigration, New South Wales Branch.

Fisher, Emanuel (1939–1944) SP11/5, FISHER, EMANUEL
Frischer, Feigel (1939–1946) SP11/5, FRISCHER, FEIGEL
Frischer, Hildegard (1939–1943) SP11/5, FRISCHER, HILDEGARD
Graff, Horst (1939–1946) SP11/5, GRAFF, HORST
Graff, Margery (1940) SP11/5, GRAFF, MARGERY MINNA [Box 91]
Kaiser, Gerty Margarete (1939-1947) SP11/5, KAISER, GERTY MARGARETE [Box 91]
Kaiser, Ned John Kurt (1939–1946) SP11/5, KAISER, NED JOHN KURT
Weintraub, Elly (1942-1946) SP11/5, WEINTRAUB, ELLY [Box 212]
Weintraub, Gertrud Irene (1940–1945) SP11/5, WEINTRAUB, GERTRUD IRENE
Weintraub, Max (1942–1946) SP11/5, WEINTRAUB, MAX
Weintraub, Stefan (1939–1946) SP11/5, WEINTRAUB, STEFAN
Weiss, Leo (1939–1945) SP11/5, WEISS, LEO

SP1011/1 Australian Broadcasting Commission, Head Office, ABC publicity photos

SP1011/1, 2122, John Goldner, Band Leader (c.1960) [Box 93A]
SP1011/1, 4658, Leo White and his band (c.1958) [Box 137]

SP1011/2 Australian Broadcasting Commission, Head Office, Press cuttings and written publicity, general television and radio

SP1011/2, 'Leo White file' (box 113)

SP1048/7 General correspondence, 'S' (Secret) series. Recorded by: (Nov 1939 – Apr 1942) Headquarters, Eastern Command [I], Australian Military Forces.

Internee file, John Kurt Kaiser [box S64] (1940–1941) SP1048/7, S56/1/1041

ST1233/1 Investigation files, single number series with 'N' [New South Wales] prefix. Recorded by: (1919–1946) Investigation Branch, New South Wales.

Graff, Horst (1939–1945) ST1233/1, N22597, [Box 81]
Weintraub, Max and Elly (1942–1945) ST1233/1, N32786, [Box 108]
*Weintraub, Stefan (1939–1945) ST1233/1, N19220, [Box 71]

NAA Other Files (Selected)

A261 Department of Immigration, Central Office, Application Forms (Culled from other file series) for admission of relatives or friends to Australia (Form 40)

A261, 1946/1973, [Helfgott, Samuel]

A367 Commonwealth Investigation Branch (1919–1946), Correspondence Files, single number series with 'C' prefix, (1927–1953)

A367, C15091, [Ex-internee N9195—Luigi Ricci–Bitti] (1930–1945)

A432 Attorney-General's Department, Correspondence files, annual single number series

A432, 1937/383, Musician Union—exclusion of imported musicians (1935–1944)

A434 Department of the Interior, Correspondence files, Class 3 (Non British European Migrants)

A434, 1944/3/690, Snider and Dean Theatres Limited—Admission of Artists (1937-1945)

A435 Department of the Interior (to 1945)/Department of Immigration (from 1945), Class 4 correspondence files relating to naturalisation

A435, 1944/4/3629, JOSEPH Max (1944-1945)
A435, 1949/4/3458, HELFGOT AKA HELFGOTT Samuel (1949-1969)
A435, 1949/4/4772, REVESZ Gabor (1949-1954)
A435, 1949/4/1197, RICCI BITTI Luigi (1930-1949)

A444 Department of Immigration, Correspondence files, multiple number series, Class 16 (Migrants T–Z)

A444, 1952/16/2762, Musicians Union of Australia (1935–1946)

A12508 Department of Immigration, Central Office (July 1945 – Dec 1948), Personal Statement and Declaration by alien passengers entering Australia (Forms A42)

*A12508, 56/460, WISNIA, Mathys (1947)

B78 Department of Immigration, Victorian Branch Alien registration documents

*B78, 1952/WISNIA M (1948–1952)

B2114 Australian Broadcasting Commission, Victorian Branch, Correspondence files, multiple number series

*B2114, 6/7/4 Permanent Units—Musicians Union—Nationality Quotas (1952–1960)

BIBLIOGRAPHY

MP1170/3 Australian Broadcasting Control Board, Head Office, Broadcasting and General (1935–1970). Policy and General in regards to Broadcasting.

MP1170/3, BA/11/6 PART 1, Australian Talent—Musicians Union of Australia (1949–1952)

SP11/2 Department of Immigration, New South Wales Branch, Applications for registration (Aliens Registration files) (Forms A1, B1 and C), alphabetical series by nationality

SP11/2, YUGOSLAVIAN/SZENASSY K, (Box 210) (1940–1942)

SP173/1 Australian Broadcasting Commission, Head Office—Concert Management/Concert Department, Artists files, (1932–1950)

SP173/1, SVERDLOFF, LAZAR [Box 28] (1937)
SP173/1, SZENASSY, KAROLY (1940-1948)

SP368/1 Australian Broadcasting Commission, Head Office—Administrative Division Artists files

SP368/1, 7/55/7, Leo White [Box 29] (1948–1951)
SP368/1, 7/46/16, Luigi Ricci Bitti (Tasmanian Orchestra) [box 23] (1945–1953)

SP613 Australian Broadcasting Corporation, Head Office, General correspondence including Administration, Policy, and Artists' Contract files

SP613/1, 6/12/8, Report on Orchestras, all states—Eugene Ormandy [Box 20] (1944)
SP613/1, 7/10/12 PART 1, Eugene Goossens, Conductor, Sydney Symphony Orchestra (1946–1947)
SP613/1, 7/10/12 PART 2, Eugene Goossens, Conductor, Sydney Symphony Orchestra (1947–1950)
SP613, 6/1/7 PART 1 Sydney Symphony Orchestra—personnel (1943–1948)
SP613, 6/1/7 PART 2 Sydney Symphony Orchestra—personnel (1949–1956)

SP767/1 Press cuttings (staff, activities and artists). Recorded by: Australian Broadcasting Commission, Head Office.

SP767/1, KAROLY SZENASSY (1941-1948) [Box 4]

SP1011/1 Australian Broadcasting Commission, Head Office, ABC publicity photos

SP1011/1, 818, Henry Adler, pianist (1955) [Box 71A]

SP1011/2 Australian Broadcasting Commission, Head Office, Press cuttings and written publicity, general television and radio

SP1011/2, SIR EUGENE GOOSSENS ABC PRESS CLIPPINGS (1949–1956)

SP1558/2 Australian Broadcasting Commission, Head Office, Central Files

SP1558/2, 741, Permanent Units—Importation of Key instrumentalists—
 Employment of foreign musicians (1937–1941)
SP1558/2 750, Permanent Units—Reports on Orchestras (1933–1940)
SP1558/2, 760, Musicians Union [ABC file] (1936–1937)

NAA Files (Chapters 7 and 8)

Note: Dossiers and Tribunal Transcripts for Horst Graff and Stefan Weintraub are included in the list of named files above. The individuals listed below were Jewish internee signatories to the letter to the Minister for the Army, 3 December 1940, regarding the establishment of appeals tribunals.

A6119 ASIO Central Office, Personal files, alpha-numeric series

A6119, 104, SALOMON, Horst Egon (1940–1953)

C329 Transcripts of internees' appeals before the Aliens Control Tribunals and Advisory Committees

C329, 476, Max JOSEPH (Objection 192 of 1941) [Box 15]

MP508/1 Department of the Army, Central Office, General correspondence files, multiple number series

MP508/1, 255/702/529, [Assistance to Internees by the Rt. Rev, the Bishop
 Coadjutor of Sydney]
MP508/1, 255/711/59, Chronicle of German Internment Camps in Australia—
 found in Sydney Hotel (1940–1941)
Official Visitors' Reports, Tatura (mainly No 1 Internment Camp):
 MP508/1, 255/715/94
 MP508/1, 255/715/140
 MP508/1, 255/715/159
 MP508/1, 255/715/183
 MP508/1, 255/715/212
 MP508/1, 255/715/319
 MP508/1, 255/715/354
 MP508/1, 255/715/395
 MP508/1, 255/715/420
 MP508/1, 255/715/531
 MP508/1, 255/715/680
MP508/1, 255/730/143 [Jewish Refugee Internees]
MP508/1, 255/742/383, Dr Kurt Singer—release from internment (1940–1942)

MP529/2 Deputy Crown Solicitor's Office, Dossiers of German internees who lodged objections to detention under National Security (Aliens Control) Regulations

MP529/2, BERNHARD/HA

BIBLIOGRAPHY

MP529/2, FLEGENHEIMER/E
MP529/2, FLESCH/M
MP529/2, GINSBURG/W
MP529/2, GOLDFELD/E
MP529/2, GORE/WM
MP529/2, HERWEG/K
MP529/2, HORN/FL
MP529/2, JOSEPH/M
MP529/2, LESSER/A
MP529/2, LOEFFLER/F
MP529/2, SCHMOLKA/HD
MP529/2, SORAUER/H
MP529/2, WARSCHAUER/GE
MP529/2, WOLFF/KP

MP529/3 Aliens Tribunal transcripts of evidence of objections against internment under Regulation 26 of the National Security (General) Regulations

MP529/3, TRIBUNAL 1/FLEGENHEIMER
MP529/3, TRIBUNAL 1/FLESCH
MP529/3, TRIBUNAL 1/GINSBERG
MP529/3, TRIBUNAL 1/GOLDFELD
MP529/3, TRIBUNAL 4/SALOMON

MP529/8 Applications by enemy aliens for leave to submit objections against detention orders made under National Security (Aliens Control) Regulations. Recorded by: (22 Jan 1941 – 20 Aug 1942), Deputy Crown Solicitor's Office, Victoria.

MP529/8, JOSEPH/M (1940)
MP529/8, STARK/F

MP729/6 Department of the Army, Central Office, Secret correspondence files, multiple number series with '401' infix (1936–1945)

MP729/6, 65/401/79, Control of Aliens Independent Tribunals.

MP742/1 Department of the Army, Central Office, General and civil staff correspondence files and Army personnel files, multiple number series (1943–1951)

MP742/1, 255/2/814, Advisory Committees & Aliens Tribunals—Clerical Assistance

*MP1103/1 Prisoners of War and Internees Information Bureau, Registers containing 'Service and Casualty' forms of enemy prisoners of war and internees held in camps in Australia [online]

*MP1103/2 Prisoners of War and Internees Information Bureau, Dossiers containing reports on Internees and Prisoners of War held in Australian camps, single number series with alphabetical prefix [online]

Archives of the Professional Musicians' Union of Australia, Noel Butlin Archive Centre, Australian National University

Note: Information about foreign musicians—internal and external correspondence, rules, conference minutes and resolutions, news clippings—is spread across the archive of the Professional Musicians' Union of Australia. The list that follows is selective. A descriptive calendar of the holding is available from the Noel Butlin Archive Centre. Subject groupings are not consistent across all files.

Deposit E156

Series 1: Rule Books
Series 2: General Secretary's Correspondence Files, arranged by subject matter, 1922–54
Series 2/2: Correspondence with District Secretaries and Members of Federal Council, 1924–54.
    E156/2/2(ib), Correspondence with NSW, 1933–47.
    E156/2/2(ic), Correspondence with NSW, [1935–39].
    E156/2/2(iii), Correspondence with Victoria, 1931–35.
    E156/2/2(xi), Correspondence with District Secretaries, 1927–35.
    E156/2/2(xiii). Correspondence with NSW, 1946–54.
    E156/2/2(xx), '1938–48' (applications from foreign musicians)
Series 2/3: General Union Correspondence (including … Foreign Applications)
    E156/2/3(ii), General Correspondence, 1947–54.
    E156/2/3(v) ('1945–50'; '1950–52'; '1953–55'), (foreign applications, 1938–55)
    E156/2/3(va), '1948–55' (includes correspondence re ABC Nationality Quotas)
    E156/2/3 (vb), 'John Kay'.
Series 2/4: Correspondence with other Musicians' Unions, 1923–35.
    E156/2/4(i), (English, American and South African Unions, 1924–35)
Series 2/6: Correspondence with ABC, Government Departments and Parliament 1923–48.
    E156/2/6(ii), Correspondence with Government Departments 1927–35.
    E156/2/6(iii), Plans for postwar development.
    E156/2/6(va), Australian Broadcasting Commission (includes 'Isaac Stern Criticism').
Series 3: General Secretary's Correspondence, arranged mainly in chronological order, 1956–67.
    E156/3/6, Correspondence with District Secretaries re Foreign Applications, 1955–60.
Series 6: Annual Federal Conference Minutes, Secretary's and Treasurer's Reports, and other papers, 1914–64.
    E156/6/1–E156/6/10, and E156/6/17.

BIBLIOGRAPHY

Series 7: Membership rolls and related papers, 1921–55.
Series 8: Arbitration material:
   E156/8/7, Legal Opinions.
Series 9: Arbitration material (ABC related), 1938–51:
   E156/9/1, folder pt. 2 (arbitration transcripts, n.d.)
Series 11: Journal of the Professional Musicians' Union, 1928–9.
   E156/11/1, *The Professional Musician*

Deposit N93

N93/1, Minutes of Special Conference, February 1955.
N93/2A–N93/6, Minutes of Federal Conferences 1956–1960.
N93/476–N93 478, *Rules of the Musicians' Union of Australia*, 1925, 1927 and 1929.

Deposit T7

Series 1: Minute Books
   T7/1/6–T7/1/12 (1918–1941).
Series 15: Arbitration material, 1943–57.

Deposit Z391

Z391, box 34: 'Australian Broadcasting Commission'('1959'; '1960'; 'Quotas in ABC orchestras').
Z391, box 73: ('Rules 1948–49'; 'Rules 1958–61')

Deposit Z401

Z401, box 2.
Z401, box 3: Rule books 1900–1983
Z401, box 5: Correspondence with State and Federal Parliamentarians 1935–40; correspondence with General Secretary 1932–34.
Z401, boxes 6 and 7: Arbitration transcripts, legal opinions; Hoyts 1928–32.
Z401, box 12: Press cuttings 1927–29.
Z401, box 13: Press cuttings 1938–52.

Documents from David Buchan (Chapter Six)

Shanghai Municipal Police (SMP) Special Branch Reports:
   31 December 1934
   18 April 1936
   26 January 1937
   23 March 1937
   18 June 1937
   7 April 1941
Special Branch Memorandum on R.S. Buchan and W.M. Buchan 27 January 1937
Berkeley Gazette, 22 March 1946 at http://news.google.com/newspapers?nid= 1970&dat=19460322&id=5EkyAAAAIBAJ&sjid=OeQFAAAAIBAJ& pg=5552,6269387
Indexes to the 'Green' or Secret Papers among the General Correspondence of the Foreign Office, 1940. Nendeln/Liechtenstein: Kraus–Thomson, 1972 [Extract]
North China Daily News

16 December 1934
19 May 1936
3 October 1939
Shanghai Evening Post & Mercury 3 March 1937
Shanghai Times 29 November 1933

Other Libraries and Archives

Akademie der Künste Berlin

Musikarchiv, Bestand Weintraubs Syncopators

Australian Archive of Judaica, University of Sydney

Max Joseph papers box 3. Personal Papers of Max Joseph 1938–44.

National Library of Australia

MS 9908 John Kay [includes music scores and interview tapes]
Biographical files:
 Richard Goldner Bib ID 372320
 Robert Pikler Bib ID 1997969
 Gabor Reeves Bib ID 482658
 Jiri Tancibudek Bib ID 185792
 Stefan Weintraub Bib ID 655605
TROVE: Australian newspapers, digitised by the NLA, reported on the arrival and performances of the Weintraubs Syncopators from July 1937 onwards.

State Library NSW

MLMSS 6693 Karl Bittman—records of the Viennese Thatre (Kleines Wiener Theater), Sydney
MLMSS 7164X. Scrapbooks concerning the Mercury Theatre, 1940s–1950s [Sydney John Kay]
The New Citizen, Sydney: Association of New Citizens, 1946-1954.

State Records NSW

Premier's Department Special bundle:
 NRS 5343, 11/1573, *Industrial Commission of New South Wales* vol. 198. *Transcripts of Proceedings August 1944*. [John Kay transcript]
 NRS 12061, 8/2143, 41–1486 Activities of enemy aliens, 1916–41
 NRS 12061, 8/2143, 42–3040 The State's contribution to the War effort, 1945 A39–1230
 Series 6/1433, 1928, Industrial [Commission of NSW] M–R. Oyoyly and Martelli vs. Musicians' Union of Australia NSW District.

USC Shoah Foundation Institute Visual History Archive

Emanuel Fisher, Interview code 17168
Addy Fisher, Interview code 18125

BIBLIOGRAPHY

Victorian Jazz Archive
Mike Sutcliffe Collection

Legislation
Immigration Restriction Act 1901
Commonwealth Conciliation and Arbitration Act 1904
Contract Immigrants Act (Amending Immigration Act) 1905
Immigration Act 1925
Conciliation and Arbitration Act 1928
National Security Act 1939
Industrial Arbitration Act 1940 (NSW)
Nationality and Citizenship Act 1948

Part Two: Secondary Sources

Australian Dictionary of Biography

Cain, Frank. 'MacKay, William John (1885–1948)', *Australian Dictionary of Biography*, Volume 10, (Melbourne: Melbourne University Press, 1986), pp. 296–297.

Ewer, Peter and Peter Spearritt. 'Mair, Alexander (1889–1969)', *Australian Dictionary of Biography* 10 (1986), pp. 385–386.

Finn, Rosslyn. 'Snider, Leon Samuel (1896–1965)', *Australian Dictionary of Biography* 16 (2002), pp. 278–279.

Francis, Charles. 'Duffy, Sir Charles Leonard Gavan (1882–1961)', *Australian Dictionary of Biography* 8 (1981), pp. 351–352.

Lawson, Valerie. 'Norton, Ezra (1897–1967)', *Australian Dictionary of Biography* 15 (2000), pp. 495–497.

McCalman, Iain. 'Bendrodt, James Charles (1891–1973)', *Australian Dictionary of Biography* 13 (1993), pp. 161–162.

Moore, Andrew. 'Scott, William John Rendell (1888–1956)', *Australian Dictionary of Biography* 11 (1988), pp. 550–552.

Morris, Deirdre and Chris Cunneen, 'Gowrie, Sir Alexander Gore Arkwright Hore-Ruthven, 1st Earl (1872-1955)', *Australian Dictionary of Biography* 9 (1983), pp. 63–64.

Ritchie, John. 'Romano, Azzalin Orlando (1894–1972)', *Australian Dictionary of Biography* 11 (1988), p. 447.

Rutland, Suzanne D. 'Cohen, Rieke (1887–1964)', *Australian Dictionary of Biography* 13 (1993), pp. 457–458.

Salter, David. 'Goossens, Sir Eugene Aynsley (1893-1962)', *Australian Dictionary of Biography* 14, 1996, pp. 294–296.

Sharp, Ian G. 'Dethridge, George James (1863–1938)', *Australian Dictionary of Biography* 8 (1981), p. 293.

Sudrabs, Zaiga. 'Krips, Henry Joseph (1912–1987)', *Australian Dictionary of Biography* 17, (2007), pp. 640–641.

Williams, John M. 'Menzies, Sir Douglas Ian (1907–1974)', *Australian Dictionary of Biography* 15 (2000), pp. 351–353.

Wood, James. 'Sturdee, Sir Vernon Ashton Hobart (1890–1966)', *Australian Dictionary of Biography* 16 (2002), pp. 340–342.

Young, J. McI. 'O'Bryan, Sir Norman John (1894–1968)', *Australian Dictionary of Biography* 15 (2000), p. 513.

Books, Book Chapters and Journal Articles

Abrahams-Sprod, Michael. '"Australien! Wo ist den das?" The Migration Experience of Jewish Refugees from Nazi Germany'. *Australian Journal of Jewish Studies* 17 (2004): 9–24.

Arthur, Bronwen. '"Ban the Talkies!" Sound Film and the Musicians' Union of Australia 1927–1932'. *Context* 13 (Winter 1997): 47–57.

Arthur, Bronwen. 'Industrial Relations'. In *Currency Companion to Music and Dance in Australia*, edited by John Whiteoak and Aline Scott-Maxwell, 348–349. Strawberry Hills, NSW: Currency Press, 2003.

Australian Music Maker and Dance Band News (later *Music Maker*), July 1937 – December 1950.

Bartrop, Paul R. '"Good Jews" and "Bad Jews": Australian Perceptions of Jewish Migrants and Refugees, 1919–1939'. In *Jews in the Sixth Continent*, edited by W.D. Rubinstein, 169–184. North Sydney: Allen & Unwin, 1987.

Bartrop, Paul R. 'The Australian Government's "Liberalisation" of Refugee Immigration Policy in 1938: Fact or Myth?' *Menorah (Australian Journal of Jewish Studies)* 2/1, issue 2 (June 1988): 66–82.

Bartrop, Paul R. 'Enemy Aliens or Stateless Persons? The Legal Status of Refugees from Germany in Wartime Australia'. *Journal of the Australian Jewish Historical Society* X, Part 4 (November 1988): 270–280.

Bartrop, Paul R. '"Not a Problem for Australia": The *Kristallnacht* Viewed from the Commonwealth, November 1938'. *Journal of the Australian Jewish Historical Society* X, Part 6 (May 1989): 489–499.

Bartrop, Paul R. 'The Future of Australian Jewish Historiography: A Panel Discussion'. Part 2: Address by Paul R. Bartrop. *Menorah* 3/1, issue 4 (July 1989): 31–34.

Bartrop, Paul R. '"A Low Class of White People": The Garrett Report of 1939 and Plans for Jewish Migration to Australia in the 1940s'. *Menorah* 4/1–2, issue 6 (December 1990): 28–39.

Bartrop, Paul R. 'The "Jewish Race" Clause in Australian Immigration Forms'. *Journal of the Australian Jewish Historical Society* XI, Part 1 (November 1990): 69–78.

Bartrop, Paul R. 'Attitudes towards Refugees in 1939 and 1989: A Comparison'. *Without Prejudice* 2 (February 1991): 14–18.

Bartrop, Paul R. 'Incompatible with Security: Enemy Alien Internees from Singapore in Australia, 1940–45'. *Journal of the Australian Jewish Historical Society* XII, Part 1 (November 1993): 149–169.

Bartrop, Paul R. *Australia and the Holocaust 1933–45*. Melbourne: Australian Scholarly Publishing, 1994.

Bartrop, Paul R. 'Before the Refugees: Foreign Immigration Policy and Australia in the 1920s'. *Australian Jewish Historical Society Journal* XV, Part 3 (November 2000): 368–385.

BIBLIOGRAPHY

Bassett, Judith, 'Colonial Justice: The Treatment of Dalmatians in New Zealand during the First World War'. *New Zealand Journal of History* 33/2 (October 1999): 155–179.

Beaumont, Joan, ed. *Australia's War 1939–45*. St Leonard's, NSW: Allen & Unwin, 1996.

Beaumont, Joan, Ilma Martinuzzi O'Brien and Mathew Trinca, eds. *Under Suspicion: Citizenship and Internment in Australia during the Second World War*. Canberra: National Museum of Australia Press, 2008.

Benjamin, Rodney. *'A Serious Influx of Jews': A History of Jewish Welfare in Victoria*. St Leonards, NSW: Allen & Unwin, 1998.

Bergmeier, Horst J.P. *The Weintraub Story. Incorporated The Ady Rosner Story*. JAZZFREUND No. 16. Menden: der JAZZFREUND, 1982.

Bevege, Margaret. *Behind Barbed Wire: Internment in Australia during World War II*. St Lucia, Qld.: University of Queensland Press, 1993.

Blakeney, Michael. 'Australia and the Jewish Refugees from Central Europe: Government Policy 1933–1939'. Leo Baeck Institute *Year Book XXIX*. London: Secker & Warburg, 1984: 103–133.

Blakeney, Michael. *Australia and the Jewish Refugees 1933–1948*. Sydney: Croom Helm Australia, 1985.

Boulton, Alan. 'Government Regulation of the Internal Affairs of Unions'. In *Power, Conflict and Control in Australian Trade Unions*, edited by Kathryn Cole, 216–236.

Braham, Randolph L. *The Politics of Genocide: The Holocaust in Hungary*. Detroit: Wayne State University Press, 2000.

Brisbane, Katharine, ed. *Entertaining Australia*. Paddington, NSW: Currency Press, 1991.

Buzacott, Martin. *The Rite of Spring: 75 Years of ABC Music-Making*. Sydney: ABC Books, 2007.

Cain, Frank. 'Australian Intelligence Organisations and the Law: A Brief History'. *University of New South Wales Law Journal* 27/2 (2004): 296–318.

Cain, Frank. *The Origins of Political Surveillance in Australia*. Sydney, Melbourne: Angus & Robertson Publishers, 1983.

Castles, Stephen, Bill Cope, Mary Kalantzis and Michael Morrissey. *Mistaken Identity: Multiculturalism and the Demise of Nationalism in Australia*. Sydney: Pluto Press, 1995 (3rd edition, reprinted) (especially Chapter 1, 'A Nation Without Nationalism?' 1–15).

Chase, Malcolm and Christopher Shaw. 'The Dimensions of Nostalgia'. In *The Imagined Past: History and Nostalgia*, edited by Christopher Shaw and Malcolm Chase, 1–17. Manchester and New York: Manchester University Press, 1989.

Cockburn, M.R. and D. Yerbury. 'The Federal/State Framework of Australian Industrial Relations'. In *Power, Conflict and Control in Australian Trade Unions*, edited by Kathryn Cole, 52–84.

Cole, Kathryn, ed. *Power, Conflict and Control in Australian Trade Unions*. Ringwood: Penguin Books, 1982.

Cole, Suzanne and Kerry Murphy, 'Wagner in the Antipodes'. *Wagnerspectrum* 02/08: 237–264. Bayreuth: Richard-Wagner Museum, 2008.

Collins, Diane. *Hollywood Down Under: Australians at the Movies 1896 to the Present Day*. North Ryde, NSW: Angus & Robertson, 1987.

Commonwealth Arbitration Reports [1920–1960, MUA cases only].
Coulthard-Clark, C. D. 'Australia's War-Time Security Service'. *Defence Force Journal* 16 (May/June 1979): 23–27.
Coulthard-Clark, C. D. 'The Legion of Frontiersmen in Australia'. *Journal of the Royal Australian Historical Society* 75, Part 2 (October 1989): 132–141.
Cresciani, Gianfranco. 'Italian Immigrants 1920–1945'. In *The Australian People: An Encyclopedia of the Nation, Its People and Their Origins*, edited by James Jupp, 500–505. New York and Oakleigh, Vic.: Cambridge University Press, 2001.
Curthoys, Ann. 'An Uneasy Conversation: The Multicultural and the Indigenous'. In *Race, Colour and Identity in Australia and New Zealand*, edited by John Docker and Gerhard Fischer, 21–36. Sydney: University of New South Wales Press, 2000.
Curthoys, Ann. 'Liberalism and Exclusionism: A Prehistory of the White Australia Policy'. In *Legacies of White Australia: Race, Culture and Nation*, edited by Laksiri Jayasuriya, David Walker and Jan Gothard, 8–32. Crawley, WA: University of Western Australia Press, 2003.
Darian-Smith, Kate. 'War and Australian Society'. In *Australia's War 1939–45*, edited by Joan Beaumont, 54–81.
Deery, Stephen J. and David H. Plowman. *Australian Industrial Relations*. Sydney: McGraw-Hill Book Company Australia, 1991 (3rd edition).
Dreyfus, Kay. '"I Cannot Find a Corner in the World where I am Welcome." The Australian War-time Experience of the Weintraub[s] Syncopators'. *Journal of Musicological Research*, 26/2–3 (2007): 281–314.
Dreyfus, Kay. 'Musicians in Trouble: The Sad Case of the Weintraub[s] Syncopators'. In *Political Tourists: Australian Visitors to the Soviet Union in the 1930s and 1940s*, edited by Sheila Fitzpatrick and Carolyn Rasmussen, 190–211. Melbourne: Melbourne University Press, 2008.
Dreyfus, Kay. 'The Foreigner, the Musicians' Union and the State in 1920s Australia: A Nexus of Conflict', *Music & Politics* 3/1 (Winter 2009) (online publication).
Dreyfus, Kay. '"Truth" and the Telling of the Past in the Bio-documentary Film *Weintraubs Syncopators: Bis ans andere Ende der Welt*'. *Zeitschrift für Australienstudien* 24 (2010), 7–22.
Dreyfus, Kay. 'The Weintraub[s] Syncopators, the Jewish Question and the Musicians' Union of Australia 1937-1953'. *Australian Jewish Historical Society Journal* XX, Part I (November 2010): 81–109.
Dreyfus, Kay. 'Breaching the Profession: Jewish survivors, Displaced Persons, and the post-War Musicians' Union of Australia'. *Musicology Australia* 34/1 (July 2012): 33–52.
Dümling, Albrecht. 'Uncovering Traces: German-speaking Refugee Musicians in Australia'. *Australian Jewish Historical Society Journal* XIX, Part 2 (November 2008): 219–236.
Dümling, Albrecht. *Die verschwundenen Musiker: Jüdische Flüchtlinge in Australien*. Köln, Wiemar, Wien: Böhlau Verlag, 2011.
Dutton, David. 'The Commonwealth Investigation Branch and the Political Construction of the Australian Citizenry, 1920–40'. *Labour History* 75 (November 1998): 155–174.
Dutton, David. '"Mere Passion and Prejudice": The Allegiance and Nationality of Aliens in Commonwealth Government Policy, 1914–57'. In *Australian*

Identities, edited by David Day, 96–115. Melbourne: Australian Scholarly Publishing, 1998.

Dutton, David. *Citizenship in Australia: A Guide to Commonwealth Government Records*. National Archives Research Guide No. 10, Canberra: National Archives of Australia, 1999.

Dutton, David. *One of Us? A Century of Australian Citizenship*. Sydney: University of New South Wales Press, 2002.

Ehrlich, Cyril. *The Music Profession in Britain since the Eighteenth Century, A Social History*. Oxford: Clarendon Press 1985.

Ferguson, Kathy E. *The Feminist Case against Bureaucracy*. Philadelphia: Temple University Press, 1984.

Fitzpatrick, Sheila. 'Supplicants and Citizens: Public Letter-Writing in Soviet Russia in the 1930s'. *Slavic Review* 55/1 (Spring 1996): 78–105.

Fitzpatrick, Sheila. *Everyday Stalinism. Ordinary Life in Extraordinary Times: Soviet Russia in the 1930s*. New York: Oxford University Press, 1999.

Fitzpatrick, Sheila. 'Making a Self for the Times: Impersonation and Imposture in Twentieth-Century Russia'. *Kritika: Explorations in Russian and Eurasian History* 2/3 (Summer 2001): 469–487.

Fitzpatrick, Sheila. *Tear Off the Masks! Identity and Imposture in Twentieth-Century Russia*. Princeton: Princeton University Press, 2005, especially 'Becoming Soviet', 3–26; 'Supplicants and Citizens', 155–181; 'Signals from Below', 205–239.

Fitzpatrick, Sheila and Robert Gellately, eds. *Accusatory Practices: Denunciation in Modern European History 1789–1989*. Chicago and London: Chicago University Press, 1997.

Foenander, Orwell De R. *Trade Unionism in Australia: Some Aspects*. Australia: The Law Book Co. of Australasia, 1962.

Forbes, A.H. 'Australian Broadcasting Corporation (ABC)'. In *The Oxford Companion to Australian Music*, edited by Warren Bebbington, 32–33. Melbourne: Oxford University Press, 1997.

Ford, Bill and David Plowman, eds. *Australian Unions: An Industrial Relations Perspective*. South Melbourne: The Macmillan Company, 1989 (2nd edition).

Gardner, Margaret. 'Union Strategy: A Gap in Union Theory'. In *Australian Unions: An Industrial Relations Perspective*, edited by Bill Ford and David Plowman, 49–73.

Gellately, Robert. 'The Gestapo and German Society: Political Denunciation in the Gestapo Case Files'. *Journal of Modern History* 60 (March–December 1988): 654–694.

Gellately, Robert. *The Gestapo and German Society: Enforcing Racial Policy 1933–1945*. New York: Oxford University Press, 1990.

Gellately, Robert. 'Denunciations and Nazi Germany: New Insights and Methodological Problems'. *Historical Social Research* 22/3–4 (1997): 228–239.

Gellately, Robert. *Backing Hitler: Consent and Coercion in Nazi Germany*. New York: Oxford University Press, 2001.

Gellately, Robert. 'Denunciation as a Subject of Historical Research'. *Historical Social Research* 26/2–3 (2001): 16–29.

Gilbert, Martin. *Kristallnacht: Prelude to Disaster*. London: HarperPress, 2006.

Gilliam, Bryan, ed. *Music and Performance during the Weimar Republic*. Cambridge

Studies in Performance Practice, Vol. 3. Cambridge: Cambridge University Press, 1994.

Goffman, Erving. *Stigma: Notes on the Management of Spoiled Identity*. London: Penguin Books, 1990 [1963].

Golvan, Colin. *The Distant Exodus*. Crows Nest, NSW: ABC Enterprises, 1990.

Gorbman, Claudia. *Unheard Melodies: Narrative Film Music*. Bloomington: Indiana University Press, 1987.

Gouttman, Rodney. 'The Pilcher Conundrum'. *Journal of the Australian Jewish Historical Society* XI, Part 1, (November 1990):79–81.

Guyatt, Joy. 'A Study of the Attitudes to Jews and of the Jewish Stereotype in Eastern Australia, 1938 to 1948, as reflected by Government policies, parliamentary debates and public opinion as expressed by newspapers, journals and sundry publications'. MA qualifying thesis, University of Queensland, 1967.

Gyger, Alison. *Opera for the Antipodes*. Paddington, NSW: Currency Press and Pellinor, 1990.

Hage, Ghassan. *White Nation: Fantasies of White Supremacy in a Multicultural Society*. Sydney: Pluto Press, 1998.

Hammerton, A. James and Alistair Thomson, *Ten Pound Poms: Australia's Invisible Migrants*. Manchester: Manchester University Press, 2005.

Harré, Rom. *Personal Being: A Theory for Individual Psychology*. Oxford: Basil Blackwell, 1983.

Healey, Bede. *Federal Arbitration in Australia: An Historical Outline*. Melbourne: Georgian House, 1972.

Hearn, Mark. 'Sifting the Evidence: Labour History and the Transcripts of Industrial Arbitration Proceedings'. *Labour History* 93 (November 2007): 3–13.

Hearn, Mark and Harry Knowles. 'Struggling for Recognition: Reading the Individual in Labour History'. *Labour History* 87 (November 2004): 1–10.

Heilbrun, Carolyn G. 'Is Biography Fiction?' *Soundings* 76/2–3 (Summer/Fall 1993): 295–304.

Henderson, David. 'Academic Aliens: The University of Sydney during the Second World War'. In *Under Suspicion: Citizenship and Internment in Australia during the Second World War*, edited by Joan Beaumont *et al.*, 84–92.

Henderson, David. 'The Internment of Germans in Second World War Australia: An Exploration in History and Memory'. PhD thesis, La Trobe University, 2009.

Hoffman, Beatrix R. 'Workers and Players. The Musicians' Union, 1928–1940'. MA thesis, University of Warwick, 1989.

Hooper, Beverley Joan. 'Australian Reactions to German Persecution of the Jews and Refugee Immigration, 1933–1947'. MA thesis, Australian National University, 1972.

Howard, W.A. 'Trade Unions and the Arbitration System'. In *State and Economy in Australia*, edited by Brian Head, 238–251. Melbourne: Oxford University Press, 1983.

Inglis, K.S. assisted by Jan Brazier. *Sacred Places: War Memorials in the Australian Landscape*. Melbourne: Miegunyah Press, 1998 (especially Chapter 3).

Inglis, Ken. 'From Berlin to the Bush'. *The Monthly*, August 2010, 48–53.

Jadeja, Raj. *Parties to the Award: A Guide…1904–1994*. Canberra: Noel Butlin

BIBLIOGRAPHY

Archives Centre, Research School of Social Sciences, Australian National University, 1994.

Jelavich, Peter. *Berlin Cabaret*. Cambridge, Mass. & London: Harvard University Press, 1993.

Jelavich, Peter, 'Performing High and Low: Jews in Theater, Cabaret, Revue, and Film'. In *Berlin Metropolis: Jews and the New Culture, 1890–1918*, edited by Emily Bilsky, 208-235. New York: The Jewish Museum, 1999.

Jelavich, Peter. 'Kabarett'. In *Europäische Traditionen—Enzyklopädie jüdischer Kulturen*, edited by Dan Diner. Leipzig: Simon Dubnow Institut für jüdische Geschichte und Kultur an der Universität Leipzig, volume 3, forthcoming.

Jenkings, Patricia Anne Bernadette. 'Australian Political Elites and Citizenship Education for "New Australians" 1945–1960'. PhD thesis, University of Sydney, 2001.

Johnson, Bruce and John Whiteoak. 'Jazz'. In *Currency Companion to Music and Dance in Australia*, edited by John Whiteoak and Aline Scott-Maxwell, especially 376–377.

Jordens, Ann-Mari. *Redefining Australians: Immigration, Citizenship and National Identity*. Sydney: Hale & Iremonger, 1995.

Kassabian, Anahid. *Hearing Film: Tracking Identifications in Contemporary Hollywood Film Music*. New York: Routledge, 2001.

Kater, Michael H. *Different Drummers: Jazz in the Culture of Nazi Germany*. New York: Oxford University Press, 1992.

Kater, Michael H. 'The Revenge of the Fathers: The Demise of Modern Music at the End of the Weimar Republic'. *German Studies Review* 15/2 (May 1992): 295–315.

Kater, Michael H. *The Twisted Muse: Musicians and Their Music in the Third Reich*. New York: Oxford University Press, 1997.

Katz, Steven T. '1918 and After: The Role of Racial Anti-Semitism in the Nazi Analysis of the Weimar Republic'. In *Anti-Semitism in Times of Crisis*, edited by Sander L. Gilman and Steven T. Katz, 227–256. [New York]: New York University Press, 1991.

Kirk, Neville. 'Traditionalists and Progressives: Labor, Race, and Immigration in Post-World War II Australia and Britain'. *Australian Historical Studies* 39/1 (2008): 53–71.

Kirkby, Diane. 'Arbitration and the Fight for Economic Justice'. In *Foundations of Arbitration*, edited by Stuart Macintyre and Richard Mitchell, 334–351.

Klapdor, Michael, Moira Coombs and Catherine Bohm, 'Australian Citizenship: A Chronology of Major Developments in Policy and Law'. Parliament of Australia: Department of Parliamentary Services, 2009, at http://www.citizenship.gov.au/_pdf/cit_chron_policy_law.pdf

Klinger, Barbara. '"Cinema/Ideology/Criticism" Revisited: The Progressive Text'. *Screen* 25/1 (January–February 1984): 30–44.

Knee, Lurline and Arthur. *Marched In. Seven Internment and Prisoner of War Camps in the Tatura Area during World War 2*. Tatura: Lurline & Arthur Knee, 2008.

Koehne, Samuel. 'Refusing to Leave: Perceptions of German National Identity during Internment in Australia, 1941–45'. In *Under Suspicion: Citizenship and Internment in Australia during the Second World War*, edited by Joan Beaumont et al., 67–83.

Koehne, Samuel. '"Disturbance in D Compound": The Question of Control in Australian Internment Camps during World War II'. *Melbourne Historical Journal* 34 (2006): 71–86.
Kunz, Egon F. 'The Engineering Profession and the Displaced Person Migrant in Australia'. *International Migration* 7/1–2 (January 1969): 22–30.
Kunz, Egon F. 'Australian Professional Attitudes and the Immigrant Professional'. ANZAAS Congress, Perth, 1973 (typescript).
Kunz, Egon F. *The Intruders: Refugee Doctors in Australia*. Canberra: Australian National University Press, 1975.
Kunz, Egon F. *The Hungarians in Australia*. Melbourne: AE Press, 1985.
Kunz, Egon F. *Displaced Persons: Calwell's New Australians*. Sydney: Australian National University Press, 1988.
Kwiet, Konrad. '"Be Patient and Reasonable!" The Internment of German-Jewish Refugees in Australia'. *Australian Journal of Politics and History* 31/1 (1985): 61–77. Special Issue: *On Being a German-Jewish Refugee in Australia*, edited by Konrad Kwiet and John A. Moses.
Kwiet, Konrad. 'Max Joseph. Lebensweg eines deutsch-jüdischen Emigranten'. In *Antisemitismus und jüdische Geschichte*, edited by Rainer Erb and Manfred Schmidt, 231-242. Studien zu Ehren Herbert A. Strauss, Berlin: Weidler, 2006.
Lamidey, Noel W. *Aliens Control in Australia 1939–46*. Sydney: Noel Lamidey, 1974.
Lang, Birgit. 'Exilkabarett und die "Politik der Repräsentation". Die Kabarettaufführungen des *Kleinen Wiener Theaters* in Sydney, Australien (1945-1973)'. In *Hundert Jahre Kabarett: zur Inszenierung Gesellschaftlicher Identität zwischen Protest und Propaganda*, edited by Joane McNally and Peter Sprengel, 96-116. Würzburg: Köninghausen & Naumann, 2003.
Langfield, Michelle. '"White Aliens": The Control of European Immigration to Australia, 1920–30'. *Journal of Intercultural Studies* 12/2 (1991): 1–14.
Langfield, Michelle. *More People Imperative: Immigration to Australia, 1901–39*. Guides to the Collection No. 7. Canberra: National Archives of Australia, 1999.
Lareau, Alan. 'The German Cabaret Movement during the Weimar Republic'. *Theatre Journal* 43 (1991): 471–490.
Lareau, Alan. *The Wild Stage: Literary Cabarets of the Weimar Republic*. Columbia, SC: Camden House, 1995.
Larsson, Marina. *Shattered Anzacs: Living with the Scars of War*. Kensington, NSW: University of New South Wales Press, 2009.
Leonard, Neil. *Jazz and the White Americans: The Acceptance of a New Art Form*. Chicago and London: University of Chicago Press, 1962.
Levey, Geoffrey Brahm, 'Jews and Australian Multiculturalism'. In *Jews and Australian Politics*, edited by Geoffrey Brahm Levey and Philip Mendes, 179–197. Brighton, Portland: Sussex Academic Press, 2004.
Levi, Erik. *Music in the Third Reich*. New York: St Martin's Press, 1994.
Louis, L.J. *Trade Unions and the Depression: A Study of Victoria, 1930–1932*. Canberra: Australian National University Press, 1968.
Love, Peter. '"The Kingdom of Shylock": A Case-Study of Australian Labor Anti-Semitism'. *Journal of the Australian Jewish Historical Society* XII, Part 1 (November 1993): 54–62.

BIBLIOGRAPHY

Macintyre, Stuart. 'Labour, Capital and Arbitration, 1890–1920'. In *State and Economy in Australia*, edited by B.W. Head, 98–114.

Macintyre, Stuart and Richard Mitchell, eds. *Foundations of Arbitration: The Origins and Effects of State Compulsory Arbitration 1890–1914*. Melbourne: Oxford University Press, 1989.

McCarthy, John. 'Australia and the German Consul-Generals 1923–39'. *Australian Journal of Politics and History* 27/3 (1981): 344–353.

McLennan, Andrew (producer). '"From Where? And Where To?" Episodes in the Life of the Musical Clown Friedrich Hollaender,' produced by and for *The Listening Room*, ABC Radio National, http://www.abc.net.au/rn/intothemusic/stories/2007/1823004.htm (17 February 2007) and http://www.abc.net.au/rn/intothemusic/stories/2007/1846278.htm (24 February 2007), accessed April 2010.

McShane, Ian 'Challenging or Conventional? Migration History in Australian Museums'. In *Negotiating Histories: National Museums*. Conference proceedings edited by Daryl McIntyre and Kirsten Wehner, 122–133. Canberra: National Museum of Australia, 2001.

Markey, Ray. 'Trade Unions, the Labor Party and the Introduction of Arbitration in New South Wales and the Commonwealth'. In *Foundations of Arbitration*, edited by Stuart Macintyre and Richard Mitchell, 156–177.

Markus, Andrew. 'Divided We Fall: The Chinese and the Melbourne Furniture Trade Union 1870–1900'. *Labour History* 26 (May 1974): 1–10.

Markus, Andrew. *Fear and Hatred: Purifying Australia and California 1850–1901*. Sydney: Hale & Iremonger, 1979.

Markus, Andrew. 'History of Post-War Immigration'. In *New History: Studying Australia Today*, edited by G. Osborne and W.F. Mandle, 94–112. North Sydney: George Allen & Unwin Australia P/L, 1982.

Markus, Andrew. 'Jewish Migration to Australia 1938–49'. *Journal of Australian Studies* 13 (November 1983): 18–31.

Markus, Andrew. 'Labour and Immigration: Policy Formation 1943–5'. *Labour History* 46 (May 1984): 21–33.

Markus, Andrew. 'Labour and Immigration 1946–9: The Displaced Persons Programme'. *Labour History* 47 (November 1984): 73–90.

Markus, Andrew. *Australian Race Relations 1788–1993*. St Leonards: Allen & Unwin, 1994.

Martin, Jean I. *The Migrant Presence: Australian Responses 1947–1977*. Hornsby, NSW: George Allen & Unwin, 1978, especially Chapters 2 ('Overview') and 7 ('Trade Unions').

Martin, Ross M. *Trade Unions in Australia: Who Runs Them, Who Belongs—Their Politics, Their Power*. Ringwood: Penguin Books, 1980 (Revised edition).

Martinez, Julia 'Questioning "White Australia": Unionism and "Coloured" Labour, 1911–37'. *Labour History* 76 (May 1999): 1–19.

Mitchell, Richard. 'State Systems of Conciliation and Arbitration: The Legal Origins of the Australasian Model'. In *Foundations of Arbitration*, edited by Stuart Macintyre and Richard Mitchell, 74–103.

Mitchell, Richard and Stuart Rosewarne. 'Individual Rights and the Law in Australian Industrial Relations'. In *Power, Conflict and Control in Australian Trade Unions*, edited by Kathryn Cole, 188–215.

Mitchell, Richard and Esther Stern, 'The Compulsory Arbitration Model of Industrial Dispute Settlement: An Outline of Legal Developments'. In *Foundations of Arbitration*, edited by Stuart Macintyre and Richard Mitchell, 104–131.

Mitten, Richard and Ruth Wodak. 'On the Discourse of Racism and Prejudice'. *Folia Linguistica* 27/2–4 (1993): 191–215.

Moore, Andrew. *The Secret Army and the Premier: Conservative Paramilitary Organisations in New South Wales 1930–32*. Kensington NSW: New South Wales University Press, 1989.

Moore, Andrew. '" … When the Caretaker's Busy Taking Care"? Cross-Currents in Australian Political Surveillance and Internment, 1935–1941'. In *Alien Justice: Wartime Internment in Australia and North America*, edited by Kay Saunders and Roger Daniels, 47–65. St Lucia: University of Queensland Press, 2000.

Morgan, Kenneth. 'Cultural Advance: the Formation of Australia's Permanent Orchestras, 1944–1951', *Musicology Australia* 33/1 (July 2011), 69–93.

Morgan, Kenneth. 'Sir James Barrett, Musical Patron in Melbourne'. In *Marshall-Hall's Melbourne: Music, Art and Controversy 1891-1915*, edited by Thérèse Radic and Suzanne Robinson, 89-107. Melbourne: Australian Scholarly Publishing, 2012.

Müller, Gerhard. 'Weintraubs Jazz Odyssee'. Programmheft Nr. 33, 11 December 2007. http://www.berlinerphilharmoniker.de/konzerte/kalender/programmdetails/konzert/2994/termin/2007 12-11-20-00/, accessed February 2010.

Münz, Lori, editorial direction. *Cabaret Berlin: Revue, Kabarett and Film Music between the Wars*. Hamburg: Edel Classics GmbH, 2005.

Neumann, Klaus. *Refuge Australia: Australia's Humanitarian Record*. Sydney: University of New South Wales Press, 2004.

Neumann, Klaus. 'Fifth Columnists? German and Austrian Refugees in Australian Internment Camps'. Public Lecture for the National Archives of Australia, the Goethe Institute (Sydney) and the Centre for European Studies at the University of New South Wales. Sydney, 2002. At http://uncommonlives.naa.gov.au/, accessed 18 May 2006.

Neumann, Klaus. *In the Interest of National Security: Civilian Internment in Australia during World War II*. Canberra: National Archives of Australia, 2006.

Nichols, Bill. *Representing Reality: Issues and Concepts in Documentary*. Bloomington: Indiana University Press, 1991.

Nichols, Bill. *Introduction to Documentary*. Bloomington: Indiana University Press, 2001.

O'Brien, Ilma Martinuzzi. 'Citizenship, Rights and Emergency Powers in Second World War Australia'. *Australian Journal of Politics and History* 53/2 (2007): 207–222.

Palfreyman, A.C. *The Administration of the White Australia Policy*. Melbourne: Melbourne University Press, 1967.

Palmer, Glen. *Reluctant Refuge: Unaccompanied Refugee and Evacuee Children in Australia, 1933–1945*. East Roseville, NSW: Kangaroo Press, 1997.

Perkins, John and Andrew Moore. 'Fascism in Interwar Australia'. In *Fascism Outside Europe: The European Impulse against Domestic Conditions in the Diffusion of Global Fascism*, edited by Stein Ugelvik Larsen, 269–286. Boulder:

BIBLIOGRAPHY

Social Science Monographs, 2001.

Peters, Nonja. 'From Aliens to Austr(aliens): A Look at Immigration and Internment Policies'. In *From Curtin to Coombs: War and Peace in Australia*. Seminar at Curtin University of Technology, 25 March 2003. At http://john.curtin.edu.au/events/seminar2003.html, accessed September 2010.

Plantinga, Carl R. *Rhetoric and Representation in Nonfiction Film*. Cambridge: Cambridge University Press, 1997.

Portelli, Alessandro. 'What Makes Oral History Different'. In *The Oral History Reader*, edited by Robert Perks and Alistair Thomson, 63–74. London and New York: Routledge, 1998.

Price, Charles 'Postwar Immigration, 1947–98'. *Journal of Population Research* 15/2 (1998): 115–129.

Reisigl, Martin and Ruth Wodak. *Discourse and Discrimination: Rhetorics of Racism and Antisemitism*. London: Routledge, 2001.

Richardson, John E. and Ruth Wodak. 'Recontextualising Fascist Ideologies of the Past: Right-wing Discourses on Employment and Nativism in Austria and the United Kingdom'. *Critical Discourse Studies* 6/4 (November 2009): 251–267.

Ringer, Alexander L. 'Dance on a Volcano: Notes on Musical Satire and Parody in Weimar Germany'. *Comparative Literature Studies* 12/3 (September 1975): 248–262.

Robinson, J. Bradford. 'Jazz Reception in Weimar Germany: In Search of a Shimmy Figure'. In *Music and Performance during the Weimar Republic*, edited by Bryan Gilliam, 107–134.

Rosen, Carole. *The Goossens: A Musical Century*. London: Andre Deutsch, 1993.

Rosenstone, Robert A. *History on Film/Film on History*, Harlow, UK: Pearson Education Limited, 2006.

Rubenstein, Kim. 'Citizenship in Australia: Unscrambling Its Meaning'. *Melbourne University Law Review* 20 (1995): 503–527.

Rubenstein, Kim. 'An Unequal Membership: The Constitution's Score on Citizenship'. In *Legacies of White Australia: Race, Culture and Nation*, edited by Laksiri Jayasuriya, David Walker and Jan Gothard, 145–162.

Rubinstein, Hilary L. *Chosen: The Jews in Australia*. Sydney, London, Boston: Allen & Unwin, 1987.

Rubinstein, Hilary L. *The Jews in Australia: A Thematic History*. 2 vols. *Volume One: 1788–1945*, Port Melbourne: William Heinemann Australia, 1991.

Rubinstein, W. D. 'Australia and the Refugee Jews of Europe, 1933–1954: A Dissenting View'. *Journal of the Australian Jewish Historical Society* X, Part 6 (May 1989): 500–523.

Rubinstein, W. D. *The Jews in Australia: A Thematic History*. 2 vols. *Volume Two: 1945 to the Present*. Port Melbourne: William Heinemann Australia, 1991.

Rutland, Suzanne D. *Take Heart Again: The Story of a Fellowship of Jewish Doctors*. [Sydney]: Fellowship of Jewish Doctors of New South Wales, 1983.

Rutland, Suzanne D. 'Australian Government Policies to Refugee Migration 1933–1939'. *Journal of the Royal Australian Historical Society* 69, Part 4 (March 1984): 224–238.

Rutland, Suzanne D. 'Australian Responses to Jewish Refugee Migration Before and After World War II'. *Australian Journal of Politics and History* 31/1 (1985): 29–48.

Rutland, Suzanne D. '"Waiting Room Shanghai": Australian Reactions to the Plight of the Jews in Shanghai after the Second World War'. Leo Baeck Institute *Year Book XXXII*. London: Secker & Warburg, 1987: 407–433.

Rutland, Suzanne D. 'Australia and Refugee Migration, 1933–1945: Consensus or Conflict'. *Menorah (Australian Journal of Jewish Studies)* 2/2, issue 3 (December 1988): 77–91.

Rutland, Suzanne D. *Edge of the Diaspora* (2nd revised edition). Sydney: Brandl & Schlesinger, 1997 [1988].

Rutland, Suzanne D. 'Postwar Anti-Jewish Refugee Hysteria: A Case of Racial or Religious Bigotry?' *Journal of Australian Studies* 77 (2002): 69–79.

Rutland, Suzanne D. *The Jews in Australia*. New York: Cambridge University Press, 2005 (especially Chapter 4, 'The Watershed Years').

Sametz, Phillip. *Play On! 60 Years of Music-making with the Sydney Symphony Orchestra*. Sydney: ABC Enterprises, 1992.

Sander, Klaus and Jörg Süssenbach. *Weintraubs Syncopators: Bis ans anderes Ende der Welt*. [Berlin]: Cine Impuls KG for WDR TV in collaboration with Arte Media, 2000 [documentary film].

Saunders, Kay. '"Inspired by Patriotic Hysteria?" Internment Policy towards Enemy Aliens in Australia during the Second World War'. In *Minorities in Wartime*, edited by Panikos Panayi, 287–315. Providence and Oxford: Berg Publishers Ltd, 1993.

Saunders, Kay. 'A Difficult Reconciliation: Civil Liberties and Internment Policy in Australia during World War Two'. In *Alien Justice: Wartime Internment in Australia and North America*, edited by Kay Saunders and Roger Daniels, 114–137.

Saunders, Kay (with Helen Taylor). 'The Enemy Within? The Process of Internment of Enemy Aliens, 1939–45'. In *War on the Homefront: State Intervention in Queensland 1938–1948*, 33–58. St Lucia: University of Queensland Press, 1993.

Sawer, Geoffrey. *Australian Federal Politics and Law 1901–1929*. Carlton: Melbourne University Press, 1972.

Shklar, Judith N. 'The Ambiguities of Betrayal'. In *Ordinary Vices*, 138–191. Cambridge, Mass.: Bleknap Press of Harvard University Press, 1984.

Shumway, David R. 'Rock 'n' Roll Sound Tracks and the Production of Nostalgia'. *Cinema Journal* 38/2 (Winter 1999): 36–51.

Sipe, Dan. 'The Future of Oral History and Moving Images'. In *The Oral History Reader*, edited by Robert Perks and Alistair Thomson, 379–388.

Smith, Graeme. 'Public Multicultural Music and the Australian State'. *Music & Politics* III/2 (Summer 2009). http://www.music.ucsb.edu/projects/musicandpolitics/past.html, accessed September 2010.

Smith, Neil C. *Dictionary of Australian Military Abbreviations*. Brighton, Vic.: Mostly Unsung, 2002.

Starr, S. Frederick. *Red and Hot: The Fate of Jazz in the Soviet Union 1917–1980*. New York: Oxford University Press, 1983.

Steinweis, Alan E. 'The Professional, Social, and Economic Dimensions of Nazi Cultural Policy: The Case of the Reich Theater Chamber'. *German Studies Review* XIII /3 (October 1990): 441–459.

Steinweis, Alan E. '"Unreliable" and "Unfit": The Reich Chamber of Culture and the Expulsion of Jews and Other "Dangerous Elements" from German Cultural

BIBLIOGRAPHY

Life, 1933–1945'. In *Holocaust Studies Annual 1991*, edited by Sanford Pinsker and Jack Fischel, 5–22. New York and London: Garland Publishing, 1992.

Steinweis, Alan E. *Art, Ideology, & Economics in Nazi Germany: The Reich Chambers of Music, Theater, and the Visual Arts*. Chapel Hill and London: University of North Carolina Press, 1993.

Stewart, Murray M., ed., *Commonwealth Arbitration Reports* (CAR) Vol. 27 (1928–29). Melbourne: The Law Book Company of Australasia Ltd.

Stilwell, Robynn J. 'The Fantastical Gap between Diegetic and Nondiegetic'. In *Beyond the Soundtrack: Representing Music in Cinema*, edited by Daniel Goldmark, Lawrence Kramer and Richard Leppert, 184–202. Berkeley, Los Angeles and London: University of California Press, 2007.

Stratton, Jon. 'The Colour of Jews: Jews, Race and the White Australia Policy'. *Journal of Australian Studies* 20/50–51 (1996): 51–65.

Tavan, Gwenda. 'The Abolition of the White Australia Policy: Elite Conspiracy or Will of the Australian People?' *Australian Journal of Political Science* 39/1 (March 2004): 109–125.

Tavan, Gwenda. *The Long, Slow Death of White Australia*. Melbourne: Scribe Publications, 2005.

Tavan, Gwenda. 'The Limits of Discretion: The Role of the Liberal Party in the Dismantling of the White Australia Policy'. *Australian Journal of Politics and History* 51/3 (September 2005): 418–428.

Tempo: The Australian Musical News Magazine. Sydney, NSW: Tempo, July 1937–1955.

Thompson, Stephanie Lindsay. 'Italian Migrant Experiences of Australian Culture (1945–1970)'. In *Australia, the Australians and the Italian Migration*, edited by Gianfranco Cresciani, 27–47 (especially Part 1. Historical Background, 28–32). Milan: Quaderno di Affari Sociali Internazionale, 1983.

Turnbull, Malcolm. *Safe Haven: Records of the Jewish Experience in Australia*. National Archives Research Guide No 12, Canberra: National Archives of Australia, 1999.

Walker, David. *Anxious Nation: Australia and the Rise of Asia 1850–1939*. St Lucia, Qld.: University of Queensland Press, 1999 (especially Chapter 8: 'The Invasion Narrative').

Walker, David. 'Strange Reading: Keith Windschuttle on Race, Asia and White Australia'. *Australian Historical Studies* 37/128 (2006): 108–122.

Wasserstein, Bernard. *Secret War in Shanghai: Treachery, Subversion and Collaboration in the Second World War*. London: Profile Books, 1998.

Weissweiler, Eva. *Ausgemerzt! Das Lexikon der Juden in der Musik und seine mörderischen Folgen*. Köln: Dittrich-Verlag, 1999.

White, Hayden. *Metahistory: The Historical Imagination in Nineteenth-century Europe*. Baltimore & London: The Johns Hopkins University Press, 1973.

White, Hayden. 'Historiography and Historiophoty'. *American Historical Review* 93/5 (December 1988): 1193–1199.

White, Naomi Rosh and Peter B. White, 'Evaluating the Immigrant Presence: Press Reporting of Immigrants to Australia, 1935–77'. *Ethnic and Racial Studies* 6/3 (July 1983): 284–307.

Wicke, Peter and Richard Deveson. 'Sentimentality and High Pathos: Popular Music in Fascist Germany'. *Popular Music* 5 (1985): 149–158.

Windschuttle, Keith. *The White Australia Policy*. Paddington, NSW: Macleay Press, 2004.

Winter, Christine. 'The Long Arm of the Third Reich: Internment of New Guinea Germans in Tatura'. *Journal of Pacific History* 38/1 (June 2003): 85–108.

Winter, Christine. 'Neutral Intermediaries? The Role of the Swiss Government in Looking after Internees during the Second World War'. In *Under Suspicion: Citizenship and Internment in Australia during the Second World War*, edited by Joan Beaumont *et al.*, 52–66.

Wodak, Ruth. *Disorders of Discourse*. New York: Longman, 1996.

Yeats, Christine. 'Research Note: Industrial Arbitration Transcripts and Related Sources in the NSW State Archives 1902–91'. *Labour History* 93 (November 2007): 145–153.

INDEX

(Note: References to figures are printed in bold-face type.)

A

Abraham, Peter   155–156
Abrahams-Sprod, Michael   230
Adkins H.E. (Captain)   81
Adler, Henry,   104, 112, 277
Ajax New Century Dual Snare
   Drum   51
Aliens
   and military service   96, 229–232,
      233–234
   arrests of   177, 184*n*. 27, 212, 214,
      245, 247, 256
   classification of   40, 43, 61, 199,
      220, 225, 247, 254, 264
   control of   133, 178, 179, 181, 189,
      190, 200–202, 218*n*. 93, 254, 255,
      273
      See also National Security
         (Aliens Control) Regulations
   internment of (Second World
      War)   61, 102, 177, 185, 187–189,
      202, 212, 213, 214, 215, 229,
      231–235, 247, 248, 255, 279–280
   registration of   19, 181, 201, 236,
      275, 276, 277
   rights of   136, 141, 217, 187–188,
      199, 201, 214, 227
Aliens Classification and Advisory
   Committee   225*n*. 112, 227
Aliens Registration Office   236, 237,
   238
Aliens Tribunals   184*n*. 25, 217–221,
   227–228, 233–234, 245–246, 247, 251,
   252–253, 259, 266
   objectors   218*n*. 89, 219, 228, 251,
      252, 253, 278–279
   Weintraubs at   15, 18, 21, 102,
      191–193, 205, 218, 221–224, 225,
      273, 274
American Federation of Musicians   80

Anschluss   123, 262
Arts Club (NSW)   186
Arthur, Bronwen   17, 73*n*. 33,
   125*n*. 37, 129*n*. 51
Asmis, Rudolf   115, 186*n*. 33, 261
Attorney-General   120*n*. 20, 227, 252
Attorney General's Department   254,
   276
Australian Broadcasting
   Commission   18, 49, 110–112, 123,
   127, 131, 139*n*. 97, 146, 152, 165, 166,
   273, 275–278, 280, 281
   commitment to Australian
      musicians   159–160
   foreigners in orchestras of   80–81,
      138, 155–159, 161–162
   nationality quotas   146, 152–162,
      167–168, 170–171, 174, 276, 280,
      281
   recruitment of foreign
      musicians   146, 153–154, 157,
      159
   standards in orchestras   81,
      137–138, 152–153, 155
Australian citizenry
   and aliens (Second World War)   54,
      183, 197–200, 201, 212, 231, 246
   British character of   21, 54, 59,
      66–67, 83–84, 118, 164–165, 167,
      172, 197–199, 201, 229
   attitudes towards foreigners   54, 67,
      186*n*. 34, 198, 199, 255
Australian Citizenship
   Conventions   157*n*. 40, 167
Australian Jewish Welfare Society   96,
   217, 218*n*. 89, 248
Australian Labor Party   74, 84*n*. 80,
   119, 120, 162, 227, 252, 254
Australian Legation (Moscow)   226
Australian Medical Association   53, 60

– 297 –

Australian Music Maker and Dance Band News (*Music Maker*)   **20, 50, 51**, 89, 107, 110, 112*n*. 68, 132, **239**, 242, 259
Australian Natives' Association (ANA)   108*n*. 51
Australian Security Intelligence Organisation (ASIO)   23
Australian security services   7, 18, 19, 23, 102, 103, 110, 141, 178, 187, 198, 221, 223*n*. 107, 225, 226, 235, 245, 265, 272, 273

B

Bachman[n], Gezá   157*n*. 40, 166
Baker, Josephine   9
Barger [Baruch], Henry (Heinz)   7, 29, 122, 202, 267
Bartrop, Paul R.   17, 40, 53*n*. 7, 54, 90*n*. 5, 130, 133, 183, 185*n*. 29, 200, 234–235, 246–247, 249
Bathurst Immigration Centre   157
Beaumont, Joan   198, 229, 234, 255
Beecham, Thomas   152
Bendrodt, James Charles   47, 49, 100, 104–107, 108–109, 131, 134, 140, 177
Benny, Jack   260–261
Bergmann (Weintraub), Gertrud Irene   7, 191*n*. 54, 195, 205, 225*n*. 113, 269–271, 275
Bergmeier, Horst J. P.   4, 7*n*. 7, 26–27, 31, 43, 203*n*. 33
Berlin cabaret   4, 8–11, 14, 26, 35, 115, 259–260, 261
Berlin Philharmonic Orchestra   115
Bestand Weintraubs Syncopators   **4, 6, 9,** 21*n*. 35, 28*n*. 10, **48,** 89, **121,** 203*n*. 33, 240
Bevege, Margaret   183, 214, 215, 218, 220*n*. 100, 232, 233
Blakeney, Michael   53, 59, 151*n*. 13
Blue Angel, The   5, **6,** 9, 25, 29, 35–36, 39
Borge, Victor   261
Brennan, T.C.   218
British Musicians' Union   69, 75, 98, 125, 126
Bruce, Stanley Melbourne   82, 84, 85
Buchan, David   ix, 182*n*. 18, **207,** 207*n*. 48, 210, 281

Buchan, Evelyn (aka Evelyn Oleaga)   209, 211
Buchan, Reginald   208, 209, 210, 211, 281
Buchan, William Muir Augustus Erskine   8, 18, 19, 23, 178, 179, 181–183, 184, 187, 191, 195–197, 202, 203, 206–211, **207,** 214–215, 217, 221–222, 224–226, 227, 228, 229, 235, 237, 240, 248, 265, 267, 281
Buchenwald concentration camp   220
Bulletin (Sydney)   215*n*. 77, 261
Burkhardt, Buchan & Co. (Shanghai)   207
Burkhardt, Buchan & Co (1934) Ltd (Shanghai)   208
Burkhardt, G.J.   207, 209
Buzacott, Martin   81, 174

C

Cabaret   9
Calwell, Arthur   59, 157, 158, 167, 187, 255
Carrodus, Joseph Aloysius   90, 91
Chronicle of German Internment Camps in Australia   216, 243, 278
Cipolla, Arnaldo   83
Cleary, W.J.   112
Cleland, Mr Justice Edward   218*n*. 94, 219, 252
Clyne, Mr Justice T.S.   218
Cockburn, M.R.   71
Cohen, Rieke   248
Colgate-Palmolive Radio Unit   32, 135, 148, 241–242
Collings, J.S. (Senator)   60, 148
Commonwealth Conciliation and Arbitration Act (1904)   66, 69, 70*n*. 24, 76
Commonwealth Investigation Branch   91, 123*n*. 30, 178, 238, 269, 276
Conn saxophones   51, **51**
Constitution of Australia   74, 76, 124, 198
Constitutional Association of New South Wales   185
Contract Immigrants Act (1905)   66, 82, 120

INDEX

Coulthard-Clark, C. D.   189
Crawford, Craig   47, 103, 147
Crooks, Richard   111
Curtin, John   198, 227, 252, 254, 255

D

Daily Guardian   76*n*. 41, 77
Daily Telegraph   **65**, 137*n*. 92
Danilov, Eugene   169
Dekany, Bela   155, 174
denunciation   18-19, 107, **111**, 182-187, 197, 226-228, 246, 248-250, 255, 267
   categories of   16*n*. 28, 185-186, 196*n*. 3, 197*n*. 8
   responses to   182, 184-185, 186, 187, 202*n*. 29, 211-12, 226-227, 246-247, 252, 253
   See also Buchan, William Muir Augustus Erskine
Department of the Army   97*n*. 26, 146*n*. 124, 182, 236, 244, 254, 278, 279
Department of Defence   133, 146*n*. 124, 182, 220
Department of External Affairs   82, 270, 271
Department of Immigration   150, 160, 165, 173, 269-270, 272, 273, 275-277
Department of the Interior   91-92, 120, 129, 130*n*. 57, 132, 133, 148, 177, 178, 185*n*. 29, 212, 269-271, 276
Department of Labour and National Service   169
Department of Trade and Customs   272
Depression, the   14, 17, 70, 85, 124-127, 199
Der Stürmer   250
Dethridge, George James   67, 72-73, 78
displaced persons   38-39, 54, 61, 63, 124, 149-150, 163, 168
Dietrich, Marlene   5, **6**, 35
Dorati, Anton   152-153
Dreyfus, George   160
Dümling, Albrecht   61*n*. 22, 116-117, 118, 122, 134, 142, 145

Dunera   61*n*. 22, 188, 244, 245
Dutton, David   172, 173*n*. 92, 185*n*. 30, 197*n*. 7, 198, 200, 225*n*. 112, 229, 234, 255

E

Eastern Command, Australian Military Forces   103, 187, 192*n*. 55, 212, 214, 215, 216, 219, 233, 247, 275
Ehrlich, Cyril   125*n*. 33
Elizabethan Theatre Trust   79
Evatt, Herbert Vere   227, 252, 253
Evian Conference (1938)   52-53

F

Feminist Club of New South Wales   185
Ferguson, Kathy E.   87
Finn, Rosslyn   262
First World War   10, 41, 59, 67, 109, 110, 118, 144, 186, 196, 199, 200, 207, 212, 230-234, 241, 245, 246, 253
   Australian casualties   231-232
Fisher, Andrew   119-120
Fisher, Edzia   ix, 38-39, 40, 43, 196*n*. 6, 200*n*. 22
Fisher, Michael   102*n*. 36, 266
Fitzpatrick, Sheila   ix, 21*n*. 34, 184, 186*n*. 34, 204*n*. 38, 226-227
Flegenheimer, Ernst   249, 278, 279
Flesch, Max   220*n*. 99, 230, 251*n*. 77, 253, 279
Foll, H.S.   90, 92, 130 *n*. 57, 133, 177, 213
Forde, Frank   154*n*28
frame conflict   232-234, 252-253
Frischer/Fisher, Adolf (Ady)   7, 14, **34**, 39-40, 93, **99, 100**, 100, 134*n*. 78, 147, 148, 181, 225, 237, 238*n*. 35, 266, 269-273, 283
   and anti-Semitism   38, 42, 122
   arrival in Australia   31
   army service   101, 225-226
   joins Weintraubs   38, 42, 122
   naturalisation   21*n*. 36, 148
   role in documentary film   31, 38, 39, 42

Frischer/Fisher, Emanuel (Mannie/Manny)   5, 7, 10, 31, **34**, 36*n*. 31, 39–40, **94**, 94, **100**, **101**, 122–123, 147, 148, 237, 263, 266, 269–275, 282
   army service   101, 134*n*. 78, 225–226
   Midnight Sextette   40, **99**, 100–102, 107, 134
   name change   100, 102*n*. 36
   nationality   14–15, 181, 225, 238*n*. 35
   naturalisation   21*n*. 36, 148, 182*n*. 16
   radio broadcasts   40, 102
   Russian wife   182, 203, 266
Frischer, Hildegard   195, 273, 275

G

Gardner, Margaret   86
Gellately, Robert   16*n*. 28, 141, 182*n*. 17, 184, 196, 197, 202, 206, 240*n*. 38
Geneva Convention (Convention relative to the Treatment of Prisoners of War) (1929)   188, 216
George (Gyors), Hans   156, 157, 174
Gilbert, Martin   230
Gluszkow, Lidia (aka Jeanette or Jeanna)   203.
   See also Frischer, Emanuel, Russian wife
Goebbels, Joseph   5, 116, 144, 260
Goffman, Erving   104, 242
Gofilegt State Philharmony and Vaudeville Trust (Georgia)   29, 204–205
Goldfeld, Erich   251, 279
Goldner, Fritz (aka Ray)   5, 13, 18*n*. 31, 29, 31, 32, 38, 204, 263, 269–272, 274
Goldner, Richard   81, 166, 174, 282
GOMEZ (GOMETs) (Moscow) (State Organisation for Music, Variety Theatre and Circus)   28, 202, 203*n*. 33, 204, 205
Good Neighbour Council (NSW)   172
Goossens, Sir Eugene Aynsley   112, 148, 152, 154, **156**, 156, 157, 158, 159, 174*n*. 95, 277

Gorbman, Claudia   35, 36
Gowrie, Sir Alexander Gore Arkwright Hore-Ruthven, 1st Earl   97
Gowrie, Lady (Zara Eileen)   97, 238*n*. 36
   as refugee advocate   97
   correspondence with Musicians' Union   97–98, 105
   Garden Fair and Ball (1940)   90, 97–98, 214, 235–241
Graff, Dorothy   ix, 266
Graff, Horst   **2**, **4**, 5, 7, 90, 96, **111**, 122, 123–124, 132, 177–178, 179, 183, 196, 202, 203–204, 206, 211, **239**, 254, 269–271, 273–75
   arrest and internment   19, 22, 23, 39, 41, 90, 100, 102–104, 184, 188, 212, **213**, 214, 215–217, 229, 233, 235, 241–242, 244, 245–246, 251*n*. 77, 264, 265, 266
   and Lady Gowrie incident   19*n*. 33, 236–238
   and Musicians' Union   90, 92, 95, 134, 140, 147, 247
   as manager   89, 92, 96, 122*n*. 25, 240, 263
   at Appeals Tribunal   15, 21, 103*n*. 38, 191, 192, 193, 218–219, 221, 223–224, 247, 253, 259
   at Romano's   104–112
   co-founds Weintraubs   3
   nationality   14, 240
Graff (née Graeme), Margery Minna (Margot)   7, 180, 191*n*. 54, 211, 223, 273, 275
Grey, Joel   9
Guyatt, Joy   18*n*. 32, 180*n*. 10, 183

H

Hardt & Co (Sydney)   215
Hardt, Herbert E.   215
Harty, Hamilton   152, 153
Helfgott, Samuel   150, 155, 167*n*. 71, 276
Henderson, David   186, 202, 227, 235, 246, 252–253
Hesterberg, Trude   9, 26
Hollaender, Friedrich   **4**, 4, 5, 7*n*. 8, 8–9, 26, 35

INDEX

Holloway, E.J.   120
Holt, Harold   **95**, 163, 164–165
Home and Territories Department   85, 127
Hooper, Beverley Joan   60*n*. 16
Housewives' Association of New South Wales   185
Hoyts theatre chain   63, 70*n*. 23, 72, 83, 84, 108*n*. 51, 281
Hughes William Morris (Billy)   84, 125, 144*n*. 113, 164

I

Igudesman, Aleksee   261
Immigration Restriction Act (1901)   55, 66, 74, 83, 118, 119, 120, 136*n*. 84, 198
Inglis, Kenneth   231
Iron Cross (German)   106, 109, 230, 245

J

Jelavich, Peter   **9**, 10, 26*n*. 1, 260
Jenkings, Patricia Anne Bernadette   172
Johnston, Danielle   267 and *n*. 16
Joo, Hyung-ki   261
Jordens, Ann-Mari   173
Joseph, Max   242*n*. 47, 244, 250–251, 254, 264, 276, 278, 279, 282

K

Kaiser, (Ned) John Kurt/Kay, (Sydney) John   **2**, **4**, 5, 7, 16, 31, **33**, **34**, 90, 92*n*. 12, 93, **94**, 94, **95**, 96, **100**, 142*n*. 110, 177–178, 183, 193, 211, 223, **263**, 269–272, 274–275, 280, 282
  and Musicians' Union   17, 62, 88, 117–118, 120–123, 128, 132, 134–137, 138–141, 143, 147, 149, 155
  career   23, 32, 116, 134–135, 140, 142*n*. 10, 148
  in Russia   28–29, 202–206
  internment   19, 39, 100, 178, 196, 212, **213**, 214–217, 223, 235, 241–242, 265

name changes   117*n*. 8
nationality   15, 117n8, 136, 147*n*. 1, 199, **213**, 214, 216–217, 225, 226, 238, 242
security blacklisted   225
Kater, Michael H.   4*n*. 3, 7*n*. 7, 10, 12, 125*n*. 35
Keefe, Inspector (MPI)   180, 181, 235
Kinsella, Justice E.P.   135*n*. 82, 136–137, 138, 139, 141, 149
Kitson, Frank   49, 53, 54, 57, 58, 60, 74, 77–78, 80, 99, 112, 130–31, 154, 167
  See also Musicians' Union of Australia
  and Lady Gowrie   97–98
  and the John Kay summons   135–136, 138
  and the Romano's incident   104–110, 144, 265
  and the Weintraubs   47, 89, 90–92, 95, 100, 102, 132–134, 141, 143–144, 148, 177, 180
Klinger, Barbara   32
Koehne, Samuel   243, 244, 250*n*. 72
Kollat, Captain Georg   215
Korda, Klara   155
Korong Vale Soldiers' Welfare Committee   185
Kramer, Frederick (Friedrich)   161–162
Kraus(z), George   156–157, 174
Krips, Henry Joseph   140
Kristallnacht pogrom (1938)   123–124, 130, 220, 242, 250, 262
Kunz, Egon F.   60, 61, 157, 158, 162, 165*n*. 63, 166
Kwiet, Konrad   184, 185*n*. 29, 244, 245, 250

L

Lamble, W.H.S.   58, 135, 136, 165, 167, 241*n*. 41
Landa, Abram   141
Lareau, Alan   5, 9, 10
Larsson, Marina   231–232
Levi, Erik   5*n*. 4, 144*nn*. 114, 116, 145*n*. 120
Liberal Party of Australia   162, 163, 168

Little Viennese Theatre   112
Long Bay Jail (NSW)   215–216, 241
Lunghua Civilian Assembly Centre (Shanghai)   210

M

Macintyre, Stuart   69
MacKay, William John   180*n.* 9
Mair, Alexander   212–214
Markus, Andrew   ix, 61, 82, 86*n.* 86, 118, 123*n.* 32, 149, 151, 241*n.* 41
Martelli, Athos   77, 282
Martinez, Julia   74, 119
Masel, Alec   218, 221
Massey, Victor   58, **95**, 164*n.* 59, 167, 168, 170
McEwen, John   90
Melody Maker   75
Menzies, Sir Douglas Ian   218, 220–222, 253
Menzies, Sir Robert Gordon   91, 120*n.* 20, 162, 201, 212, 253
Military Police Intelligence (MPI)   8, 104, 106*n.* 47, 179, 180, 181, 182, 189, 201, 214, 215, 235, 236, 238, 273
Minelli, Lisa   9
Mitchell, Inspector D.R.B.   123*n.* 30, 178
Mitchell, Richard   69, 77, 141
Mitten, Richard   110*n.* 60
Moore, Andrew   15, 180, 182–183, 189
Moses, Charles   153, 155*n.* 32, 159, 160–161, 171
Musica Viva ensemble   166
Musica Viva (society)   174
Musicians' Union of Australia, The [Professional]
   See also Kitson, Frank; Lamble, W.H.S.; Trevelyan, Cecil; Wheatland, C.M.
   and arbitration   16–17, 48, 55, 64, 68ff., 79–80, 86–88, 168–169, 281
   and Australian federalism   48, 69, 71–72, 76–77, 136, 137–139, 143, 149, 155, 168
   and 'coloured' musicians   66*n.* 4, 85, 119–120, 142, 172
   and Jewish refugees   17, 52–54, 57, 59–61, 63, 81, 89–90, 98, 107, 109–110, 112, 116–117, 119, 124, 129, 130, 141, 143, 146, 151, 158–159, 174, 265
   and musicians under contract   16, **48**, 64, 66, 67, 74, 82, 84, 120, 124, 129, 130, 142, 262
      See also Contract Immigrants Act (1905)
   and protective legislation   58, 66–67, 82–85, 127–128, 149–151, 163
   and Weintraubs. *See the individual musicians*
   and White Australia Policy   17, 55, 66, 74, 117, 118, 119–120, 142–143, 172
      See also Immigration Restriction Act (1901)
   challenges to rules of   17, 57, 62, 63, 73*n.* 30, 76–78, 117–118, 128, 129*n.* 53, 134–139, 143, 166ff
      See also Kaiser, (Ned) John Kurt
   rules and rule making   14, 48, 54, 55, 58, 63–64, 66, 70–71, 73–74, 75, 76, 86–87, 92–93, **93**, 90, 95, 96, 97*n.* 27, 119, 128–129, 131, 135, 137, 139, 143, 147, 148, 155, 166–172, 173, 265, 280–281
      See also challenges to rules; Australian federalism; White Australia Policy above
   policy on foreign musicians   16, 17, 22, 47, 48–49, **50**, 53–54, 55–60, 61, 62, 63ff., 98–99, 106, 107, 116–120, 122, 124, 126–128, 130–131, 138–139, 141–143, 146, 147ff., 261–262, 265, 276, 278, 280
      See also Australian Broadcasting Commission (nationality quotas)
   policy on naturalisation   59–60, 61–62, 63–64, **65**, 78, 86, 112, 127–128, 131, 135, 137, 139, 140*n.* 100, 143, 148–149, 154, 155, 160, 161–162, 167, 168–174

INDEX

N

National Archives of Australia **11**, 18, 30, 39, **111**, 184*n*. 27, 190–191, 195, 199*n*. 19, 202, 203, 204, 212, **213**, 215, 230, 236, 238, 246, 248–249, 267, 269–280
National Security (General) Regulations 216, 274, 279
National Security (Aliens Control) Regulations 200–202, 239, 247, 254, 274, 278, 279
National Security Act (1939) 200, 216, 218
Nationality and Citizenship Act (1948) 165, 166–167, 172
Nazism 116, 187, 217
Nelson, Rudolf 8, 26
Neumann, Klaus 40*n*. 48, 185*nn*. 29, 30, 187, 188, 196*n*. 4
New Citizen, The 140*n*. 100, 169
Newman, Captain G.H.V. 223–225, 247, 259, 264
Norton, Ezra 109
NSDAP (in Australia) 22, 41, 212, 215, 235, 242, 251, 254

O

O'Brien, Alfred 67
O'Brien, Ilma Martinuzzi 185, 187, 199*n*. 19, 201, 224, 232–233
Ochronka Jewish Orphanage (Lublin) 205
Ormandy, Eugene 137–138, 152, 154, 158, 174, 277
Orange Temporary Internment Camp 123, 216, 217, 241, 242, 245
Oyoyly, Guiseppe 77*n*. 44, 282

P

Paris (Wise), Antoinette 7, 271
Peters, Albert Robert 132–133, 178
Pfund (Kaiser), Gertrude (Gerty) Margarete 7, 177, 271, 273, 275
Pikler, George 158
Pikler, Robert 156, 174, 282
Pilcher, Bishop Charles Venn 199, 217, 248
Plantinga, Carl R. 31, 38, 42, 43*n*. 62

Postmaster-General 153
Potts Point (NSW) 8, 179, 183, 212
Prime Minister's Department 80, 85*n*. 81

R

Reeves (Revesz), Gabor 159, 282
Regent Theatre (Sydney) 83
Reich Chamber of Culture 116
Reichsmusikkammer 62, 116–118, 142, 144–146
Reichstreue 242
  at Tatura 242–244, 249–251
Reichstag fire 116
Reinhart, Max 8
Reisigl, Martin 99
Returned Soldiers' and Sailors' Imperial League of Australia (RSSAILA) 96*n*. 23, 105, 108, 133
Ricci Bitti, Luigi 78, 276, 277
rights, human 228, 255
  to work (of immigrants) 58, 62, 75, 137, 141, 143, 163, 164, 201
  of employers 68, 72, 153
  of citizens 58, 167, 172–173, 187, 201, 224
  of appeal 68, 72, 136–137, 199, 216, 217–218
Ringer, Alexander L. 14
Rinso Melody Riddles radio program 50–51, 240
Rivett, Sir David 261
Romano, Azzalin Orlando 98
Romano's 98, 104–113, **111**, 196, 265, 266
Rosen, Carole 174*n*. 95
Rosenstone, Robert A. 32, 36–37, 42
Rosewarne, Stuart 77, 141
Rubenstein, Kim 58, 141
Rubinstein, W. D. 53*n*. 7
Rutland, Suzanne D. 60, 108*n*. 51

S

Sametz, Phillip 154*nn*. 26, 28, 155
Sankey Declaration of the Rights of Man 228
Sargent, Malcolm 53, 152, 153
Saunders, Kay 212, 214*n*. 75, 219, 232–233

Schnéevoigt, Georg   152, 153
Schulvater, Antonia   203*n*. 36, 273
Schulvater, Cyril   5, 7, 10, **94**, 94, 147, 148, 181, 204, 205, 206, 272, 273
   denounced   195, 196
   joins Weintraubs   **2**, **4**
   leaves band   7, 121, 222, 223–224
   nationality   14, 223
   relationship with Graff and Weintraub   193, 222–224
   smuggling foreign currency (Russia)   204
Schulvater, Ernest   7, 273
   in Russia   181, 203, 204–205, 206
   denounced   196
Schulvater, Jenny   182, 203–205, 206, 211
Schwarz, Rudolf   169
Scott, (Major) William John Rendell   134, 180, 181, 189
Sheridan, Mr   201
Shoah Foundation   41*n*. 38, 39*n*. 44, 266, 282
Shumway, David R.   36, 37
Sipe, Dan   27
Smith, Graeme   166
Smith's Weekly   215
Smolka, Herbert   232
Snider and Dean   7, 13, 30, 62, 89, 120–121, 123, 132, 276
Snider, Leon Samuel   262
Spender, Hon. P.C.   245
Spoliansky, Mischa   26
Stafford, E.R.   218
Steinweis, Alan E.   115*n*. 1, 144, 145
Stern, Isaac   170, 280
Strasser, Otto   26
Sturdee, (Lieutenant General, later Sir) Vernon Ashton Hobart   214, 233–234
Süssenbach, Jörg   3*n*. 2, 15*n*. 27, 30*n*. 14, 134
Sverdloff, Lazar   128–129, 277
Sydney Morning Herald   40, 53, 80, 84, **156**, 177, 183, 212
Sydney Symphony Orchestra   112, 148, 152, 154–158, 162, 173, 277
Szell, Georg   152
Szenassy, Karoly   104, 110–112, 166, 277

T

Tancibudek, Jiri   159, 282
Tatura Internment Camp (Victoria)   22, 102, 184, 188–189, 216*n*. 85, 217, 235, 241–246, 249, 250*n*. 72, 251, 253, 254, 256, 264, 266, 278
Templers   242
Tempo   21, 100, 131, 132, 148, 163–164
Theresienstadt concentration camp   230
Thomson, Alistair   ix
Tiller Girls, The   9
Tosca   157
Trades and Labour Council (NSW)   130, 131
Trevelyan, Cecil   58, 69, 71–73, 75, 76*n*. 43, 77, 78, 79, 80, 82, 83, 108, 125, 126, 128–129
Tycho, Tommy   158

U

United Australia Party   90, 91, 213
Usiskin, Boris Leonid   166*n*. 64, 169

W

Wachsmann (Waxman), Franz   **2**, **4**, 26
Warschauer, G.E.   240, 256, 279
Warschauer, Rev. Elizabeth   255–256
Warschauer, Sheila   256
Wasserstein, Bernard   209–210
Weintraub, Bonnie   37*n*. 36, 38–39, 42, 265
Weintraub, Stefan   **2**, **4**, 5, 7, 21, 23, 26, **34**, 35–36, 37*n*. 36, **51**, 39, 93, 96, 104, 106–107, 108, 109–110, **111**, 112–113, 122, 177, 179, 183, 203–204, 205, 206, 237–238, **239**, **263**, 263–264, 265–266, 269–275, 278, 282
   and Musicians' Union   23, 90, 91, 104–106, 107–108, 140, 143–144, 146, 147, 265
   founds Weintraubs Syncopators   3
   interned   19, 22, 39, 41, 100, 102–103, 134, 184, 188, 189, 191–193, 196, 212, **213**, 214–215, 216–217, 218, 219, 221–223,

INDEX

224–225, 230, 233, 235, 241, 242, 244–245, 249–250, 251, 254, 264, 265
   nationality   14
   security blacklisted   141, 223–225, 264
Weintraubs Syncopators. *See* Frischer/Fisher, Adolf (Ady); Frischer/Fisher, Emanuel (Mannie/Manny); Goldner, Fritz (Ray); Graff, Horst; Kaiser, (Ned) John Kurt/Kay, (Sydney) John; Schulvater, Cyril; Weintraub, Stefan; Weiss/White, Leo; Wise, Gordon Freddy
Weiss, Leo   **2**, 5, 7, 27, 31, 40, 93, 99*n*. 32, 122, 134, 147, 177, 183, 204, 212, 225, 264, 269–273, 275
   at Prince's   23, 31, **34**, **99**, 100–101, 134*n*. 78, 147–148
   denounced   23
   name change   147
   nationality   14
Werder, Felix   188
West Australian Musicians' Union   170–171
West Australian Symphony Orchestra   171
Wheatland, C.M.   168
White Australia Policy   55, 116–117, 120, 198
   See also Immigration Restriction Act (1901)
White, Naomi Rosh   107
White, Peter B.   107
Williamson Grand Opera Season 1924   78, 79
Williamson, J.C.   72
Williamson-Melba Grand Opera Season 1928   83, 84
Windschuttle, Keith   116–117
Winter, Christine   187–188, 235, 242, 243, 244, 254
Wise, Gordon Freddy   **2**, 5, 7, 14, 36*n*. 31, 121, 122, 271, 275
Wisnia, Mathys   150, 167*n*. 71, 276
Wittouck, Serge   210
Wives. *See* Bergmann (Weintraub), Gertrud Irene; Fisher, Edzia; Frischer, Hildegard; Gluszkow, Lidia; Graff, Margery Minna (Margot); Pfund (Kaiser), Gerturde (Gerty) Margarete; Paris (Wise), Antoinette; Schulvater, Antonia; Weintraub, Bonnie
Wodak, Ruth   22, 99, 109*n*. 57, 110*n*. 60, 233*n*. 21, 253
Wolff, Peter   233, 279

Y

Yerbury, D.   71
Yerkes, Harry   79